Medieval Archaeology

'This is a well-written, interesting and informative book which should not only be on the shelves of every medieval archaeologist but should prove of interest to historians and prehistorians as well.'

Mick Aston, University of Bristol/Time Team

'The book has wide scope, and will be of interest to all those with an interest in the Middle Ages whether students, teachers or those who enjoy visiting castles and abbeys.'

Paul Stamper, English Heritage

The archaeology of the later Middle Ages is a comparatively new field of study in Britain. At a time when archaeology generally is experiencing a surge of popularity, our understanding of medieval settlement, artefacts, environment, buildings and landscapes has been revolutionised. Medieval archaeology is now taught widely throughout Europe and has secured a place in higher education teaching across many disciplines.

In this book Gerrard examines the long and rich intellectual heritage of later medieval archaeology in England, Scotland and Wales and summarises its current position. Written in three parts, the author first discusses the origins of antiquarian, Victorian and later studies and explores the pervasive influence of the Romantic Movement and the Gothic Revival. The ideas and achievements of the 1930s are singled out as a springboard for later methodological and conceptual developments. Part 2 examines the emergence of medieval archaeology as a more coherent academic subject in the post-war years, appraising major projects and explaining the impact of processual archaeology and the Rescue movement in the period up to the mid-1980s. Finally the book shows the extent to which the philosophies of preservation and post-processual theoretical advances have begun to make themselves felt. Recent developments in key areas such as finds, settlements and buildings are all considered, as well as practice, funding and institutional roles.

Medieval Archaeology is a crucial work for students of medieval archaeology to read and will be of interest to archaeologists, historians and all who study or visit the monuments of the Middle Ages.

Christopher Gerrard is a Lecturer in Archaeology at the University of Durham. He is a Fellow of the Society of Antiquaries of London, a member of the Institute of Field Archaeologists and Monographs Editor for the Society for Medieval Archaeology.

Medieval Archaeology

Understanding traditions and contemporary approaches

Christopher Gerrard

Routledge
Taylor & Francis Group

LONDON AND NEW YORK

First published 2003
by Routledge
2 Park Square, Milton Park, Abingdon, Oxon, OX14 4RN

Simultaneously published in the USA and Canada
by Routledge
270 Madison Ave, New York NY 10016

Routledge is an imprint of the Taylor & Francis Group

Transferred to Digital Printing 2005

© 2003 Christopher Gerrard

Typeset in Baskerville by Exe Valley Dataset Ltd, Exeter

British Library Cataloguing in Publication Data
A catalogue record for this book is available
from the British Library

Library of Congress Cataloguing in Publication Data
Gerrard, Christopher, 1962–
   Medieval archaeology: understanding traditions and contemporary approaches/
Christopher Gerrard.
      p. cm.
Includes bibliographical references and index.
1. Great Britain–Antiquities. 2. Archaeology, Medieval–Great Britain. 3. Excavations
(Archaeology)–Great Britain. I. Title.
DA90.G46 2002
941–dc21   2002075165

ISBN 0–415–23462–X (hbk)
ISBN 0–415–23463–8 (pbk)

Printed and bound by Antony Rowe Ltd, Eastbourne

For Alejandra, who was very patient

Contents

Illustrations

Figures

Boxed text

Preface

The 'Middle Ages' traditionally describes the thousand years sandwiched between classical antiquity and modernity, between Rome and Renaissance. The term is usually used in the plural because there are several sub-eras. This book covers roughly the first half of the second millennium, between about 1000 and 1550 AD, a period variously referred to as 'post-Conquest' (in England) or the 'Later' or 'High Middle Ages', usually in order to differentiate it from the 'early medieval' or 'Anglo-Saxon period'. 'Later medieval archaeology' is the term I have adopted in this book, but it is a convenience only, there is not even consensus in the spelling of 'medieval' and, of course, other countries adopt very different schemes and nomenclatures, so I have deliberately not defined my chosen start and end dates too closely. In this context, political and constitutional events, such as the battle of Hastings in 1066 or Bosworth Field in 1485, may serve historical or (English) national agendas well but their signature in the archaeological record may be less apparent and calls undue attention to the 'joins' between periods.

The emergence of later medieval archaeology as a productive sub-discipline has been one of the most significant achievements in the study of archaeology in the last hundred years. Before about 1950 medieval archaeology was not a recognised and coherent 'subject', though some of its components do have a much longer history of study. Today, few of the seventy-three departments in fifty-two institutions in the United Kingdom offering undergraduate and postgraduate courses with archaeology elements are without at least an optional medieval module or two (Henson 2000). Further opportunities abound for research at MA, MPhil and PhD level. In the space of fifty years or so what had been an interest for a small group of individuals has been woven into a respected sub-discipline defined by a particular set of practical and philosophical problems, equipped with its textbooks and mulled over by field units, lecturers, local government officers and museum staff.

Interest in later medieval archaeology in Britain is neither parochial nor restricted to academia. Sites and their excavators, books and their authors, are all widely known and discussed at European and world conference venues and can count on strong support, particularly in Australia, Canada, North

America and South Africa. Most British practitioners see themselves as part of wider communities of later medieval archaeologists, archaeologists, historians and geographers, scientists and social scientists. They may not always lead the discussion but they feel they have a place. Outside 'professional' life there are opportunities for everyone to participate in medieval fieldwork projects, join special interest groups or the Society for Medieval Archaeology, and visit monuments of all kinds. Many people in Britain still live in medieval houses, in villages with medieval plans, walk their dogs over medieval earthworks and regularly visit their parish church or cathedral. In England there are almost as many later medieval monuments as there are people. Inspired or infuriated by a television programme, a computer game, an internet web site, a piece of music, a film, or just plain curiosity, a growing demand for information is fed by a wide range of publication, from fiction to 'faction', as well as more sober tomes on topics ranging from monasteries to gardens. Today the Middle Ages in Britain are revisited in many parts of the world and often in surprising ways ranging from 'wash-and-wear sorcery and Holy Grail frappé' to more conventional scholarship (Eco 1986: 65). Such cultural plunderings are nothing new; as we shall see, the Middle Ages have always served contemporary needs.

This book is *not* a summary of recent academic results for the archaeology of the Middle Ages. If you wish to clarify the precise date of a particular building or artefact then you may well be reading the wrong book. My ambition here is to provide a coherent map of how and why later medieval archaeology developed, to tell the story of its origins, how it matured and to explain how contemporary approaches have evolved. I will be saying more about what happened than what was found. I want to do this for several reasons. First, many people still equate archaeology with the study of prehistory. Thumb through most standard textbooks on modern archaeological methods or theory and there is very little about medieval archaeology. Yet, as we shall see, its contribution to methodological innovation has not been insignificant and theoretical debates, even if they have not had the impact they have had elsewhere in archaeology, have never been entirely ignored. That there would be scope now for a comprehensive account of recent theoretical applications to later medieval archaeology says much about the engagement of the subject with the wider conceptual issues of social science over the past decade.

Second, I believe that some of the archaeologists (using this term rather loosely) who have participated in the rise of later medieval archaeology deserve to be known rather better than they are at present. A few years ago I was asked in one tutorial why Martin Biddle would have dedicated his massive *Object and Economy in Medieval Winchester* volume (1990) to two 'unheard-of' archaeologists. Initially, I was bemused that the student in question had not come across Gerald Dunning and John Ward Perkins but, on reflection, I wondered where they might have done so. Few medieval archaeologists have written autobiographies and tributes by others tend to be widely scattered through journals and *festschrifts*. It was obvious then that students (and they are not alone, even among practising archaeologists) had only the haziest understanding of how and why the subject had developed or who the key players and places were.

These basic aims might have led on to any one of several different books. This could have been an 'encyclopaedic' gazetteer of excavations and ideas and an invaluable quarry for reference. A successor perhaps to Platt (1978a), Clarke (1984), Steane (1984) or Hinton (1990). It could also have been more openly biographical in content and sketched some of the personalities more fully. More detailed biographical accounts are certainly needed, of Hope, Hoskins, O'Neil and Peers to name but a few. Instead, I wanted to know *why* the subject had grown, *where* it had come from and *what* had motivated its past scholars. These themes crosscut all the chapters in this book and, I hope, show that the development of interest in medieval material culture has always been contingent upon wider social, cultural, economic and political issues. Academic scholarship, antiquarianism, élite taste, national and local history, nostalgia, political subtext, popular fashion, public education, religious identity, visual spectacle and scenery for action; medieval monuments have served all these at one time or another.

There were two questions to which I kept returning. The first concerned the nature and form of intellectual shifts. In any subject most practitioners follow unhesitatingly their predecessors' philosophies and techniques; only a handful of publications and individuals in each generation stimulate innovation and crossover, between countries and between disciplines, and so push the development of the subject forward, often in quite unconscious ways. Most innovations come from the outside, as a result of academic fashion or through the impact of social and economic events. New trends may take time to make themselves felt, and while some endure and take on wider currency, others evaporate. Frivolously perhaps, I wondered when it might have been possible for a single individual to claim, with any justification at all, that they knew everything that contemporary knowledge had to offer about later medieval archaeology. You might care to speculate on this too, but my guess would be not far into Chapter 4!

Mostly it is hard to see revolutionary or dramatic 'paradigm shifts' in later medieval archaeology, to use Kuhn's terminology (1962). I believe there have been four important events in the years since the Second World War. The first might be described as the 'genesis' of rural settlement studies in June 1948 which sparked projects and interests which were long term and influential in both philosophy and practice. The second was the first meeting of the Society for Medieval Archaeology in April 1957 which counted then on a broad constituency of academic, institutional and public support and continues to do so. And if the third event was the advent of rescue archaeology in 1970–2 which so vastly increased the rate of recovery of medieval structures and artefacts over the next twenty years, then the fourth must be the issuing of PPG 16 in 1990, ostensibly merely a planning guidance document, but one which has reduced large-scale excavation to a trickle and released funding for other activities in which many of us now find ourselves engaged in one form or another. All these events can be pinpointed exactly but there have also been much longer, slow-moving changes inspired by excavations at Wharram Percy or digging in Winchester, by the impact of processual and post-processual ideas and the remarkable surge in university teaching, particularly through extra-mural departments. The impact of these various initiatives may not have been immediately striking but, as they unfurled over a number of years, they have contributed in substantial and important ways.

My second question is about character. Like traditional history, later medieval archaeology might be described as an intellectually invertebrate affair. Indeed, some believe that one of the distinctive characteristics of the subject has been its ability to survive without drawing on theoretical ideas developed in cognate disciplines and that earlier periods have a monopoly on ideas. I do not agree with this diagnosis and, in this book, I have made every effort to present a balanced picture of conceptual and methodological milestones. In doing so, later chapters which set out the detail of contemporary approaches are necessarily more detailed and lengthy. For further background the reader is best referred to general works on recent trends in methods and theory. These are fully referenced in the text.

This book is divided into three parts and six chapters. These appear to follow on from one another in straightforward chronological fashion but, like the period of study they describe, their start dates and end dates are far from precise. I have chosen significant dates but the events they mark do not affect all aspects of the discipline with equal force, nor do they slice through the development of practice and theory in any convenient kind of way. Thus, ideas which may be suggested at one time may find wider application later, sometimes much later, and often jagging in from quite another academic direction.

Just as the dates for my chapters are blurred and arguable, so is my definition of 'medieval archaeology'. Standing building recording, architectural study, environmental science and artefacts, I consider all these although I understand fully that each has its own traditions and literature. I have no wish to suggest, for example, that the unique achievement of dendrochronology lies in the later medieval period in Britain, merely to show that its impact as a method for this period is very important. Excavation and fieldwork data, documents and maps, aerial photographs and remote sensing techniques are not sources uniquely employed by medieval archaeologists.

Nor is it sensible to think of later medieval archaeology in isolation; developments in other subjects, particularly local history and historical geography, will be central to our story. For this reason I have been indifferent to disciplinary boundaries, often introducing economists, historians and geographers who would never have considered themselves 'medieval arch-aeologists'. Likewise, my 'medieval archaeology' embraces all past discussions about material culture of the later medieval period, including those of the nineteenth century and earlier, long before 'medieval archaeology' as a recognised topic of study really came into existence.

This book is concerned primarily with events in England, Scotland and Wales. I do not accept, however, that there is one unified trajectory of study for these three countries, nor have I excluded mention of influences further afield where this is appropriate. Other authors have adopted similar approaches for other parts of the world, for Germany (Fehring 1991) and Scandinavia (Andersson et al. 1997) for example, but I hope one day another book might adopt a European or even worldwide perspective and set these different stories into a wider context. In my own fieldwork I have seen for myself just how much the experience of working in northern and southern Europe can vary in fundamental ways. The value of standard British research tools like Ordnance Survey maps and Sites and Monuments Records are only fully appreciated when you reach out and find they are not there. Intellectual traditions and socio-political circumstances in different countries may dictate that there is little tradition of fieldwork, perhaps only the most negligible contribution from environmental archaeology, but that standards of publica-tion, for example, are far higher. These contrasts require fuller exploration.

The greatest danger in a book of this kind, written as a kind of narrative history and from today's perspective, is that a stream of scholars and their ideas can be placed too easily in chronological order and spuriously linked on the basis of the date and content of their publications. To counteract this tendency, every effort has been made to consider individuals in their intel-lectual context, to evaluate the processes of change. Again, I hope that the more detailed analysis of the social and political circumstances of particular institutions and individuals might be seen as worthy of attention in the near future. I have made no attempt here to produce an inventory of every individual, institution and publication involved with the subject, nor have I excluded what might be considered 'bad archaeology', for those who make 'errors' can be as stimulating to change as those who tread the 'right' track. It is not my intention to take sides between the different approaches and interpretations on offer, even so I feel sure my 'medieval archaeology' is not necessarily the same medieval archaeology that everyone would wish to subscribe to.

Acknowledgements

The origins of this book are to be found in my undergraduate experience at Bristol University between 1980 and 1983 where two third-year courses, one entitled 'The Prehistory of the Western Mediterranean', the other 'Settlement and Evolution of the Landscape', introduced me to two very different approaches to the past. The former, under the tutelage of Richard Harrison, was theoretically informed, intellectually rich and provocative; the latter, taught by Mick Aston, infected every student with the excitement of historical archaeology and the joys of unpicking and deciphering the half-legible earthworks of medieval monuments and landscapes. Later I was 'apprenticed' as a doctoral student under their supervision and went on to post-doctoral research before weaving a career path through units, consultancy and higher education. I have drawn on all these experiences in writing this book.

Fortunately, I have not been without help and many people have had their part to play. Mick Aston, Tim Darvill, Richard Higgins at University of Durham Library, Helen Fenwick, James Greig, Tom James, Neil Linford, Phil Mayes, Philip Rahtz, Sarah Reilly, Steve Rippon, Paul Stamper and David Viner all provided photographs or figures without charge. Some data on excavations was provided by the National Excavation Index in 1997. Thanks also to Mick Aston, David Austin, the British Library, the Bodleian Library, Bristol and Gloucestershire Archaeology Society, British Film Institute Stills (Posters and Designs), the Central Archaeological Service (English Heritage), the Council for British Archaeology, James Greig, University of Durham library, Roberta Gilchrist, English Heritage, Hampshire Field Club, Sue Hirst, the Humber Wetlands Project, the MARS Project, Phil Mayes, Python (Monty) Pictures Ltd, Museum of London Archaeology Service, the North Somerset Levels Project, Perth High Street Archaeological Excavation Committee, Salisbury and South Wiltshire Museum, the Society of Antiquaries of London, the Society for Medieval Archaeology and Paul Stamper for copyright permissions for the figures. Alejandra Gutiérrez re-drew the illustrations where necessary.

Pre-1972 county names, with their standard CBA abbreviations, have been used in the text.

I wish to thank David Austin for getting me onto the right track and another anonymous, but possibly clairvoyant, Routledge referee who foresaw many of the pitfalls which I have since encountered for myself. Patrick Ashmore, Grenville Astill, Mick Aston, David Bromwich, Graham Brown of the Centre for Archaeology, David Hinton, Phil Marter, Richard McConnell and Steve Minnitt all helped me locate facts and figures. Mick Aston, John Hurst, Tom James and Paul Stamper read and suggested changes as first drafts of chapters were completed. Tim Darvill, Margarita Dìaz-Andreu, Chris Dyer, Pam Graves, Matthew Johnson, Philip Rahtz and Andrew Millard advised on specific sections of the text. I owe a considerable debt of gratitude to all of them. Polly Osborn and Julene Barnes at Routledge were always supportive. Finally, King Alfred's College, Winchester gave me sabbatical leave for a semester in 1999 during which I completed a draft of the first two chapters; the remainder was written during the summer and autumn of 2001 following my move to the Department of Archaeology at the University of Durham. Thank you to colleagues and students, north and south.

SWAINBY
December 2001

Part I

The discovery of ignorance

At my fyrst cominge to inhabit in this Island Anno 1607 I went to Quarr, and inquyred of divors owld men where ye greate church stood. Theyre wase but one, Father Pennie, a verye owld man, coold give me anye satisfaction; he told me he had bene often in ye church whene itt wase standinge, and told me what a goodly church itt wase; and furthor sayd that itt stoode to ye sowthward of all ye ruins, corn then growinge where it stoode. I hired soome men to digge to see whether I myght finde ye foundation butt cowld not.

(from the memoir of Sir John Oglander describing one of the first excavations of a later medieval monument, at the Cistercian abbey at Quarr on the Isle of Wight in 1607, quoted in Long 1888)

Go forth again to gaze upon the old Cathedral front, where you have smiled so often at the fantastic ignorance of the old sculptors; examine once more those ugly goblins, and formless monsters . . .; but do not mock them, for they are signs of the life and liberty of every workman who struck the stone; a freedom of thought, and rank in scale of being, such as no laws, no charters, no charities can secure; but which it must be the first aim of all Europe at this day to regain for her children.

(Ruskin 1851–3)

In former daies the Churches and great houses hereabout did so abound with monuments and things remarqueable that it would have deterred an Antiquarie from undertaking it. But as Pythagoras did guesse at the vastnesse of Hercules' stature by the length of his foote, so among these Ruines are Remaynes enough left for a man to give a guesse what noble buildings, &c. were made by the Piety, Charity, and Magnanimity of our Forefathers. . . . These stately ruines breed in generous mindes a kind of pittie; and sette the thoughts a-worke to make out their magnificence as they were when in perfection.

(from J. E. Jackson, 1862, *Wiltshire. The Topographical Collections of John Aubrey F.R.S., AD 1659–70*, page 255)

How strange it would be to us if we could be landed in fourteenth-century England.

(from William Morris, 1966, *The Collected Works of William Morris*, XXIII, page 62)

There is nothing so stimulating to research as the discovery of ignorance.

(from J. B. Ward Perkins, 1940, page 20)

Chapter 1

Inventing the Middle Ages

Antiquarian views (to c.1800)

Early studies of the monuments and artefacts of the Middle Ages have largely been written out of general histories of archaeology, which have tended to focus upon prehistory. Yet the period between the sixteenth century and the turn of the nineteenth saw the development of ideas and perceptions about the medieval past which still impinge on our understanding today. This chapter sets out some of the motives behind antiquarian activities and the contributions of major institutions, societies and intellectual movements are briefly explained. Attitudes to medieval monuments are seen to be influenced strongly by religious and social affairs and employed in their negotiation. The roles of John Leland, William Camden, William Dugdale, John Aubrey, William Stukeley and John Carter are highlighted. The chapter takes as its closing date the growing influence of the Gothic Revival at the turn of the nineteenth century.

The early antiquarians

Even before the Middle Ages had come to an end, there was already an interest in medieval monuments and material culture. The human remains of bishops, kings and saints were exhumed regularly; the sensational 'discovery' in 1191 of the body of King Arthur next to that of his wife Guinevere at Glastonbury being only one of the best recorded examples of a staged spectacle of medieval digging (Rahtz 1993: 42–50). Relics could be stolen or change hands at high prices (Geary 1978) and the opening of a coffin established whether a saint's body was 'uncorrupted' and so promoted their cult. If successfully managed, benefactors became less forgetful and pilgrims too appreciated the replenished cache of relics on view (Gransden 1994). Perhaps, in a very loose sense, these exhumations were excavations but they are rather special and specific examples and suggest no substantial interest in gathering new information about the past.

More promising in the context of this book are those studies of the Middle Ages written before the end of the Tudor age. These were of two broad types. General historical narratives included both inventive contributions by Geoffrey of Monmouth and Matthew Paris, and more questioning writing like Polydore Vergil's *Anglica Historia* (1534) which covered English history to

1509. Material culture rarely figured strongly in these accounts, though John Rastell, for example, speculated about the authenticity of Arthur's seal at the shrine of St Edward in Westminster Abbey (McKisack 1971: 95–125). A second type of study were local chronicles containing antiquarian observations, typified by the remarks of Warwickshire chaplain John Rous on fashions of dress and armour in the mid-fifteenth century (Kendrick 1950: 27). A contemporary of Rous, the topographer William Worcestre jotted down details of the churches and monasteries he visited in his diaries (J. H. Harvey 1969). Noting paced and yardage measurements for buildings, he even made a sectional drawing of a door jamb at the church of St Stephen in Bristol, the city where his most detailed survey was undertaken (Kendrick 1950: plate V; Leighton 1933). This taste for architecture and measurement, together with the record he kept of his journeys, were all unusual for their time but writing an historical survey does not seem to have been William's intention. His interests were clearly wider and included diary descriptions of his contemporary surroundings as well as notes on local legend, folklore and antiquities. His was a medieval world to celebrate.

Not until the middle of the sixteenth century did historical consciousness become more fully sensitised. Between 1536 and 1540 monasteries gave up their possessions to Henry VIII's commissioners. In the aftermath, fixtures and fittings were especially vulnerable. Statues, altars, sculpture, window glass, vestments, tombs and books were pilfered, damaged and mislaid. In Aubrey's phrase, 'the manuscripts flew about like butterflies' (1847). Damp and deserted buildings collapsed quickly once deprived of their roofing tiles and were demolished and carted away for construction or hardcore. Those buildings which escaped did so either because they were inaccessible or because they could be adapted to another purpose. Many were partially recycled into country residences or rented out for storage and industrial uses. In England and Wales, nearly 850 religious houses ceased to exist (Aston 1993: 141–50).

Nor were these the only changes. Between 1547 and 1553 parish and diocesan records show that the attack on traditional religion left parish churches with only a handful of their images and vestments. Walls were whitewashed and altars removed. Everyday items of liturgy were stripped and sold (Duffy 1992: 478–503). Few were vocal in their protests, and some would profit from the dismemberment, but, within twenty years, familiarity with the day-to-day late medieval worlds of countryside and townscape, secular and religious, had been fractured and disrupted for all. Heaps of monastic masonry lay strewn about as testament to Henry VIII's efficiency, and it is claimed that out of the loss and shock emerged a new sense of engagement with the past (Levy 1967).

Monasteries, and particularly the fate of the books in their libraries, were of particular concern. The Welsh lawyer John Prise acquired the foundation charters of those houses he visited on Cromwell's behalf (Ker 1955). John Bale, himself educated as a Carmelite, published catalogues of the medieval books he knew of (e.g. Bale 1557–9) as well as collecting them for himself and drafting a history of his order (Aston 1973). Similarly, his friend John Leland toured the country examining collections and salvaging monastic tomes for the King's Library (Carley 1985). Leland's confessed first purpose was conservation, to preserve the best of the authors whose books were now being dispersed (Leland 1546), but the timing and wider purpose of his travels are especially fortunate for today's student of medieval archaeology. His writing is rich in contemporary detail of the monastic sites he visited (Chandler 1993) and, subsequently, would provide the basis of more complete catalogues of religious houses. But, as he toured the country, Leland visited all manner of sites of different periods and classes. His notebook entries, though they are not always entirely accurate and sometimes rely on uncorroborated local sources, brim with first-hand topographical observation of castles, industries and town walls. Leland's reference to a deserted medieval settlement at Deerhurst in Gloucestershire, dating to the 1540s, is probably the earliest to a monument of that kind (Aston 1989).

William Camden was not the first to use the term 'Middle Ages', but the single illustration in the first edition of *Britannia*, his pocketbook bestseller of 1586, shows a medieval monument, the Saxo-Norman chancel arch in the church of St John's-under-the-castle at Lewes in Sussex (Kendrick 1950: 151; Figure 1.1). This was the first published illustration in British archaeology. Later revisions featured one of the first published drawings of a medieval object, the 'falsified' lead mortuary cross from the twelfth-century diggings by monks at Glastonbury Abbey (Rodwell 1989: 19; Figure 1.2), as well as county maps and ground plans of medieval buildings.

Whether Camden and his contemporaries would have recognised all this as a growing interest in the artefacts and monuments of the later medieval period is highly doubtful. Mostly, antiquarians had no wish to endorse the Catholic culture and religion of the later medieval period and, indeed, rejected it in favour of more intimate links with a pre-Norman Saxon heritage. When Lawrence Nowell, Dean of Lichfield, began to collect all of Leland's contributions on the study of Old English place names into a single volume and set about transcribing countless medieval manuscripts, he did so out of sympathy with the views of Archbishop Matthew Parker and his antiquarian colleagues with the church of Saxon England (Flower 1935). When the first county history was published for Kent by lawyer and historian William Lambarde in 1576, the author was careful to strike a balance between horror and applause at the havoc of 'places tumbled headlong to ruine & decay' (Lambarde 1576). While it is true that Nowell, Lambarde and John Stow, whose own *Survey of London* was published in 1598, all indulged a strong sense of local and national pride from which later medieval mouments were not excluded, post-Conquest history was not to be endorsed lightly. Religion often provided the framework for writing and attitudes to the medieval past should be seen as part of this contested arena.

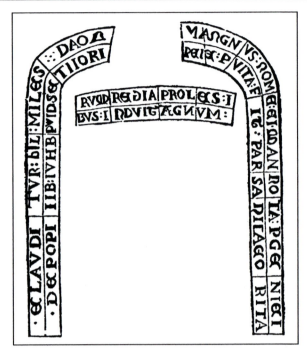

Figure 1.1 William Camden's recording of the medieval inscription over the chancel arch at the church of St John's-under-the-castle in Lewes (Sussex), for his *Britannia* (1586). The first antiquarian book illustration. The arch was incorporated into a new church on a nearby site in 1839.

Even though later medieval archaeology was largely incidental to the purpose of these later sixteenth-century antiquaries, their activities proved influential. In the absence of a Royal Library, Bale, William Cecil, Robert Cotton and Parker all favoured the accumulation of documents in vast private libraries of their own making (McKisack 1971). Contemporary scholars frequently acknowledged their indebtedness to these sources, as Camden and Speed acknowledged Cotton's library, and these same manuscripts later came to form the core of national collections. The later sixteenth century also set the formula for future antiquarian studies. The contents list for Lambarde's Kentish *Perambulation*, for example, opened with a general topographical description before providing lists of hundreds, religious houses and gentry. His text drew upon Bede, chronicles, Domesday Book and royal charters as well as general histories. There was even a coloured location map and he relates the history of many buildings though he did not describe them. Camden's interests, on the other hand, were certainly more orientated towards material culture and he speculated that 'monuments, old glasse-windows and ancient Arras' might provide a novel and independent line of

Figure 1.2 The lead cross from Glastonbury illustrated in the sixth edition of William Camden's *Britannia* in 1695. When translated from the Latin, the inscription reads 'Here lies buried the famous King Arthur in the island of Avalon'. The object itself is now lost, but the lettering cannot be fifth or sixth century. This may be a twelfth-century forgery by Benedictine monks eager to establish an Arthurian cult at the abbey and was possibly 'found' during the staged exhumation of Arthur and Guinevere in 1191.

historical inquiry (Camden 1607). Modern archaeological study does find an echo here but we must be careful not to claim too much. Camden may have published later medieval archaeology and architecture but it is only with the benefit of more recent scholarship that the items he presented can be seen as Norman or later in date.

This antiquarian movement cannot be divorced from a growing interest in cartography. After the institutional and physical disruptions of the mid-sixteenth century, there was now growing awareness of national and local geography in Britain. Saxton's county maps were in hand by 1574 and his atlas of county maps was in print by 1600 (Greenslade 1997). Surveying and map-making were becoming priorities for landowners, who were perceiving the landscape in new ways and saw maps as an aid to the improvement of their estates (Johnson 1996). Some of these estate maps already indicated abandoned medieval monuments, but they captured the surveyor's attention only as landmarks. Moats, windmills, deer parks and strip patterns in open fields were often depicted; the deserted medieval settlements at Fallowfield (Northumberland) and East Layton (Durham) were recorded in c.1583 and 1608 respectively (Beresford 1966; 1967a). By the end of the century map-making was already a semi-professional business and would underpin future generations of antiquarian research.

Excavations and histories of the seventeenth century

For most classically-educated antiquaries, the 'middle ages' were just that, wedged in the middle between classical antiquity and the Renaissance. In this growing Enlightenment view the Romans had been Britain's last link with the civilised world (Trigger 1989). Those who undertook the 'Grand Tour' through France, Germany, Italy and the Low Countries only returned more confirmed of this view and identified with the idea of social, cultural and technological progress. And while medieval life was considered barbaric and restrictive there was little inclination to study its monuments. John Evelyn, amongst others, damned without reservation all the greatest monuments of the Middle Ages criticising:

> [the] universal and unreasonable Thickness of the Walls, Clumsy Buttresses, Towers, sharp pointed Arches, Doors, and other Apertures, without Proportion.
>
> (Evelyn 1706)

Attitudes to medieval monuments, particularly ecclesiastical architecture, continued to be influenced by the flux in Protestant and Catholic allegiances. An open preference for Gothic architecture, however, did not necessarily signal pro-Roman Catholic affiliation, this assumes too much. For one thing, the Crown's religious policies were unevenly applied, for another, behaviour and attitudes, inward and outward, were not clearly trammelled. The connection between monuments and religious belief was not so directly made. Having Protestant beliefs did not mean that medieval parish churches and cathedrals should be left in disrepair, far from it, much was done under Elizabeth, James I and later under Archbishop William Laud, to restore the fabric of ecclesiastical monuments as part and parcel of changes to regulations on preaching and services (Oldridge 1998: 37–64). To add to the confusion, understanding of architectural chronology could still be muddled. The Gothic architectural flavours of the new library at St John's College and the chapel at Peterhouse in Cambridge, both early seventeenth century in date, were intended to link an 'authentic', 'national' architecture with the pre-Catholic Anglican church (Howarth 1997: 15).

Seen in this context, antiquarians like John Weever, referring to monasteries, felt able to express feelings of loss, even shame, at the 'shipwracke of such religious structures' (1631). A mixture of piety and curiosity led him and others to visit ruins and the first attempted excavation of a later medieval monument by John Oglander took place in 1607 at Quarr on the Isle of Wight (see p. 3). It is hard to say just how common such 'diggings' might have been, perhaps more common than is now realised. Certainly, the familiar antiquarian stereotype was already in place:

> He will go you forty miles to see a saint's well or a ruined abbey . . . printed books he condemns, as a novelty of this latter age, but a manuscript he pores on everlastingly, especially if the cover be all moth-eaten. . . .
>
> (Earle 1633)

That some seventeenth-century antiquaries cherished an interest in the Middle Ages at all is remarkable but, even when classicism and official iconoclasm was at its height, collection and study continued. Medieval artefacts, often coins, featured among the exotic exhibits in cabinets of curiosities (MacGregor 1985) and medieval documents were scrutinised for county histories (Currie and Lewis 1997). These histories, of which those for Leicestershire (Burton 1622; Phythian-Adams 1997) and Nottinghamshire (Thoroton 1677; Henstock 1997) might be singled out, generally itemise the Domesday manors, linking buildings with historical events with misplaced confidence (Hunter 1971). The map-maker and surveyor John Norden included extraordinary bird's-eye view illustrations of medieval monuments in his *Description of Cornwall* of *c*.1610 (Figure 1.3) and mapped antiquities such as park boundaries in his surveys (Norden 1728; Kendrick 1950). Robert Plot's history of Staffordshire (1686) claimed 'not to meddle with the pedigrees and descents' but to 'chiefly apply my self to things . . .'. For the most part, however, the gentry's obsession with genealogy and land ownership provided the most obvious market for this kind of writing, and where pedigrees and local social identities could be reinforced, they were (Broadway 1999; Currie and Lewis 1997).

Particular contributions were made by two seventeenth-century antiquaries, William Dugdale and John Aubrey. In his *Antiquities of Warwickshire* (1656), Dugdale conformed in most respects to the socially one-dimensional format and content of other county histories, though his interests were more strictly historical than topographical (Moir 1964: 14). An introductory description of

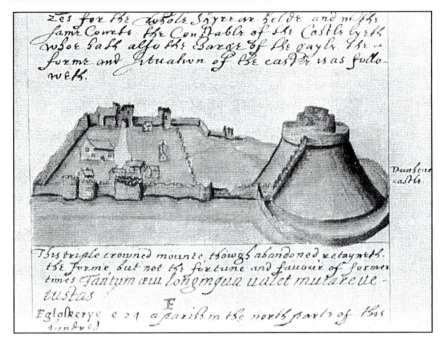

Figure 1.3 Dunheved or Launceston Castle, Cornwall, illustrated by John Norden's for his *Description of Cornwall* (c.1610, published 1728). A bird's-eye topographical record of the motte and bailey castle with shell keep and walled bailey. (By permission of the British Library; MS. Harley 6252, 93).

the county was followed by shorter entries on places and parishes. He collected monuments and classified them, marking up 'depopulated places' on his maps as open diamonds with dots in the centre (Beresford 1989: 49–50). Adopting the principles which his scientific colleagues of the day devoted to flora and fauna, Dugdale applied the same accuracy of observation and illustration.

Three volumes of William Dugdale and Roger Dodsworth's *Monasticon Anglicanum* appeared between 1655 and 1673 and featured excerpts from primary documents and a synoptic history of each monastic house, illustrated by engravings (Figure 1.4). These volumes, while they are based on the earlier endeavours of Weever (1631) and Speed (1611), who in turn had relied upon Leland and others, 'continue to form the foundation of all serious study of the religious houses of England and Wales' (Knowles and Hadcock 1953: xvii). How it is that Dugdale and Dodsworth came to write on such matters has been explained by the social circles in which they moved, mostly outside London and the wealthy social circles of dedicated followers of classical fashion (Allen 1937: 47). A work described as so 'obsolete and neglected' in

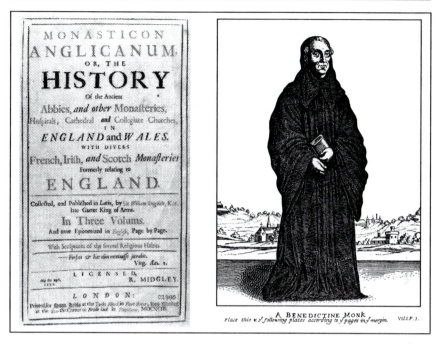

Figure 1.4 From the abridged 1693 edition of *Monasticon Anglicanum* by William Dugdale and Roger Dodsworth. Described in its preface as 'the most Evidenciary, and Repertory of Titles that is in print'.

the preface of its 1693 abridgement, had a very practical underlying purpose and appealed directly to those whose forefathers were founders or benefactors of religious houses. The true purpose of the *Monasticon* was not so much to provide the first synthesis of monastic history as to list the liberties and immunities which might be enjoyed by new owners of monastic estates, and thus might need to be defended in a court of law.

The antiquary John Aubrey worked mostly in Wiltshire and is best known among archaeologists for his descriptions of Stonehenge and Avebury (Powell 1963). One of his first achievements was to have Wenceslaus Hollar produce an engraving from his original drawing of Osney Abbey in Oxford for Dugdale's *Monasticon* (Aston 1973). Aubrey's *Monumenta Britannica* described medieval as well as prehistoric monuments, and the unfinished fourth part was to have included a chronological sequence of styles for medieval doors and windows in which architectural evidence was matched against documented buildings (see p. 3). This *Chronologia Architectonica* of *c.*1670 was remarkable for two reasons. First, Aubrey produced illustrations derived from his own observations rather than the textual descriptions preferred by Leland and others. Second, at this date the stylistic sequence of architecture was quite unappreciated, the term 'Gothic' might be used for Romanesque buildings and 'Saxon' for post-Conquest, for example (Cocke 1973). The first published analysis of the English Gothic was not available until 1763 and Rickman's more definitive classification appeared only in 1817 (see Chapter 2). While Aubrey's understanding was restricted to ecclesiastical architecture and he placed medieval military architecture into the Roman period (Hunter 1971), he hoped his classificatory scheme would 'give a guess about what Time ye Building was' (Piggott 1976: 17). Unfortunately, it was destined to remain in manuscript form (Figure 1.5).

Oxford antiquary Anthony Wood is less well known than either Aubrey or Dugdale. Wood left a number of rough manuscripts when he died in 1695, enough to understand his ambition to write an 'Itinerary' like Leland and an 'Antiquities of Oxfordshire' to match Dugdale's Warwickshire as well as an autobiography and various other works. His interest in antiquities seems to have been sparked shortly after his twenty-first birthday when he came across William Burton's *Description of Leycestershire* in the public library in Oxford (Clark 1891–1900: 182). Thereafter he studied Leland's collections in the

Figure 1.5 Late fourteenth-century windows in Westminster Abbey, as drawn by John Aubrey for his unpublished *Chronologia Architectonica* in c.1670. (The Bodleian Library, University of Oxford, MS. TOP. Gen. C. 25, Fols. 171v-172).

Bodleian Library and began to take notes on abbeys and churches, especially heraldry and tombs. He visited the monastic churches at Dorchester-on-Thames, Godstow and Osney, taking measurements and making sketches, and noted digging and finds at several sites including the recovery of lead coffins at Blackfriars in Oxford in c.1618 (Clark 1891–1900: 255; Figure 1.6). His observations and those of his contemporaries like John Evelyn, contributed to the *Chronologia* collated by Aubrey.

Wood's interests give a good impression of the eclectic range of most antiquarian tastes, in which later medieval monuments have their place, as well as the importance of scholarly collections and networks. Visiting sites was becoming popular and travel was more comfortable because of improved roads, maps and better bred horses; an important consideration for antiquaries on horseback. There is also evidence of a more emotive, subjective and romantic view of the medieval past in Wood's writing. His 'strange veneration' at Malmesbury Abbey was matched by his 'melancholy delight in taking a prospect of the ruins' at Eynsham in 1657 (Clark 1891–1900: 228). At the same time, he expressed distaste over the damage done to monuments during and after the Civil War, commenting on the removal of inscriptions, paintings and coats of arms from local churches and the daubing of paint on the stall backs in the choir of Merton College in 1651 (Clark 1891–1900: 309).

Elsewhere, Peterborough Cathedral suffered 'rifling and defacing' in 1643 (Gunton 1686) and castles were damaged during siege action (e.g. Pontefract, Yorks.; Queenborough, Kent; Raglan, Gwent; Sherborne Old Castle, Dorset). Momentarily, the overthrow of established authority and widespread destruction of monuments during the Civil War had spurred wider concern (Cocke 1987). The *Monasticon*, for example, first appeared during the Protectorate. Likewise, it has been claimed that the Fire of London also encouraged a revival in historical interests (Evans 1956: 27). Westminster Abbey, for example, benefited equally from restoration in the 1620s, 1660s and 1690s onwards and Christopher Wren was involved in numerous refurbishment schemes. But it was classicism not medieval style which dominated in the second half of the century, symbolised by the new St Paul's Cathedral in London.

Picturesque, Romanticism and the eighteenth century

At the beginning of the eighteenth century cosmopolitan intellectuals leant towards classical ideals but, as the viewing and connoisseurship of landscape changed during the new century, so new attitudes to medieval monuments took hold, reflecting a new fascination with roots and nationhood (Crook 1987: 13–41). Garden designs imitated pictures in the style of Claude or Gaspard Poussin and were peppered theatrically with monuments, many prescribed in the classical taste. At Blenheim in 1709 John Vanbrugh had

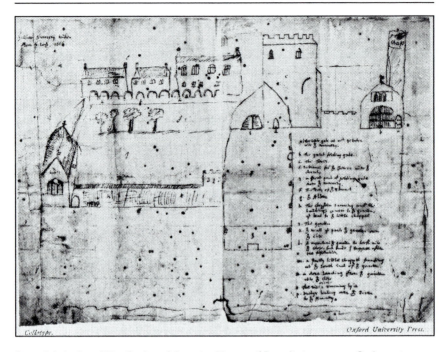

Figure 1.6 Anthony Wood's plan of the ruined house of Benedictine nuns at Godstow in Oxfordshire, dated 1687. (Clark 1891–1900: pl.VI).

pleaded to no avail with an impatient Sarah Churchill that the ruins of Woodstock Palace should be preserved (Bond and Tiller 1987: 55–6). A generation later and pleas for more variety and contrast with Palladian rules of architectural design had converted the Middle Ages into an ideal in landscape architecture; Sanderson Miller, above all, gained a reputation as the architect of Gothic taste, designing 'ruins' for Hagley Park (Worcs.), Lacock (Wilts.) and Wimpole Hall (Cambs.) among others (Macaulay 1953: 20–39).

Some 'ruins' were no more than painted canvases and plaster, but not all were entirely modern confections. At Shobdon (Herts.), the Norman chancel arch from the parish church was set up as an eye-catching folly on a nearby hilltop (Thompson 1981: 17). Masonry was also pilfered from genuine medieval monuments to assemble 'new' ones. The window tracery for Sanderson Miller's castle folly at Edge Hill (Warwicks.), probably inspired by Guy's Tower at Warwick Castle, was removed from the Premonstratensian abbey at Halesowen in 1743 (Worcs.; Macaulay 1975: 20–39; Headley and Meulenkamp 1986: 324–5). Parts of the transept of Netley Abbey (Hants.) were set up as a sham castle in Cranbury Park in 1770 (Sambrook 1980). The layouts of designed landscapes could also be enhanced by real medieval buildings, both inside and far outside parks. At Studley Royal (Yorks.), the Aislabies not only brought the Cistercian abbey at Fountains into their landscaping schemes along the River Skell after 1742 but also incorporated distant views of Ripon Cathedral. Similarly, landscaping of a long grassy platform along the rim of the Rye valley at Rievaulx contrived lines of sight down onto the monastery below through swathes of planting (Fergusson and Harrison 1999: 188–9; Figure 1.7) and Roche Abbey (Yorks.) was part demolished and part buried for Lord Scarborough's grand garden scheme at Sandbeck Park designed by 'Capability' Brown in 1774 (Coppack 1990). It was 'a delicious game' in which not all parts of Britain participated with equal enthusiasm but, at the same time, it was underpinned with serious study (Macaulay 1953: 24). Genuine medieval monuments like Tintern Abbey provided the prototypes and garden architects drew upon antiquarian publications and plans. Batty Langley felt able to design his 'Gothic summerhouses' only after a twenty-year study of the 'lost orders' of 'Saxon' architecture (Langley 1728). Thus a taste for the 'picturesque' increased the popularity of 'native' architecture, as opposed to classicism, and in turn this contributed to a better understanding of medieval architectural forms.

There was no intention, however, to invite lengthy architectural inspection of the ruins created or viewed. In a superficial way, this vogue for the medieval met a need for novelty in a society which was becoming more uniform. Wrecked and abandoned buildings, overtaken by creeping vegetation, gave simple aesthetic pleasure. Philosophically-inclined observers could turn their melancholy thoughts to the impermanence of human life and endeavour. Medieval buildings were particularly well suited to this purpose; they were not necessarily thought 'tasteful' but they did symbolise physical robustness. A decaying medieval ruin could be read as 'a triumph of time over strength' and intelligently contrasted against 'exhilarating' Neoclassical monuments (Kames 1762).

Like an oil painting, medieval 'ruins' might also convey messages of a more specific and exclusive kind. They could be versatile political symbols, designed to question established authority (**Box 1.1**). Old Wardour Castle, survivor of two sieges during the Civil War, was incorporated as a 'romantic' ruin into a new 'picturesque' park between 1769 and 1776. The castle served as a monument to family courage and to Royalist sympathies after its owners, the Arundells, returned at the Restoration (Pugh and Saunders 1968). Quite another set of associations were imagined by the Reverend William Gilpin, visiting Halesowen Abbey, who saw with satisfaction:

> the mould'ring pile
> Where hood and cowl devotion's aspect wore,
> I trace the tottr'ing reliques with a smile
> To think the mental bondage is no more . . .
> (Gilpin 1782)

Figure 1.7 The Cistercian abbey at Rievaulx in Yorkshire, looking east from the nave. Centrepiece of landscaping schemes in the eighteenth century and later transformed when the monument came into public care in 1919. Some 90,000 tons of spoil were removed from the site to create the clear and ordered presentation seen today. (Photo: author).

In this interpretation the abbey serves as a reminder of past social oppression and tyranny. But it is not a simple reference to medieval corruption overthrown, in the mid-eighteenth century it was also a timely reminder of Jacobite rebellion and the threat of Catholicism.

As part of a wider set of responses to scenery, writers and travellers were also intent on experiencing the 'primitive' and 'natural' embodied in medieval monuments. Early participants were Thomas Hearne, antiquary and for many years assistant keeper at the Bodleian Library in Oxford, whose walks through Oxfordshire in 1718 took in medieval halls and churches, the journalist and novelist Daniel Defoe who judged the three spires of Lichfield Cathedral

Box 1.1   King Alfred's Hall in Cirencester Park (Glos.)

Cirencester Park is the best surviving example in Britain of 'forest' or 'extensive' gardening of early eighteenth-century date. In Oakley Wood, at the heart of the park, stands a ruined castle-like structure called Alfred's Hall, built between 1727 and 1732 (Figure 1.8). The design for this building might have been influenced by the poet Alexander Pope, but in any case this 'pretty little plain work in the Brobdingnag style', as Lord Bathurst, the Park's creator, called it (Sherburn 1956), was successful enough to dupe visitors and antiquaries into believing that they were observing the real thing.

Figure 1.8 King Alfred's Hall or The Woodhouse in Cirencester Park (Glos.). Built on the site of an existing cottage, much of the masonry came from the demolished manor house at nearby Sapperton. (Photograph by W. Dennis, by courtesy of David Viner Collection).

At this period social refinement was synonymous with a taste for classicism. The castellations, broken doorways and Latin inscriptions of this 'sham ruin' were redolent with melancholic associations which were then enhanced further by planting up the surrounding wood with yew trees. The intended political 'reading' of the building is given away by its name, in which the 'virtuous' King Alfred could be contrasted with the reputation of the king of the day, George II, of whom Bathurst disapproved. The strange juxtaposition of King Alfred with the architectural grammar of later medieval castles seems odd to our eyes, but the difference between 'Saxon' buildings and those of the later medieval period was not well understood at this time, either by architect or by visitor.

incomparable in Europe, and printer Thomas Gent who, in 1733, thought Kirkstall Abbey 'enough to strike the most harden'd Heart, into the softest and most serious reflection' (Gent 1733: 26). Gent had been responsible for one of the very first purpose written guidebooks to a medieval monument, for York Minster (1730). By 1742 the ruins of Glastonbury Abbey were already attracting a 'great concourse of strangers' who had gone there 'purposely to see this Abbey' (Defoe 1742).

While it may be true that these early tourists did little to advance the discipline of the study of ancient monuments established by Aubrey or Dugdale, the appreciation of the medieval past now reached beyond the restricted circles of antiquaries and appealed to a wider section of the population. John Perceval built himself a whimsical castle at Enmore in west Somerset before 1779 complete with drawbridge and moat (Pevsner 1985b: 167). Horace Walpole's remodelling of his property at Strawberry Hill (London) after 1748 used Dugdale's engravings as a guide to style (Crook 1970), the roof of the tribune being suggested by the Chapter House of York Minster, the wallpaper by decoration on Prince Arthur's tomb in Worcester Cathedral and the entrance screen modelled on the choir at Rouen Cathedral. Floor tiles from Gloucester Cathedral, coins, battleaxes and medieval corslets were among the apparently authentic materials on show and later sold at auction (Robins 1842); ancient stained glass was removed from the parish church at Bexhill (Sussex) and installed (*The Times* April 22 1922). Aristocratic houses were regularly opened up to casual visitors in the eighteenth century and Strawberry Hill became so popular with visitors that Walpole wrote his own guidebook, drawing up ticketing arrangements and visiting hours (Crook 1970).

The medieval motif was everywhere, from design to literature. Furniture makers, like Chippendale, employed Gothic elements, even if the pieces themselves (bookcases, tea-tables, etc.) were far from authentic (Allen 1937: 82–4). Medievalist verse, 'Graveyard Poetry', marked by an obsession with ruined buildings and tombstones, was best experienced at night. Gloomy cloisters, overgrown walls, clanking chains and dungeons were all exploited by Blake, Burns, Goldsmith, Pope and Warton, and the abbeys at Glastonbury, Melrose, Netley and Tintern were among their favoured settings (Macaulay 1953: 338–42). Though there was scant regard for accuracy of interior detail and furnishings, Horace Walpole's *The Castle of Otranto* (1764) utilised images and monuments of the Middle Ages to invoke a sense of fear and the supernatural. Medieval archaeology provided the stage for Gothic fiction.

Antiquaries, monuments and excavation

Enlightenment philosophy promoted reason and scientific method and eighteenth-century antiquarian studies placed greater emphasis on observation and classification. In this they were aided by the availability of new sources. John

Bale's great book collection had been borrowed, stolen, divided up and bequeathed by the time about one quarter of the volumes eventually found themselves safe at Corpus Christi (Cambridge), the Bodleian Library (Oxford), Trinity College (Dublin), the British Museum and at Lambeth Palace Library. During the eighteenth century many of the libraries of earlier patrons and collectors, William Cecil, Robert Cotton and Matthew Parker among them, came to form the core of new national libraries like the British Museum Library which opened in 1753. The organisation of these libraries aided eighteenth-century county histories which routinely carried information about later medieval sites. Among them were Samuel Rudder for Gloucestershire (1779) and John Collinson for Somerset (1791) (Aston 1989; Beresford 1954). Departing from the usual antiquarian menu of church monuments and family trees, John Bridges' *History and Antiquities of Northamptonshire* of about 1720 gives notes and sometimes lengthy descriptions of deserted settlements (Taylor 1974a) and these were also marked up on Thomas Beighton's *Map of Warwickshire* five years later (Beresford 1989). Less well known is the antiquarian and correspondent John Strachey who described and drew Devizes Castle (Wilts.), among one of a number of West Country monuments which are hard to appreciate today in anything close to their original settings (McGarvie 1983). Earlier volumes, most notably Dodsworth and Dugdale's *Monasticon*, also continued to be updated and expanded (e.g. Tanner 1722; Burton 1758; Oliver 1846).

The ebb and flow of medieval studies through the eighteenth century can be traced best through the activities of the early antiquarian societies. Among the early communications of the reformed Society of Antiquaries of London, formally constituted in 1718, were articles on medieval antiquities which now paid greater attention to the accuracy of their findings. An early 'research agenda', drawn up in the first quarter of the century, listed everything from castles and weapons, to 'manufactures' and 'handicraft'. Indeed, members were urged to draw 'castles, churches, houses . . . tombs . . . and, if need be, to buy up the most curious and useful pieces of Antiquity' (Evans 1956: 43). From the start the Society was active in publishing prints of engravings, many of which took churches, castles and crosses as their subjects. Large-scale prints were bound together as the volumes of *Vetusta Monumenta*. They also acted to prevent damage to ancient monuments and in July 1721 paid for two oak posts to be placed so as to protect the Waltham Cross from passing carriages; the timbers were subsequently dug up again by agents of the turnpike in 1757. Other monuments, like the gatehouse near St Albans church pulled down in the 1720s, were less fortunate, though at least it had been sketched by William Stukeley.

Fellows brought manuscripts and finds to the meetings of the Society and churches and other monuments continued to be recorded throughout the century, but appetite for medieval matters did fluctuate. In the 1730s, for example, relations between Church and State were not propitious for the study of ecclesiastical history and the study of British medieval history could not be turned easily to the benefit of a German royal family. But by the 1740s and 1750s the tide of scholarly fashion was swinging back again. Detailed consideration was given by the Society of Antiquaries to the publication of Domesday Book (Evans 1956: 72–125) and medieval buildings featured prominently in the new fashion for topographical art, typified by the work of the Buck brothers.

Chance discoveries were now recorded more frequently when they came to light, like the fourteenth-century sword found during the construction of Westminster Bridge in London in 1740 (Celoria and Spencer 1966–70). But, generally, interests remained narrow. A review of the small numbers of known eighteenth-century excavations on medieval sites shows a predictable obsession with the larger monuments of Church and State, which were readily identifiable by their standing architectural remains. At Monkton Farleigh in Wiltshire:

> Three labourers being employed to level a very uneven Piece of Ground, found the Pillar of a Church, and, about four foot under the Rubbish, discover'd a Chancel . . . 'tis impossible to give an exact Account how far it extended. The Labourers have found a Silver cup, spoon and thimble.
>
> (Anon. 1744)

To a great extent the interpretation of finds and monuments like these was dictated by written history. When James Essex came to survey the infirmary complex at Ely Cathedral in 1762, he produced a neat, measured plan of the structures he considered original but the dates he finally placed on what he had observed were based on known and documented events (Holton-Krayenbuhl 1997: 123–6). The implicit assumption was that historical documents contained a reasonably complete account and a reliable chronological framework into which architectural sequences could be spliced. Essex's dates for Ely Cathedral would only be challenged seventy years later when architectural classifications and the sequence of styles had been better worked through and agreed (Miele 1998).

Evidence for more disciplined investigation is to be found in the work of Richard Gough, who typifies the resurgence in interest in British archaeology as the Middle Ages became a favoured field of antiquarian inquiry in the second half of the century (Evans 1956: 136). Among the 'desiderata' in his *Topographical Antiquities* (1768) were 'forts and castles . . . from the earliest date to the last century'; Gothic architecture too he saw as being worthy of further research, as well as heraldic glass, medieval epigraphy and illuminated manuscripts. Gough's list shows some understanding of the nature of medieval archaeology and its potential for the future and should be seen in the context of a renewed interest in English artistic and architectural traditions brought about by the 'picturesque' aesthetic. When the first volume of the Society of Antiquaries of London's new journal, *Archaeologia*, was published in 1770 it was logical that it should contain several papers on medieval topics including one by William Stukeley (**Box 1.2**) and another on the Welsh castles of Edward I.

During the eighteenth century, many British towns and cities still retained their medieval appearance. When the Romanesque west tower of Hereford Cathedral fell in 1786 it was just one reminder of the age and condition of so many other buildings (Cocke 1973). There was deliberate vandalism of medieval buildings. At Crowland Abbey (Lincs.), for example, Stukeley noted that 'the roof, which was of Irish oak finely carved and gilt, fell down about twenty years ago: you see pieces of it in every house' (Stukeley 1724: 33). At Stamford he collected and purchased the old medieval glass being smashed from parish churches in 1737, giving it away to friends and incorporating it into his own house at Barnhill (Allen 1937: 58). Protesting at the restoration of Peterborough cathedral in 1747 he wrote:

> They are new whitewashing, or rather dawbing the cathedral, and new painting the roof in ridiculous filligree work, party-coloured, that has no meaning in it; and above all they have, for greater ornament, as they fancy, painted the ceiling over the high altar in imitation of marble. They have made a new quire of paltry fir, painted over, in a most tastless and mean manner, and after laying out a great sum of money have really deformed this most august and venerable structure.
>
> (Stukeley 1882–7)

Such incidents were common enough. In 1718 one antiquarian reported 'with grief' the 'great havoc' wrought in Gloucester Cathedral (Bliss 1869) and in 1742 the editor of the third edition of Defoe's *Tour* complained that the Abbot's lodging in Glastonbury had been torn down and 'they were actually stripping St Joseph's Chapel . . . and the squared stones were laid up by lots in the Abbot's kitchen' (Defoe 1742). The removal of the chapter house at Durham Cathedral and the demolition of chapels at Hereford Cathedral in 1737 spurred the Society of Antiquaries into making drawings and plans (Cocke 1973) but complaint was only rarely translated into action. Waverley Abbey (Surrey) was spared from demolition for paving stones for a road, Roslyn Chapel was repaired when its roof threatened to fall in and Roche Abbey (Yorks.) was saved from stone-mongers by the Earl of Scarborough (Allen 1937: 66–7). In 1766 the architect-planner John Gwynn's ambitions for London's infrastructure included the preservation of Henry VII's Chapel, intact and unaltered (Earl 1996).

Early Romanticism

Although primarily expressed through music and literature, late eighteenth-century Romanticism also had a considerable impact on the study of medieval monuments. Not all those who indulged antiquarian interests could be said

Box 1.2 William Stukeley and medieval monuments

The antiquary William Stukeley (1687–1765) is known to archaeologists for the unrivalled detail he provides for so many of the sites he visited, particularly for his observations of prehistoric monuments. Castles, cathedrals and palaces were also included in his itineraries (Rodwell 1989: 21, 24) and a pocket volume of his architectural drawings of medieval buildings survives from 1708. An admirer of Gothic, Stukeley thought York Minster superior to either the Pantheon or St Peter's (though he had never visited either), designing a number of 'ruins' of his own in the 1730s and 1740s (Piggott 1976: 119). The first volume of *Archaeologia*, published by the Society of Antiquaries of London in 1770, contained his own account of 'a most agreeable journey to visit the venerable remains of Lesnes Abbey', the Augustinian monastery in Kent (Figure 1.9). Stukeley's plan sketch depicts the position of the cloister and church, from which he was able to deduce the location and function of buried parts of the precinct. In fact, Stukeley was not the first visitor to Lesnes Abbey. The site had already been partially dug over in 1630 in the presence of the poet and antiquarian John Weever 'after having been long covered with rubbish'. Informed by his frequent visits to the library of Sir Robert Cotton and the College of Arms, Weever's interests lay mainly with genealogy and heraldry and he was probably looking for tombs and grave slabs with which to illustrate his volume *Funerall Monuments* (1631).

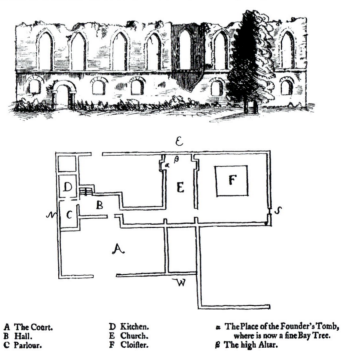

A The Court.	D Kitchen.	α The Place of the Founder's Tomb,
B Hall.	E Church.	where is now a fine Bay Tree.
C Parlour.	F Cloifter.	β The high Altar.

Figure 1.9 The east-facing elevation and plan of the ruins of Lesnes Abbey in Kent, drawn by William Stukeley in April 1753 (1770: 45).

to reflect Romantic tastes but the choice of sites for excavation shows a mild swing towards those which offered greater intensity of personal experience, particularly 'sepulchral matters', the most obvious link to sensibility and imagination and a ready opportunity to confront death and decay. Edward I's tomb in Westminster Abbey was opened for a short time in May 1774 to examine the state of preservation of the body and to ascertain whether any measures to prevent decay had been taken at the time of burial. Considerable attention was paid to the burial ritual revealed by the vestments and artefacts found inside the tomb and the intact corpse was carefully measured in order to re-evaluate the king's height, a matter of considerable speculation (Ayloffe 1786; Crook 1987: 368–9).

In an age of new beginnings, the architecture and sculpture of the Middle Ages was condemned in the revolutionary France of the 1790s. Devastation was widespread and directed mostly at royal or Church monuments, most notably in the destruction of fifty-one royal tombs in the abbey of Saint-Denis. When the Musée des Monuments Français opened in 1795 it contained many rescued and restored medieval sculptures and tomb covers, but it only did so because the authorities had been convinced that such a collection was needed to prevent undesirables having access to counter-revolutionary artefacts. The exhibitions seemed to have quite the opposite effect, up to 1816 when the museum closed, numerous catalogues were published and many visitors, artists and scholars visited the new museum (Haskell 1993: 236–52).

In Britain, events abroad in France and America served to refocus scholarly interest on national heritage. In the last quarter of the eighteenth century, Joseph Strutt published his engravings of the portraits of English kings and queens taken mostly from manuscript collections in the British Museum, the King's Library and the Bodleian. He followed this with several volumes of illustrations with early and later medieval themes, which gradually brought a more accurate, if socially restricted, picture of the medieval past to the modern reader (Haskell 1993: 279–303).

As landscape became a persistent theme of romantic poets, so too engravings and commentaries on local medieval sites and monuments became more popular. Francis Grose's volumes (1773–87) are, in effect, an architectural and archaeological inventory complete with accurate plans of buildings (Baggs 1994; Figure 1.10). County histories and architectural editions were regularly reprinted (Evans 1956: 205; Figure 1.11) and the number of publications dealing with medieval architecture rose sharply, the period 1789–96 saw twice as many papers on the subject in the pages of *Archaeologia* than the period 1771–87 (Frew 1980).

One result of isolation from mainland Europe was that the British travel account now emerged as a distinctive branch of historical writing. Following the example of the Reverend William Gilpin, Richard Colt Hoare was one of those who took to the road in the 1790s and journeyed through Wales making notes and sketches (Thompson 1983). Sir Richard prepared well for his travels, gathering material on castles, cathedrals and abbeys from his substantial library before leaving his home at Stourhead in Wiltshire. What drew him to Wales in his chaise was the variety of scenery and his search for the 'picturesque' which had become so popular in the last decade of the century. He visited all the major sites, noting tombs and memorials, making sketches and commenting on their situation. So considerable was this interest in 'ruins' that by 1800 Tintern Abbey in the Wye valley was filled with visitors who came by road and river on pleasure cruises (Robinson 1986). Amongst the visitors in the last decade of the century was Joseph Turner who brought his sketchbook and watercolours, and William Wordsworth, the poet. Guide-books sold well (Gilpin 1782; Heath 1793) and visits were even made by torchlight (Knight 1977). Some sites, such as Raglan Castle (Gwent), invested in a custodian and equipped themselves to cater for tourists (Kenyon 1988).

In the 1790s the architect James Wyatt planned the monstrous and melodramatic Gothic extravagances at Fonthill Abbey (Wilts.), including an 84-metre-tall tower, a baronial hall 23 metres in height and a boat house built in imitation of a flooded church complete with nave and aisles (Pevsner 1985a). The tower collapsed less than twenty years after it was completed in 1807. Part of the appeal of Gothic for architects and public alike was that it reflected an authentic indigenous architecture which Renaissance designs could not be. When national identity was threatened both in America and in Europe, Gothic could be adopted safely as a national symbol, in opposition to the Neoclassicism and rationalism of the earlier years of the century. As Horace Walpole observed:

> Our empire is falling to pieces; we are relapsing to a little island. In that state, men are apt to imagine how great their ancestors had been . . . the few, that are studious, look into the memorials of past time; nations, like private persons, seek lustre from their progenitors.
>
> (Lewis 1955: 165)

It was partly this 'lustre', coupled with alarm at the damaging effects of urbanisation, which awakened a fiercer preservationist stance vocalised in particular by John Carter and Richard Gough. Both men objected strongly to the over-zealous 'repair' schemes carried out by James Wyatt and others at cathedrals in Durham, Hereford and Salisbury. Under Gough's directorship the Society of Antiquaries of London had been at the centre of a growing interest in medieval buildings and monuments, but he resigned in acri-monious protest at Wyatt's election (Evans 1956: 207–14). In Carter and Gough's protests over the 'devastating and disgusting hand of architectural innovation and improvement' (Gomme 1890: 1) lie the origins of views which were to develop further over the course of the next century and finally emerged as the clarion call of the Society for the Protection of Ancient

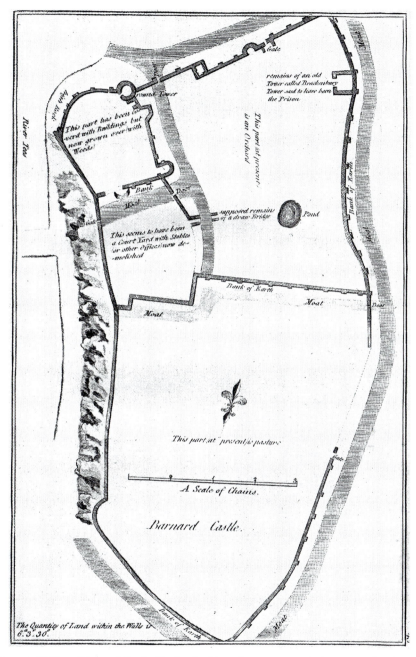

Figure 1.10 Plan of Barnard Castle (Durham) with explanatory text. A close copy of a plate published in F. Grose's *The Antiquities of England and Wales*, volume 1 (1773). The original Grose plate was copied, cropped and remounted in several subsequent histories of north-east England.

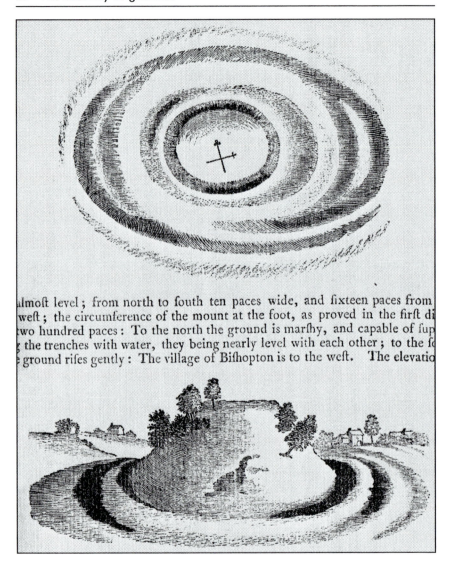

almoſt level; from north to ſouth ten paces wide, and ſixteen paces from weſt; the circumference of the mount at the foot, as proved in the firſt di two hundred paces: To the north the ground is marſhy, and capable of ſup the trenches with water, they being nearly level with each other; to the f ground riſes gently: The village of Biſhopton is to the weſt.　The elevatio

Figure 1.11 A plan and view of the motte and bailey earthwork at Castle Hill in Bishopton (Durham). This woodcut print illustrated William Hutchinson's *The History and Antiquities of the County Palatine of Durham*, volume 3 (1794). One of a wide selection of early maps and topographical prints from the collections of Durham University Library, Durham County Council Arts, Libraries and Museums, and Durham Cathedral Library viewable on the web at <www.dur.ac.uk/Library/asc/pip/>.

Buildings (Miele 1996). Ironically, it was precisely the improved standard of architectural recording pioneered by James Bentham, Carter (1795–1814), James Essex, Gough (1786–96), and others which provided architects like Wyatt with the details of decoration and ornament they needed for their restorations (Frew 1980; Rodwell 1989: 22).

Naturally, all this interest in upstanding architecture also had some effect on attitudes to buried monuments. Typical circumstances were described at Winchester some years later:

> In digging for flints last week . . . the workmen struck upon a stone door-way, which led into a large chamber built of flints and Portland stone, plastered over, and heretofore groined, the fluted corbels and springing of the arches being perfect.
>
> (Milner 1797)

Milner proposed to make a 'sketch of the keep in question . . . as they existed in ancient times' and hoped the workmen might make further discoveries. Generally speaking, the scholarly and public 'profile' of medieval monuments was now higher and architectural studies were influential in raising standards of recording. But an understanding of 'medieval archaeology' was still limited. Few excavations had been planned, executed and published and antiquaries could only conjecture about their accidental discoveries, usually on the basis of what they found in county and national histories. Conflicting interpretations of a 'subterraneous passage' discovered at Old Sarum (Wilts.), included a sallyport, well or dungeon for confining prisoners (Anon. 1796). No solution could be reached, the matter only being settled when the trench was re-opened 162 years later (Musty and Rahtz 1964).

Chapter 2

Lights and shadows

Medievalism, the Gothic Revival and the nineteenth century (to 1882)

Treatment of the Middle Ages in the nineteenth century has been a major topic for study, particularly in architecture, art and literature. During this period interest in later medieval monuments was closely linked to national histories and developments in popular culture. This chapter provides a general background to the continuing Gothic Revival before focusing on its impact on the rise of the preservation movement and study of the archaeology of the Middle Ages. The contributions of John Britton, the Cambridge Camden Society, John Lubbock, William Morris, Augustus Pugin, Thomas Rickman and John Ruskin are all briefly touched upon. The chapter takes as its closing date the passing of the first Ancient Monuments legislation in 1882, from which medieval monuments were exempted.

As the medieval revival intensified during the first half of the nineteenth century so it became less exclusive, influencing public taste and a broad spectrum of arts, politics and daily life. Samuel Coleridge, William Wordsworth and Robert Southey were among the many poets and essayists who invoked Gothic atmosphere and values. But it was in *The Lady of the Lake* (1810), *Ivanhoe* (1819) and *The Monastery* (1820) that Walter Scott portrayed to a wider public the 'Merry England' of the twelfth to fifteenth centuries most successfully (Trevor-Roper 1969). Scott's interest in the medieval period was at least partly antiquarian. His novel *Kenilworth*, first published in 1821 and later appearing as two volumes of the Waverley novels, even included a version of Dugdale's plan as a guide to the events it described (Thompson 1977). Scott drew freely for his ideas on reprints of poems and chronicles, family and county histories from which he could extract the details of architecture and daily life he needed (Chandler 1971: 25–30). New interpretations of history such as Sharon Turner's *History* (1815–23), John Lingard's *History of the Middle Ages* (1819) and William Cobbett's *History of the Protestant Reformation* (1824–6) informed him of the latest discussions of Norman and later culture.

A collection called *Robin Hood's Garlands* had gone through thirty reprints in as many years at the turn of the nineteenth century (Chandler 1971: 117) but Scott's *Ivanhoe* sold 12,000 copies in the first weeks of publication in 1819

(Banham 1984) and within a year there were no fewer than six London theatres running dramatised versions. *Ivanhoe* offered vicarious adventure, pageantry, hearty humour and heroic drama to an increasingly industrialised and urban readership. Here, good and bad were clearly coded in racial stereotypes. Treacherous Normans were pitched against the Saxons, always honest, loyal and free. Qualities of chivalry and community are always to the fore. Quite unlike early nineteenth-century England, there was always enough food for the feudal feast, with its boar's head, geese, hams, and barons of beef and ale.

Historical paintings of the day, such as those on show at the Royal Academy in the 1840s and 1850s, illustrate the wide range of topics inspired by the medieval past (Banham and Harris 1984: 83–9). Popular choices included Chaucer, the battle of Hastings, Robin Hood, the reign of Edward III and the battle of Poitiers, and through the writing of Scott, scenes from *Ivanhoe* and his other novels. Accuracy for medieval costume was ensured only by meticulous research through historical works such as Mackintosh's *History of England* (1830–1) as well as in primary sources such as the Bayeux Tapestry and the writing of Chaucer, Dante and Shakespeare. Masquerades in medieval dress were remembered in portraits, most famously Landseer's painting of *Queen Victoria and Prince Albert as Queen Philippa and Edward III*, commissioned in 1842 to celebrate a royal *bal costumé* intended as a recreation of the court of Edward III (Banham and Harris 1984: 75–7).

Medieval passions could be indulged not only through books and painting but also during visits to monuments. Warwick Castle attracted at least 6,000 visitors in 1825–6, many from nearby Birmingham and Leamington Spa. The Tower Armouries drew up to 40,000 visitors a year after its opening in 1828, with numbers climbing into six figures thirty years later (Mandler 1997). In 1839, the same year that Hampton Court opened to the public for the first time, the lords of the land paraded in medieval armour at the Eglinton Tournament. This pageant, perhaps the pinnacle of medieval mania, was intended to be a re-enactment of the medieval games described in *Ivanhoe*. It was not the first event of its kind but it was the grandest, with its processions, jousting, staged battle, banquet and costume ball attracting visitors from as far away as India and South America amongst the 100,000-strong crowds. Unfortunately, the British weather made a mockery of the programme, as later did the British press (Banham and Harris 1984: 72–4).

New building and the Gothic revival

Few main streets were left untouched by the Gothic revival (Clark 1950). More than three-quarters of the churches erected under the Church Building Act of 1818 were Gothic in design (Chandler 1971: 187) and many other public buildings, from railway stations to town halls and most notably the New Palace of Westminster, reflected the new taste for architecture, fittings and decoration (Crook 1970; Banham and Harris 1984: 78–82). As one commentator has put it 'the face of the City (of London) was more 'medieval' in 1900 than it had been at any time since 1666 (the year of the Great Fire)' (Dellheim 1982: 6–10).

Architectural fashions varied. At the turn of the century, contemporary design manuals offered the novelty of castles (Lugar 1805; Brown 1841), residences and town halls 'in the Anglo-Norman Style' (Robinson 1827, 1830). Newly-built castles such as Eastnor Castle (1815) and the vast Penrhyn Castle near Bangor with its 'Norman' decoration and furniture (1827–37; Anon. 1953) and new churches such as Leamington Priors (pre-1827) were all precursors of a fashion for 'Norman' or 'Byzantine' building in the 1840s (e.g. St Mary the Virgin in Cardiff) which faded out again in the 1850s. Some new buildings were even 'reconstructed' on surviving medieval foundations, as was the case at Stafford Castle (Stafford Borough Council nd). By the mid-nineteenth century new Gothic architecture was dominant in England, mainland Europe and America, but the zenith of the revival is usually placed twenty years later. During the 1870s the Albert Memorial was completed, one of the Revival's principal architects, George Gilbert Scott, was knighted and the standard text on Victorian Gothic was published by art historian Charles Eastlake (Eastlake 1872). By this time, it was common practice for young architects to be trained by making scale drawings of medieval buildings and there was a groundswell of interest in preservation and study groups. Newspapers reports of restoration projects further heightened public involvement and general knowledge (Parsons 1994).

A major influence in this architectural movement was Augustus Welby Pugin, who was responsible for many publications on medieval interiors which later became source books for artists and designers. Author of *Contrasts* (1836), this volume was composed entirely of juxtaposed plates of medieval (fifteenth century) and nineteenth-century life. Pugin's plates make explicit his low opinion of contemporary living and intentionally promote what he saw as the 'superiority' of the Middle Ages as the zenith of art, religion and society (Brooks 1998; Figure 2.1). Gothic architecture was the vehicle through which he chose to champion his Catholic beliefs of a world in decline. Pugin's vision of medieval architecture was not fanciful or frivolous, as some early Romantics had made it seem, it was serious and required close study.

The monastery, in particular, became a symbol for those committed to a revival of the values of the medieval Church. The Abbey of Mount St Bernard in Charnwood Forest (Leics.), founded in 1839 and designed by Pugin, became England's first monastery built since the Reformation (Banham 1984). Not everyone idealised the spiritual virtues of monastic institutions, particularly those hostile to Roman Catholicism, but the moral and social superiority of the medieval past was a theme echoed throughout the century, in the writing of Thomas Carlyle (1843) and John Ruskin (1851–3), for example.

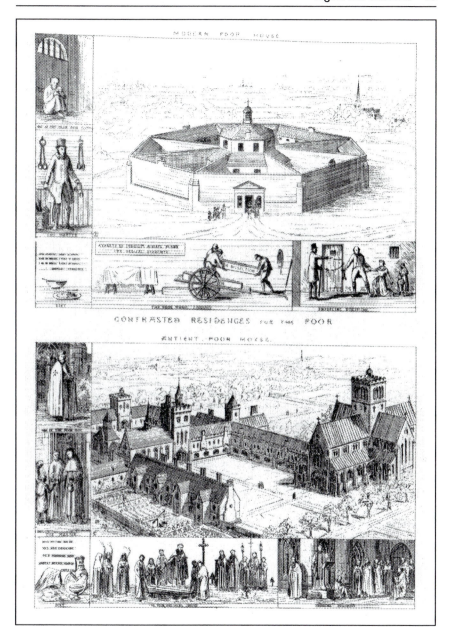

Figure 2.1 Augustus Pugin converted to Roman Catholicism in 1835 and this illustration is taken from his *Contrasts*, published a year later. Gothic architecture is here presented as an ideal and direct expression of Faith and contrasted visually against its debased over-elaborated nineteenth-century equivalent. Pugin's concern for historical authenticity in medieval design encouraged serious architectural studies.

Medieval interiors and furniture also attracted a great deal of interest, influenced by the publication of handbooks (Shaw 1836) and the great industrial exhibitions of the mid-nineteenth century. Following Pugin's 'Medieval Court' at the Great Exhibition of 1851, William Morris's firm made their debut at the 1862 exhibition with all manner of furniture, metalwork, church furnishings, tiles and textiles on show. These events resulted in important commissions which kept medieval style in the public eye.

Architecture and interior furnishings were combined together with some extravagance by the designer and architect William 'Billy' Burges for his client the third marquis of Bute. Bute, an aristocrat of almost unlimited funds and a convert to Catholicism, had a passion for antiquarianism as well as an enthusiasm for medieval monuments, purchasing and preserving both Pluscarden Priory and Rothesay Castle in Scotland. Burges' interests were in French Gothic and he was aware of the work of Eugène Viollet-le-Duc, the French architect, well known for his reconstructions at Carcassonne and for his ten-volume *Dictionnaire raisonné de l'architecture française* (1854–68). Equipped with this catalogue of furnishings, artefacts and buildings, Burges now suggested to his client how Cardiff Castle might be enlivened with towers and water in the moat. But it was the recently excavated medieval ground plan and basements of nearby Castell Coch which, in 1875, was to provide them with the ready-made foundation for a florid Gothic fantasy castle complete with conical towers, gatehouse and drawbridge, banqueting hall and wall-walk (McLees 1998).

Medievalism on this scale indulged an interest in archaeology, an enthusiasm for both building and design and reflected the attraction of Catholicism for some mid-Victorian aristocrats. The appeal was broad with a range of different 'readings'. The Middle Ages were acceptable to a nervous and conservative ruling class who were keen to maintain the social *status quo*. Anxious about events in revolutionary America and France, there was much to be gained by those nearer the top of the social ladder in promoting the conservative values of a medieval feudal hierarchy. It was well recognised that the preservation of medieval monuments could contribute actively to the stability of society, in particular 'the domestic monuments of the halls and hearths of our ancestors are surely most conducive to . . . pious and reverent feelings' (Ferguson 1849). For those further down the social scale the Middle Ages were diverting and portrayed an apparently 'golden age' when there was enough food on the table and chivalric codes pertained (Wainwright 1989). Integrated, harmonious communities had surely enjoyed a safer world, free of social upheaval, in which responsible Church and social leaders had stemmed the disintegration of society. Where a taste for classicism had been élite, because it implied money and education for the acquisition of language and foreign tastes, medievalism tapped a more democratic national appeal (Mandler 1997: 28–32).

Preservation

In 1839 the Cambridge Camden Society was established 'to promote the study of Ecclesiastical Architecture and Antiquities, and the restoration of mutilated Architectural Remains'. The members of the society, 'Ecclesiologists' as they were known, saw Gothic architecture as the outward expression of the 'true' Christian faith. Taking deteriorated church architecture as a metaphor for the redundancy of Anglicanism, they set about aggressive programmes of restoration and popularised their doctrinnaire views through a series of pamphlets. Titles such as *A Few Words to Church Builders*, *Twenty-three Reasons for Getting Rid of Church Pews* and *A Few Hints on the Practical Study of Ecclesiastical Antiquities* sold thousands of copies. Working drawings for church 'restoration' plans were sometimes submitted to the Society for approval, just as they were to its counterpart The Oxford Society for Promoting the Study of Gothic Architecture. Both organisations built up archives of notes and drawings on medieval churches and their fittings (Piggott 1976: 179–81).

What became known as the Oxford Movement in the English Church in the 1840s turned the attention of clergy and faithful alike to 'the structure and fabric of their church, the movement injected a stiff dose of medieval archaeology and architectural history into the clerical and lay population of parish after parish' (Piggott 1976: 180). Religious revival became synonymous with 'improved', 'cleaner' and 'smarter' churches. Medieval architecture, and Gothic architecture in particular, was the logical setting for revitalised medieval ritual and ceremony and, by the mid-nineteenth century, thousands of medieval churches were undergoing restoration and 'improvement' (Gomme 1890; Miele 1996).

One of those who reacted against this over-enthusiasm for restoration was John Ruskin, the quintessential Victorian intellectual. His contribution to art, architecture, culture and political economy are well known but he is also an important figure for medieval archaeologists. Like Pugin, Ruskin promoted the idea that monuments and architecture are records of the past. For him the building was a symbol of continuity, marked by endless repair admittedly, but essentially intact. The work of hands was an expression of mind; architecture could carry a moral message and medieval buildings could serve as a reminder of a 'better' past (see p. 3).

Not all his ideas were welcomed. *The Builder* (19 May 1849) called his ideas 'simply nauseous', another 'verbal excrescence', protesting at 'sentiments and associations of the mediaeval kind'. Followers of Viollet-le-Duc argued that modern materials should be introduced and reconstruction attempted if it guaranteed a future for a medieval building. Nevertheless, Ruskin's ideas were at the heart of the growing preservation movement in the second half of the nineteenth century and enshrined in the doctrine of the Society for the Protection of Ancient Buildings (SPAB), founded in March 1877. The following Ruskin quote, taken from *The Seven Lamps of Architecture*, exemplifies his views on stewardship and building preservation:

It is again no question of expediency or feeling whether we shall preserve the buildings of past times or not. We have no right whatsoever to touch them. They are not ours. They belong partly to those who built them and partly to all the generations of mankind who are to follow us. Neither by the public, nor by those who have the care of public monuments, is the true meaning of the word restoration understood. It means total destruction which a building can suffer: a destruction out of which no remnants can be gathered. . . . There was yet in the old some life, some mysterious suggestion of what it had been, and of what it had lost; some sweetness in the gentle lines which rain and sun had wrought. There can be none in the brute hardness of the new carving.

(Ruskin 1849)

SPAB countered the culture of enthusiastic restoration of ancient buildings represented by the Cambridge Movement and others (Chandler 1971: 218–19). Though they were soon overwhelmed with casework and an intended scheme for recording unrestored churches had to be abandoned, the Society was able to avert some notably destructive restoration schemes, as at Tisbury in Wiltshire, the chapter house of Westminster Abbey and the York city churches, and to influence the plans of many others by getting architects to submit their proposals for approval (Miele 1996). Case studies illustrate the extent to which SPAB could rely upon persistent and outspoken local support in its campaigns against so-called 'restoring' architects (Isherwood 2000).

An important member of SPAB was the polymath William Morris (Harris 1984a) and the inspiration which Morris found in the medieval past is reflected throughout his art, writing and political ideals (Faulkner 1980; see p. 3). In the early 1860s Morris, Marshall and Faulkner had founded a company producing furnishings and textiles loosely medieval in inspiration, some inspired by Morris's visits to the newly opened South Kensington Museum. It was Morris who, horrified in September 1876 by the sight of an Oxfordshire church being torn down for 'improvements' and George Gilbert Scott's plans for the restoration of Tewkesbury Abbey, became such an important member of 'Anti-Scrape', as SPAB was christened. Later treatments of medieval monuments were to be greatly influenced by Morris and SPAB. Slowly, buildings were becoming valued for their historical associations, for the many architectural phases they might preserve which suggested long and eclectic histories, for the aesthetic inspiration they provided for ordinary people as well as architects, and for their individuality in an increasingly mass-produced world. But there were other reasons too. Buildings might be symbols of nationhood, they were part of the fabric of national identity and, at a more local level, they contributed to a sense of community, specialness and tradition.

Medieval buildings under the most obvious threat during the nineteenth century were inevitably those abandoned sites for which no sympathetic contemporary use could be found. The south transept of Byland Abbey (Yorks.) collapsed in 1822 and the last remains of Sandwich Castle (Kent) were carted away '. . . for agricultural purposes' in the early 1880s (*Hansard* 1881: 870). Less spectacular but equally important were the losses suffered during restoration projects. Ruskin's endeavours to persuade the Society of Antiquaries to organise 'watchers and agents' in every town and then to use the Society's influence to prevent impending destruction, came to little (Evans 1956: 309–12). In the 1870s and 1880s the restoration of St Albans Abbey, the destruction of churches in the City of London and in York, and various church restorations in Wales, all went ahead.

The Society of Antiquaries had more success in their protests over a proposal to put the railway line through the precinct of Norwich Cathedral and they were kept in touch by, amongst others, the infatiguable travels of William St John Hope, who sent back reports on threatened buildings (Evans 1956: 334–6). Throughout the century there had been numerous acts of personal charity. Lord Yarborough bought Thornton Abbey (Lincs.) in 1816 to prevent it being quarried for road stone and within twenty years it had been opened to the paying public (Coppack 1990: 20). In north Wales the floors of the 'high tower' in the town wall at Conwy were restored in 1876 at the expense of the keeper of the Ashmolean Museum in Oxford, John Henry Parker, while the London and North Western Railway Company sponsored the rebuilding of the Bakehouse Tower (Taylor 1986). Another building, this time saved by private wealth accrued in South America, was Kirkstall Abbey outside Leeds, which, having first been threatened with total restoration, was about to be sold off in 1888 for development to a 'promoter of public entertainments' (Dellheim 1982: 101–5).

Support for the preservation of historic and ruined buildings could be truly popular and derived as much from a sense of national and local pride as it did from a fear of disgrace that notable buildings were about to fall into disrepair. In July 1847 a *Times* correspondent claimed that 'speculators' (rumoured to be Phineas T. Barnum) were interested in purchasing Shakespeare's birthplace in Stratford and 'trundling it about on wheels like a caravan of wild beasts, giants, or dwarfs, through the United States of America'. Fund-raising to purchase the property at auction led to the establishment of the Shakespeare Birthplace Trust (Fox 1997: 3–8; *Hansard* 1874: 584). Elsewhere, archaeological societies and civic authorities played their part. Concern that the 'Black Gate' of the castle in Newcastle-upon-Tyne would 'fall a sacrifice to modern convenience' led to appeals by the archaeology society. The Corporation offered £50 for 'the best design for the approach in question, with a clause specially insisting on [its] preservation' (Anon. 1857).

When the care of medieval monuments came to be debated in Parliament therefore, it is no surprise to find that there was considerable support for their inclusion in what would eventually become the Ancient Monuments Protection Act 1882 (Saunders 1983). The 'value' of later medieval versus prehistoric and other monuments was unarguable. There were, after all, many medieval buildings already in state care, from royal palaces to Lindisfarne Priory and the Tower of London.

> the country was covered from one end to the other with the noblest and most interesting specimens of ecclesiastical architecture. . . . Take such a monument of antiquity as the old Kitchen of Glastonbury. Which was the better worth preserving – such a building as that, or one of the innumerable barrows on Salisbury Plain . . .?
>
> (*Hansard* 1874: 583)

Special pleas were made for the inclusion of churches in the Bill, on the grounds that some acts of 'restoration' were closer to destruction; the alterations at Salisbury Cathedral and the work of George Gilbert Scott being cited as evidence of bad practice (*Hansard* 1877: 1548). In spite of the precedent set by the earlier Irish Church Act 1869, however, medieval buildings were eventually omitted. The winning argument seemed to hinge upon the potential cost of their inclusion (*Hansard* 1874: 594), the lack of any need for their protection (*Hansard* 1875: 888) and, perhaps crucially, a fear of infringement of privacy (*Hansard* 1875: 882, 1877: 1538). Did not many MPs, after all, live in medieval monuments? One member complained that:

> they could not tell where the ravages of mediaeval curiosity-mongers would stop, and . . . there was nothing to prevent, but, on the contrary, every reason to fear that the tombs of our forefathers and of ourselves would be neither safe nor sacred.
>
> (*Hansard* 1875: 884)

This nervousness was overcome finally by unfavourable comparison with the Irish situation, where responsibility for the care of ecclesiastical ruins had been broadened again under the terms of the Ancient Monuments Protection (Ireland) Act 1892 (Saunders 1983). Accordingly, the scope of English legislation was then widened in the Ancient Monuments Protection Act of 1900 to include 'any structure, erection of historic or architectural interest or any remains thereof', stipulating that inhabited buildings were to be excluded. It would be another forty-seven years before that omission was remedied.

Architectural and archaeological studies

During the first half of the nineteenth century there were outstanding achievements in the study of medieval architecture. John Britton's two sets of volumes *Architectural Antiquities* (1807–26) and *Cathedral Antiquities* (1814–35) were remarkable not only for their scope but for the speed with which they were assembled, setting new standards in the illustration and description of medieval buildings. Thomas Rickman published his pocket-sized *An Attempt to Discriminate the Styles of Architecture in England from the Conquest to the Refor-*

mation (1817; Figure 2.2) which pioneered the classification and terminology of architectural styles for the later medieval period which is still in use today. Doors, windows and arches were presented in a sequence of styles, treating buildings rather like 'kit components' (Miele 1998).

Architectural recording became increasingly precise. Significant contributions to the understanding of architectural style and terms were made by John Parker (e.g. 1836), Frederick Paley (1845) and antiquary Thomas Hudson Turner (with Parker 1851–9), whose publications subsequently enjoyed many editions and who certainly felt their research to be of interest to archaeologists (Parker 1871; Figure 2.3). Edmund Sharpe, for example, was measuring architectural detail at Rievaulx Abbey in 1843 and published his drawings in *Architectural Parallels* (1848). In particular, the summer meetings of the Archaeological Institute encouraged intensive studies by the gifted academic Robert Willis and others (Cocke 1998). Willis' method was to enforce strict separation between the written evidence and the analysis of the building's fabric, a model for later guidebooks and studies. In a series of detailed studies of cathedrals between the 1840s and the 1860s he began to phase buildings, highlighting architecture of different periods by shading and the use of colour (reprinted as Willis 1972–3; Thompson 1996). Above all, it was Willis who 'put the historical study of medieval buildings on to a firm, scholarly footing' (Parsons 1994).

Less well recognised are the myriad local contributions made by church histories and newspaper articles. Original drawings by John Buckler and other artists in the early decades of the century sometimes provide the last record of the architecture and fittings of medieval churches and other buildings prior to their Victorian renovation (RCHME 1987: 3; Figure 2.4). As the century progressed, so improvements in photography and printing brought medieval monuments to a wider public and the first photographic 'surveys' of buildings began to appear in the 1850s (Evans 1956), just as the new railways were improving access to hitherto isolated sites. Travellers were now able to enjoy handbooks which figured lengthy descriptions of medieval churches and other monuments (e.g. Murray 1858). Dover Castle, for example, had a guidebook by 1828 and many local sites had companion guides in which plans were interleaved with local advertising.

In spite of occasional bouts of Protestant prejudice, which judged the study of later medieval architecture as 'papistical' (Evans 1956: 235), the Revival sustained popular interest in certain classes of medieval monument, particularly monasteries, churches and castles. There was now a new reading market for county and local histories:

> the church visitor, with his knapsack on his back, his sketch book, and notebook, and foot-rule, and measuring-tape in his pocket, his good oak stick in his hand, with fair weather, and a fine tract of churches before him.
>
> (Neale 1843)

Figure 2.2 An illustration by the self-taught architect Thomas Rickman (1817: pl.V). Rickman classified window tracery and architectural detail and created the typological sequence and nomenclature (Norman, Early English, Decorated English, etc.) followed by subsequent scholars. Rather than take a picturesque approach to his subject, as many of his contemporaries did, Rickman made his own detailed observations and applied evolutionary principles to medieval architecture.

NORTH PIER.

ⱤECCLIA DEDICATA Eſt
IN ⱤONORE·SCE·ꞄNITATIS
ET BE MARIE VIII N MARTII
A DꞨO ⱤVGONE LINCOLNI
ESI·EPO·ANNO AB ICꞦNATI
ONE DNI M̃ C XC Ⅱ
ꞆEPORE·RICARDI REGIS

DEDICATORY INSCRIPTION.

Figure 2.3 Illustration taken from John Henry Parker's discussion on the origins of Gothic architecture (1871: pl. XII). Shown here are the north pier and dedicatory inscription of 1192 at Clee church (Lincs.), which had been recently restored, much to Parker's disapproval. 'It has become work of the nineteenth century instead of the twelfth', he wrote. Parker demonstrates how the date stone is an ineffective guide to dating the pillar into which it has been inserted.

Figure 2.4 The Free Grammar School at Wainfleet (Lincs.) founded in 1484 by the Bishop of Winchester. One of over 10,000 sketches by John Buckler, in this case for his *Sixty Views of Endowed Grammar Schools* (1827). This building was the subject of antiquarian correspondence in the early nineteenth century in the pages of *Archaeologia*.

Caricature sometimes gave way to mockery. And the antiquarian outing was given particularly brutal treatment in the popular comic prose and verse collection of the *Ingoldsby Legends* (Barham 1837–43). Here, in a visit to Netley Abbey, a poet contemplates with satisfaction the 'mouldering walls', 'the stained pane and sculptured stone', 'the lone refuge of the owl and bat' only to discover inside, to his surprise, 'a hag, surrounded by crockery-ware, vending, in cups, to the credulous throng, a nasty decoction miscall'd Souchong'. An apparently 'authentic' Gothic experience rudely shattered by crowds and commercialism.

Societies dedicated to architectural, antiquarian and archaeological interests flourished and it is no surprise to find that structural materials such as decorated floor tiles received early attention (e.g. Hennicker 1796; Nichols 1845; Greenfield 1892). When in 1804 Samuel Lysons, then Keeper of Public Records in the Tower of London, copied sixteen Spanish tiles in the Lord Mayor's Chapel in Bristol for his *Collection of Gloucestershire Antiquities* (Lysons 1804), he was one of first to record *in situ* medieval artefacts in exact detail. Tiles might be relaid, were sometimes copied (e.g. Great Malvern Priory Church, Worcs.) or stored loose and acquired by collectors. Everyday artefacts such as keys, locks and buckles held less attraction.

Medieval finds inevitably came to light as ground was dug for services, railway lines and new buildings. Few were as well dated as the collection of metal objects recovered in Salisbury (Wilts.) between 1852 and 1854 during the laying of sewers and piped water supplies. These were reckoned to postdate the foundation of the town in 1227 (Saunders and Saunders 1991; Figure 2.5). Exceptional pieces were exhibited at the Society of Antiquaries

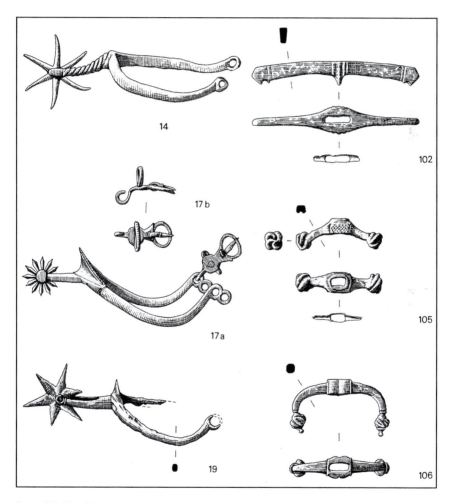

Figure 2.5 The Salisbury Drainage collection was the foundation collection of Salisbury Museum. The finds have no stratigraphical context but, given that the city was founded in the thirteenth century, they provided useful dating clues. Shown here are examples of rowel spurs and iron dagger and sword quillons. (Saunders and Saunders 1991: figures 18 and 24).

where they sometimes formed the subject of short talks and figured in the *Archaeological Journal* under the heading of 'archaeological intelligence'. Opinion on function and date could be both well informed and widely disseminated (e.g. for medieval small finds; Hume 1863).

Connoisseurs also amassed substantial collections, though they tended to restrict themselves to intact, whole pieces (Rhodes 1979; MacGregor 1998). Indeed, collectors can be traced for almost every group of medieval artefacts (**Box 2.1**). Numismatic interests flourished, for example, and several catalogues and articles appeared (e.g. Ruding 1817; *Numismatic Chronicle* from 1838–9). Coin hoards were reported according to the laws of treasure trove (e.g. Baron 1883). Sales were frequent, and English buyers and museum curators were by now travelling to Europe to make their acquisitions (Gaimster 1997a: 15–19 for German stonewares). Medieval finds did not always attract the same interest as finds of other periods, however. They were often poorly dated, lacked context and thought devoid of beauty. As late as 1884 Pitt Rivers could still comment that 'from the relics of this period little is to be learnt . . . the interest which attaches to such objects is more sentimental than useful . . . they do no more than supply some of the lights and shadows' (Pitt Rivers 1884).

The dress historian Joseph Strutt had published his *Complete View of the Dress and Habits of the People of England* in 1796–9 and this volume and subsequent reprints were enormously influential in nineteenth-century history paintings (Harris 1984b: Figure 2.7). New books on costume history reflected the popularity of medieval garments in painting and pageantry as much as the mid-nineteenth century preoccupation for technical accuracy (Planché 1834; Shaw 1843; Fairholt 1846; Mercuri 1860–1). Large collections of armour, such as that of Samuel Rush Meyrick, who published the standard text in the field (1824), could still be amassed relatively cheaply (Banham and Harris 1984: 65). Generally, the motive for doing so was neither financial nor educative but social. A display of the medieval past in the home implied a long and noble family.

Some buildings, like Scott's Abbotsford and the armouries of Queen Elizabeth I at the Tower of London, were open to visitors, but there was no British parallel for Nyerup's proposed museum for Denmark-Norway which included a room for the Middle Ages (Klindt-Jensen 1975: 46) until 1866 when the Department of British and Medieval Antiquities and Ethnography was established at the British Museum. That the new Department should have come into being at all was largely due to the efforts of Augustus Wollaston Franks (Caygill 1997). Franks had been prominent in the organisation of the Medieval Exhibition of 1850, a preliminary to the Great Exhibition, at a time when there was increasing demand for the British Museum to accept and exhibit national collections. A Royal Commission report on Museum activities in 1847 supported the idea and by January 1852 a new room had been set up to display British and medieval objects. Franks participated in this new

Box 2.1 1850 and medieval pottery studies

The middle years of the nineteenth century were important ones for the study of medieval ceramics. William Chaffers' article 'On medieval earthenware vessels' was published in the *Journal of the British Archaeological Association* for 1850. In it the author took issue with the contemporary view that green-glazed pottery was necessarily recent, pointing out that glazed vessels had been found at some depth, even mixed with or below Roman remains. He assembled a counter argument from a wide range of sources including manuscripts, literary references and documentary accounts, wills and household books and correctly deduced that a Bellarmine stoneware jug attributed to the Saxon period was more likely to be of sixteenth- or seventeenth-century date.

Chaffers' paper is one of several publications at about this time which helped to put the study of medieval ceramics onto a more advanced footing (Hurst 1991). It is important that it should draw on archaeological observation for part of its argument but also that a variety of sources contribute to its conclusions. Other events which stimulated interest in medieval artefacts were the exhibition and catalogue of *Ancient and Mediaeval Art* at the Society of Arts in London and the purchase of well-provenanced vessels from collectors, Ralph Bernal and Charles Roach Smith, 'the father of broken pottery displays', for the evolving national collections at the British Museum and the new Victoria and Albert Museum in London (Gaimster 1997a: 15–30; Weatherall 1994: 12; Wilson 1995).

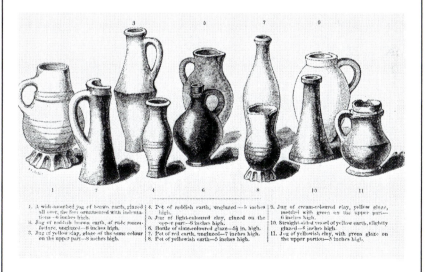

Figure 2.6 A selection of medieval pottery illustrated by William Chaffers in 1850.

Figure 2.7 Illustration of fifteenth-century hunting dress taken from Joseph Strutt's *Complete View of the Dress and Habits of the People of England* (1796–9).

venture and, a short time later, found himself Keeper of the new Department. Until his retirement in 1896 Franks dedicated himself to creating a national archaeological collection, purchasing and exchanging brasses, enamels, ivories, jewellery, medieval pottery, seals, textiles and tiles. He was himself a generous benefactor but most pieces were purchased at the sales of private collectors such as Pugin, Charles Roach Smith and Walpole though a few finds from recent excavations were also accepted, such as the textiles found in a grave at Worcester Cathedral in 1861 (Cherry 1997).

Across Europe, interest in medieval antiquities encouraged the detailed recording and excavation of medieval monuments. In Germany, the *Monumenta Germaniae Historica* was launched in 1818. In Ireland, George Petrie included medieval monuments in his volume on Derry for the *Ordnance Topographical Survey of Ireland* in 1839. In England county histories often contained descriptions and plans, particularly of parish churches. Rather less common was the inclusion of details of excavations of medieval sites. Richard

Colt Hoare's *History of Ancient Wiltshire* (1810–21) included a plan of Thomas
Phillipps' excavations at Clarendon Palace outside Salisbury (Figure 2.8).
Phillipps, a London merchant with his own massive collection of books, coins
and other antiquities, also recovered painted glass, Norman tiles and
fragments of painted stucco from the site (James and Robinson 1988).

A review of those classes of monument being investigated through excavation during the first half of the nineteenth century reveals a predictable
obsession with national history in its mix of well-documented secular and
monastic sites (data from the National Excavation Index). Of the ten
excavations on later medieval sites in the Wessex region (here defined as
within 60 kilometres of Southampton) between the years 1800 and 1850 no
less than four involved monasteries. Two of the remaining six were a chapel
and the cathedral at Old Sarum (Wilts.). Similar patterns can be observed
elsewhere; one of the first plans of a monastic ruin was drawn up after
extensive excavations on the site of the Benedictine Abbey of St Mary at York
in the 1820s (Coppack 1990) and Samuel Woodward contributed one of the
more systematic investigations of a medieval site at Wymondham Abbey
(Norfolk; Woodward 1836). Notably, these were all excavations at abandoned

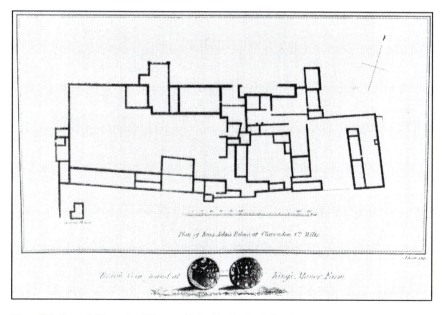

Figure 2.8 Plan of Clarendon Palace published by Richard Colt Hoare in 1837, based on
excavations by Thomas Phillipps in 1821. The site of Clarendon was known to
Leland, Saxton, Speed, Camden, Aubrey, Defoe and Stukeley and an account of it
was related to the Society of Antiquaries in 1770. Later John Britton described the
'ruined walls and heaps of rubbish' and Buckler sketched some watercolours there
before Phillips traced the outlines of all the major buildings (see also Figure 3.5).

sites; the aim of Woodward's work being to expose the foundations of the abbey in order to obtain a plan, though he was distracted somewhat by the discovery of two sealed medieval lead cases containing human remains. These were cut open only with considerable difficulty, one being found to contain human remains packed in cumin and coriander. The seeds were promptly replanted but failed to germinate! By way of contrast, excavations such as those by John Browne in York Minster in 1829 and 1840 within a place of active worship were a rarity in the first half of the century but later became more common as discoveries were made during restoration projects (Rodwell 1989: 25). Occasional 'casual' observations were also made in towns and cities, 'huge trunks of oak trees, very roughly squared by the axe', evidently substantial medieval timber waterfront revetments, were seen to the south of Thames Street in London in 1831, for example (AJK 1831).

Between 1850 and 1882 a further twenty-three later medieval sites were investigated within the Wessex area, of which three were churches, five monasteries, two cathedrals and six castles. Few excavations continued for more than one season's campaign, though a handful of sites were revisited on more than one occasion, notably Winchester Cathedral in 1797 (crypt), 1868 (tomb opening of William Rufus), 1870 (tomb opening) and Lacock Abbey (1744, 1841, 1880 and 1911). Excavations at the rural settlement and chapel at West Lavington (Crittall 1975: 103) and the magnate residence at Basing House (Colleton Rennie 1876) were exceptional and it should be no surprise, therefore, that when the 1841 Select Committee of the House of Commons met to consider the question of protection for monuments of national impor-tance, it anchored discussion around monuments associated with great events and royalty (Champion 1996). Major historical re-evaluations such as Thomas Macaulay's *History of England* (1849) which aimed 'to relate the history of the people as well as the history of the government' seem to have had no dis-cernible effect on the balance of monument classes under examination.

Most excavations were of unexceptional quality, even by standards of the day. In 1851 when the Leeds and Thirsk Railway decided to incorporate the castle motte at Pickhill (Yorks.) into their embankment, the directors 'ordered it to be excavated [and] cut it through in all directions' in search of the black chest containing treasures reputed to have given the mound its name: Money Hill (Whellan 1859). Contemporary excavators rarely attempted to resolve the complexities of stratigraphical phasing, they failed to recognise earlier buildings and did not record or publish adequately what they had seen. Disentangling verifiable observation from supposition, even where discoveries were clearly substantial and material still survives today, can be a considerable puzzle (e.g. Barton 1979: 184–90). Finds could be wildly misdated, the kiln debris and medieval coarseware wasters from Limpsfield in Surrey were thought to be Roman, for example (Leveson Gower 1891). When the Reverend Money's excavations at a round mound near Bromham (Wilts.) in 1840 revealed a cruciform-shaped bed of rammed clay together with odd Roman artefacts, the irresistible combination of artefacts and nearby Roman settlement led him to deduce a Roman date for his monument and suggested that the feature might be the burial place of a Christianised Roman Briton (Mellor 1940–2). In fact, it was a medieval windmill, and he was to be far from the last excavator to be puzzled by this particular class of monument (Bond 1995: 16).

Although most of these early excavations were unremarkable, there were exceptions. The third volume of the *Archaeological Journal*, published in 1846, contains among its articles on church architecture and bells, monasteries and manuscripts, an account of the excavations of the Reverend John Wilson, Fellow of Trinity College in Oxford, at the deserted medieval village of Woodperry (Oxon.). The church and village here had supposedly been destroyed in a fire and Wilson's aim, in which he was successful, was to 'establish the fact of the existence of a church, and cemetery around it'. His finds, drawn for the article by Albert Way and engraver Orlando Jewitt, confirmed Roman occupation and show that he was clearly able to distinguish Roman from later artefacts, including pottery (Figure 2.9; Wilson 1846).

Other excavators were also pursuing well thought-out and sustained research plans. The achievements of Yorkshire antiquary Richard Walbran at Fountains Abbey between 1840 and 1854 are well known (Coppack 1990) but those of railway surveyor Stephen Williams rather less so. Williams published full accounts of his digging at Strata Florida (Williams 1889), Abbey Cwmhir (Williams 1894–5) and Strata Marcella (Williams 1892), spending about two months in each case exposing the plan of the church and some conventual buildings at his Cistercian sites before moving on to the Premonstratensian abbey of Talley (Williams 1897). He produced both interim reports and final publications which drew together known documents, architectural drawings, plans and tables of comparative building measurements. Typically, his method consisted of identifying a wall and, with his staff of workmen, tracing its length until it joined others:

> finding that the line of the wall was due north and south, and fairly perfect for a height of from 1 ft. to 1 ft. 6 in., we hoped that by following it out we should eventually come upon the chapter-house and east wall of the transept. In this, however, we were disappointed . . . we failed to find any foundation in continuation of those we had laid bare, and after cutting several cross-trenches we did not discover anything further at this point.
>
> (Williams 1892: 2)

Occasionally, medieval discoveries caught the imagination. John Ingrams saved and published two medieval jugs and two bottles 'of very rare occurrence' found while digging a new cellar in 1838 for Trinity College, Oxford (Ingrams 1846: 62–4; Hinton 1977). In 1845–6 'wonder-struck admirers'

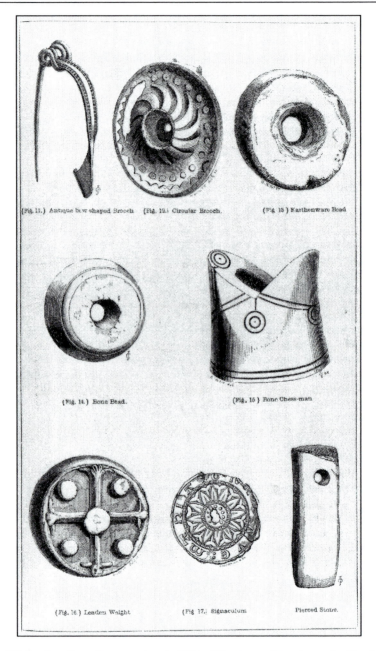

Figure 2.9 Artefacts from the excavations in 1846 at Woodperry (Oxon.) organised by the Reverend Dr Wilson, President of Trinity College, Oxford (Wilson 1846: 121). The declared aim was 'the search for a church, churchyard and village, supposed to have formerly existed there'. Several of the objects shown here are late Roman in date, as Wilson fully appreciated.

were delighted by discoveries made by railway workers near the Priory of St Pancras in Lewes (Dellheim 1982: 33–9). When the news reached the national press, hopes were raised that the charnel pits they had uncovered might prove an attraction for holidaymakers in nearby Brighton. Medieval and earlier discoveries certainly heightened Victorians' sense of their past and caused them to ponder upon the differences between past and present. In the Lewes case there was also debate as to how human burials should be treated and the decency of public display. But the discoveries added little of substance to any understanding of the medieval past. Once uncovered, the human remains were immediately linked with the closest suitable historically known event, the battle of Lewes in 1264 (Coppack 1990: 22). This equation between archaeology and history was made all too quickly at a number of sites. Williams thought his discovery of child burials at Strata Marcella must confirm documented accusations of the 'fearfully dissolute life' led by the monks there (Williams 1892: 9).

During the nineteenth century more specialised societies came into being which were to influence the study of medieval archaeology (**Box 2.2**). These included the Surtees Society (1834) devoted to the publication of unedited manuscripts, the Early English Text Society (1864), the genealogical Harleian Society (1869), the Royal Historical Society (1868), the Society for the Protection of Ancient Buildings (1877), and the Pipe Roll Society (1883). The opening of the new Public Record Office in Chancery Lane, the initiation of the Rolls Series publications and the Historical Manuscripts Commission by the 1870s all spurred interest in the publication of original texts. In addition, by 1886 there were some forty-nine county and local archaeology societies (Weatherall 1998). They encouraged active membership through summer excursions and quarterly meetings and through contributions to local 'queries'.

The aims of local societies can be gleaned from their manifestos. Their declared motives include curiosity about the past in a world of rapid change, a wish to preserve documents, antiquities and monuments under threat and a desire for intellectual betterment, to 'elevate the mind'. Medieval monuments such as churches, castles and mansions were legitimate targets; documents, topography, architecture and maps the favoured sources, and the accumulation of 'empirical fact' often the outcome (**Box 2.3**). Study of the past deepened a sense of place and historical continuity, consolidating local identity in a world which was fast becoming unfamiliar (Dellheim 1982: 52–6). Interests were wide-ranging but lacked perspective and could be unsound in their wholehearted promotion of the local context, especially in their haste to link monuments with genealogies.

Of those who indulged a taste for the past in the later nineteenth century, the largest group, the antiquarians, pursued a wide range of activities including excavation, collection, and the compilation of local histories and topographies. They were equally at home with manuscripts, antiquities and books

Box 2.2 Medieval documents, nineteenth-century transcriptions and the modern field archaeologist

During the nineteenth century a great number of county record societies and other bodies such as the Surtees Society and the Record Commissioners transcribed primary documentation. In Somerset, three later medieval documents were published in 1889: the Kirby's Quest of 1284, the *Nomina Villarum* of 1315 and the Lay Subsidy of 1327 (Dickinson 1889). The Subsidy lists manors or vills, together with the names of the people assessed and the amount of subsidy paid. The surnames often refer to named places and, while the nineteenth-century transcription is far from perfect, by comparing this list against named farms on modern and nineteenth-century maps it has been possible to correlate those farmsteads and hamlets which existed in 1327 with those in existence until recently. Names on the list which cannot now be located are likely to have become deserted in the period since 1327. The published nineteenth-century transcription thus provides the basis for modern field archaeology and augments our understanding of the medieval settlement pattern and their condition and survival (Aston 1983b).

Figure 2.10 Earthworks of a farmstead at Twitchen in Culbone (now Oare parish, Som.). William de Kytenare is recorded in the 1327 Lay Subsidy. Kitnor is another name for Culbone, and this is probably the place from which William took his name in the fourteenth century. A long-house was still standing here in 1842 when it was recorded on the tithe map. (Photo: Mick Aston).

Box 2.3 *The Yorkshire Archaeological and Topographical Journal 1869–1882*

When the Huddersfield Archaeological and Topographical Association adopted its new title in 1870 the Yorkshire county journal was born. A study of the contents of the journal in its early years reveals a typical range of antiquarian and local interests in the later Middle Ages. The first issue of 1869–70 contained articles on painted glass in a parish church, a pedigree of families and a note on heraldic bench ends. The second issue continued with a similar range of themes on Subsidy Rolls, church dedications and various manuscript volumes in the minster library at Ripon. A crucifix found under the floor of the nave of a church during repairs is the first medieval artefact to receive comment. Field archaeology makes its appearance in three articles on castles by George Clark after 1880. Clark was an authority on castle studies and believed the 'moated mounds' he saw at Sandal, Tadcaster and elsewhere to be 'ancient Saxon seats'. Clark's articles for the *Journal* included scaled plans and full architectural descriptions. His call for 'close examination' of the evidence may have led to the 'considerable excavations' at Pontefract Castle in 1881–2 when buildings were 'opened out' and 'large finds unearthed'.

The Yorkshire society is one of the forty-nine county and local societies which came into being between the 1840s and the 1880s and was among the later 'wave' of societies emerging in the industrial north of England after 1860 (Levine 1986). For the most part, general curiosity and local pride were the strongest motives for membership; archaeological and architectural discoveries served those interests well. Only when the Congress of Archaeological Societies came into being in 1888 did research become better co-ordinated at a national level (see Chapter 3).

in museums and libraries. Medieval studies were most closely associated with this popular form of enquiry. The majority were male, middle class, Anglican, and university educated at Oxford or Cambridge. Most were engaged in unrelated full-time employment, often the professional sector of the middle classes such as clerics, lawyers, bankers, Members of Parliament and military men. Very few earned their money from their studies, but many were Fellows of the Society of Antiquaries of London and bonded socially through marriage and family (Levine 1986; Weatherall 1998).

Generally speaking then, interest in the later Middle Ages was considerable but restricted largely to the study of architecture, artefact collections and documents. The contribution of archaeological excavation remained slight. The total of medieval sites as a proportion of the total number of excavations undertaken was less than 10 per cent throughout the century so that excavations on Roman and prehistoric sites were often five to ten times more numerous. Even the *Gentleman's Magazine* gave up articles on the medieval field in 1868 (Evans 1956: 289). This lack of apparent archaeological interest requires some explanation and may be in part because later medieval archaeology so rarely yielded the treasures familiar to barrow diggers (Hurst 1989) or because of the overwhelming emphasis on the study of medieval architecture and documentation.

The relationship between antiquarianism, historians, architects and archaeology was uncertain territory. One incident seems to provide a defining moment. As the middle of the century approached it was felt by some that the Society of Antiquaries was too preoccupied with earlier periods (Pettigrew 1851: 165) and so, in December 1843, the British Archaeological Association was founded 'for the encouragement and prosecution of researches into the arts and monuments of the early and middle ages' (Evans 1949). As explained in the first issue of the Society's *Archaeological Journal*, the new society would adopt a strong stance on preservation and make efforts to record those monuments which could not be saved. Internal politics led almost immediately to a division into two groups, one retaining the original title, the other calling itself the Archaeological Institute (Weatherall 1994). The Association, led by Thomas Wright, held that archaeology was a historical discipline, whereas the more progressive Albert Way, who led the Institute faction, believed in linking archaeology to geology and was in favour of closer links with anthropology and the 'sciences' (Bowden 1991: 161; Evans 1949: 9). Edward Freeman, later Regius Professor of Modern History at Oxford, was among a group who objected to this stance. In his view archaeology was no way to approach the study of sculpture, architecture or painting, '[the Institute] is merely archaeological on points where mere archaeology is worse than useless . . . the Institute is wrong in applying to higher matters the merely antiquarian tone which belongs to inferior ones' (Freeman 1871).

One drawback was that medieval studies had remained comparatively isolated from developments in prehistory in the first half of the nineteenth century in Scandinavia, England and France; unaffected by the elaboration of new chronologies, new techniques of relative dating and the question of human origins (Trigger 1989). There was, for example, no notable contribution by later medieval archaeology to the development of racial theory or to discussions about the biological origin of nations, even though the 'Saxon' and 'Norman' physical and cultural stereotypes were popular literary subjects. Such questions could be addressed by history books but do not seem to be reflected in 'archaeological' writing, at least for the post-Conquest period. Unlike later medieval architecture, archaeology seemed less capable of generating scholarly or public debate.

Central to any debate about the lack of later medieval archaeology undertaken in the nineteenth century is the concept of time, the divisions between Biblical time, geological time and prehistory, between prehistory and history. Once the emphasis was placed on distinguishing documented societies from non-literate societies, and textual studies from artefactual analysis then any archaeology of the later medieval period, of literate peoples, sat uneasily across these accepted definitions. By the second half of the nineteenth century, prehistory had taken the primary academic role within archaeology, interacting with geology, evolutionary zoology and social anthropology in the new language of science which had gained currency from the work of Charles Darwin and others. When a few Chairs of Archaeology began to be created in universities, medieval archaeology was never central to the interests of the appointments. A new set of specific methods appropriate to the archaeologist was emerging, among them excavation, inductive analysis and classification and the academic marginalisation of broader antiquarian values set back the cause of medieval archaeology. This is not to say that excellent work was not carried out. George Clark, an engineer and pioneer of British castle studies was making measured plans of sites, noting stylistic similarities and assessing their strategic importance by the middle of the century (e.g. Clark 1850). But most historic archaeology remained firmly wedded to history, reflecting concerns with the great and the famous, with nationhood and documented events.

At the very moment when archaeology came to be recognised as a separate sub-discipline and was developing its own suites of aims and methods, historical archaeology was more or less excluded. It was not wholly isolated, of course, the impact of empirical science, for instance, influenced the under-standing of stratigraphy (Bintliff 1986a). However, there now began a period of partial estrangement from methodological and theoretical advances in the study of prehistory which many would argue as damaging. An effective counter argument, however, might maintain that medieval archaeology, like Roman and Egyptian studies where inscriptions are commonly studied, was right not to maintain a rather simplistic text/artefact division and to continue to publish research bridging archaeology and history in journals of quality such as the *Archaeological Journal* and the *Journal of the British Archaeological Association*. As we shall see, the essence of this debate is still with us 150 years later.

Chapter 3

An emerging discipline

Monuments, methods and ideas (1882–1945)

The period 1882–1945 was a time of slow transition for the study of the archaeology of the Middle Ages, but concealed here, and often ignored by modern researchers, are the roots of the subject's rapid post-war growth. A high priority was placed upon the public display of medieval monuments and this was a time of methodological advances led by air photography and field survey. Excavations often targeted well-documented monuments at the higher end of the social scale but gradually moved towards the broader analyses of artefact types and monument classes. Many concepts formulated during this period continue to have a profound influence on the discipline, particularly those derived from economic history, historical geography and local history.

Excavation

Before the Great War: clearance and display

General Pitt Rivers' excavations at Caesar's Camp near Folkestone (Kent) in 1878 have been claimed as the first scientific excavation of a medieval site in Britain (Bennett 1988: 17). Published in *Archaeologia*, the excavation account is a model of logical argument and clarity in which the identity and date of the visible earthworks are deduced from stratigraphy and finds (Pitt Rivers 1883). The format of the report would be familiar to any twenty-first century field archaeologist; a discussion of topography and geology is followed by a justification of trench location, a summary of past work on the site, and a description of stratigraphy and finds from each trench (Figure 3.1). This is presented with reference to plans, section drawings, a 'Relic Table' and superb drawings of finds. The conclusion is that the 'camp' is not a hillfort, as had originally been supposed, but Norman in date and

> that it was for the defence of the coast that this Camp was erected, but at this point the labours of the Archaeologist, for the present at least, must cease. Having brought the Camp within the pale of historic times, I leave further speculation on the subject to historians.
>
> (Pitt Rivers 1883: 453)

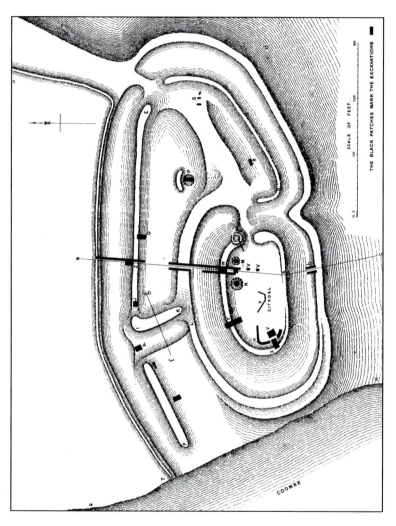

Figure 3.1 Pitt Rivers' plan of his two-week digging campaign at Caesar's Camp or Castle Hill, Folkestone, in the summer of 1878. The eleventh- and twelfth-century earthworks of this oval ringwork and bailey were thought to be prehistoric but detailed recording proved otherwise. (Pitt Rivers 1883).

Another exceptional project was undertaken by the General at King John's House at Tollard Royal (Wilts.), where an archaeological eye and method- ology were brought to bear on an historic building (Smith 1985: 7–11). Pitt Rivers had an advantage in that the house was empty but he stripped the walls of their plaster and stucco, scraped paint from panelling and removed all features later than the medieval period (including Elizabethan windows), replacing only that which was necessary for the safety of the building. This architectural recording was combined with excavation and, adopting a similar approach for both exercises, all the rooms and architectural features were numbered. Models of the thirteenth-century pointed arches showed their exact condition at the time they were found, and 'the position of each stone and brick is given by means of which architects and antiquarians will be able to see clearly what has been done, and what authority exists for the slight restorations that have been made' (Pitt Rivers 1890: 13).

In another sense too the work at King John's House was exceptional. It was in this study that Pitt Rivers highlighted the value of medieval artefact study, arguing that medieval finds could be treated just like finds from any other period:

> 'there are conditions in which they afford the only evidence available even in medieval times . . . in fact the subject has not been much studied, and it is with the hope of promoting this branch of enquiry that I have had so many little objects figured . . .'
>
> (Pitt Rivers 1890: 13–14)

The final publication on King John's House contains some of the first section drawings of medieval pottery and moves towards the idea of a sequence, the sort of 'typology' of pottery which had been unavailable to Chaffers fifty years previously and which was to become such a central concern for later gener- ations of medieval archaeologists. This promotion of the importance of common objects, 'odds and ends, that have no doubt, been thrown away by their owners as rubbish' (Pitt Rivers 1898: 336), helped to distinguish archaeologists from the treasure-hunting antiquarians.

The General's name and work are synonymous today with the break between the 'art-historical phase' in pottery studies and the 'typological phase' (Orton *et al.* 1993), although there are other unsung pioneers such as T. McKenny Hughes in the Cambridge area (Hurst 1955) and this was to be no lasting revolution in medieval artefact studies. For many years to come, the major source of comparative material for archaeologists in the field con- tinued to be museum catalogues. In pottery studies, for example, the writing of Arthur Church (1884), R. L. Hobson (1902; 1903) and of Bernard Rackham and Herbert Read (1924) was influential. The motive for these studies was no longer political or religious. Instead, under the influence of the Arts and Crafts movement, more serious attention was paid to the craftsmanship in objects. The focus was firmly upon recognisable styles, mainly for intact finewares which, in the absence of any understanding of their archaeological context, continued to be studied as 'pieces' by art historians who made comparisons between motifs and heraldic devices, described signed and dated pieces, and established the 'evolution' of decorative styles (e.g. van de Put 1904). Unfortunately, medieval coarsewares seemed to defy any logical progression in which simple forms could be seen to evolve into more complex and highly decorated ones. One depressed early twentieth-century excavator complained that 'the differentiation of unglazed sherds from Roman to Norman times, and even later than that, is practically impossible' (Chater and Major 1909).

The exceptional nature of Pitt Rivers' work only becomes clear when placed in the context of contemporary excavation. Most other sites were only sampled very lightly, few were published fully or to the standards of the General and none embraced the wider range of monument classes, choosing instead to focus on castles, cathedrals, palaces and monasteries. That is not to say that excavations were unambitious in scale. There were four seasons of excavations at Carisbrooke Castle on the Isle of Wight between 1891 and 1895, for example (Stone 1895–7), and six years at Beaulieu Abbey 1900–6 (Hope and Brakspear 1906). Even so, scholars complained that 'immense sums are spent in excavating civilisations in far-away countries with which we have little concern; our own Byland, Rievaulx, Glastonbury remain lost beneath the soil' (Bond 1905). This was all soon to change.

Although the restoration of medieval buildings had slowed, scholars now turned their attention to the detailed recording of extant features (see, for example, Bond 1908; 1910; Clapham 1934). The Archaeological Institute had proposed a national photographic record and survey as early as 1897 but, in particular, architect Charles Innocent's *The Development of English Building Construction* (1916) laid an emphasis on the more detailed analysis of structures. At the same time, ruined monuments were 'cleared' for the benefit of the visiting public. There was nothing new in this idea, the foundations of the abbey church at Beaulieu had been marked out in the turf with gravel in the 1870s (Hope and Brakspear 1906) while at Carisbrooke Castle excavated walls had been 'built up a couple of feet and roughly coped with stones set on edge' (Stone 1895–7), but a new influence on both the selection of sites for excavation and the methodologies adopted was the Ancient Monuments Act of 1900. This Act allowed buildings and ruins of medieval date to be taken more readily under the wing of the Office of Works as guardianship sites (though some, like Old Sarum, had already been acquired) so that they could be 'furbished up into smug neatness' (Cram 1906).

Abbey and priory remains were often chosen, not surprisingly since the post of Chief Inspector of Ancient Monuments was held between 1910 and 1933 by an architectural historian with strong interests in monastic sites, Charles Peers (Radford 1953). Sites with good preservation were preferred such as Titchfield (Hants. in 1923; Figure 3.2) and, with the emphasis on repair and display to the public, it was the major buildings of the monastic precinct which were normally picked upon. Negotiations for land acquisition, access and custodial transfer of property could be protracted and wartime conditions sometimes made it difficult to acquire the materials needed for repair. Nevertheless, by 1935 the Office of Works had, with the exception of Conwy, taken all the Edwardian castles in North Wales into its care and in Yorkshire alone, ten abbeys and priories representing five Orders, as well as seven castles, were in guardianship. The First Commissioner noted with satisfaction that interest in archaeological heritage was 'rapidly spreading', acknowledging the contribution of the railway companies and the Automobile Association who had produced free pamphlets with maps and short notes on monuments (Ormsby Gore 1936).

Minimum intervention was the watchword for masonry so that sites were never 'invented'. Under the aegis of engineer Frank Baines, principal architect of the Ancient Monuments branch of the Office of Works, every effort was made to preserve the colour tones and textures of stonework and jointing. As much was retained as possible, including evidence for structural problems and defects. Even cracks and bulges were restored wherever safety and stability allowed, new work was introduced very rarely and then only to ensure the

Figure 3.2 The Premonstratensian abbey at Titchfield, Hants. Converted by Thomas Wriothesley 1537–42 and largely demolished in 1781. Wriothesley inserted this turreted gateway into the monastic nave. The site was taken into guardianship in 1923. (Photo: author).

stability of existing structures. Innovative structural solutions were devised as, for example, when reinforced concrete beams were used at Tintern Abbey in 1913–14 (Fergusson and Harrison 1999: 204). Their introduction was fiercely criticised but more controversial still was the reconstruction of the bays of the cloister at Rievaulx. This site was acquired by the Office of Works in 1917, and use was made of material found in the course of excavation 'for the purpose of displaying what the cloister arcade looked like'. It was duly labelled 'reconstruction'. Similarly, a few bays of wall arcading were reassembled in the choir at Byland, a move considered to be 'without precedent' at that time (Ormsby Gore 1936).

Curiously dual standards operated. While any architectural intervention had to be carefully justified, much of the archaeological evidence for the adaption and re-use of these monastic sites was destroyed. All archaeological levels after the latest occupation, sometimes more than 2 metres in depth, were removed wholesale with the aim of revealing the plan and 'all hitherto hidden parts of the structure' (Ormsby Gore 1936: 8), rescuing only the larger decorative stonework (Coppack 1990: 25–30). The over-riding aim was clearance and often there was no policy for documenting the work by photography or by drawing. At Rievaulx, some 90,000 tons of excavated fill were spread a metre deep over the adjacent fields, covering medieval earthworks in some areas but achieving the desired effect of a levelled site. Much of the carved stone remained on site for the next seventy-five years, weathering the Yorkshire winters (Fergusson and Harrison 1999: 200). There was little chance of any meaningful integration of architectural and archaeological complexities when trenches were cut around the edges of buildings or targeted only key intersections. For the most part, walls were 'chased' just as they had been in the nineteenth century, leaving deposits proud in the centre of buildings which were then shovelled away. The final interpretation of phasing depended largely upon architecture not archaeological stratigraphy, and, for the most part, deposits beneath the highest medieval levels were left quite untouched. At each monument Peers strove to find a balance between preserving neat walls stripped of vegetation, explaining monuments in new guidebooks and enhancing their settings with smooth lawns. The end result created a 'tended and tidied ambience within which remains would stand in an ordered and disciplined manner' (Fergusson and Harrison 1999: 210). It comes as no surprise to find that Peers was such a keen gardener (Radford 1953).

Not all campaigns were publicly funded in the early years of the century. The Society of Antiquaries sponsored excavations at the Tower of London, Old Sarum (Wilts.), and Cleeve Abbey (Som.), amongst others (Evans 1956: 357). The private owner of the Carthusian monastery at Mount Grace Priory (Yorks.), the historian William Brown, encouraged the excavation of the site in 1896. His successor, the industrialist Isaac Lowthian Bell, had one of the monastic cells on the northern side of the Great Cloister rebuilt, an early example of medieval reconstruction for the purposes of display (Coppack

1991). At Glastonbury Abbey thirty-four seasons of digging took place in the years 1908–79 after the site was bought back at auction from private owners by the Church of England (Rahtz 1993). Famously, early excavations were entrusted to the architect Frederick Bligh Bond, who later claimed to be directed in his work by automatic writing guided by a medieval monk (Kenawell 1965). Spiritualism, it must be added, was not then confined to the scientific fringes but it was hardly likely to appeal greatly to his employers and contributed towards his dismissal in 1922.

The man who had been responsible for the excavations at Mount Grace Priory was William St John Hope, a key figure in medieval archaeology at the turn of the century and a keen observer of archaeology and architecture (for example, at Wells Cathedral; Rodwell 1996a). Perhaps unfairly, his name is today particularly associated with the 'robust' excavation of monastic sites, 'ungentlemanly burrowing' as one author recently termed it (Butler 1989b: 9). His tally of twenty-two investigations at monasteries, one nunnery and two friaries in the space of thirty years is certainly remarkable and could only be achieved by his rapid if destructive methods of laying open the foundation plans of monasteries by following walls. In 1904 ten trenches were dug by Hope's workmen in one week at Glastonbury Abbey! (Rahtz 1993). Inevitably the results were often mono-period with little differentiation within the 400 or so years represented in the stratigraphy. Clearly he saw absolutely no irony in matching his vigour with the trowel with his considerable efforts to protect buildings and monuments all over Britain.

Later in his life Hope collaborated with two architects, Harold Brakspear and John Bilson, establishing the standard plans of monastic precincts we are familiar with today (Coppack 1990: 22–5). Most excavations tended to be dominated by the disinterring of major standing buildings such as the church, cloister and gatehouse but Brakspear, in particular, was also interested in the rest of the precinct. He opened up larger areas on occasions and was generally more aware than Hope had been of the stratigraphy on site. Among the long list of Brakspear sites are Tintern, Waverley and Beaulieu abbeys; his own account of his conduct at Stanley Abbey (Wilts.) at the end of 1905 being perfunctory but typical. Brakspear first contacted the site owner, the Marquess of Lansdowne, through his agent 'with the suggestion that some excavations should be made on the site . . . this suggestion meeting with approval . . . four men were at once put at the writer's disposal'. Excavation continued for 'some months' until 'all that remained of the claustral buildings was traced . . . the result . . . [enabling] the plan of another Cistercian abbey to be definitely settled as far as possible under the circumstances'. The final publication, in *Archaeologia*, includes descriptions of all the major monastic buildings. After some brief words on materials and building stone, Brakspear concludes with a cursory mention of the finds, which included pottery 'of bright green glazed ware of good character', lead tracery panels, a bronze brooch, nails and three door keys (Brakspear 1907; Figure 3.3).

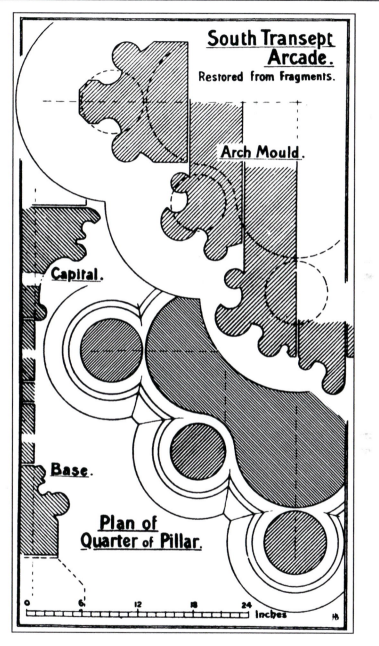

Figure 3.3 Architectural details of the south transept arcade of the Cistercian house at Stanley near Chippenham (Wilts.), recorded by Brakspear in 1907. Brakspear found that these columns had been demolished at the Dissolution by mining beneath them. The skeleton of an unfortunate workman who had been killed by the falling masonry was discovered among the rubble. (Brakspear 1907: figure 3).

There was no recognition at this time that excavation was, in itself, destructive, nor were remote sensing techniques available, though sharpened iron bars were sometimes used to identify the alignments of buried walls; however, some important methodological advances were made. The use of phased plans for monastic sites became increasingly common, with different periods of construction depicted by shading on lavishly coloured fold-out plans. This technique was popularised by Hope in his architectural and archaeological studies (e.g. Rochester Cathedral) but had been pioneered many years before by Robert Willis at Christ Church Cathedral, Canterbury, and at the colleges of Cambridge University (Thompson 1981). The same technique was exploited for the guide books written to accompany newly cleared sites in the 1920s and proved popular with the public.

Most excavators of the time never thought to articulate why they considered it important to undertake their work or to approach it in a particular way. Architectural and historical questions were undoubtedly uppermost in the minds of Bilson, Brakspear, Hope and others. Academic archaeological questions were hardly conceived of. In fact, the over-riding objective behind these costly programmes of excavation and consolidation was public education. The financial ruin of the landowning class provided an opportunity for a socialistic programme to purchase monuments and present them to an expanding middle class. Clearance revealed a plan which could then be displayed to the public and it was this obligation which seemed to drive Peers and others. This public-spirited mission to civilise the nation was by no means universally popular; there were those who protested (e.g. Fergusson and Harrison 1999: 211), and it is far from clear precisely what aspect of public education was being addressed and why. Medieval monuments might have provided a rural airing for an industrialised urban society, but they must also have appealed to the growing middle classes who had read the rambling guides, heard the radio broadcasts, joined the National Trust and now motored out into the countryside in search of an improving experience. The extent to which the acquisition and presentation of castle and abbey sites was intended to bolster colonial identity or reflected an imperialist mindset is uncertain. It was certainly symbolic of the ideals of common heritage and shared property, as against the élite wealth symbolised by the private country house (Mandler 1997: 225–64). Whatever the motive, from now on medieval heritage was seen largely as a public responsibility. Loosened from its aesthetic, religious and social connotations, medieval archaeology became part of the national heritage.

Castle sites also proved attractive to excavators and successful campaigns took place at Neroche (Som.; Gray 1903), Rayleigh (Essex; Francis 1913) and Dyserth (Flint; Glenn 1915). *Archaeologia* was an important outlet for publication and here the hope was often expressed that documentary evidence might hold helpful clues to the dating of structures and artefacts. To achieve this, architectural features were loosely parallelled with one another and then dated through association with known historical figures (e.g. see Stone 1895–7). At the time, these and other sites were at the centre of a furious debate over the origin of the castle which had been sparked off by claims by George Clark (1884) that mottes might be equated with *burh* sites. This was rejected by John Horace Round, amongst others, and later by both Alexander Hamilton Thompson (1912) and Ella Armitage in her important volume *Early Norman Castles of the British Isles* (1912), still reckoned amongst the most influential books on the subject (King 1988). It was the 'admirable' Armitage who reinforced the distinction between mottes and *burhs*, for the first time fixing a firm chronological sequence for the construction of medieval fortifications. As one author has put it 'the main reason why the study of early castles and their origins in this country has not got very much further since her day is that she did not leave us very much further to go' (Brown 1970). Indeed, her achievement is all the greater when we consider the profile of female academics at this period.

Excavations at medieval urban sites and industrial sites were almost unknown. They were not deemed suitable for display and there was little understanding of their potential; windmills, for example, were easily mistaken for prehistoric earthworks and excavated by chance (e.g. at Tattenhoe, Bucks.; CAS 1910: 6). In contrast, an exceptional contribution to the understanding of medieval industries was being made at this time by Louis Salzman. Salzman's *English Industries of the Middle Ages* (1913) remains an inspiration for even the most recent scholarship (Blair and Ramsay 1991) and followed an artefact and materials-based approach. Writing for academic and layman alike, Salzman drew upon his comprehensive knowledge of Record Office sources, published extracts from medieval writers and the work of both nineteenth-century and contemporary historians such as Bond, Parker and Turner (for architecture), and Power (for economy and religion).

Rural sites, such at Yoden (Durham) in 1884, were examined with less frequency, but some campaigns were undertaken with the benefit of what today might be thought of as research designs (e.g. see Stone 1912 for a project on dewponds and enclosures on the Isle of Wight). The first large-scale excavation of a deserted settlement site took place at Trewortha in the foothills of Bodmin Moor (Corn.) in 1891–2 (Baring-Gould 1892–3) and there was a handful of investigations of settlement sites before the First World War (Hurst 1989). A site at Stonewall Farm, Bosham (West Sussex) was excavated twice without apparent result, in 1905 and 1911, in the mistaken belief that the earthworks were a Roman fortification. Only the third campaign of excavation, responding to threat from the 'gyro-tiller' and tree planting, correctly identified the site as a medieval moated farmstead. The resulting publication, by Miss G. M. White, is a model of perceptive field archaeology and illustrates the technical advances that were to be made after the First World War (White 1935). Miss G. M. White became Molly Clark when she married Cambridge prehistorian Grahame Clark in 1936.

The inter-war years

The impact of the First War on British archaeology was considerable. War itself caused some damage in Britain, notably during the German bombardment of Whitby Abbey in 1914, and the publication of journals such as *Archaeologia* was disrupted by paper restrictions (Evans 1956: 386). More seriously, in Wheeler's (1954) understated phrase, the war had 'blotted out' a whole generation. For those who returned, the main focus of medieval excavation continued to be the recovery of building plans, often as a single plan rather than unravelling any sequence. This work was often carried out with astonishing speed. Alfred Clapham's excavations at the Augustinian priory at Haverfordwest (Pembs.) revealed the whole layout of the claustral buildings but still took only five days to complete in June 1922 (Clapham 1922).

Among the largest 'restoration' projects of the 1920s were those at the castles at Pembroke (Dyfed), Caerphilly (Glam.) and Goodrich (Hereford.), while similarly massive campaigns were also carried out at the abbeys at Tintern (Gwent; Taylor 1946), Byland and Rievaulx (Yorks.). At Rievaulx, for example, work began in 1919 with thousands of tonnes of spoil and fallen masonry being trucked away on a specially constructed light railway (Thompson 1981). First World War veterans shovelled, pick-axed and trenched their way through the rubble as costs rose to £32,000 for clearance and repair (Fergusson and Harrison 1999: 211). Elsewhere, as at Beaumaris Castle (Anglesey; O'Neil 1935b), moats were cleared and flooded once again. In Wales alone upwards of a quarter of a million pounds was spent on the excavation and preservation of ancient monuments in the care of the Ministry of Works; the greater proportion of this sum being used on castles (O'Neil 1946b). Major investigations included those at castles at Bodiam (Sussex; Myres 1935), Dunstanburgh (Nhumbs.; Charlton 1936), Faringdon (Berks.; Leeds 1936), Kidwelly (**Box 3.1**), Lydney (Glos.; Casey 1931), Grosmont and White (Mon.; O'Neil 1935a) and Marlborough (Wilts.; Brentnall 1935–7). With some notable exceptions, however, the forgotten standards reached by Pitt Rivers in his excavation, recording and publication of structures and finds were only rarely to be reached again on medieval sites before the outbreak of the Second World War. The importance of some artefact collections recovered at the time was sometimes not appreciated until very much later (e.g. Cruden 1952–3 for Melrose Abbey excavations 1921–3).

One of the major excavations of the 1930s was that underway at the medieval royal palace at Clarendon (Wilts.). This venture was under the distant direction of Tancred Borenius (Professor of Medieval Art at University College, London and Fine Arts Advisor to Sothebys) and supervised on site by John Charlton and, in the closing stages by Howard Colvin (James and Robinson 1988: 50–1; Figure 3.5). The work was driven mainly by Borenius' interest in history of art and particularly in Clarendon's documented thirteenth- to fifteenth-century wall paintings (Borenius 1932). Large-scale

Box 3.1 Kidwelly Castle (Carms.), 1931

Excavations at Kidwelly Castle took place for just ten days in 1931 and were directed by Cyril Fox and C. A. Ralegh Radford. This is an early exemplar of a promptly published excavation on a later medieval site designed to answer a specific question raised by the study of the standing structure, namely the location of the earliest castle on the site in the inner ward. Three small trenches were dug and these clarified the structural history of the castle as well as providing a local chronology for medieval pottery which has only recently been revised in the light of dendrochronological work (Fox and Radford 1933; for a critique see Hurst 1962–3: 145–6).

Especially important at Kidwelly was the discovery of jugs with green and brown polychrome decoration, dated 1275–1320. These were reported upon by Gerald Dunning who noted both the curious form of their spouts as well as their coastal distribution. He surmised a centre of production in southern France somewhere close to Bordeaux and suggested a link with trade in wine. Today the Saintonge region is known to be one of the main production centres supplying pottery to northern Europe and our knowledge has been supplemented greatly by many more finds and by survey work in France (Hurst 1986: 76–8). Dunning's pioneering article remains important, however, not only for its intelligent use of distribution maps but as the first substantial contribution to the study of medieval pottery imported into Britain (Hurst 1974).

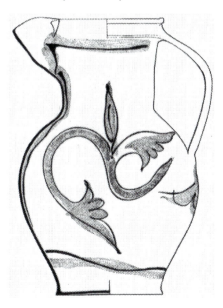

Figure 3.4 Polychrome jug from the excavations by Cyril Fox and Ralegh Radford at Kidwelly Castle (Carms.) in 1930–1 and identified as of probable southern French origin. (Fox and Radford 1933: figure 6).

Figure 3.5 Excavations in the royal wine cellars at Clarendon Palace in September 1938, directed on site by John Charlton. The lower flight of stone stairs was found to be intact and, in the photograph, the original floor surface of the eastern flank of the northern cellar has just been exposed by workmen. The work was halted at the outbreak of war in 1939 and remained unpublished for almost fifty years. (Photo: Clarendon Archive, King Alfred's College, Winchester).

clearance was undertaken by workmen on 'unemployment relief schemes', a popular tactic on many sites of the period (Hudson 1981: 127–8), and again speeded by the construction of a light railway to help shift loose earth. Reports on the excavations were read each year to the Society of Antiquaries.

Some insight into the social and academic worlds within which the Clarendon excavations operated is provided by the visitors' book maintained by the Borenius household at nearby Combe Bissett during the excavations (James 1989). Amongst the writers, artists, musicians, archaeologists, art historians and aristocrats who showed an interest and must have visited the site were Harold Brakspear, George Chettle, Gordon Childe, Alfred Clapham, Kenneth Clark, Alan Gardiner, Walter Hildburgh, James Mann, Nikolaus Pevsner, Lord Ponsonby of Shulbrede, Duke of Rutland, Frank Stevens, J. F. S. Stone, Heywood Sumner and the composer William Walton. Mortimer and Tessa Wheeler, then excavating at Maiden Castle, advised on where to dig on the site. There was even a talk on Clarendon on pre-war television from Alexandra Palace by Borenius 'heavily made up in bright yellow' (Lada-Grodzicka nd).

Not all excavations had such a high profile but the range of monuments examined did slowly broaden. Industrial sites, such as glass works in the Weald (e.g. Winbolt 1933) and iron- and brick-works (Straker 1931; Brooks 1939) all received some attention, particularly the building trades (e.g. Knoop and Jones 1933). The aim of the excavations undertaken by Christopher Hawkes, John Myres and C. G. Stevens on St Catharine's Hill outside Winchester (Hants.) between 1925 and 1928 was to 'recover knowledge of the site and character' of the medieval chapel there. Their final report contained revealing photographs of their circuit of trenches around the chapel together with drawings of the elevations of the uncovered walls and lengthy contributions on finds. That for medieval pottery is unusually detailed and was contributed by R. L. Hobson, Keeper of the Department of Ceramics in the British Museum (Hawkes *et al.* 1930; Figure 3.6). This was archaeological evidence to comple-

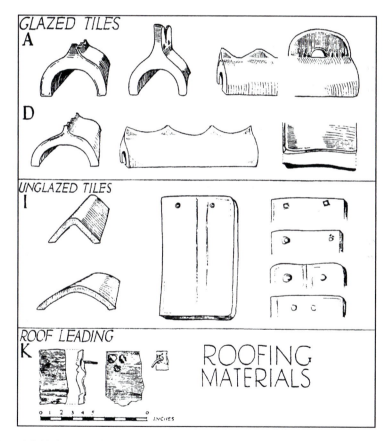

Figure 3.6 Medieval roofing materials excavated from the chapel site on St Catharine's Hill outside Winchester (Hants.). Claimed as 'something more than an Excavation Report', this figure illustrated a very full historical and archaeological account. While the excavation techniques used were unremarkable, the final publication included a lengthy speculation on the source of blue slate found at the site and comments on the patterned colour-scheme used for the roof. (Hawkes *et al.* 1930: figure 24).

ment, though not yet to match, the contribution of architectural historians such as Charles Cox (1916) and Francis Bond (1916). Publication standards rose too with the inclusion of black and white photographs, well-composed illustrations, and specialist reports on 'animal remains', 'pottery' and 'small finds'. The best reports even set out the aims of the project. At Alstoe Mount (Rutland) the purpose was 'to date the earthwork by pottery, etc. . . . and to search for signs of wooden structures on top of the mount' (Dunning 1936). Reports might be rounded off with some kind of agenda for further work. The Old Sarum suburbs report concluded, for example, with the plea that 'the time has now arrived when a closer identification should take place of English earthenware of the eleventh and twelfth centuries . . .' (Stone and Charlton 1935). Comments such as these show an improving awareness of gaps in knowledge.

Towns and cities also produced stray finds which helped to fill out the chronological sequence of artefacts. Occasionally, construction work produced finds. Together with Martyn Jope, Rupert Bruce-Mitford spent much of 1937 watching machines excavating the basement for the Bodleian Library Extension, where 'for the most part objects had to be salvaged as the ground was in the act of being broken up by the grab . . .' (Bruce-Mitford 1939); 'a taste of rescue archaeology before that term was invented' (Biddle 1997). The resulting publication established a datable sequence of medieval pottery for Oxford, the first firm datable pottery sequence for any medieval town in Britain and led its author to set up a National Reference Collection of Dated Medieval Sherds at the British Museum some time later (Bruce-Mitford 1964). Generally though, this kind of work depended very much on the initiative and availability of committed individuals, something that could not be promised everywhere. With urban history largely confined to studies of constitution and institutions (Schofield 1999), research excavations on urban sites were few and far between. Perhaps the first urban rescue operation took place in London in 1938, at Whitehall Palace. A remarkable site at which an entire Tudor wine cellar was excavated and re-sited (White and Gardner 1950).

In the countryside, although Edward Leeds had shown the potential of excavations on early medieval settlement sites at Sutton Courtenay (Berks.) in the 1920s (Leeds 1947), excavations on later medieval peasant-houses all but ceased for more than twenty-five years between 1911 and the mid-1930s (Hurst 1989). Indeed, a major review of British archaeology between 1914 and 1931 excluded any comment at all on the later medieval period (Kendrick and Hawkes 1932). Then, within only a few years, friendships, fieldwork and discoveries led first to the identification, then to the excavation of new medieval sites. In upland Wales 'platform houses', rectangular platforms terraced back into the hillside, were first noted by the Foxs at Margam Mountain, Glamorgan (Fox and Fox 1934) and soon led on to full-scale excavation by Aileen Fox at Gellygaer Common (Glam.; Fox 1937; 1939) which showed them to be upland farms. Among the excavation team were friends Audrey Williams (later Mrs Grimes) and Peter Murray-Threipland, who had learnt his excavation skills at Ur with Leonard Woolley. Together, Aileen Fox and Murray-Threipland were to identify many further sites in East Glamorgan (Fox 2000: 82–6) and the latter went on to excavate another medieval farmstead on Bredon Hill (Worcs.; Murray-Threipland 1946–8). 'Amateurs' too made notable contributions, such as Helen O'Neil who began excavating at Sennington (Glos.) while, in the south-west, Martyn Jope, with Ian Threlfall, excavated a three-room long house at Great Beere near North Tawton (Devon; Jope and Threlfall 1958).

It was quickly realised that later medieval deposits on less disturbed rural settlement sites were not always very deeply buried and could sometimes be found directly beneath the turf line. While ditches and pits usually produced the majority of the cultural material in the form of pottery, bone and metalwork, buildings proved difficult to identify. The pre-War excavators of the 'lost village' of Seacourt in Berkshire uncovered 'loosely constructed and heavily robbed' buildings, causing Bruce-Mitford (1948: 4) to comment on the extreme complexity and difficulty of rural medieval excavation. Interpretation of the stratigraphy and structures in the long thin trenches at Seacourt had been complicated by extensive robbing and the insertion of field drains. Nevertheless, the signs were encouraging and Bruce-Mitford was optimistic that 'it should be possible to recover complete ground plans of domestic buildings and of the church, and details of the architecture and domestic system with which to reconstruct the physical environment of the medieval peasant'. Elsewhere in Europe excavations were diversifying into similar areas, the first major excavation on a deserted medieval site was under way in Germany (Hurst 1989), for example, and academics like Christopher Hawkes were encouraging in their support:

> Villages abandoned (after the Black Death of 1348/9) and never re-occupied are known in almost every county, and documentary evidence concerning them too; an archaeologist's picture of an English 14th century peasant community would be a unique contribution to the historians' knowledge of the Middle Ages, on the eve of the revolt of 1381 and its far reaching sequels in the structure of our rural life.
>
> (Hawkes 1937)

At the time young prehistorians like Hawkes were pioneering an interest in prehistoric daily life and economy through excavations at Little Woodbury and elsewhere, and, in a parallel development, archaeologists like Bruce-Mitford, Fox, Jope and Leeds were beginning to spread the range of excavated sites beyond castles and abbeys to examine details of 'ordinary life'. The tone had been set by the Society of Antiquaries scheme of research in 1926 which pointed out the need for better dating of pottery and careful excavation (Evans 1956: 401). But after 1930 the Congress of Archaeological Sciences new Research Committee had begun to frame clear priorities, including, for the medieval period, the 'investigation of settlements with a view to the establishment of a sequence of pottery' highlighting both 'domestic sites which can be reasonably dated to the pre-Conquest or early post-Conquest times' and 'mound and bailey castles of which the date of desertion is known . . .'. There was a move away from the excavation of monastic, military or domestic buildings where, it was recommended, work 'should only be undertaken in such examples as are likely to fill any gaps in our knowledge, either of architectural development or planning' (CAS 1930: 36). The reasoning here seems wholly academic but the broader social context was probably at least as important in mobilising the new archaeological agenda. As motor cars and suburban housing edged into the countryside, so there was greater interest in the full breadth of rural traditions, not just those represented by medieval Church or State.

As the numbers of excavations steadily grew, so the opportunities for work on finds increased. Thorpe's *English Glass* (1935; 1949: 83–6) included medieval glass lamps, urinals and phials. The work of Gerald Dunning, however, merits special mention. Over a period of fifty-five years from 1926 to the year of his death in 1981 Dunning produced 305 scholarly publications, no less than 188 of which were on Anglo-Saxon and medieval ceramics, building up a basic chronological framework for pottery and reporting and illustrating regional variations and distributions (for bibliography see Evison *et al.* 1974). His interests embraced discussions of the sources and distributions of pottery, including imports and British exports, as well as other artefacts such as hones, mortars and roofing slate. In short, it was Gerald Dunning who cemented the foundation on which medieval pottery, and ultimately the sites from which it came, could be dated, an achievement which is all the more remarkable given the comparatively small body of material available to him and the paucity of firmly dated contexts until the 1950s. Dunning's contribution is easily underrated because he published no general textbook on medieval pottery, preferring instead to publish in journals and to foster the participation of others. Nevertheless, there are many who regard him as the 'main founding father of medieval archaeology as we know it . . .' (Hurst 1982; **Box 3.1**).

In other areas too, the gradual accumulation of excavation data was rewarded by attempts at synthesis. The 1940 *London Museum Medieval Catalogue* had no peer for thirty-five years (see **Box 3.2**). Its principal author, John Ward Perkins, drew upon an exceptionally wide range of sources in his volume, archaeology being just one of them (see p. 3). Pitt Rivers's excavations at Caesar's Camp and Tollard Royal are still well cited, and, in the absence of large well-dated assemblages from a more representative range of British medieval monuments, he looked to evidence from other countries, in the case of weapons, for example, to the fourteenth-century Danish mass-burial at the Visby battle site. There are newly published artefacts (e.g. a fifteenth-century seal; Jenkinson 1938), as well as older gazetteers and catalogues (e.g. for medieval effigies, Stothard 1817; for arms and armour, Laking 1920–2) published medieval manuscripts, European stone sculpture, the Bayeux Tapestry, statuary, retables and painting. All of these were marshalled to construct rough typologies as a 'convenient basis for classification', though Ward Perkins made very little attempt to address the reasons behind any of the changes he observed in form and style. Here and elsewhere, diffusionism, the movement of people and ideas from one area to another, was seen as the major cause of innovation.

It is hard to overestimate Ward Perkins's achievement and the rewards he found in the study of, not exceptional museum pieces, but personal items of jewellery, gaming pieces and musical instruments, and the everyday artefacts of daily life such as lamps and wooden vessels (**Box 3.2**). Such a publication would have been inconceivable only forty years previously when the study of artefacts was restricted mostly to those engaged in the buying and selling of works of art. It says a great deal that his catalogue was reprinted as recently as 1993, even though the available data is now far more voluminous, swelled by post-war excavations in urban areas. The attraction of the catalogue remains partly in the range of artefacts covered, partly in the satisfyingly bulky hardback pocket-handbook packaging, partly in the illustrations, many by Ward Perkins himself, but mostly in the breadth of scholarship on offer. As Wheeler put it in his understated preface 'it has involved not a little new research into the history or archaeology of familiar but neglected antiquities of the Middle Ages' (Wheeler 1940).

By the late 1930s a fuller and more honest appraisal of the challenges of later medieval archaeology had become possible. Some methodological tools, such as seriation, developed as a way of ordering grave goods were, of course, inappropriate. Typology, sequence and association were, more often than not, the ways medieval archaeologists chose to order their evidence but typologies of artefacts, for example, assumed a process of change showing evolution of design or style, and it was quickly discovered that some medieval artefacts showed little change. In addition, some very common artefacts such as coarse-ware pottery were found to be traded only over short distances so that pottery studies on one site had only limited applicability even 25 kilometres away. Finewares were less problematical but the development of sequences required deep stratigraphy which rural medieval sites, for example, did not often provide.

These difficulties were further compounded by the need to introduce absolute dates into relative sequences. The complexities of dating sites from coins and small finds were not always fully appreciated. Documents too could be disarmingly precise. It was deceptively easy to use the first documented mention of a site to date its initial phase of occupation. Structures discovered during excavations could also be equated without hesitation to buildings

Box 3.2 The Museum of London catalogue 1940

For thirty-five years after its publication in 1940 this catalogue was the standard reference work for those working on medieval finds. It was mostly written and illustrated by John Ward Perkins between 1936 and 1938 when he was on the staff of the London Museum, though he had a number of collaborators, notably Gerald

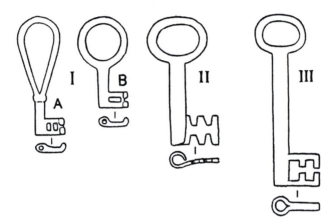

Figure 3.7 Selection of medieval keys. Keys are regularly represented in contemporary illustration but they are stylised. This was Ward Perkins's attempt at a rough classification on the basis of archaeological finds. (Ward Perkins 1940: Figure 42).

Dunning. The catalogue, though it was considered incomplete at the time, is of value because of its many illustrations, its breadth and the typologies of everyday artefacts. As Ward Perkins wrote in his introduction 'These are not collectors' pieces. They are a typical cross-section of medieval practice and craftsmanship, both rich and poor ...'.

The catalogue obviously predates the massive bulk of material from excavations by the Museum of London Archaeology Service and their predecessors in the capital. The publication of the volumes of finds from recent excavations in London is arguably the greatest sustained achievement in British medieval archaeology in the last decade (Cowgill *et al.* 1987; Grew and de Neergard 1988; Egan and Pritchard 1991; Crowfoot *et al.* 1992; Clark 1995; Egan 1998) and has been complemented by other specialist catalogues (e.g. van Bueningen and Koldeweij 1993 for pewter badges; Müller 1996 for wooden objects). Because the finds are from excavations coupled with controlled metal-detecting on reclamation-dump deposits in the 1970s and 1980s, mainly from the waterfront area of London, these latest catalogues are more representative of the broad range of objects and workmanship available in medieval London, and can be more closely dated than the finds available to Ward Perkins.

recorded in documents. Hurst (1962–3) cites the example of Leeds' excavation of a 'castle' at Faringdon clump, near Oxford, a site dated by documents to 1144–5 (Leeds 1936). With hindsight, it appears that it was a late thirteenth-century building which was excavated and not the castle at all. Likewise, when a mid-thirteenth-century stone and flint building was discovered in Romsey (Hants.) in 1927 it was quickly linked to recorded events in medieval documents and became known as 'King John's House'. This promoted the town's respectable royal and national 'credentials' and, naturally, later discoveries of graffiti in the building were then linked to royal visits, further reinforcing the desired 'pageant of history' but also compounding possible errors of misattribution (Allen 1999).

Nevertheless, the evidence accumulated during the inter-war years provided the springboard for the post-war take-off of the subject. This debt is clear, for example, in the study of medieval buildings. Writing a quarter of a century later, Pevsner and Wood (1965) drew upon the work of earlier researchers reaching back to Parker and Pugin in the nineteenth century, Brakspear and Hope, Borenius (Borenius and Tristram 1927), Alfred Clapham (1934), Thomas Garner and Arthur Stratton (1929), Walter Godfrey (1928), the Royal Commission, Victoria County Histories and a selection of Peers' pre-War Ministry of Works guides, underlining the importance of those individuals and institutions in making plans of and commentaries on standing buildings which later formed a solid basis for regional and national syntheses.

New organisations and new survey methods

The period between 1882 and 1940 is characterised by three important institutional and methodological developments. These are: the emergence of field archaeology, the impact of air photography, and the formative role of newly-created organisations such as the Earthworks Committee, the Victoria County Histories, the English Place-Name Society, and the Royal Commissions.

O. G. S. Crawford considered that the modern phase of field archaeology began in 1900 with the formation of the Committee on Ancient Earthworks and Fortified Enclosures (O'Neil 1946a). This was a joint initiative by the Congress of Archaeological Sciences, which had been founded in 1888 to co-ordinate the research of more than forty local societies across the country, and the Society of Antiquaries, who had begun the Survey of London in 1894. Its aim was undertake survey and recording and to assess reports of damage to monuments of all periods, for example from cultivation or new urban schemes. Perils recorded in the Committee Reports ranged from mundane rubbish tipping into the moat at Desborough Castle (Bucks. in 1924), to the bizarre infilling of the Norman castle ditch at Mold (Flints.) by the local committee of the 1923 National Eisteddfod of Wales to make space for the 'Gorsedd Circle', and the more serious destruction of part of Norwich Castle to provide a site for the extension to the Shire Hall in 1907 (**Box 3.3**).

Box 3.3 Acquiring medieval heritage

Even large architectural features, such as fireplaces, staircases and dismantled masonry proved surprisingly mobile well before the age of motorised transport. Decorative and sculptural stonework at Highcliffe Castle was reclaimed from a partly demolished French building and shipped to Christchurch to be reassembled for Lord Stuart de Rothesay in the 1830s. The house was gutted by fire in the

Figure 3.8 St Donat's Castle in south Glamorgan, bought by William Randolph Hearst in 1925, supposedly on the profits of the magazine *Good Housekeeping*. The prior's lodging, guest house and great tithe barn were brought here from the Augustianian priory of Bradenstoke (Wilts.) and reassembled, provoking appeals to the Office of Works and the Society of Antiquaries, letters to newspapers and questions in the House of Commons. (Photo: author).

1960s and turned into flats. Rather rarer, one might think, is the wholesale removal of medieval buildings. But in 1911 it emerged that art dealers had already removed the fireplaces at Tattershall Castle in Lincolnshire and, having purchased the rest of the mid-fifteenth century brick keep were now proposing to demolish it and ship it across the Atlantic. There was public outcry. A distressed Marquis of Curzon rescued the situation by buying back the castle and reinstating the fireplaces, at the same time carrying out considerable repairs and partially refilling Tattershall's two concentric moats with water. On Curzon's death the castle came into the possession of the National Trust and the saga later inspired a film, *The Ghost Goes West* (1936) (Mandler 1997: 184–91, 259–61).

During the 1920s and 1930s William Randolf Hearst began 'acquiring' authentic medieval monuments, dismantling and relocating them. The marked-up stonework of the Cistercian Monasterio de Ovila, 140 kilometres northeast of Madrid arrived in San Francisco in 1931 destined for conversion into a 61-bedroom, 8-storey castle to be built at the Hearst family estate. The monastery's wine cellar was to become a movie theatre and the chapel a swimming pool with side chapels converted to lounge and toilets but when the finances dried up the stones were left as landscaping in Golden Gate Park (Smith 1999).

Similarly, at the Augustinian priory at Bradenstoke (Wilts.) the large Priory Barn, guest house and prior's lodging with its fifteenth-century chimneypiece were all acquired by Hearst's agent in 1929 and, amidst some secrecy, rapidly dismantled. Letters of strong protest appeared in the local and national press, but the damage was done and both stonework and a massive fourteenth-century double collar beam roof were removed to Hearst's property at St Donat's Castle (Glam.) which he had purchased unseen in 1925 (Anon. 1930). Here new buildings were assembled from a miscellany of other medieval buildings, including a fifteenth-century stone screen from a Devon church and the decorative ceiling from the parish church at Boston (Lincs.; Aslet 1980).

Among the best travelled of all medieval architecture are the items acquired by William Burrell from the Hearst Collection in 1953/4. Some of these had crossed the Atlantic in crates but were now returned again to take their place in public collections. The largest piece was the Early Tudor three-storey portal from Hornby Castle near Richmond in Yorkshire which Hearst had bought twenty-three years earlier. When the main building had failed to sell at auction, architectural features were sold off individually and the contents dispersed. One range of the castle still stands, a remnant of one of England's great late medieval fortified manor houses.

In part, the 'annoyance at the drain from England of its artistic patrimony' expressed by the Congress of Archaeological Societies (1926: 13–14) derived from nationalist resentment that 'whereas formerly the great collectors were English, the supremacy had now passed to America' but it also touched issues of cultural identity and raised genuine concerns about the effectiveness of existing legislation. As a result of these and other perceived threats to Hadrian's Wall, Stonehenge, and elsewhere, powers of protection which had been reinforced in ancient monuments legislation in 1913 were expanded further in 1931 (Saunders 1983). Public concern was registered by the foundation of the Council for the Preservation of Rural England in 1926.

Of particular interest are the Congress 'special reports' which not only informed contemporary debate on matters as wide ranging as the study of place-names (1900) and the future preservation of ancient records (1907) but also set out guidelines for best practice, for example in the recording of churchyard and church inscriptions (1907) and the recognition of archaeological evidence for open field systems (1931). The latter recommended which dimensions should be recorded such as the length, breadth and height of ridges, their straightness or curvature and explained how to summarise the information on 1-inch Ordnance Survey maps.

New standardised schemes of earthwork classification were more widely publicised by textbooks on the emerging discipline of field archaeology. Charles Wall's *Ancient Earthworks* (1908), issued in the Antiquaries Primers series ('Helps to the Knowledge of British History') contained a section on medieval fishponds and diet. In the same year Hadrian Allcroft's *Earthwork of England* had separate chapters on Norman castles and 'moated farmsteads', and described the classic features of a midland-county deserted medieval village for the first time (Allcroft 1908: 551–3). Like all good survey, this early work provided clues to the form of the earthworks and did not preclude 'minor' features such as vermin traps and pillow mounds (Allcroft 1908: 682–97), helping to build up a relative chronology for recorded sites (Bowden 1999). Similarly, Heywood Sumner (Cunliffe 1985; Figure 3.9) and John Williams-Freeman (1915) both carried out regional surveys making use of the Earthworks Committee schemes of classification, and these then influenced standards set out by the Royal Commissions on Ancient and Historical Monuments and others. Moated sites, for instance, were defined as Category F by the Earthworks Committee and some estimate of their frequency and variation could be gathered readily from lists and descriptions in Victoria County History volumes (Aberg 1978).

The Victoria History of the Counties of England (the VCH) had been launched in 1899 (Tiller 1992: 18–19). This was 'an enormous, almost unmanageable, enterprise, such as could only have been conceived in an age of optimistic imperialism' (Greenslade 1997: 22) and aimed to produce county by county, parish by parish accounts of local history. The first volume, *Hampshire I*, was published in 1900 and by 1914 the total number of volumes already stood at 74. While these first volumes catered mainly for upper class interests in genealogy, heraldry, antiquities, manorial and church history new features were introduced so that research into archaeology, economic history and religious history appeared systematically and fully referenced in the introductory county sections (Lewis 1989: 53–64). In spite of increased costs, the VCH survived in a limited way after the First World War and during the 1930s broke new ground in the first volume of the Cambridgeshire series when Charles Phillips' chapter on ancient earthworks, by his own admission much influenced by O. G. S. Crawford, included surveys of medieval sites alongside prehistoric earthworks (VCH 1948; Phillips 1987: 62–4). More recent VCH volumes continue to follow Phillips's example and include detail on landscape, settlement morphology and economic history.

A critical foundation stone for the future study of medieval settlement was to be the analysis of place-names. Notes and books on this topic had begun to appear before the first war (e.g. Duignan 1902; Skeat 1913), the first systematic study of place-names on a county basis being that by Walter Skeat for Cambridgeshire (1901) but, with the publication in 1925 of a volume for Buckinghamshire (Mawer and Stenton 1925), the newly formed English Place-Name Society (of 1923) began to publish reliable scholarly editions on a county-by-county basis (for example, Gover *et al.* 1931–2 for Devon). Three scholars particularly, Allen Mawer, Frank Stenton (Mawer 1929; Mawer and Stenton 1933) and Eilert Ekwall (e.g. 1922; 1951), laid the groundwork for later synthetic volumes (Cameron 1961; Gelling 1978; Field 1989), examining both printed and unpublished documents and drawing out the historical, social and linguistic implications of their material (Dickins 1961).

In October 1908 the Warrant to create the Royal Commission on Historical Monuments (England) was signed, a few months after the Commissions for Scotland and Wales. The remit of the new Commission was 'to make an inventory of the ancient and historical monuments and constructions connected with or illustrative of the contemporary culture, civilisation and conditions of life of the people of England . . .'. Monuments up to 1700 were to be included (this date range was later extended) and it was decided that the inventories would be compiled on a county basis by parish. Every monument included would be visited and, in spite of difficulties of funding and staffing shortages, by 1914 the inventories for Hertfordshire (RCHME 1910) and Buckinghamshire (RCHME 1912; 1913) were published and a volume for Essex was complete (RCHME 1916). Six counties and the city of Oxford (15 volumes) were published later during the inter-war years (RCHME 1999). The impact of this work, which was carried out to the highest standards, was to increase awareness of less visible and less well-known earthwork sites and to promote further the value of surface survey. A more balanced assessment of the full range and condition of the archaeological record was now becoming possible for the first time, part of a wider perception of crisis in the rural landscape after the First World War.

All these new organisations were not, of course, as disparate as a text of this sort might make them seem. Many scholars had experience of working in more than one and staff continued to be linked formally and informally through archaeological societies. Alfred Clapham, who made so much contribution to medieval art and archaeology, began his career with the Victoria County History and contributed to the Survey of London before joining the Royal Commission on Historical Monuments (England) but he also played leading roles in the Royal Archaeological Institute, the Society of Antiquaries and, latterly, the Council for British Archaeology (Godfrey 1953).

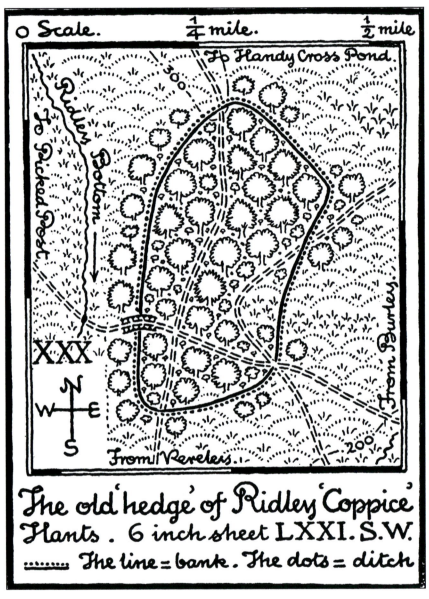

Figure 3.9 Heywood Sumner was 64 years old when he published this illustration in *The Ancient Earthworks of the New Forest* (1917: 114–17). It depicts a medieval earthwork marking the bounds of Ridley coppice, an area of about 20 hectares. The style is influenced by the Arts and Crafts Movement, in which Sumner was a leading figure. Until the advent of computers, illustrative styles were often recognisable and characteristic of particular authors, though few were as well composed as this one.

In 1925 Crawford published the first aerial photograph of a deserted medieval village, at Gainsthorpe (Lincs.; Crawford 1925). The publication of such apparently slight new evidence must be seen in the context of its time and had implications not just for the recognition of new sites, but also for their dating. Three years later, for example, in *Wessex from the Air*, Crawford and Keiller (1928: 162) recorded a medieval windmill mound on Steeple Longford Cowdown (Wilts.), a class of monument first defined a few years earlier by Allcroft and Williams-Freeman (Bond 1995: 16). They also included 'an area of typical medieval strip cultivation', part of the pre-enclosure field map for Calstone (Wilts.), together with an aerial photograph of the same scene taken on 15 July 1924 (Crawford and Keiller 1928: plates XXVIII and XXXIX; Figure 3.10). Whereas Seebohm (1883) had insisted that open-field systems were of Roman date, Crawford now accumulated the evidence from aerial photographs to prove that such systems overlay those associated with Romano-British settlement. As Crawford predicted, aerial photography was to prove 'a new instrument of research comparable only to that provided by excavation' (Crawford 1928: 9–10) and other researchers followed Crawford's lead. In 1938, for example, the Orwins published a 1635 map of Laxton, as well as an air photograph of strips at Crimscote in Warwickshire (Orwin and Orwin 1938). The authors' first purpose here was to contribute to agricultural history, though they did so from a practical standpoint, departing from the previous practice of historians who had restricted their discussions on open fields to their social and political implications. It was, however, still rare for examples to be identified from the air, sought out on the ground and then surveyed in detail. As Crawford noted:

> The identification of certain types of earthwork as medieval is a recent achievement, brought about by the impact of field archaeology on history. Prehistorians in the course of the field-work found mounds, banks and ditches which, from their associations or from explicit documentary evidence, could only be regarded as medieval. It is some measure of the bookishness of medievalists that only in the present century was it established that castle mounds were Norman, not Saxon. The proof, when it came, was historical, not archaeological, for the medievalists could not even date their own pottery until Dr Wheeler and his former pupil Mr Dunning came and helped them out; and in such a sorry state of affairs even excavation cannot produce results.
>
> (Crawford 1960: 188)

It was also Crawford who began to experiment with the way maps could be used to illustrate archaeology. From the 1870s the Ordnance Survey had begun to replace the old 1-inch maps with a completely new second edition at three scales: 1-inch (now 1:50,000), 6-inch (now 1:10,000) and 25-inch (now 1:2,500). The six- and 25-inch maps, which marked field boundaries

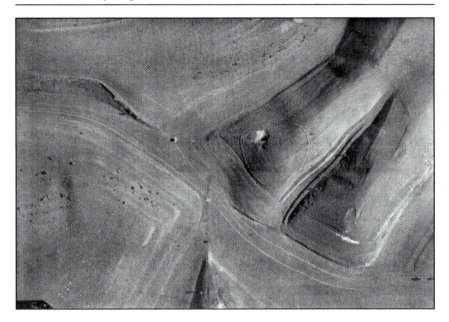

Figure 3.10 Vertical aerial photograph of fields at Calstone, Calne Without (Wilts.) from *Wessex from the Air* and intended to show 'an area of typical strip-cultivation'. The hillside lynchets correspond with those shown on an early eighteenth-century estate map. (Crawford and Keiller 1928: pl. XXVIII).

and gave an accurate outline for standing buildings, proved ideal for marking archaeological monuments and features. By 1936 a selection of post-Roman antiquities (AD 420 to AD 1688) were marked in 'German text' including castles, moated homesteads, monasteries and a miscellany of other monument classes such as trackways and lynchets (Ordnance Survey 1936). The first historical map published by the Ordnance Survey had been the 1870 facsimile of the fourteenth-century 'Gough' map of Great Britain, and now Crawford sponsored the production of William Rees colour map of the South Wales and Border area in the fourteenth century (1932). Sadly, no later medieval map was ever produced to match the popular 'Map of Roman Britain' (1924) or 'Britain in the Dark Ages' (1938–9).

Changing influences

The main objective for those working on aspects of the archaeology and buildings of the Middle Ages in the first quarter of the twentieth century was to discover 'new facts' or 'new knowledge'. Mostly this consisted of obtaining dates for artefacts and plans for monuments. Charles Peers' statement of 'research policy' stressed the need for 'careful excavation' to date medieval pottery and selective excavation of monastic buildings and fortifications only where these would fill gaps in knowledge. In an early statement of 'rescue' philosophy he declared that 'the threatened destruction of a site by industrial or housing expansion should be deemed a prime motive for excavation, even if the site involved is not of first-class importance' (Peers 1929). Practical issues of method and organisation were at the forefront rather than the philosophy of the subject, perhaps no surprise considering the wide range of professional backgrounds from which practitioners were drawn. Only when sufficient data had accumulated was synthesis possible, though the final interpretation and presentation of results remained largely a matter of intuition and common sense. O. G. S. Crawford baldly summarised the views of many archaeologists of the 1920s in stating that there was only a role for archaeology in helping history 'by confirming or contradicting its facts', believing as he did that: 'archaeological material so used . . . is inferior in value to the material remains of prehistoric man, which remains are the only evidence we have. Hence the word 'antiquary' might be reserved for the students of 'historic' archaeology' (Crawford 1921: ix). This seems a curious statement from Crawford, given that his temperament, later writing and fieldwork seem to suggest that he felt otherwise. A major problem was that historic archaeologies seemed to have had little contribution to make to understanding how human behaviour had evolved, simply because they represented more recent phases in the development of society. There was also the depressingly changeless quality of some medieval material culture, such as coarseware pottery, and continuing concerns over chronology, the lack of stratified excavation and the apparent dearth of techniques necessary to extract dates from excavated sites.

In fact, the origins of later medieval archaeology can be best traced in the diversification of geography and history. Geography emerged as an independent field of study in the early years of the twentieth century (Stoddart 1986) and archaeological applications were recognised early on by Crawford who predicted that 'most of the advances in archaeological knowledge will be made by means of geographical studies' (1921: 132). It was only when numbers of publications on human and regional geography increased during the 1930s that historical sources, such as tithe maps, were regularly called upon to document the recent development of the landscape. This blurring of academic divisions between history and geography is well illustrated by the composition of the Fenland Research Committee which included archaeologists, botanists, geologists and geographers and inspired a series of publications which stressed the value of approaching regional geography from an historical angle (Darby 1932; Fowler 1934). These concepts were then developed further by figures such as Richard Hartshorne (e.g. 1939) and Carl Sauer (e.g. 1941), the American cultural geographers, who provided a platform for influential texts both before and after the war (e.g. Darby 1953).

The objective of most studies was to write a detailed narrative description of the geography of a study area for the historic period (Baker 1952), a reconstruction of past geographies (e.g. Darby 1934). Such was the approach effectively applied by Herbert Salter in his work on deeds, leases, rentals and other documents from Oxford, for which a mass of documentation was arranged topographically by parish and tenement so that the history of houses, occupiers and owners could be traced from the thirteenth to the nineteenth centuries (Salter 1934). Applied in a slightly different way to broader tracts of countryside, a similar range of ideas was seen to best effect in archaeology in Cyril Fox's *Archaeology of the Cambridge Region* (1923), a volume based on one area which made use of distribution maps coloured to show physical features such as rivers and vegetation. The physical geography of the region was argued to have a profound impact on its cultural development and this theme was developed further in *The Personality of Britain* (1932), 'a sketch of the essential Britain', which advocated an environmental and ecological approach to the subject and necessitated increased co-operation between archaeologists, geologists and biologists in order to examine landscape change over long timeframes.

Fox's volume excluded any consideration of the post-Conquest period, but its publication had an important influence on later researchers like Grahame Clark and Eric Higgs (Daniel 1981) and thence permeated the study of historic archaeology, particularly the study of buildings (e.g. Barley 1961). Three general points might be emphasised: first, the importance of physical geography and climate, particularly the difference between upland and lowland Britain; second, the use of maps, not only simply as locational reference or illustrative of the arguments in the text but as part of the toolkit through which arguments were developed; third, the concept of the 'region' with a focus on monuments, farms, hedges and fields.

Distribution maps found their way into publication of later medieval sites with increasing frequency in the 1930s. Coles, for example, plotted distribution maps of moated sites in Essex (Coles 1935) and showed that they mostly lay in formerly forested areas and that their origins might be related to woodland clearance. Similarly, lists of water mills mentioned in the Domesday Survey (Bennett and Elton 1898–1904) were mapped for the first time (Hodgen 1939). In the same decade, a dramatic change took place in medieval artefact studies as authors such as Gerald Dunning, John Ward Perkins and Martyn Jope, at that time a research biochemist, began producing articles quite different in tone and layout which made use of distribution data. These first attempts were sometimes tantalisingly incomplete, the names of findspots could be omitted and the maps failed to show negative findspots, something which was corrected later (e.g. Jope 1952a; Jope and Threlfall 1959). However, this was a new departure which broadened the study of artefacts from single sites onto a wider canvas. Jope, for example, surveyed regional developments in the Oxford area (Jope 1947). At the same time, spatial studies helped with 'cross-dating', building up a master sequence from several sites which might then be confirmed by documentary evidence.

This approach was typified by an article published in 1937 on the subject of embossed medieval tiles (Ward Perkins 1937). The aims of the article were 'not only to establish certain general facts about their origin, date and distribution, but to throw some light upon the conditions which controlled their manufacture'. Close attention was paid to technical and stylistic attributes and relationships between English and 'continental' material and a series of period-based distribution maps were contrasted. Two explanatory theories were advanced. The first was 'diffusion of the craft of embossed tile-making from any one of the English sites where such tiles have been discovered'; this explanation was dismissed on the grounds that the designs were too various. The second explanation was 'a migration of craftsmen analogous to that which later undoubtedly took place for the manufacture of the embossed stove-tiles of the Tudor period' followed by a period in which the craft became 'naturalised'. In terms of motifs 'the political contacts of Sicily at this time render it a peculiarly likely centre for the diffusion of oriental ideas . . .'.

As this example demonstrates, finds were now being more carefully compared and classified. This opened up the alternative of defining geographical rather than chronological patterning and, mimicking ideas developed elsewhere in archaeology and history, Ward Perkins and other practitioners now relied upon migrations and diffusion as ways of explaining the changes they observed in material culture. This 'culture-history paradigm' encouraged attention to specific local details of the archaeological sequence rather than upon general stages of development (Trigger 1989).

The professional discipline of history, characterised by thorough documentary analysis and with political and constitutional matters at its core, is usually considered to have been established in England as a university subject after 1866 when William Stubbs and his successor Edward Freeman occupied the Regius Chair of Modern History at Oxford. Following the German example, Frederic Seebohm's *English Village Community* (1883), Paul Vinogradoff's *Villainage in England* (1892) and Frederic Maitland's *Domesday Book and Beyond* (1897), with its use of maps and field evidence, all widened the scope of traditional historical academic research to include medieval agrarian institutions. Seebohm, for example, was the first to propose a theory for the development of open-field systems. Together with the work and teaching of William Cunningham, Thorold Rogers and Arnold Toynbee, these scholars helped to establish economic history as a topic worthy of debate and development for the medieval and modern periods (Hoskins 1967: 17). By the outbreak of the First World War, when history had replaced classics as the major Oxbridge subject (Harte 1971), social and economic aspects of history had already become popular.

The drawing of history closer to the social sciences was the natural breeding ground for new ideas and methods linking historical thinking with the study of environment and archaeology. This major new branch of historical enquiry crystallised in the *Annales* approach, named after the journal *Annales d'histoire économique et sociale* founded in 1929 by Marc Bloch and Lucien Lebvre. Sometimes referred to as 'total history', it represented a departure from the traditional chronological narrative and a move towards a more multidisciplinary and inclusive approach, which incorporated other disciplines such as anthropology and geography. Building upon the work of social geographer Paul Vidal de la Blache and others, *Annalistes'* attention was directed towards the study of *pays*, geographical cells at the regional scale. Differing 'personalities' of landscape were seen as resulting from the interplay of man and environment. Central figures of the school, other than Bloch and Lebvre, were George Duby (e.g. 1974) and Emmanuel Le Roy Ladurie (especially *Montaillou* 1975) but the general *Annales* philosophy also influenced recent journals such as *Past and Present* and the *Journal of Interdisciplinary History*.

Among the foreign British scholars open to the value of the behavioural and social sciences, particularly to regionally-based histories in which historical geography and cartography played a central role, were English historians like Michael Postan, Eileen Power and Richard Tawney (Coleman 1987: 118–19). In an age when Britain's international position was changing, economic history was now presented as a social science which could add the historical dimension to economic inquiry and benefit from contributions from anthropology and sociology (Harte 1971). In her inaugural lecture of 1933 Eileen Power stressed the need for integration between anthropologists, sociologists, economists and historians (Power 1933: 114–119) and a trio of her books took this approach (Power 1922; 1926; 1940). Many of the themes she tackled, such as gender and resistance, and the intimate social experience of medieval individuals, have only recently re-emerged on the archaeological agenda (see Chapter 6).

Power and Postan collaborated closely both on the *Cambridge Economic Histories* and in setting up the *Economic History Review* (1927). This was one of a number of journals addressing issues in specialist economic history which began to be published at that time (e.g. *Revue d'histoire économique et sociale* in 1908, *Rivista do storia economica* in 1936) and important in drawing attention to the possible value of archaeology to the cause of economic history and to the understanding of the rural history of medieval England. The importance of Postan, in particular, to the medieval archaeologist lies not only in his writing on economic activity in the Middle Ages but the stimulus he provided for others, in drawing attention not to the themes of medieval government, religion, literature and art favoured by the previous generation of historians but to a less attractive rural world affected by plague, bad weather and food shortages.

Increasingly influenced by the writings of Marx, historians were turning inwards, away from histories of the state towards 'that of everyday things . . . the rhetoric of the "small man' prevails" (Samuel 1984). On the one hand, this was a more socially inclusive version of the medieval past which could be appreciated by pre-war adult education classes or enjoyed by audiences for the Gaumont-British Instructional Ltd film *A Medieval Village*. On the other, it touched wider public concerns about the British landscape and drew upon a nostalgia for a rural past fast disappearing beneath ribbon development, arterial roads and pylons. The gap between history and archaeology was closing.

As the century progressed a number of medieval economic historians began to draw attention to the value of the historical landscape, usually as a means of illustrating their arguments about population fluctuation, crops, land use and agricultural techniques. Tawney is credited with the famous exhortation 'History needs not more books but more boots' (Beresford 1985: 112), though with so few aerial photographs readily available, it was slow and muddy work. Tawney, in particular, was making use of estate maps and standing buildings for his work on the sixteenth-century countryside (Tawney 1912). The spirit and moral tone of his work was echoed by other historians:

> The face of the country is the most important historical document that we possess. Upon the map of England 'that marvellous palimpsest' is written much of English history: written in letters of earth and stone, of bank and ditch, of foliage and crop. As is the case with every map, the writing is not such as he that runs may read. It needs patience to discover, knowledge to decipher, insight, sometimes amounting to genius, to interpret. But the writing is there, all else awaits the competence of the reader.
>
> (Randall 1934: 7)

As Randall recognised, most historians saw the countryside as simply an arena for human activity. When the *Historical Geography of England and Wales* was published in 1936 there were plenty of maps but they were devoid of topography and places. This was a landscape 'in the aggregate' (Beresford 1985: 111), wallpaper on which to plot historical data. 'No one in any lecture said anything that could be construed as a comment on the historical landscape or drew upon it as a part of historical exposition'. This was how Maurice Beresford recalled his pre-war history lectures at Cambridge (Beresford 1985: 109) and this was the problem; few historians saw the value of comparing their maps and documents against what could be seen in the field. Collaborations between historians, geographers and archaeologists were still rare and restricted to a tiny number of individuals who were widely scattered in different institutional guises with little philosophical or methodological focus to their efforts.

The war years

Some fieldwork was broken off at the outset of hostilities, other studies now suffered long delays in publication. The substantial medieval pottery collection excavated at Bothwell Castle in 1937–8, one which would have provided the first corpus of Scottish medieval pottery, did not appear for fifteen years (Cruden 1951–2). Stocks of the south sheet of Neville Hadcock's 'Monastic Britain' 1:625,000 OS map had been printed by 1940 but were destroyed during an air raid on Southampton. Preliminary drawings survived and the two maps, north and south, finally appeared in 1950 and quickly went to a second edition (Phillips 1980: 30–9). To some extent, the 'little golden age' of field archaeology in the early 1950s resulted from the 'stockpiling' of pre-war and wartime research (Fowler 1980).

But while many careers and scholarship were effectively suspended, the War now accelerated the advance of medieval archaeology in other areas. Many medieval buildings were destroyed by bombing. The twenty hectare area devastated in London included seventeen churches and another seven were severely damaged (Milne 1997: 2). In Bristol the historic centre of the city suffered major losses, including St Peter's Hospital, an early fifteenth century merchant's house and St Nicholas' Church. Local architects were invited to prepare a basic list of historic buildings for their area which was then circulated to local authorities. This was the first of the national lists to be compiled and later became the basis for the National Buildings Record. Following enemy action, or indeed damage resulting from occupation by allied forces, and depending upon their entry in the register, buildings might be shored up, damage repaired or arrangements put in place to collect fittings from demolition rubble (O'Neil 1948 for a list of interventions). Brooke House in Hackney, one of the country residences which originally lay on the periphery of medieval and Tudor London, was more fortunate. Although partially destroyed by bombing in 1940, its demolition was lavishly recorded by the local authorities' Historic Buildings Department in plans and photographs before being excavated by William Grimes. The final publication linked architecture with archaeology and documentary sources in a comprehensive study (Sheppard 1960).

One result of enemy action during the war was that wholesale changes to land use in urban areas now became feasible. Indeed, even while the war was still on, the rebuilding of bomb-damaged towns and cities was already being planned for. Given the legislative position, the relatively low profile of archaeology and the understandable need to avoid delays, it is no surprise that those eager for improvements to housing and the rehabilitation of commerce, industry and infrastructure barely registered any awareness of archaeology. Southampton City Council was exceptional in commissioning reports on its historic buildings and monuments and recommended that sensitive areas, including medieval sites, might be reserved for public open space (Crawford 1942).

In the countryside only a handful of medieval monuments, mostly moated sites, were affected by the new factories, camps and airfields (O'Neil 1948). At Weston Zoyland (Som.) a topographical survey of the medieval ridge and furrow was undertaken in advance of destruction by a new airfield. The investigation of the moated site at Nuthampstead (Herts.) by Audrey Williams was among the more thorough wartime excavations, with the US Army providing the labour force (Williams 1946).

Part 2

Into the light

Medieval and post-Medieval archaeology may be said to have arrived.

(from Bruce-Mitford 1948: 2)

By field-work, that is to say by going out with a large-scale Ordnance Map and walking the boundary, the course followed by the park-bank can often be recovered; to do so may involve two or three days' work, but when it has been done, one unit in the medieval system has been restored to knowledge. That is surely worth doing.

(from Crawford 1953: 190)

The common tendency to discriminate archaeologists as prehistorians and antiquaries as medievalists does good to nobody. If anything, it attempts on the one hand to rob prehistory of a little of the humanity that comes more easily to the Middle Ages; and on the other to deprive medieval studies excessively of the cold and calculating objectivity that is attributed to the prehistorian.

(from Wheeler 1954: 201–3)

No traveller comes easily to a lost village.

(from Beresford 1954: 27)

No wonder so many grown-ups loathe the very word 'history'.

(from Hoskins 1962: viii)

'What shore are we making for, O Timandahaf?'
'I chose one at random, O Nescaf, we're making for Gaul.'
Which should teach us all to distrust random samples . . .

(from Asterix and the Normans 1966)

History, the reconstruction and understanding of the past, requires all kinds of evidence, of which archaeological evidence is only one, and not the best, being notoriously vague in the matter of date, and consisting exclusively of material remains, artifacts, from which the spirit is almost by definition missing.

(from Brown 1970: 132)

If we want progress, history has got to go . . . every time anybody wants to do anything history is brought up. Progressively we have got to get rid of these ancient monuments.

(chairman of an urban council referring to a listed farm building; Somerset Guardian 16 October 1970)

We should deal with reality, not play with models in Legoland.

(from Hurst 1983)

Post-excavation is indeed an ideal refuge for the methodological idler; the lack of a well developed body of theory and techniques enables inconsistency and irrelevance to dominate.

(from Boddington 1985: 50)

Chapter 4

Out of the shell
Medieval archaeology comes of age
(1945–1970)

The period after 1945 was a time of remarkable growth for later medieval archaeology. In the immediate post-war period few scholars thought of themselves as 'medieval archaeologists'; they were more likely to be local historians or historical geographers, but they worked side-by-side in the societies and groups which quickly established themselves and provided direction for research. The release of additional resources and the purposeful application of new techniques vastly increased the perceived potential of the subject and attracted a new generation of researchers who undertook influential fieldwork and excavation across a broadening spectrum of monuments. These included the excavations at Hen Domen, Wharram Percy and Winchester and the Five Castles programme. Elsewhere, the archaeological response to development was mostly low-key and sites could be destroyed without adequate record. This chapter ends in 1970, as new conceptual trends were filtering into publication and the 'Rescue' movement was gathering momentum.

Excavation and fieldwork

In 1946 the bestselling guide to field archaeology omitted any mention or illustration of medieval archaeology (Atkinson 1946), but during the next quarter of a century the numbers of excavations on later medieval sites increased in explosive fashion. Between 1956 and 1970, the period for which accurate excavation statistics can be compiled from *Medieval Archaeology*, the total number of medieval sites investigated in Britain more than doubled from 87 to 188 per year. By 1970 there were twenty times as many excavations underway each year as there had been pre-war.

Urban sites

Between 1946 and 1962, William Grimes led the Roman and Medieval London Excavation Council (1946–62) in the investigation of a handful of destroyed church and monastic sites as well as some secular buildings and portions of the city wall (Figure 4.1). These were the first sustained campaigns of urban archaeology inside a living city and the work was funded by public subscription and conducted before the astonished eyes of commuters, a combination Grimes found sometimes took on a 'curiously nightmarish

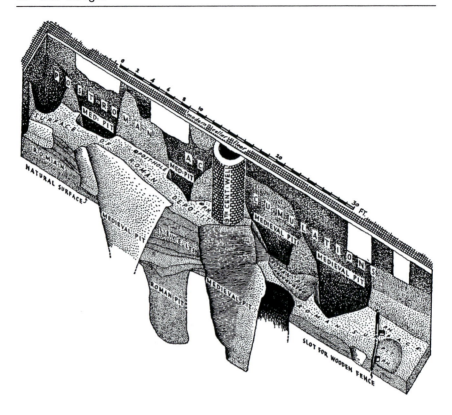

Figure 4.1 Reconstruction by William Grimes of a section at Gutter Lane, Cheapside, showing the relationship of Roman deposits to medieval pits and later features. One of the sixty-three rescue and research excavations in the City of London which now form the Grimes London Archive at the Museum of London. (Grimes 1968: figure 1).

quality'. Nevertheless, the work was innovative in several ways, for while he hired mechanical diggers to help with his work, Grimes adhered strictly to archaeological methods. Given the cramped spaces in which he was forced to open trenches, stratigraphic sequences were normally given priority over area digging, with resulting benefits for artefact dating (Frere 1988). Unfortunately, Grimes was unable to produce definitive accounts of his findings in his own lifetime (e.g. Milne 1997), but his general philosophy towards urban excavation was to have lasting impact. In particular, in his work he made use of many different sources including maps, illustrations and documents. His even-handed treatment of medieval and later archaeology was also unusual and reflected his wide 'period' interests (Grimes 1956; 1968: 151–241).

Following the example set for London, urban archaeology began in earnest in the bomb-damaged city centres of several medieval towns, often under the supervision of excavation committees as in Canterbury (Millard 1971; Williams

1976; Bennett *et al.* 1982) and Southampton (Platt and Coleman-Smith 1975). Just how daunting a task actually faced excavators on the ground is well described by Aileen Fox in her personal account of archaeological work carried out between 1945 and 1947 on behalf of the Committee for War-damaged Exeter, one of the cathedral cities which had suffered so badly during the 'Baedeker raids' in 1942 (Fox 2000: 103–6). With only limited public and charity funding available, it is indisputable that Roman archaeology was what interested most excavators but later remains were hard to ignore (e.g. Cotton 1962 for a section through the bank of Colchester Castle). Only a few, however, were alert to the possibility of combining archaeological and documentary evidence in a more sustained fashion. In Norwich, Martyn Jope plotted medieval finds against topography with illuminating results for occupation sequences across the city (Jope 1952b) and later work showed how urban archaeology could answer questions about the significant components of medieval towns (Hurst and Golson 1955). Meanwhile, in Bristol, clearance of bomb-damaged areas revealed long sections of the medieval town walls among the debris and collapsed cellars (Figure 4.2). Kenneth Marshall's work here combined excavation with boreholes which were sunk to strike archaeology and establish the depth of bedrock, an early, small-scale example of 'deposit-mapping' (Marshall 1951: 46–8; see Chapter 5).

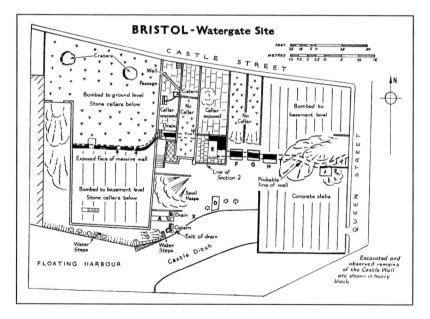

Figure 4.2 Between 1948 and 1951 the 'Ancient Bristol Exploration Fund' appealed for funds to excavate bomb-damaged areas near the city centre. One of their principal tasks was to trace the line of the medieval City Wall through the bombed shells of later buildings. (Marshall 1951: 27).

The chance for more sustained campaigns of archaeological investigation was provided by successive waves of new town development and urban regeneration schemes, though many opportunities were squandered. In Worcester, for example, a fifth of the historic city centre was removed in the 1960s. Here, as in so many other places, the lesson that modern development was a serious threat to buried archaeology was painfully learnt. Other cities were more fortunate however and by 1970 there had been substantial and sustained campaigns of excavation in a number of British towns, notably in Bedford (Baker 1970), Bristol (Hebditch 1968), Chichester (Down and Rule 1971; Down 1974), Hereford (Butler 1960), King's Lynn (1963–70; Clarke 1981), Plymouth (1959–69; Gaskell Brown 1986), Stamford (1963–9; Mahany 1982) and Winchester. Between 1956 and 1970 the numbers of excavations on medieval urban sites rose tenfold (Figure 4.3).

Taken together, these campaigns did much to break down the perception that historical documentation held all the answers (Clarke 1984: 177–8). Recurrent themes included the search for urban origins, the recovery of plans of medieval domestic buildings, the evolution of construction techniques and the refinement of artefact typologies. The realisation that some medieval towns sought to increase their areas, not only along entry routes but also along their waterfronts was also an important one. River banks and sea shores had constantly been encroached upon and reclaimed, often on several occasions as the water level rose, burying medieval buildings whose plans could later be recovered by excavation (Schofield 1999). Urban rubbish, sometimes deep and waterlogged, was found to have been dumped together with gravel and stone behind vertical revetments preserving finds such as leather and wood, discarded industrial products and household waste (Milne and Milne 1982). Crucially, because quays and warehouses were supported on wooden piles, these finds could sometimes be closely and independently dated by dendrochronology while the combined study of architectural and documentary sources demonstrated patterns of silting, reclamation and sea-level change. The complex excavation of waterfront sites was pioneered at Bryggen in Bergen (Norway) in the 1950s (Herteig 1981) and followed later by important work at sites in the Netherlands and elsewhere (Milne and Hobley 1981; Milne 1992a). In Britain, excavators had had some experience of dealing with well-preserved medieval timbers (e.g. in York; Richardson 1959) but the first timber waterfront in England was exposed at the Thorsby College wharf in King's Lynn in 1964 (Parker 1965; Clarke and Carter 1977; Clarke 1981).

Of all the urban campaigns of the 1960s it is the work of Martin Biddle and his 'research unit' in Winchester which is regarded today as most novel and influential in ethos and technique (Figure 4.4). Even the briefest comparison will show that Biddle's work is a far cry from Grimes' excavations in London ten years previously. Funding, manpower, recording, direction; all these were elevated to a higher plane in Winchester where 'rescue' was seen as subordinate to 'research' (Biddle 1968). Building upon his earlier experiences in Cambridge (Addyman and Biddle 1965), 'research' translated as a robust strategy to examine the archaeology and documents of a changing city, privileging no one period over another and exploiting every opportunity to compare different zones, from one end of the economic, religious and social spectrum to the other. Excavations took place mainly on the public buildings of the medieval town such as the royal castle and the bishop's palace, two parish churches and three chapels, but there was significant work too on the medieval street plan and a group of tenements in Lower Brook Street. In total just under 2 per cent of the walled area of the town was examined (Biddle 1983) and, though the process of writing up the Winchester campaigns still continues, the regular publication of interim statements ensured that preliminary results were widely disseminated (e.g. Biddle 1970; T. B. James 1997).

By the late 1960s some sixty English towns had experienced serious archaeological investigation, but only three in Wales and none in Scotland (Biddle 1968). A number of larger towns had established their own research frameworks (e.g. Barker 1968–9 for Worcester), though in nearly all cases 'a modern hierarchy of investigation echoes the hierarchy of prestige which the selected sites are once thought to have enjoyed, usually on the advice of medieval literature' (Carver 1981: 68). Small- and medium-sized towns were less well explored.

Rural settlement

During the late 1940s new fieldwork began to indicate the potential of rural settlement. Moated sites, a discrete and visible monument class which had received only cursory examination before the War, now became a target for excavation (Figure 4.3). Initially, curiosity was limited to providing dated sequences for buildings within the moated area. Somewhat like the monastic excavations of the inter-War years, investigations focused on living and service buildings rather than ancillary farm buildings but, by the mid-1950s, campaigns such as those at Milton (Hants.), Ashwell (Herts.; Hurst and Hurst 1967) and Moat Hill (Yorks.; Thompson 1956) were showing how larger scale excavations could produce fuller and more rewarding site histories.

The results of early work on moated sites were published in a geographical journal (Emery 1962). This synthesis set the agenda for further work and the period between 1964 and 1973 was to be the heyday of excavation on moated sites, with totals reaching an annual peak in 1969. Almost every site dug seemed to add to the sum of information, at first suggesting, then confirming, likely dates for construction and occupation, and gradually increasing the range of buildings sampled (RCHME 1968). As excavation continued during the 1960s at Brome (Suffolk; West 1970), East Haddesley (Yorks.; Le Patourel 1973) and elsewhere, archaeological data was increasingly correlated against

Figure 4.3 Monument classes investigated per five-year period and registered in the journal *Medieval Archaeology*.

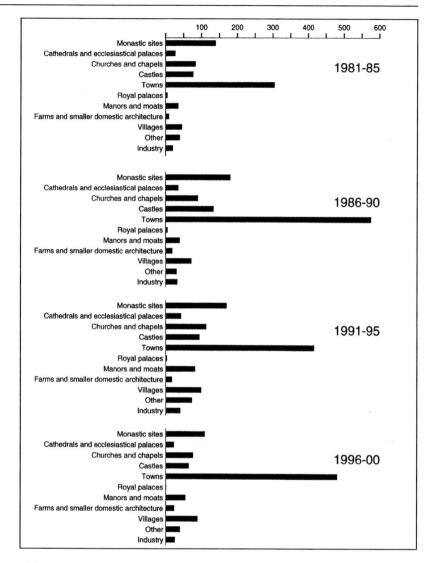

Figure 4.3 (continued).

land use, settlement geography, soil types and topography as well as combined with documentary research so as to explore the status of the sites' medieval owners (e.g. Roberts 1965). Within fifteen years research had broadened both in scale and diversified in scope, propelled by two central questions: why and when had moated sites been dug?

The pattern of research at deserted medieval village sites follows a similar trajectory. The number of excavations rose steadily to an annual peak of 29 in

Figure 4.4 Winchester excavations in progress at Lower Brook Street in August 1970, looking north. The stone building is St Mary's Church with intersecting tenth- to fourteenth-century medieval pits in the foreground and House XII beyond. (Photo: Mick Aston).

1968, before dropping away again in the 1970s (Figure 4.3). Among those sites which made an early contribution in the 1950s were Hangleton (Sussex; Holden 1963) and Stantonbury (Bucks.; Mynard 1971) and, later, the Cotswold nucleated village at Upton (Glos., 1959–73; Rahtz 1969; Rahtz and Watts 1984) and the long-house and courtyard sequences at Gomeldon (Wilts., 1963–8; Musty and Algar 1986). At West Whelpington (Nhumbs.) about 20 per cent of the site was cleared, some 14,000 square metres, and this remains one of the most completely excavated deserted village sites in England as well as one of the longest running campaigns (1958–76; Jarrett and Evans 1987; Evans *et al.* 1988).

The geographical coverage and the form of settlements excavated was soon extended. There were important projects at the deserted settlements on Dartmoor (Devon; 1961–75; Beresford 1979), and at the hamlet of Braggington (Salop.; Barker 1969a) as well as at Pickwick Farm on Dundry Hill, south of Bristol, excavated by Ken Barton in the 1960s (Barton 1969). This last site was an early example of an excavation of a medieval and later farmstead or hamlet with underlying evidence for prehistoric and Roman settlement. Excavations on later medieval sites were often components of bigger projects, sometimes unintentionally so. The first detailed excavations of medieval sheilings were excavated under the mistaken impression that the earthworks were of Iron Age date (Gelling 1962–3).

Box 4.1 A kind of genesis: 1948

Within the space of ten days in June 1948 a series of meetings and coincidences began a chain of events which sparked post-war methodological and academic development. On 17 June Michael Postan, the economic historian, who had secured British Council funding for a visit from the Danish archaeologist Axel Steensberg, organised a seminar at Peterhouse, Cambridge, to mark the occasion. Unlike Oxford, from where many of the pre-war pioneers had emerged, Leeds, Jope and Bruce-Mitford among them, Cambridge had hitherto been little involved in the archaeology of medieval rural settlement, but Postan was interested in seeing if archaeology could provide evidence for his theory of the expansion and contraction of settlement, later to be published in his chapter on medieval English rural society for the revised first volume of the *Cambridge Economic History* (1966).

At the seminar both William Hoskins and Maurice Beresford spoke on their recent work on deserted medieval settlements in the Midlands. Beresford, illustrating his talk with maps and slides from RAF aerial photographs, spoke to an audience which included Rodney Hilton, Axel Steensberg, Edward Miller, and Grahame Clark. The seminar was followed the next day by an inspection of earthworks at Knaptoft and Hamilton (Leics.) where Hoskins had recently dug some trial trenches (Beresford 1981, 1986–7).

On that same day, 18 June 1948, Kenneth St Joseph took a photograph of the village earthworks at Abbotstone (Bucks.) which was apparently the 'origin of his perception of medieval sites'. Then, by bizarre coincidence, within the next eight days, both St Joseph and Beresford, unknown to each other (they did not meet until 1951), were to come across the earthworks at Wharram Percy in the Yorkshire Wolds, for so long an epicentre of activity for medieval archaeologists, one on foot, the other from the air (Beresford 1994). Later in the same year, in October 1948, Rupert Bruce-Mitford issued his famous clarion call for medieval archaeology, pointing out that previous work on the period had favoured cathedrals, abbeys and castles (Bruce-Mitford 1948; see p. 93).

The Cambridge connection with later medieval archaeology was one which persisted long after 1948. In 1951 Jack Golson, one of Postan's history students, began work on the deserted medieval villages of Lincolnshire, by which time John Hurst was studying medieval pottery in East Anglia (Hurst 1986: 201). When Golson visited Beresford to discuss his thesis, he heard of the initial work at Wharram Percy and told Hurst about it. This then introduced Hurst to Beresford and there began an influential and enduring partnership of archaeologist and historian.

The early years of the Wharram Percy project are regarded as a 'bench-mark in the making of medieval archaeology' (Hodges 1990). There are good technical reasons to justify this claim but, first and foremost, it was at Wharram that archaeologists demonstrated that they could contribute in significant ways to academic debates in medieval rural history. The initial impetus for the project was to establish the dates and reasons for settlement desertion, fuelled by debates set out in Beresford's *Lost Villages of England* (1954). But the objectives of the project were never static and rapidly embraced new themes such as the complexities of house construction and materials (e.g. Beresford 1979), the evolution of house types (Hurst 1965), the origins of villages, environment, setting and economy. What began as the basic acquisition of information on a number of specific topics quickly encompassed broader themes.

Figure 4.5 Maurice Beresford and John Hurst at Wharram Percy in 1989 for the presentation of a volume of rural studies dedicated to them (Aston *et al.* 1989). Beresford with tea in hand. (Photo: Mick Aston).

The outstanding contribution to rural studies was made by excavations at the site of Wharram Percy (**Box 4.1**). Work first began here in 1950 and ran for another forty-two seasons, mostly under the joint direction of historian Maurice Beresford and archaeologist John Hurst, who had first met there in 1952. Something of the 'sociology' of 'Wharramite' life has been well captured in a recent booklet (Hayfield 1990) and the roll call of diggers who passed through Wharram and later went on to exercise influence in British arch- aeology is an impressive one. The influence of the site has extended well beyond the trench edge, the Yorkshire Wolds or the academic world and pervades the social fabric of later medieval archaeology in Britain through to the present day.

Much of the credit for popularising a multi-disciplinary approach to medieval rural studies was due to the extraordinary revival of local history after the War. After the Department of English Local History was founded at University College, Leicester in 1948 a trio of practical guidebooks to the subject emerged in the space of ten years, namely *History on the Ground* (Beresford 1957), *Local History in England* (Hoskins 1959) and *Fieldwork in Local History* (Hoskins 1967). These were interspersed with broad ranging and synthetic volumes such as Maurice Beresford's *The Lost Villages of England* (1954) and William Hoskins' *The Making of the English Landscape* (1955; **Box 4.2**). There were also local and regional case studies such as Herbert Finberg's work at Withington (Glos.; Finberg 1957) and Hoskins' *Devon* (1954). The academic boundaries of subjects were becoming harder to draw and, in the following decade, some of the best work in historical geography was also to integrate multiple sources in a series of regional case studies on the draining of the Levels in Somerset (Williams 1970), rural settlement and estates (Jones 1961), medieval field systems (Baker and Butlin 1973) and the impact of Cistercian monasteries (Donkin 1963).

Not one of these seminal publications contained the word 'archaeology' in its title. Nevertheless, references to relict landscape features such as settlements and field boundaries abounded in some and, where they did not, they provided a ready-made agenda for later archaeological work. Exceptionally, in Beresford's *History on the Ground* (1957) local archives and fieldwork were married together to provide clues to 'English topography'. Hoskins too devoted two whole chapters to fieldwork in his *Local History in England* (1959), emphasising the importance of sources such as Ordnance Survey maps and the volumes of the English Place-Name Society. Here were new kinds of guide books to the English landscape, full of advice and encouragement to be enjoyed by the general reader as well as the specialist historian. The academic focus was wider too and more socially inclusive, embracing whole communities in both town and countryside, not just the privileged few.

It was only right at the end of the 1960s that more sustained fieldwork projects began to embrace this wider 'landscape' vision. Chris Taylor's work

Box 4.2 William Hoskins

The writing of W. G. Hoskins on the English landscape has been widely influential for archaeologists and first took shape in a series of papers on field systems (Hoskins 1937) and deserted villages (Hoskins 1944–5). These ventures in the 'archaeology of rural history' confirmed his passions as being local, rural, outdoors and concerned mostly with those inhabitants of parish communities at the lower end of the social scale.

Hoskins' special blend of 'archaeological geography' is seen to best effect in *The Making of the English Landscape*, published in 1955. Here he encouraged the analysis of topography, not merely as a descriptive backdrop but as a source as informative as documents. Emphasising the need for multi-disciplinary work, he placed the study of maps and documents alongside hedgerows, earthworks and architecture stressing that the landscape is a 'palimpsest', a tablet onto which several generations have etched their activities, partially erasing the efforts of their predecessors. This brand of 'open air studies' (Marshall 1997: 26) appealed to those with even the most oblique interest in geography and history and inspired local history classes (Harrison 1961). A series of county volumes (e.g. Taylor 1970) as well as Hoskins' own textbook *Local History in England* (1959) soon followed.

Hoskins' writing and motives deserve a more thorough analysis than can be offered here (Phythian-Adams 1992). He was certainly reacting against rural change and radiated nostalgia for pre-industrial landscapes; his was a kind of neo-Romantic view of a past countryside not yet vandalised by industry or housing sprawl. In this he echoed both the concerns of the Council for the Preservation of Rural England and the more public worries about post-war change expressed by local amenity groups and reflected in the formation of the Civic Trust in 1957. The past was a welcome retreat from incomprehensible modernity and offered 'something of which they [his readers] can grasp the scale and in which they can find a personal and individual meaning' (Hoskins 1959: 6). Politics were never far from the surface in his work, both in his inclusive approach to social study and in the manner of his writing. Hoskins cultivated a style which avoided explicit academic definitions, exclusive methodologies, expensive techniques or binding theoretical tradition, and, by appealing for wider inter-disciplinary participation, successfully engaged his reader (see p. 93). As a result his work has been accused of being largely consensual and conservative in tone (Marshall 1997: 14–15), a kind of John Betjeman for local history. Few could deny, however, that they were devoid of any interest, however slight, in the way in which Hoskins dressed history, geography and archaeology. He had a particular constituency in mind, 'the great army of amateurs' (Hoskins 1959: 3–6), and a clear aim, to spread an enthusiasm for the past so that 'every country walk will then have a new meaning, every corner of the parish will be peopled with the ghosts of old men and old buildings' (Hoskins 1962).

at Whiteparish in Dorset would be one example of this (Taylor 1967), Peter Wade-Martins fieldwalking in Norfolk between 1967 and 1970 another. Fieldwalking was already being extensively used in the United States at the time, but was relatively new to British archaeology. Wade-Martins' survey was restricted to areas which seemed most likely to produce settlement evidence, collecting pottery which could be relatively well dated by reference to earlier work by Hurst and others. The main objective was in line with the early excavation aims voiced at Wharram and focused on settlement 'origins' but, given the spatial patterning of the data, questions of settlement movement and 'continuity' could also be addressed. The project made use of place-names, manuscript maps and documents too (Wade-Martins 1980).

Church and monastic studies

Economic history was not alone in adopting a more topographical slant. Work by monk and scholar David Knowles to complete his 1,800-page, four-volume history of the religious orders in England (1940, 1948–59) was interrupted so that he could collaborate with Neville Hadcock on a locational guide and handbook of monastic sites (Knowles and Hadcock 1953 and 1971 with enlargements). At that time no full list of medieval monasteries existed and the volume was to become an essential guide for the field archaeologist, complementing Hadcock's earlier Ordnance Survey map of *Monastic Britain* published in 1950.

Like Beresford and Hoskins, Knowles would never have considered himself to be an archaeologist (Brooke 1975). Nevertheless, he is a more important figure in the history of medieval archaeology than the titles of his articles and books might suggest. Knowles collaborated with Grimes in his work on the London charterhouse and, as Professor of Medieval History, provided influential support for the appointment of Kenneth St Joseph as Curator in Aerial Photography in 1948. Later he used the St Joseph collection as the illustrative basis for a series of books for which St Joseph was General Editor. The first of these was *Monastic Sites from the Air* (1952), in which Knowles' distilled descriptions accompanied St Joseph's photographs, and this volume was followed six years later by another St Joseph collaboration, this time with Maurice Beresford, in *Medieval England: An Aerial Survey* (1958).

Set against this background of considerable historical and geographical endeavour the numbers of excavations on monastic sites remained static; indeed the annual totals declined somewhat in the early 1960s. There were good reasons for this. Comparatively few monastic sites were affected by urban redevelopment and, with limited funds available, excavation priorities lay elsewhere, given that so many monastic sites had been examined in the pre-war years. Nevertheless, historical evidence continued to provide stimulus for fieldwork (e.g. at Vale Royal, Ches.; Thompson 1962) and major excavations such as those at the Cluniac priory at Faversham (Kent; Philp 1968) now reflected ambitions to reveal the full ground plans of less well understood monastic orders and to discover how monastic precincts might have developed and changed. As historical research widened (e.g. Platt 1969 for Cistercian granges) so 'rescue' funds were employed to explore a fuller range of monastic site types (Butler 1993: 83). This work was justified by the need to establish the extent of sites for the purposes of scheduling, or as a prerequisite to consolidation and repair, but amounted, in effect, to a State-sponsored research programme. Among those sites targeted were the Bene-dictine nunnery at Elstow (Beds.; 1965–70; Baker 1971), the Benedictine/ Franciscan house at Denny (Cambs.; 1968–75; Christie and Coad 1980) and the preceptory of the Knights Templar at South Witham (Lincs.; 1965–7). At this last site, the soil was stripped to reveal buildings arrayed around a central courtyard including a hall, chapel and kitchen ranges (Mayes pers. comm.); one of the largest medieval excavations ever to take place. Sadly, with some exceptions such as Bicester Priory (Oxon.; Hinton 1969) and Reading Abbey (Berks.; Slade 1973), many excavation campaigns of this period have suffered delays in publication, such as the Benedictine abbey at Chertsey (Surrey), dug in 1954 (Poulton 1988) and the Trinitarian priory at Thelsford (Warwicks.), excavated in 1966 (Gray 1993). Others may never now appear in any substantive form.

Whereas churches surviving above foundation level had hitherto been regarded as the preserve of architectural historians, those destroyed during the War had effectively been 'converted' into an archaeological resource. Thus, in 1952 at St Bride's, Grimes undertook the first extensive research excavation of a parish church in the City of London. The digging was not without its difficulties and was interrupted by vandalism, thieving, complaints from nearby office workers and strikes from the workmen dig-ging the burials. Sums raised by selling off lead coffins helped compensate the fund set up to finance the excavations and the restoration which followed (Milne 1997: 13). The interim results suggested what might be achieved elsewhere under more controlled conditions and, through the identification of successive building phases, how earlier churches might be nested inside later buildings. In a final chapter to the story, the medieval structures exposed during excavation were preserved in an on-site museum (Milne 1997: 112).

During the 1960s the examination of church sites became more technically refined and began to address the archaeology beyond the church walls. An influential campaign which pioneered the investigation of the whole churchyard site was that by Philip Rahtz at the bombed site of St Mary-le-Port in Bristol in 1962–3 (Watts and Rahtz 1985). While the later medieval burials were only superficially examined, Rahtz examined both the church below ground as well as the relationship of the church to adjacent properties (Rahtz pers. comm.). At about the same time Martin Biddle was directing excava-tions in Winchester revealing a tract of later medieval townscape which included two churches (St Pancras in Brook Street and St Mary in Tanner

Street; Biddle 1972). The opportunity was taken here to compare two urban churches, exploring their structural development and internal arrangements, including burials. In both cases the archaeological evidence long predated historical documentation. However, that there was not yet full appreciation of the archaeological potential of even key sites is illustrated by events at York Minister in 1967–73 where archaeologists worked desperately in engineering cuttings, sometimes day and night, to rescue details of the Norman cathedral and the archaeology beneath (Carver 1995).

While the first phase of post-war church excavations was directed mainly towards sites damaged by enemy action, a second phase focused on disused churches. Among the pioneering excavations of rural church sites was the seven-week rescue excavation directed by Philip Rahtz at Broadfield (Herts.) in 1965 which revealed a thirteenth- to fifteenth-century sequence in three phases (Klingelhofer 1974). At the same time, one of the first investigations of a redundant church was taking place at Wharram Percy (Yorks.) where excavations of both the church and sample areas of the churchyard were completed between 1962 and 1974 (Bell and Beresford 1987). Unlike Grimes' work at St Bride's both these sites were excavated in plan rather than dug as series of narrow intersecting trenches (Milne 1997: 9). The work at Wharram was influential in showing how the total archaeological excavation of a church could complement the architectural evidence of the standing structure. The 687 skeletons recovered also represent a useful sample of the rural population, as recent studies of their palaeopathology by Simon Mays have shown (Mays *et al.* 1998; Mays 1998).

Castles

Partly because of the volume of excavation which had taken place on stone castle sites early in the century, post-war excavators switched their attention to 'earth castles' of motte and bailey or ringwork type (Webster 1963: 32–3). Jope and Threlfall's work at Ascot D'Oilly (Oxon.) in 1946–7 first showed how earth could be piled against the outside of a square tower (Jope and Threlfall 1959); while Brian Hope-Taylor's 1949 excavation at Abinger (Surrey) produced the first plan of a castle motte (Hope-Taylor 1956). Excavations of similar thoroughness became more widespread in the 1950s at Oakham Castle (Leics.; Gathercole 1958) and the motte and bailey castle at Therfield (Herts.; Biddle 1964). During the 1960s the numbers of castle excavations doubled in number with notable campaigns at Tote Copse Castle (Sussex; Brewster 1969), Pontesbury Castle (Salop.; Barker 1964), South Mimms (Herts.; Kent 1968) and Castle Neroche (Som.; Davison 1972), a 'ring work' converted into a motte and bailey. In Winchester, Martin Biddle showed what could be achieved digging in the spaces between existing buildings to reveal a sequence of lodgings, halls, service areas and defences (Biddle 1970). Excavation was also carried out as a component of consolidation programmes, as at Lydford (Devon; Saunders 1980) and Caerlaverock (Dumfries.; MacIvor and Gallagher 1999), where the silted moat was cleared and refilled with water, mostly without archaeological investigation. Perhaps because of the volume of finds and structural information generated by castle excavations, a number of major campaigns remain unpublished.

The pattern of investigation on castle sites followed a now familiar track. At first, excavation was focused on key visible components of the monument, in this case the motte. Thereafter excavation became ever more refined, scientific and/or extensive so that components previously seen as having lesser importance, such as the castle baileys, began to repay attention. A pause for consideration, synthesis and a statement of further potential helped to place the archaeological results within a wider academic context (e.g. Renn 1968; King and Alcock 1969). A basic tool for the archaeological study of castles, for example, was the collation and publication of the medieval building accounts for royal sites (Colvin 1963). Questions raised by *The History of the King's Works* led to various excavations including those at Clipstone (Notts.; Rahtz and Colvin 1960) where four men where employed for four weeks in October 1956 'to find the extent and date of the medieval buildings known as King John's palace'. Later research then tended to be more angled towards archaeological agendas and, in the case of castles, this latter phase is marked by the Royal Archaeological Institute's research into the origins of the castle in England which had its genesis at the Third Château-Gaillard Conference on the 900th anniversary of the Norman Conquest in 1966. This project was co-ordinated by Andrew Saunders to test the idea that the castles in England are post-Conquest, Norman institutions; a brave attempt to adhere to a clear research agenda. Three aspects were targeted: those early castles of Normandy considered to be of pre-Conquest date (Davison 1969), late Saxon fortifications (e.g. at Sulgrave, Northants., Davison 1978; and Goltho, Lincs., Beresford 1987), and the castles of the Conquest (e.g. Hastings, Sussex; Barker and Barton 1978). The project touched upon themes of 'continuity' and 'origins' seen in other arenas of later medieval studies and was to involve collaborative archaeological and historical research, at times controversially (Saunders 1978). In particular, frank exchanges between the historian R. Allen Brown and archaeologist Brian Davison still have much to offer on what defines different approaches to castle studies (Parsons 1978; see p. 93). Such tooth and claw debate is, sadly, all too rare.

Buildings

The losses of war seemed to focus minds on the remaining medieval building stock. There were increased measures for standing buildings in the 1944, 1947 and 1968 Town and Country Planning Acts which, among other things, provided a list of notable buildings, increased their protection and made owners responsible for maintaining their character. At the same time, public awareness and education were improved greatly through Ministry of Works and National Trust guidebooks. Case studies on medieval buildings appeared in sources as diverse as *Country Life*, county archaeological proceedings, the *Archaeological Journal* and, later, in *Medieval Archaeology*. Nikolaus Pevsner's *Buildings of England* series, which began with Cornwall in 1951 and ended with Staffordshire in 1974, soon became a national institution (Murray 1984).

Two publications will be singled out here. The first, *Monmouthshire Houses* by Cyril Fox and Lord Raglan (1951–4), contained important new work on 460 'small houses'. Their high quality illustrations and analysis of vernacular buildings included both constructional and decorative detail, chronologies, and distribution maps. In short, they brought an archaeological eye to a set of architectural problems; the result has been called 'the most important book on vernacular building that has yet appeared in English' (Smith 1963). The second book was *The English Medieval House* (1965) by Margaret Wood, a major new synthesis which drew upon the work of major buildings researchers of the day such as Maurice Barley (1961), Freddie Charles (1967), John Harvey (1954), Charles Hewett (1962–3), Stuart Rigold (1956), Louis Salzman (1952) and John Smith (1965). Barley, in particular, like Fox and Raglan before him, championed archaeology in the study of smaller, less well documented buildings (Barley 1961: xviii–xix). The best of this work not only combined documentary evidence with structural observations illustrated with comparative plans, sections, reconstructions and photographs but also provided a social context for a set of buildings under review (e.g. Barley *et al.* 1969; for an appraisal see Quiney 1994). Contributions to the understanding of building development also continued to come from archaeological sites (e.g. Thompson 1957), particularly for wooden buildings such as those found at Cheddar (Som.) in 1960–3 (Rahtz 1979).

Among the most influential contributors to building studies was William Pantin, Lecturer in Medieval Archaeology and History at the University of Oxford. Like Gerald Dunning, Pantin wrote illustrated papers rather than books, not all of them of direct interest here, but in the field of medieval architecture he was keenly aware of how archaeology might be combined fruitfully with architectural recording to produce phased building plans and conjectural three-dimensional views. He was a great supporter of local and national archaeological initiatives (Knowles 1974) and in his collaboration with Jope at the Clarendon Hotel in Oxford in 1956 (Jope and Pantin 1958) and his work on the medieval buildings of King's Lynn (Pantin 1962–3; Figure 4.6), he broadened the investigation of medieval buildings to include small-scale domestic constructions and warehouses. In doing so he laid the groundwork for classificatory schemes of vernacular architecture which could then be applied more widely and which still dominate the subject.

Artefacts and industry

The study of medieval industry had traditionally been the preserve of the historian and, naturally, focused on administration and organisation for which documentary evidence provides so much material (Clarke 1984: 130).

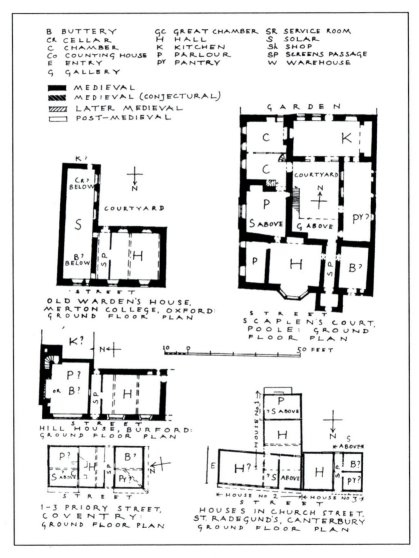

Figure 4.6 Medieval English town-house plans, thirteenth to fifteenth century. Pantin compared houses in different towns to show how their plans could be adapted to restricted urban sites. This group have their frontages placed parallel with the street in an 'extended' plan. (Pantin 1962–3: figure 69).

Early archaeological excavations were used mostly to illustrate parts of the textile manufacturing process and complemented evidence from sculpture and illustration (e.g. Carus-Wilson 1957). Gradually, however, archaeologists came to concentrate their efforts on those industries which had generated the artefacts found on their excavations and for which documentary evidence was, on the whole, rather less good. Early excavations at windmill sites include those at Butcombe (Som.) by Philip Rahtz in 1946 (Rahtz and Rahtz 1958) and at Lamport (Northants.; Posnansky 1956). Tile and brick kilns received some attention too (Mayes 1965) as did iron-working sites such as at Goltho (Lincs.; Beresford 1975: 46) and Rotherfield (Sussex; Money 1971). Some of the more specialist areas of research had their own particular 'champions'; Ronald Tylecote, for example, directed several excavations with the specific aim of investigating the development of the iron industry (e.g. at High Bishopley, Durham; Tylecote 1959).

Large excavation campaigns at pottery production sites included those at Chilvers Coton (Warwicks.), where some forty-two kilns and related features were excavated (Mayes and Scott 1984), Donyatt (Som.; Coleman-Smith and Pearson 1988), Hallgate (Doncaster; Buckland *et al.* 1979) and Laverstock (Wilts.; Musty *et al.* 1969). By the mid-1960s John Musty was able to provide a catalogue and classification of medieval pottery kilns, promoting standard terminology which is still used today (Musty 1966; 1974) though it reflected a bias in excavation towards kilns rather than the investigation of the pottery workshop as a whole (e.g. as at Lyveden, Northants.; Steane and Bryant 1975). At the same time, the importance of detailed documentary research was being realised and began to link personal names, place-names and production sites (Le Patourel 1968).

The 1950s and 1960s are remembered for the earliest attempts at regional synthesis of medieval pottery studies, epitomised by the work of John Hurst in East Anglia (e.g. Hurst 1955) and the continuing contribution of Gerald Dunning. Medieval finds were more commonly on display in museums and this promoted further interest; the London and Guildhall Museums even sold colour slides of medieval pots (Rhodes 1979: 88). Nevertheless, behind the scenes, massive backlogs of material were mounting up quickly and it was to be more than a decade before large assemblages from 1960s campaigns began to emerge in print. Outstanding examples are those from Hereford (Shoesmith 1985) and Plymouth (Gaskell Brown 1986).

Slowly, a more distinctive archaeological approach to ceramics study was promoted, especially after the publication of *Ceramics for the Archaeologist* (Shepard 1956), an influential volume which set the scene for archaeological study of ceramics over the next quarter century (Orton *et al.* 1993: 13). Pottery began to be quantified and results worked at with new methods in an attempt to reach beyond basic classification and dating. Imported pottery now received more extended consideration (Dunning 1961). The work of Martyn Jope was influential, developing the use of distribution maps with negative as well as positive findspots (Jope 1963), examining pottery frequencies (Jope and Threlfall 1959), comparing between sites in greater detail and discussing techniques of pottery making (Jope and Hodges 1956). Jope's scientific background perhaps enabled him to experiment with new methods and concepts in a way which can now be seen to be exceptional for his time and so vastly different from the aesthetic approach offered in Bernard Rackham's *Medieval English Pottery* (1948) published only a few years previously.

New resources and techniques

The post-war period was important for enhancing the basic archaeological record of sites and monuments of all classes. Crawford's manual *Archaeology in the Field* (1953) emphasised from its very first paragraph how the techniques of archaeology could be applied to seemingly unglamorous monument classes of 'Saxon and medieval times'. Chapters covering 'Medieval Castle Mounds and Parks' and 'Medieval Cultivation-Banks' underlined the importance of combined study of documents and visible remains in the field. 'The student must be at home in both spheres', Crawford wrote, 'and whether he is called a field archaeologist or historian is a matter of words; he must be both' (Crawford 1953: 198). It was a philosophy which he extended to his editorship of 124 issues of *Antiquity* and which advocated that survey need not be merely a prerequisite for excavation but could make its own independent contribution.

Since the later 1940s VCH county histories had been extended. Studies of landscape and settlement growth were all now treated parish by parish (Lewis 1989: 60). The 1948 VCH for Cambridgeshire included plans and descriptions of medieval moated sites, for example (VCH 1948). At the same time, the Royal Commission on Historical Monuments continued to produce county inventories (Dorset 1952–76; Cambridgeshire 1969–72) and surveys of historic towns (Cambridge 1959; York 1962–81). Amongst the other new initiatives were the National Buildings Record in 1940 (Croad 1989) and the Archaeology Division of the Ordnance Survey (OS) in 1947 which set about systematising its archaeological recording, referencing and indexing. Full OS archaeological surveys of the counties of Dorset, Hampshire and Northumberland were complete by 1958 (Phillips 1980). In the following decade two important developments for the future were the creation of the National Monuments Record in 1963 which led to considerable improvements in the recording of threatened buildings (Cooper 1988) and, following pioneering work by, among others, Don Benson in Oxfordshire, some county councils and local authorities began to develop lists of monuments and location maps, the fledgling Sites and Monuments Records which are so central to the planning process today.

The potential of aerial photography for medieval archaeology was seized upon immediately after the War (Bruce-Mitford 1948) and, as early as 1947,

Maurice Beresford made regular visits to the RAF collection housed in Nissen huts at Medmenham in his search for 'lost' villages (Beresford 1994). However, for the most part, what he found there were high altitude verticals and it was not until the involvement of Kenneth St Joseph that well-composed oblique photographs taken from a lower altitude became available more widely. St Joseph's links with the newly formed Deserted Medieval Village Research Group led to many sites being identified for the first time and new detail to be added for those already mapped. Later, the benefits of aerial photography were advertised more widely in the two Cambridge University Press volumes which made effective use of St Joseph's aerial photographs (Knowles and St Joseph 1952; Beresford and St Joseph 1958). *Monastic Sites from the Air* was the first archaeological study of aerial photographs to be published in book form since *Wessex from the Air* in 1928 and did much to provide impetus for the Royal Commission's (RCHME) national programme of air photography, which began in 1967. During the 25-year period covered by this chapter, no single technique was as influential generally in archaeology as the study of aerial photographs and its impact on medieval archaeology was quite distinctive. Chiefly, it enhanced the recognition of new earthwork sites and revealed a truer picture of the distribution, form and survival of monuments, thereby promoting archaeo-logical methods and terminology. At the same time, aerial photography provided a novel and wider visual perspective for sites which had hitherto been appreciated only from the ground or in mapped form. This was to contribute to a progressive shift in the scale of research and site management from single sites to larger tracts of countryside (Darvill *et al.* 1993).

In 1970 many of the techniques taken for granted today were not yet applied on a routine basis. Fieldwalking was still associated in most people's minds with flint collecting and did not rate a mention in archaeological manuals, though members of the Oxford University Archaeology Society were undertaking 'parish surveys' between Witney and Oxford after 1964 (Jonathan Coad, Tania Dickinson, Philip Dixon, Tom Hassall, David Hinton, George Lambrick, Helen Sutermeister and Andrew Williamson were all involved). Both earthwork survey and 'sherding' were carried out here and by Kettering Grammar School under the supervision of John Steane in 1968 (Stamper pers. comm.). Likewise, 'sub-terrestrial' survey, whether using resistance or magnetic techniques, was also at an experimental stage. Pottery kilns had been detected magnetically and then excavated, for example at Brill (Jope 1953–4), and trials had also been undertaken on medieval settlement sites, for example on Fyfield Down (Wilts.) in 1962 (Fowler and Blackwell 1998: 18) but the procedures were still labour intensive and slow so that coverage of large areas remained impractical.

Generally speaking, archaeological fieldwork was restricted to the study of aerial photographs and maps, followed by a reconnaissance visit and perhaps a measured survey (in imperial measurements), mostly using the plane-table method. By today's standards the appetite for fieldwork of this kind seems quite remarkable. During the 1950s, for example, Beresford and Hurst themselves led visits to some 1,500 deserted village sites. County checklists and distribution maps of deserted medieval settlements were published regularly from the mid-1960s (e.g. Allison *et al.* 1965) so that, nationally, the 1,353 identified sites published in Beresford (1954) more than doubled in the next 25 years (Beresford *et al.* 1980). Dots on maps, however, were no substitute for fuller topographical survey, and here the situation was far less satisfactory. In 1971, of the 101 deserted medieval villages known in Oxfordshire, only one had a plan of its earthworks (Benson 1972). By making use of the 6-inches to 1-mile (1: 10,560) Ordnance Survey maps, rapid sketch survey techniques had to be developed to locate and record sites before they disappeared altogether and, in some cases, these now provide the only record of their existence (Aston and Bond 1973; Aston 1989). Generally speaking, survey was overshadowed by excavation and tended to be underfunded and underestimated in academic terms.

Excavation directors, at least those operating freelance and funded by the State, were expected to write up their excavations in their own time and moved from job to job completing post-excavation and publication when time allowed. Philip Rahtz, for example, directed excavations in no less than fourteen English counties in the decade after 1953, from which the rate of excavation can be imagined (Rahtz 1974; 2001). Many directors, whether paid or voluntary, learnt their field craft through experience by participating in excavation. Those who had the benefit of training had, more often than not, honed their skills on prehistoric sites, as John Hurst did at Star Carr (Le Patourel 1992). Directors had to be polymaths, managing hired labourers who did most of the digging, often undertaking all the drawing and most of the specialist finds studies single-handedly with only occasional help from visiting specialists. Even by the mid-1960s, the archaeological community was still very small. Only twelve archaeological staff were employed by the English Royal Commission and the Ordnance Survey (Taylor 1987) and most archaeologists were at least on nodding acquaintance with each other.

Real innovation on-site came about through the new methodologies introduced at Wharram Percy. The small excavation trenches dug by Hoskins, Beresford and others on deserted village sites in the 1940s and early 1950s had proved confusing (Hurst 1971: 83), and their methods were sometimes unconventional (Stamper 1999). The first time open-area excavation was used on a British medieval site was in 1953 at Wharram Percy, where John Hurst and Jack Golson put the technique into practice in a 50 by 20 foot trench at House 10. By the standards of the time, Hurst's trench was a large area to open up. 'I was slightly cautious at the time', he recalls, 'as I had just been trained at Cambridge in the grid method, so we still left two baulks across it; but we regretted this later as we lost a lot of evidence' (Hurst quoted in Selkirk 1975). The House 10 experiment was much influenced by Golson's experiences a year earlier at Store Valby in Denmark where he had dug with Axel Steensberg using the open-area method (Steensberg 1982; Kristiansen and Mahler 1998; Hurst 1999). This required excavation without the use of the baulks which characterised the grid or box system advocated by Mortimer Wheeler. It had important implications for the way in which a site was understood and placed greater reliance on what emerged in plan rather than the interpretation of vertical sections. At Wharram every find was recorded in three dimensions.

There was always an explicit link between the research underway at Wharram and excavations of rural settlements financed by the Ministry of Works and its successors. This link was provided by John Hurst who chose deserted medieval villages for the Ministry of Works to dig. Quite simply, before Wharram there had been no professional excavation of a large 'lost village' site. Once open-area excavation had proved itself, the method was then used on 'official' excavations (e.g. at Moreton (Som.) in 1953–4; Rahtz and Greenfield 1977, and at Holworth (Dorset) in 1958; Rahtz 1959). But it was not until the end of the 1950s that the method was more generally embraced, even by experienced field archaeologists. Peter Fowler, for example, did not use the technique at Wroughton Mead on Fyfield Down (Wilts.) in 1959 (Fowler and Blackwell 1998: 17). After the trenches were excavated on a grid of 10-foot squares at Seacourt (Oxon.) in 1958–9, the excavator recognised that the method had 'provided a large number of vertical sections, but tended to obscure the plans of both the stone and timber buildings, and on a future occasion a much larger unit of excavation would be used' (Biddle 1961–2). Similarly, once it became clear at Wharram that only excavations beyond the four corners of the house earthworks could reveal the full history of the whole enclosure, then the 1960s policy of funding excavations of single houses, which had by then delivered its aims of sampling peasant house types, was abandoned in favour of larger open areas and the full excavation of whole enclosures (e.g. at Grenstein, Norfolk, 1965–6; Wade-Martins 1980: 93–161). Soon earthmoving machines began to play an important role (Petch 1968), and the challenge became how to record such large areas efficiently and to a high standard. At South Witham (Lincs.; 1965–7), the accurate recording of 3,600 square metres of medieval buildings of the Templar preceptory made innovative use of a vertical tripod-mounted camera to produce a composite mosaic of photographs (Mayes pers. comm.; Figure 4.7).

Another site whose excavation was a microcosm of the way techniques changed after 1960 was the motte and bailey castle at Hen Domen near Montgomery on the English–Welsh border (Higham and Barker 2000; Figure 4.8). Initial work here began with trenches cut across the motte ditch, progressing onto the excavation of 8-foot-square boxes, separated by 2-foot baulks and, finally, the extremely precise recording of open areas, gently picked off in broad sweeps across the castle interior. Much of the evidence

Figure 4.7 Chapel under excavation at the Templar preceptory at South Witham (Lincs.) in 1965–7. This site was threatened by ploughing and rescue excavation was financed by the (then) Ministry of Public Buildings and Works. Rapid recording was facilitated by the use of photomosaics like this one. (Photo by courtesy of Phil Mayes).

consisted of pebble circles and rows and very shallow post-sockets and the open-area excavation method enabled large areas to be exposed, so providing a complete view of the site. Under different circumstances, such ephemeral remains would have been swept away by the plough or, worse still, gone unnoticed by archaeologists. Only near-total excavation (aided by frost action over the winter months) provided the complete picture (Barker 1969b) and would demonstrate that timber castles were more substantial, impressive and complex than had been suggested hitherto.

New technical standards in the recording of urban archaeology were set in Winchester (Hants.) by Martin Biddle in the 1960s and 1970s, particularly during open-area excavations at the Old Minster and at Lower Brook Street. Up to this time open-area excavation had been used mostly on shallowly buried, single-period sites but was as yet untested on deeper urban

Figure 4.8 The motte at Hen Domen under excavation in July 1991. (Photo: Paul Stamper).

stratigraphy in Britain where the Wheeler box-method was still current. The switch to the new technique in Winchester was to have immediate implications for all aspects of the excavation process, from routine site discipline to recording systems. Innovations included the use of transparent drawing film and planning in full colour; and it was the Winchester team who recognised the advantages of the metric system, both for producing drawings at standard scales and for accurate on-site recording and plotting of finds and features (Biddle and Kjølbye-Biddle 1969). Of course, these developments owed much to other parts of the discipline of archaeology and went deeper than field practice. Biddle's belief that documentary sources should be thoroughly integrated with excavation data (Keene 1985) was influenced by earlier practitioners like Salter and Grimes, his use of large open-area excavation followed the example of Bergen and other Scandinavian cities and his inclusion of 'evidence derived from a wide range of the natural sciences' (Biddle 1983), owed much to the influence of prehistorian Grahame Clark at Cambridge, who had been responsible in part for Biddle's undergraduate training. Biddle's work was, however, much more than a mere dovetailing of other people's ideas, it was an original application which drew urban medieval archaeology firmly into the mainstream of archaeological thinking and methods and then developed it further. Many different aspects of the Winchester operation, from the numbers of foreign volunteers to the high proportion of female supervisors, have attracted comment (e.g. Hudson

1981: 6–9) but it is still the scale of the work which is striking today. In 1969 the average number of people on Winchester sites for the 14-week season was 170. Not inappropriately, the cooks were provided by the Army, who served over 23,000 meals that year (Biddle 1970: 277).

Scientific techniques were only rarely applied to medieval artefacts and sites in the 1940s and 1950s. A report on the analysis of the contents of a medieval jug (Dunning 1942) and a series of spectrographic analyses on medieval pottery glazes (Jope 1952a; Jope and Threlfall 1959: 254; Spillett *et al.* 1943) stand out as early technological and usage studies which would later be expanded upon (e.g. Musty and Thomas 1962). Expertise was often sought in university departments, for petrology and provenance studies, for example, though here too Jope and Dunning were active (e.g. for blue roofing slates; Jope and Dunning 1954). Thereafter, a handful of institutions, most notably the Institute of Archaeology, the newly established Ancient Monuments Laboratory (and here particularly Leo Biek), the British Museum Research Laboratory and the Oxford Research Laboratory for Archaeology and History of Art, led the way in experimenting with scientific methods. A growing number of general textbooks and collections of papers outlined principles of archaeological science and showed no bias against medieval material, sometimes including rewarding case studies (e.g. Biek 1963 for microscope work; Brothwell 1972: 137–8 on leprosy; Chaplin 1971: 138–42 on horn cores from medieval Coventry).

The experimental nature of some of this early work is illustrated by work on dating techniques. A radiocarbon date from a post in the barley barn at Cressing Temple (Essex) threatened the faith of architectural historians by producing a date of AD 970 ± 70 years, a date considered by most to be at least 150 to 200 years too early. In the alarmed discussion which followed it became clear that the wood sample had been extracted from the centre of the tree, creating a margin of error of up to 300 years which depended on the felling age of the timber. Nor was it appreciated until some years later that deviations in the radiocarbon concentration of organic matter on earth during the historical span could induce errors as high as 200 to 250 years. These two factors alone produced a cumulative error of such magnitude as to render the exercise useless. Lessons were quickly learnt for subsequent investigations of timber-framed medieval buildings, including the over-simplistic equation of particular structures with documentary references which apparently dated them and the serious challenge of proving even a well-dated roof to be contemporary with the stone walls supporting it (Horn 1970; Rigold 1966).

Generally, the impact of radiocarbon dating on medieval sites is far less significant than it has been for prehistory. It tends to be reserved for sites with little cultural debris but where some understanding of a sequence is required; medieval cemeteries are one example (Gilchrist 1999a). In contrast, the dating of timber samples used in buildings and recovered from archaeological sites has become widespread. European master chronologies were already advanced by the late 1960s when the taking of wood samples from archaeological sites for dendrochronological dating became commonplace (e.g. Huggins 1970 for a medieval bridge). Aware of the potential, one far-sighted excavator redeposited excavated medieval bridge timbers into a waterlogged castle moat in the hope of conserving them for future dendro-chronologists (MacIvor and Gallagher 1999). They were successfully dated sixteen years later.

Experimentation with some techniques, such as the dating of weathered glasses using the depth of their layered crusts, proved them to be flawed (Newton 1971). However, the potential for other dating techniques such as thermoluminescence and archaeomagnetism was well appreciated by the mid 1960s. Among the first published medieval archaeomagnetic dates were hearths from Kirkstall Abbey (Yorks.; Cook and Belshé 1958) and Seacourt (Oxon.; Aitken and Harold 1959). Dates for numerous medieval sites were regularly assessed in the pages of *Archaeometry* over the next decade (e.g. Hurst 1963; 1966; Aitken and Hawley 1967). In particular, new dates for pottery kilns helped to verify local and regional type series (e.g. for Laverstock (Wilts.); Musty *et al.* 1969: 93). For the most part, however, there was little guidance on new techniques except through word-of-mouth and publication. State-funded work was exceptional in this respect because visits from Inspectors of Ancient Monuments and staff of the Ancient Monuments Laboratory provided links both between excavations and between excavation and laboratory. John Hurst, for example, advised on medieval pottery, particularly imports (Le Patourel 1992), while Leo Biek and others could advise on scientific applications (e.g. for the Northolt Manor report; Hurst 1961; Hurst pers. comm.)

By 1970 most excavation reports of medieval sites had, for some years, contained reports on animal and human bone, though normally only a selection of bones were retained for further study. In 1968 in Hereford, for example, bones on one site were kept from the earliest occupation layers only, on another only if they came from pits (Noddle 1985: 84). Innovative work included the identification of marine mollusca and fish bones from 1950s excavations at Kirkstall Abbey, Pontefract Priory and at Petergate (York; Ryder 1969) and regional reviews of 'livestock remains' (Ryder 1961). However, the taking of soil samples for pollen, plant and insect analysis was not yet either systematic or routine and Dimbleby's classic textbook *Plants and Archaeology* (1967) omitted anything other than prehistoric evidence. There were occasional studies, on the implications of fly pupae for medieval living conditions (Oswald 1962–3), on parasite eggs from wood-lined medieval pits in Winchester (Taylor 1955; Pike and Biddle 1966), and on pollen analysis of soils and silts (e.g. Biddle 1961–2: 195–7; Huggins 1976, excavated 1969–71) but these were exceptions. Typically, there was no on-site flotation work, environmental samples being taken only when the context was deemed 'special'. Any assessment of the 'value' of deposits was usually made on visual criteria alone, sampling being restricted to the width of the trench with no suggestion of complementary off-site investigation.

New organisations

The first moves towards founding a new society and journal for early and later medieval archaeology took place in the autumn of 1956. The idea had arisen independently in the minds of Donald Harden, John Hurst and David Wilson and so carried with it a range of institutional and chronological interests from the beginning. A selection of interested parties were canvassed informally for their views by letter and, since there was only one outright dissenter, a broad consensus of the outline of aims and outcomes of a future journal was quickly arrived at. John Hurst predicted that the journal should be high standard and would include:

> fieldwork, excavation, the study of museum objects and other things which impinge on the study of Saxon and Medieval settlement as a whole. There should be co-operation with Historians, Geographers and Architects so that the whole field of medieval studies can be covered. It is hoped to increase still further the links which are beginning to form after such a long dichotomy between Archaeologists and Historians. We shall have to lay down the division of the journal at least on broad lines so as not to cause trouble later, the scope should not however be too restricted on paper. We should exclude heraldry, bells, genealogy, ecclesiology but of course the dividing line is thin as we would wish to include glazed floor tiles but not stained glass from churches. While purely documentary work should be discouraged it is badly needed to fill out excavation reports, or fieldwork. The journal should include notes and brief reports on excavations etc carried out during the year. There should be book reviews but not a large bibliography. Advertisements might be admissible on the back cover but not inside.
>
> (SMA archive, December 1956)

The first public meeting, chaired by Sir Mortimer Wheeler, then President of the Society of Antiquaries, took place in Burlington House on 16 April 1957 with about eighty-five people present. Donald Harden outlined some initial suggestions as to what functions any future society might perform and what the geographical and chronological coverage would be. In the open forum which followed the undecided voiced their worries about overlaps with existing national and county societies and the precise definition of content but, although one detractor stated openly that the Society would not survive (in point of fact he joined himself in 1959, apparently greatly impressed with the new journal), the motion to form a society was carried by an overwhelming majority.

Box 4.3 The Society for Medieval Archaeology

During the formative years of the Society in 1956 and 1957, much thought was given by founding members to appropriate names and titles for the Society and its new Journal (SMA archives). Initial correspondence from John Hurst in 1956 used the name *Journal of Saxon and Medieval Archaeology*. Hurst himself admitted to finding the name rather cumbersome and realised that it was always likely to be an awkward choice for those working in the 'Celtic west'. Yet it was important that everyone should feel represented and so several alternatives were explored. Donald Harden thought *BRITAIN AD*, Grahame Clark the *Journal of Dark Age and Medieval Studies* and Wilson suggested something Latin such as *Acta Archaeologica Medieval*. None of these titles seemed to fit the bill, Hurst felt the term 'Dark Age' was best avoided and otherwise the titles were either too long or not specific enough in their implied date range. Martyn Jope put forward two candidates: the *Journal of Post-Roman Studies* and the *Journal of Medieval Archaeology*. The latter suggestion Hurst thought the best yet, but at the first meeting in April 1957 the discussion was of a *Society for Dark Age and Medieval Studies*.

  The steering committee was charged with mulling over the issue further and soon discarded Jope's first suggestion because they felt it gave the impression that the Journal and Society would be devoted to immediately post-Roman times (letter DMW to HPRK 5–6–57). The *Society for Dark Age and Medieval Studies* seemed confirmed until one committee member, Herbert Finberg, wrote to protest saying that he found the terms 'lamentably imprecise' and 'the term "Dark Age" defeatist and depressing. In another thirty or forty years it may look very silly indeed. As a title for a society, it is both cumbrous (17 syllables!) and slipshod (an adjective coupled with an adjectival noun)'. Finberg's many years of experience in publishing led him to suggest the alternative title of *LUCERNA. A Review of the Unwritten Evidences of British History Since the Roman Period*. Unable to reach a unanimous verdict, the steering committee remained split between archaeologists and historian and, at the second meeting of the new Society on 13 June 1957, it was Jope's suggestion of *The Society for Medieval Archaeology* which was finally settled upon. Finberg later recycled his proposed title for a volume of studies in 1964.

A steering committee of Harden, Hurst, Wilson, Bruce-Mitford, Finberg and Phillips was requested to report back at a future date on ways and means. The 'prolonged discussion and private conversation' which followed centred around the name of the society (**Box 4.3**) and its objectives. The wording of the draft constitution had to be carefully judged so as to be as inclusive as possible. Finally, a draft constitution was approved on 13 June 1957 and the first journal appeared barely 12 months later, by which time the new Society for Medieval Archaeology already had a membership of nearly 400 (Harden 1957). Rupert Bruce-Mitford, excavator of Sutton Hoo (Suffolk) and Mawgan Porth (Corn.), became the Society's first President, though great credit must be due to David Wilson and John Hurst for initiating discussions on the possible formation of a society, and to Donald Harden, editor of the first seventeen volumes of the elegant new journal (Figure 4.9). The familiar pastel blue cover of the annual journal, with its articles, reviews, and news has continued to be the Society's most visible face, though a monograph series (since 1966), a newsletter (since 1989), a website (since 2000) and major conferences are also now at the core of the Society's activities.

The establishment of the new Society helped prove medieval archaeology as a credible academic pursuit and provided evidence of a self-critical sub-discipline with a broad constituency. The composition of its first committee, with its blend of local and economic historians like Hoskins and Finberg, architectural historians like Colvin, and prominent archaeologists of both the early and later medieval periods such as Radford and Grimes, set the distinctive tone of its early journals and conference topics. The binding was provided by Oxbridge connections. Bruce-Mitford, Harden and Leeds had all been based in Oxford and provided support and advice for younger scholars like Cambridge student John Hurst (Hurst 1994). There were grow-ing European connections too. In France, for example, the establishment of the *Centre de Recherches Archéologiques Médiévales* at the University of Caen in 1955 was followed by the castle colloquium *Château Gaillard* in 1962 and by the French journal *Archéologie Médiévale* in 1971.

In Britain, the early post-war impetus for later medieval archaeology was generated by a relatively small group of scholars, many of them with an interest in medieval rural settlement. Crucially, whether they represented museums (like Bruce-Mitford and Harden), the Ministry (Dunning and Hurst) or academia (Beresford, Jope or Pantin), all seemed to prosper and rapidly climb their respective career ladders. Their benevolent political and

Presidents of The Society for Medieval Archaeology	
1957–2002	
1957–60	Mr R. L. S. Bruce-Mitford
1961–62	Mr W. A. Pantin
1963–65	Dr J. N. L. Myres
1966–68	Prof. E. M. Carus-Wilson
1969–71	Dr C. A. R. Radford
1972–74	Dr A. J. Taylor
1975–77	Dr D. B. Harden
1978–80	Mr C. Blunt
1981–83	Mr J. G. Hurst
1984–86	Prof. H. R. Loyn
1987–89	Prof. A. C. Thomas
1990–92	Dr H. Clarke
1993–95	Dr M. W. Thompson
1996–98	Prof. M. Biddle
1999–2001	Prof. C. Dyer
2002–	Dr R. A. Hall

Figure 4.9 Society for Medieval Archaeology. List of presidents.

academic influence ensured that medieval archaeology would be considered increasingly as an equal partner in the world of archaeology. At the same time, their enthusiasm for their subject and patronage of others guaranteed the kind of broad-based following typified by the Deserted Medieval Village Research Group (DMVRG), founded in 1952 by Beresford, Hurst and a handful of others (Beresford *et al.* 1980). Together with the Vernacular Architecture Group which held its inaugural meeting in the same year, the DMVRG was the earliest of the medieval special interest research groups and remains one of the most successful at integrating archaeologists, historians and historical geographers, both professional and amateur. Between 1955 and 1970 the identification of deserted medieval villages became a pursuit in which all were encouraged to participate, particularly those in the adult education sector. Individuals, local societies, extra-mural groups could all make a start on their own areas by building up files and county gazetteers of sites, almost always with rewarding results. To take one example, in 1954 there were fifteen known deserted medieval settlements in Gloucestershire, in 1959 there were twenty-eight, in 1962 fifty-four and by the time of the 1971 publication *Deserted Medieval Villages* (Beresford and Hurst 1971), based on a 1968 gazetteer, there were sixty-seven, more than a 400 per cent increase within the space of fourteen years.

Among the other key initiatives for post-war archaeology was the formation of the Council for British Archaeology (CBA) in 1943. The CBA set up the 'excavation committees' to promote and monitor inner city reconstruction projects after the war and the inclusion of medieval archaeology in its *Survey and Policy of Field Research in the Archaeology of Great Britain* and, after 1953, in its six period-based research committees, was a crucial step towards placing historic archaeology on an equal footing with other period interests. The Medieval Research Committee of the CBA, for example, organised a conference on medieval pottery in 1964 at which was launched the idea of a National Reference Collection. In the late 1960s and 1970s the thematic work of the CBA specialist committees, such as that for Urban Research, was especially influential in ideas and action. The Churches Committee, for example, encouraged the establishment of archaeological advisors for cathedrals and churches and, much later, the formation of the Society for Church Archaeology.

A further boost was provided in the post-war era by the building up of record offices and the opening of new archives. Huge quantities of previously undigested material, much of it from the later medieval period, was assembled, sorted and catalogued. In one English county, Essex, the collection of deeds grew from five thousand in 1946 to half a million by 1969. It was a similar story over all of Europe (Barraclough 1979: 185), posing serious questions for scholars as to how best to identify and access likely sources. Initially, some archaeologists found the publication of topographical material frustratingly slow (Crawford 1953: 198), but access was soon improved, not least through the new technology of photocopying.

A series of post-War initiatives accounted for the increase in public participation in the study of local history and archaeology. The 1944 Education Act created greater equality of opportunity by extending adult education and, in response, local education authorities and universities rapidly expanded their provision. Some idea of the rate of growth can be gauged by the fact that the number of full-time staff in extra-mural departments trebled from 83 in 1945–6 to 244 by 1951–2 (Fieldhouse 1996a: 212) and between 1947 and 1950 the number of students attending evening institutes rose from 825,000 to nearly 1,250,000 (Fieldhouse 1996b: 58). Operating in a dominantly liberal ideological climate, an enthusiastic generation of new posts now set about extending the range and variety of their programmes across the country and, since subjects such as social studies and economics had been among the most popular before the War, this was an obvious area for increased provision.

Archaeology benefited greatly from the popularity of history and local studies, which had quickly generated a literature of its own, from the quarterly *The Local Historian* to popular newsletters and magazines (Finberg and Skipp 1967). Cheaper books and a growing public library service increased the choice available to students at all levels. The Standing Conference for Local History (now the British Association for Local History) represented the county committees who were themselves made up of dozens of local history groups busy organising research projects and working towards publications on their own village or town. These groups, lacking the conservatism and weight of tradition of nineteenth-century archaeology and history societies, proved an effective channel for the enthusiasm of amateur local historians, many of whom now came into contact with archaeology (Riden 1983: 9–23). Such opportunities could be as important for teachers as for their students. John Hurst's evening classes on medieval pottery held at Goldsmiths' College, London, from 1963 onwards helped develop his own ideas for publication, for example.

New threats

In the mid-1960s the predicted UK population growth suggested to planners that a city the size of Leeds would need to be built every year for the next forty years (Lane 1966). Imaginative solutions were called for, including the rebuilding and renewal of historic centres (e.g. Bristol), urban expansion (e.g. Basingstoke) and the establishment of new garden cities and satellite towns (e.g. Stevenage). Planning procedures were portrayed as slowing down reform; local tactics designed to frustrate major strategies (see p. 93). In the event, very limited archaeological work was done in advance of the new towns like Harlow (Essex), Hemel Hempstead (Herts.) or Peterlee (Durham). Related infrastructural projects enveloped well-preserved medieval landscapes (Figure 4.10).

The seriousness of the problem was made clear in a series of local assessments (e.g. Oxford, Benson and Cook 1966; Peterborough, RCHME 1969). The Oxford report, in particular, set the template for the genre of so-called 'implications' surveys in the 1970s (see Chapter 5). If anything, the statistics compiled for the destruction of historic buildings were even more appalling than for archaeological monuments. Gloucester lost 144 (24 per cent) of its 603 listed buildings between 1947 and 1971 and few towns could claim to have anything approaching satisfactory provision for recording their listed buildings prior to demolition (Aston and Bond 1976: 214). Even this dismal picture proved unduly positive because many medieval (and later) buildings

Figure 4.10 A medieval landscape submerged, January 1969. Ridge and furrow disappears under a reservoir at Thurlaston (Warwicks.). (Copyright Cambridge University Collection of Air Photographs).

had escaped listing thanks to their more modern exterior facades. 'Resource management' was set to become an ever-present theme in medieval arch-aeology from the late 1960s onwards.

In rural areas medieval archaeology seemed to escape more lightly. Large monuments like monasteries and castles were better protected, and the considerable damage done by gravel and peat extraction and afforestation mainly affected prehistoric sites (RCHME 1960). Even motorways, whose construction went mostly unrecorded by archaeologists, tended to keep their distance from occupied medieval sites. Deserted villages like Seacourt (Oxon.), which was destroyed almost completely by the construction of the Western Bypass around Oxford, were more vulnerable though (Biddle 1961–2) and there were also localised threats from stone quarrying (as, for example, at Thrislington in Durham) and ironstone mining (in Oxfordshire and Northamptonshire especially). Less dramatic but much more serious to the legibility of historic landscapes was the removal of hedgerows and the ever-increasing acreage put under the plough. Ridge and furrow suffered badly, especially in the midland claylands of England; the Dorset volumes of the English Royal Commission give a good impression of what was being lost else-where (Taylor 1987). The growth of historic villages and infill of abandoned plots as well as the designation of areas of countryside for new uses remained serious threats.

The discovery that so many medieval sites, sometimes of national impor-tance, were vulnerable to damage from domestic and European agricultural policies operating outside any development control gave added impetus to the establishment of groups and societies. In the early 1960s it was estimated that, of the 1500 deserted medieval sites then known to exist, about 250 had been destroyed by land use changes since 1939 and a further 200 were threatened with destruction (Beresford *et al.* 1980). Most were flattened in piecemeal fashion over a number of years like the sites at Kingsthorpe (Northants.), intact until the 1950s but with only its former main street surviving in 1974 (Taylor 1974a). Aware of the level of destruction, in 1965 the Deserted Medieval Village Research Group suggested a policy on the preservation of deserted medieval sites to the then Ministry of Public Buildings and Works and continued to provide advice on priorities for rescue excavation (e.g. Hurst 1980).

Concepts and ideas

The main catalyst for post-war interest in medieval archaeology was the remarkable surge in the popularity of cultural, social and economic history (**Box 4.2**). Both post-war economic recovery and contemporary technological advances had increased the relevance of social sciences, turning students away from traditional political and constitutional interests (Coleman 1987: 94–7). Explicit left-wing slant or Marxist perspective was rare but, operating in a climate of liberal ideology, there was some bias towards working-class interests from which medieval settlement and land use studies could only benefit (Fieldhouse 1996a: 209). At the same time, innovations in academic working practices leant towards interdisciplinary study and collaborative projects.

Into this vacuum stepped a number of disciplines which blended a trinity of academic subjects in slightly different ways. Not all were new, like historical geography or agrarian history, but others, notably local history and economic history, quickly became influential. Adroit scholars hopped from one academic 'compartment' to the next and much of what appears now to have been a carefully plotted academic path from economic history to agricultural history and on to archaeology was, according to one scholar at least, merely the product of chance (Beresford 1986–7). In Beresford's case it was an ambition to plot ridge-and-furrow onto a large-scale Ordnance Survey map which led him to the earthworks of his first deserted medieval village at Bittesby (Leics.) in June 1946. The next step on to excavation and archaeology was logical if such 'lost' villages were to be dated and so both Hoskins and Beresford had experimented with digging by the time of the famous Cambridge seminar in June 1948 (**Box 4.1**).

The lead role taken by history in setting the agenda for archaeological work was a crucial one. Knowles, Platt and others provided the stimulus for excavation agendas on monastic sites, for example, just as Colvin did for castles and other secular sites. When Maurice Beresford's *The Lost Villages of England* was published in 1954 it was intended as a contribution to economic history. In fact, as Chris Dyer has recently commented (1999b), what was at the time seen as something of a sideline in agricultural history proved to be the core of quite another sub-discipline. Its importance lay not only in its subject matter, its use of aerial photographs, its weaving of history and archaeology but in its tone. From its first lines (see p. 93) *Lost Villages* encouraged engagement and access.

'Sooner or later, the wise field-workers will learn some history, and history graduates will take to field-work . . .' (Anon. 1961). And so it was, for the most rewarding projects were to be those in which history and archaeology were more closely linked, as at Upton (Hilton and Rahtz), Wharram Percy (Beresford and Hurst) and Winchester (Keene and Biddle). The relationship between history and archaeology was chosen as the theme of the Society for Medieval Archaeology's very first annual spring conference in March 1958. To some extent medieval archaeology may have 'suffered from a disciplinary inferiority-complex towards textual historians, and this stifled the development of an independent approach to archaeological data' (Bintliff 1986b). There is some truth in this, but it is also the case that some senior historians, perhaps taken aback by the rapid rise of their academic neighbour, were at pains to impose themselves and restate their case for precedence. In particular, they were offended by archaeological terminology (Brown 1970; see p. 93), laying the blame firmly at the door of the prehistorian: 'The methods of prehistory have, in the younger generation, begun to take over historic and well-documented periods in which more subtle, more aesthetic, and more civilised methods of approach should primarily be employed' (Evans 1961).

In point of fact some of the 'inappropriate' methods referred to are more likely to have derived from links between historical geography and archaeology. The archaeological study of town development was greatly influenced by, among others, the geographer Michael Conzen who pioneered the analysis of medieval town plans (Conzen 1960; 1968). Conzen drew attention to the importance of the burgage plot as a building block, observing subtle differences in their alignment and area and unpicking phases of urban formation and growth. Similarly, a study of the evolution of a landscape, it was argued, could establish the general principles which had determined its present day patterning (Mitchell 1954). To achieve this, two techniques were employed, the 'cross-sectional' approach of period reconstructions seen in the first publication in the series on the *Domesday Geography of England* (Darby 1952), and the analysis of 'vertical themes' of landscape change (e.g. Darby 1940; 1953; Dickinson 1949). Henry Darby's essay on the 'Changing English Landscape' (1951), for example, dealt with the evolution of the landscape from the Anglo-Saxon period through to the Industrial Revolution. Historical documents, such as Lay Subsidies, were drawn upon with increasing sophistication as geographical sources. Recognising the value of collaborative research it was Darby who facilitated funding for the Medieval Village Research Group to finance research into the Midland counties which later formed the basis of monographs on the deserted villages of Oxfordshire (1965) and Northamptonshire (1966) (Beresford *et al.* 1980).

It is no surprise then to find that the 'writing and conversation' of Darby, as well as other 'agrarian historians' such as Eyre (1955), Kerridge (1951; 1955) and Mead (1954) who concerned themselves with field evidence for open-field systems, are all credited in Beresford's *History on the Ground* (1957). Where Beresford and Hoskins differed from their colleagues in historical geography was in their explicit use of fieldwork. It was only right that Beresford should dedicate his volume to his mother 'who packed the sandwiches', for the place of fieldwork was central to his brand of history.

It is significant that two of the few medieval practitioners who had been exposed to scientific thinking, Patrick Faulkner and Martyn Jope, should have provided the lead in one of the more progressive areas of debate, the elucidation of spatial patterns. Faulkner's contribution in the late 1950s and 1960s was in the use of schematic diagrams to suggest the purpose of different areas of castle plans (e.g. Faulkner 1963). These were, in effect, early experiments in 'access analysis' which enabled Faulkner to develop a model of medieval social organisation. Jope's contribution lay in another sphere of spatial analysis. His characteristic distribution maps were some of the first to include both contours and negative findspots. In addition, Jope's pioneering 1963 paper on the regional cultures of medieval Britain put forward the notion that medieval archaeology might be used in some way as a testing ground for prehistory (Jope 1963). Drawing upon a wide range of medieval evidence, including regional distributions of pottery, building styles, land tenure, dialect and agricultural methods, Jope examined what such distributions might mean in the lives of medieval communities. In concluding that coincidences in pattern were insignificant he sent a warning to prehistorians who might be 'postulating prehistoric cultures largely in terms of pottery styles' (Jope 1963).

Such a confident assertion of the merits of archaeological study in the medieval period had rarely been voiced previously but Jope's views could not be said to represent the mainstream. Far from it, there was insufficient consistency in the application of theory (where it could be said to be applied at all) to constitute a tradition in medieval archaeology. Most work carried out under the heading of medieval archaeology up to this date might justifiably be categorised as 'empiricist'. Scholars collected data, classified it and, assuming the material was collected in a consistent and rigorous way, made their interpretations by applying 'common sense' judgments. Explanatory accounts were linked to peoples, nations and events as an extension of the process of historical writing. Material culture, whether buildings or artefacts, was seen as a passive reflection of the wider social and economic picture.

The post-war period was a time of tremendous change for the social sciences, one in which general trends and patterns began to be interpreted within a theoretical framework, and numerical and scientific methods were employed more extensively. For medieval archaeologists of the late 1960s the conditions were not yet in place for the full development of an academic field of study. None of the senior players had undertaken university courses with substantial elements of post-Roman archaeology so, naturally, external stimuli from cognate subjects were influential and innovations were derivative rather than indigenous. There had been an increase in the funding for projects but there was not yet a body of concepts, however loosely defined, acceptable to the majority of practitioners and enshrined in the aims and philosophies of new societies and groups.

Instead, the post-war period was one of continuing accumulation of data, particularly for settlement studies, and a time when academic confidence and impact was growing. By 1970 few of those practising archaeology in Britain were entirely ignorant of later medieval studies. In contrast to the immediate post-war period, when it was hardly appreciated that there was a need for medieval archaeology in any form, Webster's guide to practical archaeology did contain sections on medieval sites and artefacts (Webster 1963). However, quantities of incoming data were not immediately matched by synthesis, which was slow to follow partly because few medieval archaeologists were in place within higher education, and partly because the rest were altogether absorbed in collecting the primary data. The pace of data accumulation outstripped the development of paradigms of thought in a developing subject. In this phase of exploration the gathering of basic facts and improvements in record keeping and standards were the core activities. Only later would medieval archaeology have to struggle to forge any conceptual and methodological identity.

Chapter 5

Breaking ranks

New ideas, new techniques, the Rescue years and after (1970–1989)

This chapter spans two decades of extraordinary change in the organisation, direction and levels of funding for archaeology in Britain. Rescue archaeology, developer funding, archaeological units, new legislation, restructured national agencies, cultural resource management; all these were in the future in 1970. Government funding rose sharply and many towns and suburban areas, in particular, saw high levels of archaeological excavation whose cost was increasingly met by alternative sources of funding during the 1980s. Medieval archaeology did not wholeheartedly embrace the latest conceptual developments in the discipline but benefited from the introduction of a wide range of new scientific techniques, establishing itself firmly in university departments. The first, widely influential, synthesis of results was written by Colin Platt (1978a) and followed by assessments from Fowler (1980), Hinton (1983), Clarke (1984), Steane (1984), Cherry (1986) and Hurst (1986). The year 1989 is a convenient cut-off point for the funding and theoretical developments discussed here.

Excavation and fieldwork

Urban life

The year 1972 was significant for medieval urban archaeology. Not only for the formation of 'Rescue', a new campaigning voice for archaeologists, and for well-publicised damage and destruction to individual sites (**Box 5.1**), but also for the publication of *The Erosion of History* (Heighway 1972). This document, which combined academic insight with a sense of outrage at the perils of heedless development, was to be the manifesto for urban archaeology for the next twenty years and was especially influential for the medieval periods (Schofield and Vince 1994: 3). In it, the case for urban archaeology was set against the losses which might be caused by future redevelopment. Twenty per cent of all historic towns, it was forecast, would be destroyed archaeologically by 1991. A series of 'implications' reports lent weight to those shocking conclusions, predicting that existing archaeological arrangements would be overwhelmed (e.g. for the City of London, Biddle and Hudson 1973; for list see Darvill and Fulton 1998: Appendix A).

Partly as a result of these surveys, the organisation and funding for rescue archaeology improved markedly. Arguably, the most impressive results for the

Box 5.1 Baynard's Castle and New Palace Yard

In March 1972 the site of Baynard's Castle, near Blackfriars Bridge in London, was threatened with redevelopment. This mid-fourteenth century site had both royal historical and literary associations and had been covered with warehouses since the seventeenth century. A row broke out over the lack of money and time made available to the excavator, Peter Marsden of the Guildhall Museum. Parliamentary questions probed both the lack of financial support and the mechanism for incorporating archaeological investigation into redevelopment. Working against time, the layout of waterside towers was recovered, together with organic remains from the Roman and medieval waterfronts.

Later in 1972, the construction of an underground car park in Westminster's New Palace Yard was approved and work began early the following year. At the time, this was believed to be the site of the royal palace of Edward the Confessor and perhaps also of wooden buildings of pre-Conquest date (Horsman and Davison 1989). It emerged that the decision to begin excavation had been taken without archaeological advice so that the Parliament appeared to be acting in contravention of its own archaeological policies. In spite of a European campaign to halt the work and the vocal protests of archaeologists campaigning for 'Rescue', the accumulated yard surfaces were swept away, though the octagonal foundation of a later fountain was carefully recorded. In Peter Fowler's words 'How can you find remains of wooden buildings hundreds of years old in a trench gouged out by a bulldozer?' (quoted in Jones 1984: 61). It was some consolation that the affairs at New Palace Yard and Baynard Castle were effective in drawing attention to the financial stringencies under which archaeologists operated and to the lack of any effective regulatory framework for the development of sites with archaeological potential.

later medieval period were from Lincoln (e.g. Jones 1980), London, Norwich and York (e.g. Hall *et al.* 1988) and a summary of results from these and many other towns is now available (Schofield and Vince 1994). Just as had been predicted, a series of waterfront sites in London fulfilled the promise of the first major excavations at Baynard's Castle and Old Custom House (Tatton-Brown 1974). Sites concentrated around London Bridge (e.g. at Billingsgate; Steedman *et al.* 1992) and in the west of the City (e.g. at Trig Lane; Milne and Milne 1978) probed the waterlogged stratigraphy in a 100-metre wide strip, 2 kilometres long and 3 to 5 metres deep. These sites produced evidence for streets and houses, as well as waterside developments such as wooden jetties and quays, and since these sometimes reused ship timbers they were also revealing about woodworking techniques and woodland management (e.g. Milne 1992b; Hutchinson 1994).

Opinions differed as to what to dig. The Norwich Survey, directed by Alan Carter, conducted excavations at about forty sites across the city between 1971 and 1978, sampling specific residential and industrial zones. The evidence preserved by the fire of 25 March 1507 on Pottergate provided an opportunity to examine those undisturbed house contents which had survived the conflagration (Atkin *et al.* 1985: 9–85). A similarly structured approach was adopted in Taunton (Som.) where a broad, formal research design blending the archaeological and the documentary was developed for the later medieval period by Peter Leach (Leach 1984; Figure 5.1). Research designs and sampling strategies sharpened awareness of priorities when time and money were short.

By 1981 a listing of recent work was able to report on 146 urban campaigns (Schofield *et al.* 1981). Collectively, they represent a rollercoaster of disappointment, elation and surprise. Where post-medieval terracing and cellarage had removed medieval stratification in one part of a town, well-preserved and rich archaeological deposits were encountered elsewhere (Allan 1984). There were many unexpected discoveries, among them the medieval bridge and waterfronts at Kingston-upon-Thames (Potter 1992) and a late medieval shipbuilding site in Poole (1986–7; Watkins 1994). With more experience came a better understanding of the character of urban archaeology; the bulk of finds and the range of evidence, the degree of later dis-

Figure 5.1 Rescue excavations underway at Hawke's Yard in Taunton in 1977. After the buildings had been demolished and the site cleared, trial sections were cut to intersect with the suspected line of the medieval defences. The work was directed by Peter Leach, then a Field Officer with the Committee for Rescue Archaeology in Avon, Gloucestershire and Somerset and funded by the Department of the Environment and the local authority. Six weeks of work here were undertaken by volunteers and a Job Creation Programme team (Leach 1984: 65–73). (Photo: Mick Aston).

turbance, alterations to street frontages, the lack of well-defined structures, the potential for comparison between groups of tenements and the challenge of waterlogged deposits. Less positively, the excavated sample could be biased, so that in only nine of the eighty-six historic towns in East Anglia had excavation taken place by 1984 and very few excavations encompassed even a single tenement in its entirety (Atkin and Evans 1984). Site reports could be brief with only minimal interpretation, a reflection on the difficult conditions under which excavation often took place. Post-excavation too could be hurried, uneven, poorly funded, and omitted further work on documents and topography. A handful of towns grasped their opportunities, but many were left with lengthy and costly backlogs.

As these examples make clear, county capitals, provincial towns and ports figured prominently during the 'rescue' years but urban rescue excavation was not confined to southern England. The controversies at Wood Quay and Fishamble Street in central Dublin (Ireland) had considerable symbolic impact outside that country and showed how powerful public protest could be in defence of heritage (Delaney 1977; Carver 1993: 8–9). Behind the scenes politics, timetabling and funding so often dominated discussion. Scottish campaigns included the first ever excavations in Aberdeen, on Broad Street in 1973–4, which produced evidence of fourteenth-century housing and a medieval timber-framed quayside at the mouth of the Dee (Jones 1984: 114). Perth, a walled medieval town of some status, offered medieval stratigraphy unaffected by later post-medieval and modern development with good organic preservation in deep well-stratified deposits. Excavation soon revealed well-preserved textiles and environmental evidence, considerably raising public and academic expectations of what archaeology could achieve in an urban location (Bogdan and Wordsworth 1978; Figure 5.2). The expectations from English experiences tended to be transferred to other countries and it was only by the end of the 1980s that independent agendas began to be developed seriously (Spearman 1984).

The enormous quantity of data generated tends to mask some important innovations in approach to urban archaeology at this time. Under the right circumstances archaeological and historical evidence were patiently combined to reveal more about standing buildings (e.g. Driver *et al.* 1990 for Canterbury). It became clear, however, that documents could only rarely be related with any confidence to specific excavated buildings in urban tenements, except in the cases of grander ecclesiastical and civil monuments. Topographical studies now emphasised the development of streets and property boundaries in a broader 'landscape' approach derived from historical geography (Aston and Bond 1976). The published papers of two successful conferences organised by the Council for British Archaeology's Urban Research Committee pursued the same topographical theme and opened out discussion to a European scale (Barley 1975, 1977). The second volume of the Winchester Studies series provided a comprehensive topographical survey of the

Figure 5.2 Urban rescue excavation at the High Street, Perth (1975–6) funded largely by the Inspectorate of Ancient Monuments and supported by the Manpower Services Commission. In the foreground the medieval archaeology had been partially damaged by nineteenth century cellars, but elsewhere some thirty wattle buildings of mid-twelfth- to early fourteenth-century date were identified, with walls still standing to 0.40 metres in places. (Photo: T. B. James and the Perth Museum and Art Gallery).

medieval city, complete with a street-by-street gazetteer with tenure and building histories linked to a bibliographical register (Keene 1985).

At the same time, more specifically archaeological issues were coming to the fore. Greater attention was paid to the depth, location and thickness of surviving deposits (e.g. Biddle and Hudson 1973 for London: figs 5 and 6). This provided some measure of the condition and survival of buried archaeology (e.g. for Shrewsbury; Carver 1978). In doing so, there were both academic and strategic implications. Some archaeologists wished to move away from an historical agenda which they did not feel could be addressed through archaeological data. 'If understanding is ever to be advanced, courageous and positive action must be taken to allow archaeologists to exercise freely their own demanding discipline on what remains' (Carver 1980: 25). Related to this was a desire not to be driven constantly by the imperative of development, but to be free to make choices on the basis of a 'research blueprint'. This required a radical shift in emphasis '. . . away from a commitment to what history "needs to know", and towards a commitment to the archaeological evidence that is actually there' (Carver 1981: 71). The aim would be to map the depth, date and coherence of deposits above the pre-settlement contours and then sample surviving strata archaeologically before deciding whether to protect or excavate. This concept, which allowed archaeological hypotheses to be 'tested' by sampling a more fully mapped 'deposit', was influenced by both New Archaeology and by the reconceptualisation of buried archaeology as a finite and precious 'resource'.

Rural life

Against a background of unsympathetic land use change in the countryside it seems curious that the overall numbers of excavations at rural settlements actually declined and remained at a low ebb. Unlike the drama of development unfolding in towns, changes in the countryside were deceptively gradual and so less high profile. Perhaps justifications for funding seemed less urgent but, mostly in the absence of any clear local policies, rural excavation programmes suffered financially (Wainwright 1978: 23). In the 1970s those archaeological units who expressed post-Roman interests mostly appealed for funding to excavate multiperiod crop mark sites with prehistoric, Romano-British and Anglo-Saxon components (MVRG 1984a). By the time the basis of project funding changed in the early 1980s, the limited value of small-scale excavation was widely accepted and the weight of opinion was in favour of the protection of sites. The Deserted Medieval Village Research Group and its successors issued numerous statements of advice to that effect, the first being formulated in 1965 (e.g. MVRG 1983; 1984b; MSRG 1988). As a result, only a restricted number of threatened sites were investigated and the 'flagship' role of excavation at medieval rural settlements was diminished within the subject as a whole.

Numbers of investigations on moated and manor sites illustrate this decline (Figure 4.3). State funding was modest and, sadly, some of the small number which were examined on any scale have never been fully published, though excavations at Acton Court (Bristol) will provide a very complete example of a medieval and later moated site with good evidence for structural develop- ment and a well-developed finds sequence (Gaimster *et al.* 1989: 167–9). In spite of the uncertainties of funding and labour, privately-initiated excavation projects seemed to stand a greater chance of completion. At Faccombe Netherton (Hants.; 1967–80), the City of London Archaeological Society carried out one of the most complete excavations of a medieval manorial complex so far undertaken. Some twenty-five timber and stone buildings dating between the ninth and sixteenth century were recovered and fully published (Fairbrother 1990).

Amongst the larger and more impressive of the 'rescue' campaigns was Thrislington (Durham; 1973–4), a deserted village threatened by limestone extraction. Excavation here sought to address typical concerns of the day such as fixing dates for the origin of settlement and its desertion as well as examining the development of house plans. A great deal of new information was recovered and elegantly published. However, by the director's own honest appraisal, extreme time constraints inevitably led to major structures such as the chapel and manor house being targeted. As a result, little is known about gardens, outbuildings, boundaries or activities in the intervening spaces between the excavated areas, while the landscape around the settlement remained largely unexplored archaeologically (Austin 1989: 159–62). 'Rescue' archaeology and medieval rural settlement were rarely well matched.

One persistent challenge was how to meld together small-scale, routine investigations into a useful academic contribution. The volumes produced by the Milton Keynes Archaeology Unit are a model, drawing together data from excavations and watching briefs carried out between 1971 and 1991 in advance of, and occasionally during, development for Britain's largest post- war new town (Mynard and Zeepvat 1991; Croft and Mynard 1993; Mynard 1994; Ivens *et al.* 1995). This work covered some 90 square kilometres and included medieval earthworks in most of the eighteen parishes affected. Although not presented as such, this was landscape archaeology on a very large scale, with eighty-four sites examined of all periods, twenty of them by open-area excavation, accompanied by both fieldwalking and historical research. Many sites were 'trial-trenched' in order to determine their extent and condition with more detailed work often being curtailed by the small workforce, late or limited funding and sometimes laughable time constraints. Precisely because the work was dictated by circumstance rather than strategy, a great variety of monument classes were at least evaluated, including churches, moats and village earthworks.

Excavations at Wharram Percy continued each year and became a fixture of the British excavation scene. It might be argued that the presence of a single, dominating project was harmful to academic progress but this was not the case. The Wharram research strategy was flexible and far from monolithic. The directors responded to events as they unfolded on site and conducted, in effect, a three-week open-air seminar on medieval rural settlement followed by a lengthy period of reflection on the year's results when interim reports were written up over the winter months. The excavation process was reiterative rather than continuous. Debate was not internalised but inclusive; there were lectures and guided visits, many of them by experienced excavators and academics, as well as a constant stream of questions from volunteers. All this had a decisive influence on the direction of the work at Wharram Percy as well as other projects underway elsewhere in Britain and further afield.

As with all excavation, chance played its part. One of the key elements in the Wharram village plan, the parish church, became available for study after the church tower fell in 1959 and a faculty for excavation was obtained in 1962 (Bell and Beresford 1987). The choice of Area 10 for the excavation of a peasant house was also fortuitous, for beneath it the undercroft of an earlier manor house was first exposed in 1955. Both investigations contributed towards a general shift of interests away from village desertion and the evolution of the peasant house towards settlement origins and development (Figure 5.3). At the same time, not only were these and other opportunities grasped when they might have been rejected, but the directors acted with great foresight in tackling the site of the late medieval and post-medieval vicarage and the post-medieval farmstead as well encouraging the investigation of pre-existing settlement in the wider landscape (Hayfield 1987). Here they anticipated future research agendas and responded to external stimuli, both academic and strategic. A number of projects then followed along similar lines in seeking to provide a broader picture of medieval settlement and land-use, addressing themes such as desertion and continuity (e.g. the Lunan Valley Project, 1983–4; Pollack 1985). Long-running investigations like West Whelpington (Nhumbs., 1958–76; Evans and Jarrett 1987; Evans *et al.* 1988) endured both the shift to metrication and a switch from box trenches to open-area excavation, as well as a change in the focus of the project from site excavation to parish survey in reaction to the growth of landscape and environmental archaeology.

Exactly how to answer new research questions within a development-led project and using a different funding formula was addressed by the Raunds Area Project (Northants.). This large-scale endeavour was special in many ways. On the one hand, the comprehensive examination of an area of about 40 square kilometres included excavations at a late Saxon graveyard, church, village, two manor houses, and a deserted hamlet. On the other, the project made use of a wide variety of archaeological techniques such as fieldwalking and geophysics. But to achieve this, advantage was taken of sites threatened by housing development, gravel extraction and new roads, counting on the

Figure 5.3 One focus for work at Wharram Percy during the 1970s was the pond and dam to the south of the church and churchyard. Investigations here over a number of years recovered environmental evidence and waterlogged organic objects which will fill out the picture of daily life provided by excavations on the plateaux above. Successive phases of water management were revealed from Late Saxon times onwards. This is one of the Wharram sites currently in its 'post-excavation phase' though a preliminary summary is available (Beresford and Hurst 1990: 65–8). (Photo: Paul Stamper).

partnership of a number of organisations including English Heritage, Northamptonshire County Council and universities (Cadman 1983; Cadman and Foard 1984). Unlike Wharram, which had begun as a site-specific, period-based investigation and became a broader study, Raunds was conceived from the outset as a cohesive multiperiod, multidisciplinary project to investigate an 'ordinary' landscape of settlements and fields.

Between the publication of *Deserted Medieval Villages* (Beresford and Hurst 1971) and *The Countryside of Medieval England* (Astill and Grant 1988) rural medieval archaeology was changed fundamentally in its methods and perspective. A wider vision of landscape now comprised the full spectrum of settlement types (occupied, shrunken, nucleated, dispersed, etc.) as well as a broader chronological context. That a 1989 facsimile edition of *Deserted Medieval Villages* should be referred to as 'unnecessarily cranky' by one reviewer is a wonderful testimony to progress through two decades of change. In 1971 Beresford and Hurst were rightly preoccupied with the respectability of their subject, by the end of the 1980s rural settlement studies had been strengthened by a more pluralistic attitude which ensured co-operation between archaeologists, historians, geographers and the environmental sciences. Not only could projects now count on the perspectives of several disciplines but their results were of interest to different constituencies, indeed different countries (Chapelot and Fossier 1980 for mainland European and Scandinavian case studies). The work of historian Chris Dyer (e.g. 1989) and geographers Brian Roberts (e.g. 1977, 1987) and Harry Thorpe (e.g. 1975) proved to be of equal interest to archaeologists as to their 'own' disciplines and, indeed, they were not shy of using archaeological techniques to good effect (e.g. Dyer 1990a).

Churches

One of the most significant successes of the period between 1970 and 1990 was the extraordinary change in public appreciation and academic study of the archaeology of historic churches. Churches came under threat of widespread redundancy, conversion and demolition when *The Pastoral Measure* was adopted by the Church of England in 1968. The Council for British Archaeology, again an influential voice, set up its Churches Committee in 1972 and promptly issued a series of influential policy statements and reports, seeking to discourage unobserved structural repairs and churchyard 'tidying' (Morris 1977; Butler 1983; Rodwell 1987).

Under the guidance of Lawrence Butler, Richard Morris, Warwick Rodwell and others, new trends emerged. The Committee had united archaeologists, architects and art historians who embraced the integrated study of buildings, fittings, graveyards and associated structures (Rodwell 1989). The emphasis on threatened 'living churches' brought archaeologists everywhere into more regular contact with art historians researching fixtures and fittings, stained glass and sculpture. 'Archaeological' projects reflected this in more complete and thorough examinations which moved beyond the mere recovery of the ground floor plan. Outstanding examples included St Martin's Church at Wharram Percy (1962–74; Bell and Beresford 1987), St Mary Bishophill Junior and St Mary Castlegate in York (1961–80; Wenham *et al.* 1987) and St Mark's in Lincoln, where detailed consideration was given to the changing floor plan in the context of changing liturgical requirements (1975–77; Gilmour and Stocker 1986).

A key feature was the combination of tradition and innovation, in this case inspired not only by work on Anglo-Saxon architecture, particularly by Harold Taylor (Taylor and Taylor 1965; Taylor 1972), but also by 'church archaeology' projects underway elsewhere in Europe, especially in Denmark, Germany and Holland. Many projects, like Rivenhall (Essex, 1971–3; Rodwell and Rodwell 1985) and Hadstock (Essex; Rodwell 1976), integrated archaeology with architecture to good effect, an approach which was extended to Barton-on-Humber (Humbs.; Rodwell and Rodwell 1982), Brixworth (Northants.; Sutherland and Parsons 1984), Deerhurst (Glos.; Rahtz and

Watts 1997), and elsewhere. Compared to previous investigations at damaged and disused church sites, there was a very different character to these projects, mainly because the churches were themselves still in use. The major lesson was that earlier structures could survive undetected beneath later additions and renders and that, properly investigated and recorded, a relative chronology for the fabric of a building could be constructed as an alternative to purely art-historical dating. As a method this was widely influential; it drew attention to the different stone and mortar types in use and the reuse of masonry from earlier buildings, but it was also criticised for producing over-elaborate structural phasing and, through the use of seemingly more 'objective' recording criteria, for undervaluing the iconographic aspects of buildings (Fernie 1988: 357).

Other influences such as landscape archaeology invited a larger canvas for study (Rodwell 1984; Morris 1989). This encouraged regional comparative surveys of monument classes, such as that completed by the Royal Commission for fifty-five churches in south-east Wiltshire (RCHME 1987). Also firmly located in this tradition was the excavation at Raunds Furnells (Northants.), where work ahead of building development between 1977 and 1984 revealed two churches, the later structure being converted into one of the buildings of the manor house complex (Boddington 1996). Not all work was on such a grand scale, however, and a great deal of minor excavation was done in and around churches and cathedrals, usually to improve access or drainage and upgrade facilities. This too paid dividends. What could be achieved through seemingly minor investigation was well illustrated by the work around Canterbury Cathedral, financed by the Dean and Chapter. Here a series of small trenches around the north-east transept and St Gabriel's Chapel contained a deep sequence of deposits including a Roman street and building, an eleventh-century charnel pit, foundations in various phases and skeletal remains (Driver *et al.* 1990).

Monasteries

Throughout the two decades under consideration in this chapter, monastic archaeology also made striking advances. These are well summarised in two important collections of papers edited by Roberta Gilchrist and Harold Mytum (1989; 1993) which should be considered alongside studies of individual buildings (e.g. for Durham; Coldstream and Draper 1980), architectural surveys of particular Orders (e.g. Fergusson 1984 for the Cistercians) and documentary surveys (e.g. Burton 1979).

The upsurge in urban redevelopment was mostly responsible for an increase in archaeological interest in the Dominicans and Franciscans and results have been expertly summarised (Butler 1987, 1993). Major excavations were undertaken in the 1970s at Guildford (Poulton and Woods 1984), Oxford (Lambrick and Woods 1976) and Leicester where environmental conditions preserved artefacts and environmental evidence (Mellor and Pearce 1981). Amongst the remarkable collection of items were fourteenth- to sixteenth-century shoe leathers, belts, straps, knife sheaths, clothing and part of a spectacle or pen case (Allin 1981). Seeds, molluscs and insects recovered from ditch samples also revealed detailed evidence for land use around the site and suggested that the friars enjoyed high standards of cleanliness (Girling 1981).

Excavations on monastic sites in towns suffered all the tribulations of the urban archaeologist and were frequently hampered by piecemeal develop-ment (e.g. Stones 1989). In Greater London, numerous excavations took place on the sites of more than ten religious houses and churches, the Augustinian priory and hospital at St Mary Spital being the subject of nine separate excavations and watching briefs (Hinton and Thomas 1997). Major excavations were also undertaken at the Carthusian priory of St Anne in Coventry (1968–87; Soden 1992) and the Dominican Priory at Beverley (Yorks.), excavated 1986–9, was typical of such a large campaign. Once trial trenches had established the presence of archaeology, the site was then dug for eleven months through the winter by Manpower Services Commission labour under the supervision of the Humberside Archaeological Unit. This clarified the limits and plan of the friary and made a contribution, at a national level, to knowledge of diet and the environmental character of the site both before and during occupation by the Priory. Redevelopment of the area subsequently did considerable damage to surviving and unexcavated deposits (Foreman 1996).

The threat of urban expansion was the cue for large-scale excavations at monastic sites in suburban locations. Investigations at the Cistercian house of Bordesley Abbey (Worcs.; Rahtz and Hirst 1976; Hirst *et al.* 1983) and the Augustinian house at Norton Priory (Ches.; Greene 1989) were, in effect, long-term 'rescue' projects strongly linked to wider community visions, the latter being set aside as an open area for public recreation within Runcorn New Town (e.g. Warhurst 1999). In an attempt to correct the imbalances of previous research, the archaeological emphasis was on phasing all the build-ings within the precinct, paying particular attention to the earliest and latest phases represented (e.g. at Sandwell Priory, Staffs.; Hodder 1991). Excavation was frequently linked with standing building recording and environmental study, often with particular attention to activities previously considered of marginal interest, for example water systems and fishponds (e.g. Bond 1989a) or industrial activities (e.g. at Bordesley Abbey; Astill 1993).

Rural monastic sites were far from immune from threat. In 1973 levelling and ploughing of earthworks at Thornholme Priory (Lincs.), for example, led to a long-term research project (1974–80) which included excavation (Coppack 1989). Grove Priory (Beds.) was excavated between 1973 and 1985 in advance of sand quarrying (Baker and Baker 1989; Figure 5.4) and a medieval grange of Abingdon Abbey (Oxon.) was examined in advance of housing development after attention was first drawn to the site during field-walking (1975–6 and 1984–7; Allen 1994). Other opportunities for investigation of rural monastic sites were linked to visitor provision, mostly at sites in State care such as Battle Abbey (Sussex; Hare 1986).

Generally, the direction of monastic studies combined the trends for church and rural settlement studies. A shift in the scale of research reflected the increased use of non-intrusive tools such as aerial survey, topographical survey and geophysics to investigate non-claustral buildings and earthwork sites (e.g. Everson 1989). Mick Aston and James Bond were among those able to apply the principles of field survey and landscape history to a series of case studies (e.g. for Abingdon Abbey, Berks.; Bond 1979). A broader geographical approach to the study of monastic estates was exemplified by the work of Robinson (1980) and the need for more inclusive, multi- and interdisciplinary approaches well argued by Moorhouse (1989).

Castles

Significant work was carried out at castles affected by urban redevelopment. In Bedford, the castle founded in *c.*1100 and slighted in *c.*1225 was one of the thirty-two sites investigated between 1967 and 1977 (Baker *et al.* 1979: 7–64). Forty-four trenches were excavated here in five seasons totalling about

Figure 5.4 Grove Priory (Beds.) under excavation in advance of sand quarrying in December 1978. (Photo: Mick Aston).

twenty weeks, casting new light on the plan and layout of the site. Under the circumstances, to produce coherent conclusions from numerous small-scale investigations on a complex site was remarkable. A similar exercise was undertaken for Southampton Castle where the results of four excavations undertaken between 1973 and 1983, amounting to some 10 per cent of the total castle area, were unified into a single account (Oxley 1986).

Numbers of castle excavations declined quite perceptibly between 1974 and 1984, dropping lower than they had been during the late 1950s. On the one hand, the measure of protection afforded to more visible architecture and earthworks curtailed excavation, on the other the modest successes of the Royal Archaeological Institute's 'Castles Project' had underlined the difficulties of interpretation where work was small in scale (e.g. Bramber, Sussex; Barton and Holden 1978) and funding limited (e.g. at Baile Hill, York; Addyman and Priestley 1978). For the most part, preservation was favoured over excavation wherever possible (but see Goltho 1971–4, below).

Two castle projects must be singled out. Continuing large-scale excavations at the motte and bailey at Hen Domen (Powys) detailed the eleventh- to fourteenth-century phases there (Higham and Barker 2000; see Chapter 4). Meanwhile at Sandal Castle (Yorks.) the 2.5-hectare site was completely excavated and surviving stonework consolidated (Mayes and Butler 1983). This massive project (1964–73) was completed under the direction of Philip Mayes and Lawrence Butler and funded by the University of Leeds, the local government authority and the local historical society. The University of Bradford took responsibility for the final publication programme which contained an influential pottery report which maximised spatial data available from the open area excavation.

An increase in the number of small-scale interventions in the late 1980s gave a firmer idea of the potential of other sites, but very little in the way of new knowledge. Larger excavations on unthreatened sites were tied to improvements in presentation. These projects provided some flexibility to pursue research agendas, certainly to a greater extent than was afforded by developer-led work. A wider variety of castle types was investigated, not just the motte and baileys (e.g. Thompson 1987), and drew attention to features such as aspects of daily life and domestic structures. Work of this character included that at Threave Castle (Dumfries.; 1974–8; Good and Tabraham 1981), Barnard Castle (Durham; 1974–8; Austin 1980), Okehampton (Devon; 1972–80; Higham 1977; Higham and Allan 1980) and Castle Rising (Norfolk; 1970–6, 1987; Morley and Gurney 1997) as well as a series of excavations at Welsh masonry castles including Dryslwyn (Carms.; 1980–8; Caple 1990) and Dolforwyn (Powys; 1981–2000; Butler 1989a).

Possibly more than any other monument class, however, castle studies were blighted by lengthy delays to the final publication of key sites, among them Beeston (Ches.; 1968–85; Ellis 1993), Bristol (1968–70; Ponsford 1972), Launceston (Corn.; 1965–76) and Ludgershall (Wilts; 1964–72; Ellis 2000).

Fortunately, excavation was not the whole story. Major documentary surveys continued to have impact (Colvin 1971; 1975; 1982), as did comprehensive gazetteers (e.g. King 1983) and synthesis (Platt 1982). A handful of landscape studies now began to link castles with roads, forests and the wider countryside (Hughes 1989) while studies of building fabrics showed what could be added through a marriage of archaeological, architectural and documentary work (e.g. Munby and Renn 1985).

Buildings

Until the early 1970s typologies of urban housing were based largely upon standing buildings. Rescue excavation in towns tended to reveal a greater variety of house forms. Archaeological information about later medieval stone houses, for example, was published from Norwich (Ayers 1988). Waterfront sites also preserved timbers which provided new information about carpentry techniques and construction methods, particularly for foundations (Goodburn 1992). Important excavations were carried out on high-status residences at Dartington Hall (Emery 1970) and Eltham Palace (London; Woods 1982) among others, with the subject as a whole being discussed by Tom James (1990). Some classes of monuments, like bastles, were described in detail for the first time (Ramm *et al.* 1970).

Vernacular architecture studies continued to build into a detailed corpus of case studies, aided by the application of dendrochronology and powered by a growing conservation movement. Many new medieval studies figured in *Vernacular Architecture*, the journal of the Vernacular Architecture Group. Basic dating criteria for house designs and methods of construction were established for different house forms and types of materials (e.g. Brunskill 1971; Hewett 1980; Mercer 1975). Other major contributions to the study of medieval buildings were made by Nat Alcock, Freddie Charles, John Smith, and staff of the Royal Commission on Historical Monuments. In this last context special mention should be made of architectural recording in York (e.g. RCHME 1981), Stamford (RCHME 1977) and Salisbury (RCHME 1980).

Building studies did not remain immune to trends seen elsewhere in medieval archaeology. The examination of the dismantled roofs of Blackfriars Priory (Glos.) was typical of the greater emphasis placed upon the whole process of building, from tree to structure (Rackham *et al.* 1978). The work of Oliver Rackham was influential in providing palaeobotanical perspectives on timber and construction (Rackham 1980; 1989) but, more generally, a multidisciplinary approach incorporated both historical (e.g. Schofield 1987) and archaeological contributions. For example, much of the evidence for peasant housing in the later Middle Ages came from excavation (Dyer 1986) and that at Wharram was subjected to an important revision which suggested a greater degree of permanence in peasant building than had been proposed in the original excavation report (Wrathmell 1989).

Artefacts and industry

While the wide variety of evidence for medieval industry recovered during urban rescue campaigns proved especially valuable for the eleventh and twelfth centuries when documentary evidence is less voluminous (Schofield and Vince 1994: 99–127), well excavated, larger-scale projects were few and far between (Crossley 1981). Medieval inland salt houses were examined for the first time in Nantwich in advance of drainage operations (Ches.; McNeil 1983). Work at Bordesley Abbey added substantially to what had been learnt from the fifteen smithies previously excavated (e.g. at Chingley, Kent; Crossley 1975) and recovered a sequence of four well-preserved water mills (Astill 1993). Olney Hyde (Bucks.; Moorhouse 1981) and Cheam (Surrey; Orton 1982) were among excavated pottery workshops which provided invaluable data on forms and fabrics and their results were incorporated into both regional (e.g. Barton 1979 for Sussex; Vince 1985b for London) and national surveys (McCarthy and Brooks 1988).

The study of medieval crafts and industry remained strongly slanted towards finished artefacts. Falling numbers of excavations on production sites contrasted with the voluminous rise in the numbers of artefacts recovered from urban excavations which, in turn, led to a boom in specialist finds study. Much medieval material was recovered from pits and reliable dates were provided by stratified waterfront sequences, dated by dendrochronology of their timber revetments. Some categories of finds came under sustained analysis for the first time. Robert Charleston's work on collections from Southampton was the first major report on medieval glass in England, for example (Charleston 1975). Ian and Alison Goodall studied the metalwork from many medieval sites (e.g. Exeter; Allan 1984). Stuart Rigold frequently reported on jettons and lead objects (e.g. Bedford; Baker et al. 1979) and Elizabeth Eames on floor tiles (Eames 1980). Urban waterfront excavations also boosted finds of well-preserved textiles, wood and leather (e.g. Grew and de Neergaard 1988). Generally, catalogues were now more complete, with more standard use of terminology and greater sophistication in their quantification techniques. Following the lead set by the 1940s Museum of London's *Medieval Catalogue*, many authors now arranged their finds according to use and function rather than by material and greater effort was made to provide a socio-historical context.

Excavation reports continued to be dominated by pottery and large urban units recovered upwards of 100,000 sherds per year (e.g. in York; Holdsworth 1978). Major pottery corpora for urban sites included those for Colchester (Cotter 2000), Hereford (Vince 1985a), Hull (e.g. Watkins 1987), London (e.g. Pearce and Vince 1988), Norwich (Jennings 1981), Northampton (McCarthy 1979) and Worcester (Morris 1980). To accompany fuller definitions of pottery types, these reports now included quantification, illustrations of the full range of vessels, comment on methods of manufacture, evidence for use and wear, analysis of pottery distributions across sites, non-local pottery and dating. The challenge of high proportions of residual material in urban deposits also began to be addressed (e.g. Lambrick and Mellor 1980). Outside towns, where finds were fewer, methodological developments were especially notable. Influential reports included Sandal Castle (Yorks.; Moorhouse 1983b; Figure 5.5) and Kirkstall Abbey (Yorks.; Moorhouse and Slowikowski 1987).

Trade and distribution proved an important theme of study, both for British pottery (e.g. Vince 1977 for Malvern region; Moorhouse 1981) and imports (Hurst *et al.* 1986; Davey and Hodges 1983 for the North Sea). Rescue excavations at ports such as Poole and Exeter produced large groups of imported medieval pottery from which new types were identified and dated (e.g. Hurst 1977 for Spanish pottery). These imported groups proved to be of considerable significance as a dating tool and their dates and frequencies were compared against documentary evidence from customs accounts and probate inventories (Le Patourel 1983). In Exeter, for example, much of the imported pottery was found to have been redistributed via the port of London. While its appearance on archaeological sites did not reflect direct foreign commerce as might have been assumed, neither did the customs accounts provide an accurate picture of consumption of imports in the city, implying mostly British coastal trade (Allan 1984: 353–7). Only the combined study of documents and archaeology completed the picture of trade and consumption.

Techniques and scientific applications

Gradually, the 'single site mentality' was replaced by a move towards larger scales of study and the recording of whole landscapes (Taylor 1987). Numerous general books (e.g. Aston and Rowley 1974; Aston 1985) and articles with an emphasis on post-Roman landscapes appeared (Fowler 1970) and a Society for Landscape Studies was formed in 1979, publishing an annual journal entitled *Landscape History* which has since featured significant material on the later medieval period. It was appropriate that Beresford and St Joseph's *Medieval England: An Aerial Survey* (1958), which had done so much to further awareness of the landscape approach, should have a second edition in the same year.

A single word – 'landscape' – concealed a variety of purpose, method and scale (Coones 1985; Barker and Darvill 1997). Underlying all such projects was an ambition to embrace an understanding of the relationships of all sites to each other and to the natural and man-made environment over long time periods (Taylor 1974b). For the later Middle Ages it was, in a sense, a logical extension in scale of earlier fieldwork undertaken on 'lost villages' but it was also one which relied more heavily on survey and highly developed spatial and observation skills than it did upon digging (Taylor 1981). This work was

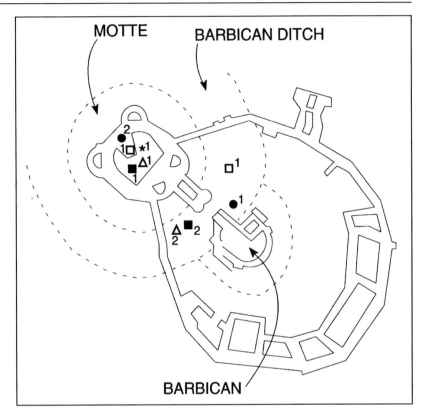

Figure 5.5 Sandal Castle (Yorks.) was excavated 1964–73. Within the curtain wall, the whole of this site was excavated using the open area technique. The inner moats were excavated out using a 'rolling' section of 1 metre vertical segments, and a film was made of this process underway. Over 18,000 pottery sherds were recovered and studied by Stephen Moorhouse. This figure shows the locations of some of the cross-fitting sherds which link Richard III's construction work on the motte with the Barbican ditch. (After Moorhouse 1983b: figure 63e).

motivated as much by 'threat' as by a need to improve 'understanding'. Two volumes, both published in 1974, Christopher Taylor's *Fieldwork in Medieval Archaeology* and Mick Aston and Trevor Rowley's *Landscape Archaeology*, provided guides to techniques and sources (Figure 5.6). In the tradition of adult liberal education, these were aimed squarely at the 'part-time enthusiast who wishes to make an original contribution to the subject' (Aston and Rowley 1974: 135).

At the county and regional levels, surveys of settlement location and site density might be 'led' by fieldwalking (for an historical overview see Orton 2000: 68–74). This was both less destructive than excavation and cheaper, though it was restricted to arable land (e.g. Fasham *et al.* 1980). Model case studies with substantial later medieval components included the East Hampshire Survey 1977–8 (Shennan 1985: 91–104), the Vale of the White Horse Survey 1984 (Tingle 1991: 82–99), and the East Berkshire Survey 1984–5 (Ford 1987: 47–50). Fieldwalking located deserted and shifted settlements and, where off-site distributions were also analysed, mapped patterns of land use. The results were routinely combined with documentary evidence and Sites and Monuments-type data (e.g. Faull and Moorhouse 1981; Wood 1984). Topographical survey was also carried out widely, and although the Royal Commissions abandoned their parish by parish inventories of earthworks in the 1970s, survey continued on selected areas, monuments and periods. Of particular relevance for the later medieval period was a detailed survey of monuments in north-west Lincolnshire (Everson *et al.* 1991; Figure 5.7).

The weaker survey projects tended to accumulate site data as an end in itself and interpretation was minimal, comprising merely the arrangement of sites into chronological order and the elucidation of spatial patterns, usually with results summarised on a series of period-map overlays. Historical underpinning was rarely strong. The input of so many specialist methods and skills proved hard to integrate, writing styles were endured rather than enjoyed by the reader, and theory went mostly unmentioned. Nonetheless, the stronger projects did provide invaluable case studies. There could be, for example, no effective account of the later medieval settlement in Britain without reference to dispersed settlement on upland, as documented in Cornwall (Austin *et al.* 1989). Landscape studies also underlined the contribution of other disciplines such as historical ecology (Rackham 1975; 1976; 1978; 1980) and garden history (Harvey 1981). Deer parks (Cantor 1983; Stamper 1988), fields (e.g. Rowley 1981), land boundaries (Fleming and Ralph 1982), pillow mounds (Austin 1988) and water management features (Aston 1988) were all embraced as never before. Even 'minor' earthwork features such as ponds and woodbanks came back onto the field archaeologists' agenda as Rackham and others showed how topographical observation, documentary analysis and field-name study could be combined with a botanical background to investigate woodland development (Rackham 1989: 155–66 for Hatfield Forest). The vigour of new multi-disciplinary trends was appropriately reflected in collected essays and synthetic works which set the research agenda for the next decade (Astill and Grant 1988; Cantor 1982; Taylor 1983).

Off-site prospection techniques continued to develop. Geophysics was increasingly applied as an aid to excavation and on area-based surveys so that by the late 1980s technological advances were rapidly improving the speed of data processing and the display of results. A steady growth in interest was indicated by two syntheses (Clark 1990; Scollar *et al.* 1990) and a review of methods used in field evaluation generally found that over 10 per cent of the 1,035 projects studied between 1982 and 1991 had used magnetometry, with about half that number using resistivity (Darvill *et al.* 1995: 33). Other new

Figure 5.6 In his parish study of Wormleighton (Warwicks.) Harry Thorpe explored the
relationship between earthworks of enclosures, fishponds, water supply, house
platforms, trackways, remnants of ridge and furrow and the present village,
suggesting changing morphologies and shifting settlement sites. This photograph,
with its key, were first published in 1975 and later used to illustrate the
development of the English landscape to a wider European readership by
Chapelot and Fossier (1980: 176–8). (Thorpe 1975: figures 6 and 9) (Photo:
Crown Copyright).

techniques to aid the location and interpretation of sites were phosphate
analysis of soils (e.g. Alexander and Roberts 1978; Gerrard 1988) and magnetic
susceptibility survey, but these were rarely employed on medieval sites.

New techniques for the study of buildings were piloted during the 'historic
fabric surveys' set up by English Heritage in the 1980s for their repair and

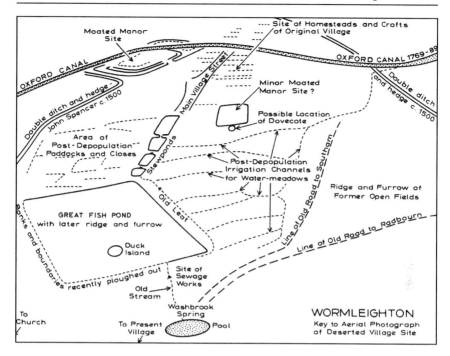

Figure 5.6 (continued)   Key to photo opposite.

conservation programmes. Much influenced by experiences at Rivenhall and elsewhere, these surveys aimed to produce plans and stone-by-stone elevation drawings combined with the study of historical and illustrative sources. Photogrammetry usually provided the base overlay for further photography and measured survey of mouldings and architectural detail. Ground-based remote sensing was also employed, particularly photo-imaging to detect subsurface features such as blocked doorways and to enhance detail in window glass or on grave markers (Brooke 1989) and the same techniques could be used to improve public presentation, for example in generating three-dimensional perspectives of monuments (Wood 1992).

The rationale, procedures, atmosphere and whole 'tone' of excavation was, by the mid-1970s, already very different from what had gone before. Goltho (Lincs.; 1970–4) serves as an example of what went on. Rescue excavation here followed a request to level a 16-hectare deserted medieval village with 37 crofts. The buried archaeology which lay beneath the summer grazing land had been put under threat by the rising value of agricultural land. Ironically, the very same machinery which threatened to level the archaeology was then used to good effect to expose it over very large areas, revealing the remains of timber and clay structures (Beresford 1975). Once the spoil had been removed in dumper trucks the clay was scraped back with long-handled onion hoes to

Figure 5.7 Medieval earthworks recorded by the Royal Commission on the Historical Monuments of England at Buslingthorpe (Lincs.). A deserted village (between points a-d) rings a moated manorial complex with a mill pond to the south (e). An exemplar of recording of its kind which can be used to inform research as well as the protection and future management of the monument. (Everson *et al.* 1991: figure 62) (Crown Copyright. NMR).

reveal features beneath. Later, at the manor house site (excavated 1971–4) some 4,580 cubic metres of soil were shifted, mostly by machine and requiring a workforce of about 10 on site over 46 weeks (Beresford 1987).

Within the context of archaeological excavation of its day, the exercise at Goltho was successful. It demonstrated clearly what could be recovered from clayland sites if appropriate methods were used. Smaller trenches would have been inadequate to understand the complexity of the recorded earthworks. The site was a natural extension in the scale of intervention which had begun with the excavation of individual houses and later expanded to include whole plots. Wharram Percy was the role model here, followed by other large-scale investigations at the shrunken village of Moreton in the Chew Valley (Som.; 1954–5; Rahtz and Greenfield 1977). The practice of stripping sites over larger areas reached its ultimate expression at the deserted settlement of Caldecote (Herts.), the first planned excavation of a complete deserted medieval village (1972–7; unpublished; Hurst 1986: 231).

This shift from trench to open area stripping brought many advantages. Larger expanses of contemporary features were exposed, including seemingly 'blank' spaces as well as structures beneath the more obvious earthworks. These benefits came at a price, however. Results could be slow and time wasted. Not only did excavators have to contend with the pros and cons of earthmoving machinery (Pryor 1974) and ground water control (e.g. Fasham 1984 for Reading Abbey waterfront) but the labour force, now spread out over wider areas, had to be tightly controlled. Not all excavators took up the new approach and, for example, the Wheeler system of excavation and recording was still in use to good effect on DoE/English Heritage excavations at Castle Rising in 1987 (Morley and Gurney 1997).

Directors experimented with different recording systems. At Winchester, every stratigraphic unit was given a 'layer' number and when these could be interpreted as events a 'feature' number (e.g. a pit) was provided, sometimes with a separate number series for different types of feature. These were recorded in cross-referenced notebooks. Until the early 1970s most excavators made use of notebooks to record their observations. While these had the advantage of good binding and plenty of space, recording could be inconsistent and there was no insurance that routine data would be noted down. In order to remedy this apparent lack of objectivity and influenced by the resurgence of positivist thinking at the time, a number of directors began to issue their own recording forms. One was produced for the University of Birmingham's School of History excavations at Bordesley Abbey (Figure 5.8). Similarly, in the rather different circumstances of a rescue excavation, Martin Carver experimented with 'context' and 'feature' cards at Shrewsbury (Hirst 1976). Gradually the idea of a universal recording form took shape (Jefferies 1977; Museum of London 1980).

With larger sites being dug, thousands of artefacts being recovered, and the paperwork of recording growing all the time, there was growing belief during the 1970s that not all monuments *should* be dug. Excavation on the outer court of Thornholme Priory, for example, showed that it would be cheaper to pay for the preservation of the rest of the monument than to continue excavating (Baker and Baker 1989: 261). Nor *could* all areas of all sites be investigated in equal detail. Merely increasing the volume of data did not lead to better understanding and, if earlier deposits were to be reached and properly recorded, then selection procedures would be needed (for a history of sampling see Orton 2000: 43–66). Sampling now proceeded at many levels (Clarke 1977; Carver 1981: 74–85). When the Shrewsbury

BORDESLEY RECORDING FORM (Foolscap)

RECORDING FORM

SITE AND YEAR:

COMPLEX	AREA	ROOM	LAYER	FEATURE

HOW DEFINED			
RELATION TO LAYERS OR FEATURES	IT IS ABOVE:	IT IS BELOW:	IT IS SURROUNDED BY:
BRIEF DESCRIPTION			

DIMENSIONS ACROSS	DEPTH FROM WHERE

COMPONENTS AND PROPORTIONS	
BUILDING AND OTHER MATERIAL	

FINDS:

ON PLAN?	WHICH PLAN?	ON SECTION?	WHICH SECTION?

REMARKS:

NAME OF EXCAVATOR OR RECORDER:

DATE:

Figure 5.8 On-site recording form from Bordesley Abbey. (Hirst 1976).

Archaeological Unit disbanded itself in 1975 in favour of pursuing a regional research agenda in towns all over the West Midlands it dedicated itself not to the history of an individual town but to the 'processes of urbanism'. This 'macro' sampling programme subsequently covered many towns rather than one or two in detail. At the 'semi-micro' level, choices about how to sample a medieval town also had to be carefully considered (e.g. at Norwich, Carter 1978; at Worcester, Carver 1980) and a list of research aims frequently provided a basis for decisions. Surveys designed to gauge the depth and preservation of deposits came to be seen as a priority (e.g. Carver 1983; Lunde 1985) with 'typical' structures being awarded the same weight as 'major' monuments. At the 'micro' level, stark choices had to be taken 'on site' about what and where to dig because of the resource implications for retrieval and storage. 'Collecting policies' usually stated that all medieval bone, pottery, slag and small finds should be retained, but bulk finds such as brick, tile and shell might be 'sampled' (e.g. Hassall 1979). It could no longer be assumed that all available sites would be excavated, nor that each excavation would result in a total record (Carver 1993: 81).

Archaeological science

In 1975 the Ancient Monuments Laboratory celebrated its 25th anniversary. Throughout the 1970s and 1980s the Lab provided the services of a national archaeological laboratory for those conducting excavations financed by the Ministry of Works and its successors, remaining at the forefront of new developments in conservation, environmental studies, geophysics, and technology. The participation of the scientist in archaeological work became steadily more common, especially after further work was funded in the regions through a series of new State-sponsored posts established in the universities in the late 1970s. The founding of the *Journal of Archaeological Science* in 1974 was merely one marker of the more sustained collaboration between archaeologists and scientists, particularly botanists, chemists and zoologists. Techniques such as pollen analysis, geophysical survey, the study of animal bone and the physical and chemical analysis of pottery fabrics, became more commonplace in medieval archaeology. Increasing numbers of degree components were dedicated to archaeological science and the universities took an important role here in developing scientific applications (for ceramics at Southampton, for example), benefiting from new sources of funding. The decision taken in 1977 to set up a committee through which the Research Councils might fund archaeological science was very important, though the idea had been initiated as early as 1969 by Martyn Jope and Derek Allen following the first joint archaeological science meeting organised by the Royal Society and the British Academy (Allibone 1970; Aitken 1992).

On most medieval sites the precise dating of occupation was founded upon documentary references and artefacts, mainly pottery and metalwork. The interpretation of stratigraphy and the value of these relative chronologies were explored by Philip Barker in his classic text on excavation techniques (1977) in a series of case studies which included medieval examples. Suites of absolute dates from physical dating methods were more difficult to come by. The main scientific method of archaeological dating, radiocarbon, seemed to have limited application for the medieval period because of the wide confidence limits set on dates, normally between 50 and 70 years. The cost of narrowing the limits using high precision measurements or using multiple samples could rarely be justified, though the Turin Shroud was one exception (Damon *et al* 1989). Similarly, the level of accuracy for thermoluminescence dates was generally considered too wide to be of use for better dated medieval artefacts such as pottery (Higham 1982) and too expensive to merit detailed sampling programmes. Archaeomagnetic dating continued to be used for kilns and ovens, with dates to a resolution of ±25 years often produced within a week and the results fed back into the process of excavation. Ambiguities caused by the crossover of the calibration curve at AD 1280/1420 could not, however, be resolved easily (see Clark 1987 for studies in London and Beverley). Experiments with dating weathered glass also proved unsuccessful (Gillies and Cox 1983). Even the dating of hedges by botanical methods, which had seemed such a welcome addition to the techniques of the landscape archaeologist (Hooper 1970), was now widely regarded with caution (Archer-Thomson 1987; Johnson 1980).

One technique, dendrochronology, proved to have huge potential. It continued to be used to date timbers in standing buildings (e.g. Bridge 1988) but was now applied regularly to excavated wooden structures. Waterfront sites provided suitably preserved timbers for tree-ring dating and so transformed chronologies previously concocted from pottery and documentary evidence. The success of the technique at Novgorod in western Russia (Thompson 1967) and elsewhere, inspired similar projects at British sites in the 1970s, in Exeter, for example, and at Trig Lane in London, one of the largest programmes mounted for an English medieval site (Hillam and Morgan 1981; Hillam 1981). Waterfront excavations such as Billingsgate Lorry Park in London continued to provide large numbers of samples and these were later complemented by results from inland sites such as Reading Abbey and Beverley (Humbs.; Hillam 1987).

The volume of medieval artefacts now available for study, taken together with a need for reliable identification, quickly led to more standardised approaches to description. In pottery studies for example, the concept of fabric type was one of the major advances of the 1980s (Mellor 1994: 5) and the value of detailed visual descriptions to assess fabric characteristics, pottery inclusions and surface treatments was well appreciated. Building upon American developments and the work of David Peacock at Southampton, petrography now began to be used for characterising the mineralogical content of medieval pottery (Peacock 1977; Streeten 1980a; 1980b). One of the first reports to figure this kind of thin-section analysis for the medieval period was the assemblage from the Saxon and medieval palaces at Cheddar (Peacock 1979). However, it was particularly through the work of Alan Vince that the thin-section analysis of pottery became established as a standard technique in medieval archaeology, providing both a relatively cheap and simple method of describing fabrics and pinpointing clay sources (Vince 1977; 1981a; 1981b; 1984; Freestone 1991). Other petrological techniques, such as x-ray diffraction, were less commonly used but compositional analyses of elemental concentrations, such as neutron activation analysis and x-ray fluorescence, were found to have potential for the classification and characterisation of finer pottery fabrics (Stopford et al. 1991 for floor tiles). These techniques also found a wide range of applications in compositional analyses of coinage (Metcalf and Schweizer 1971), copper alloys (Brinklow and Warren 1975), iron ores (Cleere 1971), pewter (Brownsword and Pitt 1984) and window glass (Gillies and Cox 1983). Novel applications of technological analysis included the analyses of organic residues in pots (Moorhouse 1986: 110–11).

During the 1970s animal bone reports were commonly published as short appendices to medieval site reports, the work tending to be undertaken by zoologists attached to university departments. Some excavators still assumed that information on diet and animal husbandry could be extracted adequately from documentary sources and concern continued to be expressed over the whims of recovery and retention policies (British Museum 1982). Studies of pioneering importance which demonstrated the value of large faunal samples included assemblages from King's Lynn (Noddle 1977), Portchester Castle (Grant 1985), Southampton (Noddle 1975) and Mark Maltby's monograph on the 75,000 animal bones from Roman, medieval and post-medieval Exeter. This was the first British monograph to be concerned solely with archaeozoological data and the first to make use of the large and well-excavated urban samples then emerging, in this case from nine rescue excavations in different parts of the city between 1971 and 1975. At Exeter it proved possible to examine changes in meat diet, trends in the quality of stock, aspects of marketing and to make an assessment of the importance of wild mammals and birds in the diet (Maltby 1979). These data could then be compared against information compiled from documents, for example population estimates and proportions of livestock listed at Domesday. Most of the 40,000 later medieval animal bones had come from cess- or waste-pits but, because of restrictions on time and labour, only a small proportion of the deposits had been sieved. One of the many lessons learnt from Exeter was that significant variations in faunal assemblages could be caused by bias in recovery techniques, and this underlined the need for well argued sample-sieving strategies. This particular lesson has been repeated many times subsequently as the study of large animal bone assemblages has become more sophisticated (e.g. O'Connor 1982 for Flaxengate, Lincoln).

In contrast, little work was done on animal bones from medieval village sites, reflecting the imbalance in numbers of sites excavated and the poor conditions of preservation often encountered. Shallowly-buried and water-logged deposits proved to relate more closely to the abandonment of sites and not their use. Nonetheless, some indication of how far bone studies had come over the two decades is revealed by critiques of those excavations which were delayed in reaching final publication. Goltho manor site, for example, was excavated between 1971 and 1974 and when the site was published thirteen years later the animal bone specialists took the excavator to task for the inconsistency of the sampling strategy, noting that only large, well-preserved whole bones with obvious joints had normally been retained (Jones and Ruben 1987). Such comments reveal much about changes in expectation and an increased awareness of research potential; earlier specialists had warned excavators that little could be done with bone slithers or the central sections of major bones (Hurst pers. comm.).

The study of human remains could count on only a handful of published later medieval cemetery excavations with more than a hundred bodies. Reports commented on difficulties of reliable dating and variable conditions of survival. Important sites include Colchester (Crummy *et al.* 1993) and London (e.g. for St Nicholas Shambles; White 1988) but some of the largest samples of populations have come from York. At St Andrew's Fishergate the skeletons were exceptionally complete (Stroud and Kemp 1993) and at St Helen-on-the-Walls a minimum of 1,041 bodies were recorded (Dawes and Magilton 1980). Studies of these and other sites have gradually extended from demography and life expectancy to consider burial positions and zoning within the churchyard, differences in treatment of individuals, stature, injury, and diet (Daniell 1997: 116–44). More controversial areas of study include ethnic affinities, and of particular interest are the distinctive Jewish burial practices examined in 482 late twelfth- and thirteenth-century graves at Jewbury (York, 1982–3; Lilley *et al.* 1994) where archaeology provided evidence for differences between prescription and practice which would otherwise be undocumented. Another is palaeopathology, for which skeletal evidence ranges from a case of twelfth-century rickets from Norwich (Wells 1982: 25) to 83 skeletons exhibiting changes consistent with a diagnosis of leprosy excavated from the cemetery of a medieval hospital in Chichester (Sussex; Lee and Magilton 1989).

Botanical studies were slow to have an impact on medieval archaeology. Normally only macroscopic plant remains from 'promising features' were sampled for further analysis with a resulting bias towards larger botanical material (e.g. Donaldson 1979; Greig and Osborne 1984 for Taunton; Green 1992 for Poole sites). A graphic example of what was lost is given by an account of the palaeobotanical evidence from thirteen sites in Christchurch (Hants.) where some fruit stones and nuts were recovered by sieving through a coarse 10 millimetre mesh but a sample of smaller seeds had to be recovered later by cleaning out the cavities in the larger nuts (Green 1983). As retrieval methods for plant macrofossils improved and particularly as flotation machines, in various forms, became increasingly common during the 1970s, so the sampling of both anaerobic and aerobic deposits became more routine. Preliminary results emerging from major programmes of work carried out on latrines, cess pits and ditches in London and York emphasised the value of all types of environmental work, including the importance of insect remains (e.g. Buckland 1974). Case studies such as that by James Greig on the contents of a fifteenth-century barrel latrine from Worcester showed what level of detail could be recovered about diet and living conditions (Greig 1981) and underlined the enormous input of organic materials into settlements, not only as latrine seats, box-lids, timber- and wicker-lined pits and wells (Shackley 1981: 99–103) but, less obviously, in the form of crops, timbers, straw, even brackens and gorses (Keeley 1987). Rewarding studies combined the analysis of pollen, seeds and insect faunas with documentary evidence, while in southern England the work of Frank Green on assemblages from Portsmouth, Southampton and Winchester and elsewhere began to build up a regional picture.

Again, medieval rural sites were less well served (Keeley 1987). Suitable preservation conditions were not always found and detailed analysis, such as that for Cowick moat (Yorks.), was all too rare. Here the botanical history for the immediate surroundings of the site was reconstructed from pollen analysis, plant macrofossils and associated beetles (Figure 5.9), and sampling and dating procedures debated (Greig 1986). Some remarkable assemblages were promptly published, such as that from a fifteenth-century drain at Barnard Castle (Donaldson *et al.* 1980), and showed the advantages of sieving and sampling, albeit mainly for 'high status' fare. Generally, articles and books continued to be illustrated by maps of medieval environments reconstructed exclusively from historical data, usually place-names and estate accounts. Occasionally, and sometimes controversially, these sources were combined with archaeological evidence (Beresford 1979; Stamper 1980).

Ironically, the real impact on the understanding of the medieval environment came from work on prehistoric and Roman pollen which, when combined with evidence from fieldwalking and aerial survey, suggested that woodland clearance and the development of farmland had already taken place by Roman times. By implication, Hoskins' assertion that by the time of the Norman Conquest 'vast areas remained in their natural state awaiting the sound of a human voice' could no longer be sustained (Hoskins 1955: 76). For medieval archaeology to make more of a contribution towards an understanding of environment there would need to be more consistent methods of analysis, improved integration of documentary data, fuller spatial and chronological sampling across urban areas, comparable data sets from rural sites, and better targeted research designed to answer specific questions. Examples of this kind of approach were rare but included a study of the land

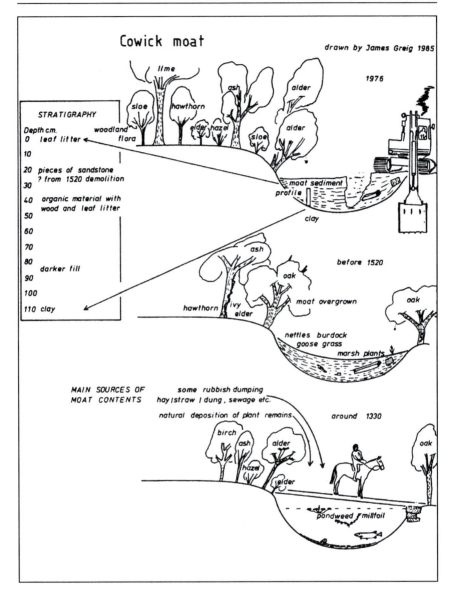

Figure 5.9 The botanical history of Cowick Moat. First dug in 1323 and excavated by machine in 1976 to make a fish pool. This illustration is based on the results of pollen and macrofossil analysis and the study of associated beetles. (Greig 1986: figure 2).

use history and vegetation of the Battle Abbey estates in East Sussex (Moffat 1986) and the use of medieval pollen data to challenge established archaeological and historical assumptions about the link between settlement change and climate (Austin *et al.* 1980; Austin and Walker 1985).

Post-excavation and publication

During post-excavation analysis of site records at the Winchester Research Unit the 'Harris' matrix was invented (Harris 1975; Brown and Harris 1993). Previously, stratigraphic sequences had normally been displayed as sections, but this new technique forced excavators to define their contexts fully in plan on site and display complete sequences on a single diagram. Since February 1973 the use of the matrix has spread right across the profession and was adopted by the former Department of Urban Archaeology at the Museum of London on rescue excavations in the City of London after 1975, initiating developments such as single-context planning and the use of computerised packages (Spence 1993).

The use of the 'Harris matrix' was just one manifestation of the ever more sophisticated use of quantification and graphics during post-excavation. With the increased use of computers, numeracy and accurate terminology quickly became essential. In pottery studies, for example, numbers and weight of sherds were already common measures of quantity but archaeologists now began to experiment with alternatives (e.g. Moorhouse 1983b at Sandal Castle). Larger areas of excavation and better standards of recording opened the way for new research on 'formation processes' (Schiffer 1987). Spatial distributions of medieval pottery, particularly sherds from the same vessel and specific ceramic forms, had been analysed to good effect in France (e.g. at Rougiers; Démians d'Archimbaud 1975) and now began to show rewards in Britain. In particular, Stephen Moorhouse demonstrated the potential of non-dating uses of medieval pottery (Moorhouse 1986).

Just as it was clear that techniques offered new opportunities, the presumption that all archaeological materials should be analysed exhaustively was also questioned. Project directors would have to prepare a 'fully argued post-excavation research design' with each phase of the excavation and the post-excavation process considered and justified in advance (Cunliffe 1982). A number of medieval collections recovered from excavation were not selected for further study, for example, the 3,000 kilograms of animal bone from Ludgershall Castle (Ellis 2000: 243). Likewise, the cost-effectiveness of archaeological publication and archive was reassessed (Frere committee, DoE 1975). Microfiche now became a common feature of streamlined archaeological reports and interest groups responded by producing their own publication guidelines (e.g. CBA Publications Committee 1976; Blake and Davey 1983).

The path from excavation through post-excavation to final publication proved beyond some and 'tortuous, repetitive and complex' for many others (Shoesmith 1985: x). Having isolated 'post-excavation' as a procedure in its own right, rather than a bad weather occupation for individuals who would prefer to be on site, there was remarkably little guidance on how it should be done (see p. 93; Boddington 1985). For the final product, various models were adopted. Excavations could be gathered together and published, either as a batch of recently excavated sites (e.g. City of Bristol Museum and Art Gallery 1979) or in a single themed volume (e.g. Atkin *et al.* 1985), sometimes with finds reports grouped together (e.g. for Bedford; Baker *et al.* 1979). When single volumes became large and expensive to produce, excavations and finds volumes were split and issued separately (e.g. for Exeter; Allan 1984). This tended to divorce finds from any discussion of their context but it did allow material to be grouped into more meaningful sequences without needless repetition. Some units, notably York and Lincoln, adopted a 'fascicule' system for multi-volume publication of finds and sites. This solution ran the risk of publishing each fascicule for a specialist market without engaging the more generalist buyer, but had the considerable merit that reports could be published on completion without undue delay. The Lincoln Archaeological Trust was among a band of units who successfully adapted their annual reports, traditionally the place for mundane business matters, to include more academic content.

In truth, the overall quality of early 'rescue' publications was not high and bore all the tell-tale signs of homemade haste and lack of experience. Some were poorly edited, inadequately bound, lacked ISBN numbers and publisher/copyright data (Fowler 1980). Only during the 1980s did the introduction of word processing and cheaper laser printers begin to have a significant impact on the process, speed and format of archaeological publishing, though even then the use of personal computers and desk-top publishing was not yet routine (Crummy 1988). Several publications began to make more attractive use of single-tone colour, fold-out plans, illustrations from woodcuts and manuscripts and tried to display their finds imaginatively (e.g. Norwich Survey reports). Particular mention might be made of the reconstruction drawings by Alan Sorrell and Terry Ball. Full colour for excavation or survey reports was rarely used on grounds of cost and tended to be restricted to books for the popular market (e.g. National Museum of Wales guidebooks; Lewis 1978).

New threats, new funding

Threats and responses

Every rural survey undertaken in the 1970s routinely stated that archaeology in the countryside faced renewed pressures (e.g. Drewett 1976; Gingell 1976). Mechanised farming, deep ploughing and the implementation of the Common Agricultural Policy accelerated unsympathetic land use changes while the growth in rural population increased demand for new housing and transport infrastructure. Closer to towns, mega-stores and out-of-town shopping centres shifted the threat of development from historic town centres to open countryside, but for many areas the archaeological response was muted. In Scotland and Wales forestry and gravel quarrying operations went unpoliced and rescue expenditure remained very low (Barclay 1997). In England, Shropshire, a county of over 348,900 hectares, received an allocation of £2,500 in 1973–4 out of the annual Department of Environment archaeology grant and was described bleakly as having 'vast historical and archaeological potential with virtually no practical resources to utilise' (Watts 1974: 12).

Where a more organised response was possible, an unexpected density of sites was revealed. Observation of construction work along over 100 kilometres of the M5 motorway in 1969–70 in the south-west of England identified some fifteen new later medieval sites 'with evidence of structures' (Fowler 1972b), an average density of one later medieval site per 7 kilometres along a randomly aligned corridor 45 metres wide cut through the countryside (Figure 5.10). For the most part, the damage was caused not by the deliberate vandalism or neglect of sites but by a profound ignorance, particularly in local government and among planners. 'Rescue', the Trust for British Archaeology, formed in January 1972, aimed to raise interest and generate a new climate of public opinion in which more funds for survey and excavation would be forthcoming and supportive legislation passed (Fowler 1972a).

Medieval archaeology played an important role in this battle for change. Peter Addyman, Martin Biddle, Philip Barker, Peter Fowler and Philip Rahtz were among the most prominent campaigners. Medieval monuments often proved to be the centre of attention. The long struggle to save Wallingford Castle (Oxon.), for example, played its part in establishing a growing philosophy that some monuments could and should be protected from both unrecorded development and excavation alike (Hassall 1977). It was mostly

Figure 5.10 The M40 cutting through the Chilterns in summer 1972. (Photo: Mick Aston).

in towns and cities that the arguments were won. Here the catalogue of destruction for medieval sites was especially lengthy as road widening removed street frontages and new building schemes encroached on abbeys and castles, infilled vacant building plots and redeveloped medieval suburbs. Outstanding opportunities for excavation were lost in Cambridge, Gloucester, Ipswich, Salisbury, Shrewsbury and elsewhere. Few towns in England, Scotland and Wales enjoyed adequate archaeological or architectural recording. Those that did have resources, like Winchester, found the annual expenditure needed to maintain any adequate archaeological response to be very considerable (Biddle 1974). Yet it was clear from every one of the 'implications' surveys produced for major medieval towns that the impact of redevelopment would be terrible. In Andover, for example, about half of the Listed Buildings were destroyed between 1968 and 1972 (Champion 1973). In broad terms, the threats to archaeology were shown to outweigh the resources, however that equation was calculated over the next twenty years (e.g. Hannan 1977 for Northamptonshire).

While not all monuments were equally regarded or understood by archaeologists (e.g. underwater archaeology; Redknap and Dean 1989), a statement to the effect that archaeology was a resource under threat of depletion would have caused few ripples of surprise in 1970 (see Chapter 4). Legislation and planning guidance for ancient monuments lagged behind professional opinion. One reaction was simply to dig as much as possible in advance of destruction; the concept of salvage. Excavation like this tended to be 'intuitive and perhaps, in some cases, a pure reaction to threats' (Hassall 1978: 131). Some digging was undoubtedly wasteful of time and resources whereas more deserving sites were excavated at great speed and site archives could be poor quality (e.g. Scott 1996 for excavations at Romsey Abbey 1973–91). The research agendas of units, where they existed at all, could be accused of being poorly structured and inward looking (Thomas 1979; Wainwright 2000). Certainly, the pattern of archaeological work had become skewed towards excavation while, relatively speaking, field survey and air reconnaissance were starved of funds (Taylor 1987).

A more considered approach was to choose sites for excavation with care in order to test hitherto unexcavated classes of monument or to explore regional and chronological variations. This required an overview of the regional and national picture and more detailed quantification of the archaeological 'resource'. One response which gained ground steadily under positivist influence, was that recording and sampling should assess problems and potentialities and be clearly linked to preservation measures, with an ordered set of priorities embedded within a philosophy of archaeological conservation. This implied 'management' of the archaeological resource rather than merely reacting to threats to its existence and many envisaged that the best way of achieving this was to ensure a strong archaeological input at the appropriate planning stages (e.g. for Barnstaple; Timms 1985). As a step in this direction, several 'implications' surveys made a point of targeting local authorities as part of their readership (e.g. Leech 1975).

Funding

'Rescue', greater awareness of threats to archaeology, a better understanding of the density of sites, high profile media events, the publication of strategic documents, public and political sympathies; all these contributed to a marked rise in income for archaeology between 1970 and 1990. In England alone, the annual state budget for rescue archaeology rose from £150,000 in 1967 to £2.1 million in 1976–7, reaching over £7 million in 1989–90 (Wainwright 2000).

Predictably, funding for salvage of archaeological sites mostly followed threat which, in turn, reflected the ebb and flow of economic cycles and redevelopment across Britain. Viewed broadly, numbers of excavations for sites of all periods therefore follow the same pattern (e.g. for Roman see Hingley 2000: 149–50) with decline in the later 1970s being followed by a rise over the next decade (Figure 4.3) and a particularly dramatic leap in London following the 'Big Bang' in 1987–88 (Carver 1993: 9). Here, later medieval archaeology was affected more than most and the main trend was the astonishing 300 per cent rise in numbers of urban excavations between 1970 and 1990, which also pushed up the totals for investigations of urban and suburban monasteries, castles and industrial sites.

Changes to State funding policies during the 1980s made a considerable impact. When, in 1980–1, core funding was withdrawn from the units, the money made available for digging came to be exceeded by grants to prepare the results of excavations for publication. Over the next decade, this 'backlog' publication programme accounted for between 35 per cent and 60 per cent of the total annual funding (Thomas 1993) and a great many of the reports mentioned in this chapter were assembled and published as a direct result. Limiting the resources for fieldwork also tended to focus minds on future priorities. Several policy documents were produced at the instigation of CBA committees (Schofield 1983) and both 'implications' surveys and special interest groups provided their own recommendations for different areas and topics (e.g. the Medieval Settlement Research Group). The CBA committee structure was especially influential in forming opinion (various reports in Hinton 1983) and the Society for Medieval Archaeology published its thoughts on future directions in 1987. Individuals too had their say. Three of the sixteen papers published in a consideration of monastic studies contained the words 'research design' in their titles, for example (Gilchrist and Mytum 1989).

Not all organisations were greatly affected by this redirection of State monies either because they were funded from another source (e.g. the Milton Keynes Archaeology Unit by the Development Corporation; Zeepvat 1994) or because they made use of new sources of funding. Many took advantage of money and labour available through job creation programmes, which reached a massive contribution of £4.8 million in 1986 for 81 archaeology projects (Mellor 1988), until this source of funding too was discontinued in the late 1980s. With this help, often combined with other local funds, some units and museums were able to keep excavation teams in the field all year round. Elsewhere, developers were increasingly making donations towards excavation and post-excavation costs and publication, particularly in major urban areas like the City of London and Bristol. By 1988–9 developer funding in England was already reckoned to be approximately double the £7 million on offer from English Heritage (HBMC 1989: 20). As a result, some units seemed able to carry on digging relentlessly, so compounding their problems of post-excavation and publication. Only in York (though the idea was mooted elsewhere) did an entirely fresh approach begin to address the funding gap. Here, funds for excavation and research were provided by a bold diversification into tourism provision.

Legislation

Changes to legislation also had an impact on fieldwork. Under the terms of the Ancient Monuments and Archaeological Areas Act 1979 five historic towns (Canterbury, Chester, Exeter, Hereford and York) became Areas of Archaeological Importance. The new system ensured at least a minimum delay for excavation in advance of redevelopment for this handful of towns, partially answering concerns about the scale and speed of urban redevelopment (Aston and Bond 1976: 209–20), but it made no provision for archaeological costs and did not cover rural areas. The protection of monuments of national importance was also bolstered by the introduction of a new principle by which changes to protected sites would require consent and a review began in 1986 of those sites protected through the scheduling process. The forecast for medieval monuments in England (as in Wales and Scotland) was that the overall numbers of protected sites would rise and that a fuller range of monument classes would now be recognised (Darvill *et al.* 1987). As yet, non-scheduled sites were still best safeguarded through the development control procedures exercised by Local Authorities. Where this could be achieved at all it was mainly through strategic policies, in the form of Local Structure and Development Plans and conditions on planning permissions (Hedges 1977 with medieval examples). The vast majority of later medieval sites, however, remained vulnerable, as was illustrated in 1989 at the site of the Rose Theatre (Wainwright 1989; Biddle 1989). Well-publicised events there were influential in bringing about a momentous change in policy guidance in February 1990 whose implications for later medieval archaeology will be considered in the next chapter.

Evolving roles and new groups

The quantity and pace of archaeological work in Britain after 1970 quickly brought existing organisations under pressure. Museums, for example, found their shelf space and facilities to be inadequate. Not only did a larger volume of photographic archive and scientific and specialist reports have to be handled, but priorities for the selection of material for conservation and storage had to be agreed. A new balance of research, finance and education, led to a tighter definition of roles and the streamlining of procedures (Leigh 1982). Greater attention was now paid to systems of materials archives (e.g. Orton 1978) and to the role of regional and national reference collections (e.g. Redknap 1988 for Welsh medieval pottery).

During the period under review in this chapter several new organisations came into being. In 1983 the National Heritage Act established the duties of the Historic Buildings and Monuments Commission for England, otherwise known as English Heritage. This was followed by the creation of CADW in Wales and later, using a slightly different operational model, Historic Scotland. These central government agencies continued to provide significant funding for fieldwork and post-excavation work. Among the organisations most severely affected by the changes were the Royal Commissions on Ancient and Historical Monuments. By the late 1970s there were moves afoot to put an end to the Commissions previous practice of publishing recorded monuments parish by parish in *Inventory* volumes (e.g. RCHME 1975). In the frenetic pace of the rescue environment, this treatment was considered 'inappropriate' (Ferrers 1987), mainly in view of the time and resource available and changing roles following the demise of the Ordnance Survey Archaeology Division in 1978. Less intensive survey continued but the National Monuments Records now took a more central role in the Commission's activities. For example, excavation archives, some of them for important medieval sites, were copied and collated and an index of archaeological excavations was created for the first time.

The curation of the archaeological resource at the local level was undertaken increasingly by local government. In England, the growing numbers of county archaeologists based in planning authorities activated local concern for conservation of the historic environment, monitored planning applications and maintained databases of local sites and monuments (SMRs). In Wales and Scotland too, archaeology databases had evolved to become a fundamental tool for both planning and research by the late 1980s. There was no discrimination against the inclusion of later medieval monuments; they were merely another segment of the archaeological resource to be treated with equal merit.

Archaeological units were among the new players. While Wales and Scotland responded to a different range of threats by providing more uniform or more centralised coverage (Musson 1987; Fojut 1987), in England the vast majority of medieval fieldwork was undertaken by the new field units (e.g. Norwich established 1971, York 1972, Lincoln 1972, Gloucester 1973). Those in the south tended to be free-standing, those in the Midlands linked with local authorities and those in the north housed in university departments. These archaeologists were more likely to come across medieval archaeology than that of any other period. Between 350 and 400 medieval sites were revealed by field evaluations from 1982 to 1991 (IFA 1993a; 1993b; Darvill *et al.* 1995). The advent of archaeology into the 'professional' world led directly to the formation of the Institute of Field Archaeologists (IFA) in 1982. Their work on standards, training, career opportunities, among other initiatives, embraced working practices within archaeology as a whole (Darvill 1993).

The reaction of universities to involvement in 'rescue' archaeology was mixed. Some continued to provide facilities and staff for the processing and publication of excavations (e.g. at the University of Sheffield) and others moved towards more vocational training (e.g. University of Oxford, Department for External Studies in-service training scheme). Most, however, opted out and there now began a long decline in the participation in British field archaeology by universities (Barker 1987).

During the 1970s, those centres with more than a handful of medieval scholars included the universities of Birmingham (where many influential fieldworkers were trained and the history department took a prominent role) and Leicester. In 1973 the first BA in Medieval Archaeology was taught at the Department of History, University College (London). For many years, the postgraduate seminar programme here was the only forum for medieval archaeology in the south of England. Nevertheless, in spite of a boom in students, few new staff with later medieval interests were appointed and during the 1980s the mood in universities was not optimistic (Austin 1987). Archaeology courses with strong later medieval components were closed at Lancaster, Leeds and elsewhere with staff moved internally or to other institutions. By 1987 there were 211 full-time staff teaching in 34 different UK universities (Millett 1987) though perhaps less than 20 of these had later medieval research interests. A review of course content amongst compulsory elements in degree courses revealed that medieval Britain and Europe were well served, falling only just behind the volume of teaching on prehistoric Europe and classical archaeology (SCUPHA 6 October 1986). Within archaeology teaching generally, the overall provision for medieval archaeology remained relatively strong therefore.

Smaller voluntary groups and societies continued to flourish, tending to define themselves not geographically or chronologically but according to monument class. The Moated Sites Research Group was formed in 1972 and its members increased the number of known sites from 3,574 in 1962 to 5,300 by 1978 (Le Patourel 1972; Aberg 1978). The Group was modelled on the villages group, with members actively encouraged to consider the distribution maps for their own areas and make standardised records of new sites (e.g. Aberg and Brown 1981). Regular conferences and an annual report provided opportunities to exchange information and views.

Meanwhile, in recognition of the expanding research agenda in rural settlement studies and especially the shift of interests towards village origins and development, the Deserted Medieval Village Research Group dropped the 'deserted' from its title in 1972 (Dyer 1992). The Group continued to organise and support fieldwork and research, its members emphasising the importance of sources of all kinds for the discovery and investigation of new sites (e.g. Beresford and Hurst 1971). The Medieval Settlement Research Group came into being in November 1986 as a result of the amalgamation of the Medieval Village and the Moated Sites Research Group. Appropriately, Christopher Taylor became the new Group's President.

Given the enormous increase in finds work, it is no surprise to find that new groups with medieval period interests were established. The Medieval Pottery Research Group was founded in 1975 and its annual journal, *Medieval Ceramics*, which covers the period between the end of the Roman period and the sixteenth century, first appeared two years later. The Welsh Medieval Pottery Research Group was formed in 1977–8 and in 1983 the Finds Research Group 700–1700 was established, maintaining its impact through meetings and the production of its *Datasheet* series, designed to communicate current research on small finds and so bypass the often lengthy wait for final publication (Finds Research Group 1999). With the formation of the Castle Studies Group in 1986, later medieval archaeology had completed a full set of committees and groups for almost every topic. This was a very different approach to that adopted for other periods and perhaps arose as a result of the success of the original settlements group. The role of the Society for Medieval Archaeology was to make the disparate pieces of the jigsaw link better. This it did very effectively for its Silver Jubilee in 1981 by reviewing the achievements of the specialist groups at its conference held at Trinity College, Cambridge (Hinton 1983).

Within this matrix of archaeological interests one group seemed to become increasingly marginalised, the general public. Teams beginning work in Exeter in 1971 had included semi-professionals as well as volunteers (Collis 1979) and this was the typical situation at that time. In Bedford the work was carried out almost wholly by volunteers until the County Council's field team was established in 1974. Thereafter volunteers were paid on a subsistence basis and blended with paid staff on short-term contracts, with added assistance from the Job Creation Programme of the Manpower Services Commission after 1976 (Baker *et al.* 1979: 2). As time went by, more and more sites came to be manned exclusively by 'professionals', those earning their living from excavation, and the involvement of volunteers was slowly curtailed.

Of course, the link between 'professional' and 'amateur' was maintained by the Council for British Archaeology (CBA) and its network of regional groups who continued to report on local activities. *Current Archaeology* championed amateur involvement, providing up-to-date news and views and sometimes contained the only published evidence that a site had ever been dug at all.

But archaeologists generally remained unconvinced that a mass audience for archaeology could be sustained (Hills 1987). Some popular booklets, like the *Children's Guide to Lincoln Castle*, sold well enough (7,000 copies between 1980 and 1987; Crummy 1987), but nothing matched the impact of television. Most members of the public in the late 1980s would probably have associated medieval archaeology with Magnus Magnusson or Michael Wood. Wood's *Domesday* series attracted healthy audiences of around 3 million for the BBC, while 20 million viewers watched the raising of the *Mary Rose* in 1982.

The impact of new ideas

During the post-war period the social sciences had begun to make greater use of numerical methods in research, particularly statistical quantification. This new focus on general trends rather than the specifics of descriptive work gave research an air of scientific respectability. Influential geography texts, such as *Models in Geography* (Chorley and Haggett 1967) and *Explanation in Geography* (Harvey 1969) made explicit use of quantified data, models and common frameworks to compare between societies and regions.

'New Geography' and 'New History' were soon followed by 'New Archaeology'. Both David Clarke's *Analytical Archaeology* and Lewis Binford's *New Perspectives in Archaeology* were published in 1968 and by the early 1980s most prehistorians, particularly those from Britain and North America, were informed by this new approach (**Box 5.2**). Later medieval archaeology made an early entry to the theoretical debate in an article by Jope (1972) which set out his views on model building. This was, however, the lone voice of a converted scientist, and it was to be nearly a decade before the impact of 'processual archaeology' made itself felt outside prehistory, in the analysis of early medieval data by Klaus Randsborg (e.g. 1980) and Richard Hodges (e.g. 1982a).

The matter was given an airing by later medieval archaeologists on two public occasions in 1981, first at The Society for Medieval Archaeology conference at Cambridge (Hinton 1983) and then by Philip Rahtz during his inaugural lecture at York University. Rahtz detected 'a wind of change . . . only now beginning to penetrate into those of later periods' (1981a) and argued for 'a formal hypothetico-deductive approach, the generation and testing of hypotheses in a rigorous manner'. In line with prehistorians, Rahtz challenged medieval archaeologists 'to discern repeated patterns which may lead to the definition of generalising laws of human behaviour' (Rahtz 1983: 14). Richard Hodges, who had attended the first Theoretical Archaeology Group meetings, reiterated that medieval archaeologists had been guilty for too long of collecting, describing and publishing data and might now benefit from an input of theory in the American tradition of anthropological archaeology or 'New Archaeology' (Hodges 1982a). Borrowing a phrase originally used to describe historians (Tiller 1992: 22–3), Hodges accused some of his colleagues of being 'truffle-hunters', noses to the ground,

Box 5.2 Processual archaeology

Medieval archaeology has traditionally adopted what might be termed 'common sense' or 'functionalist' approaches to explanation. Because it is based on a great volume of historical and archaeological evidence, this kind of work tends to detail and often emphasises the unique character of circumstances rather than longer-term trends.

Processual archaeology sought to generalise rather than particularise and to reveal long-term processes rather than the detail of individual site biographies. To achieve this a more scientific approach to data was advocated which favoured numerical and quantitative techniques. Higher aims sought to establish laws of human behaviour common to different periods and regions. One important tool was 'systems analysis', in which a past society could be broken down into a number of components, for example religious practice or population density. Each component was then examined in turn and in terms of its relationships with the others and over time (Dark 1995; Johnson 1999). The Wharram Percy Data Sheets are an example of this 'systemic approach' (e.g. Rahtz 1981b) and seek to provide a structure, typically in the form of a flow diagram, for understanding the regulation of goods and information.

Two points are worth emphasising. First, there was never enough internal consistency in the application of processual archaeology to later medieval archaeology to constitute a coherent tradition of thought. Second, while 'new' history had had no discernible impact on medieval archaeology, the 'new' approach was eventually imported from elsewhere in archaeology where it had, in turn, been adapted from conceptual developments elsewhere in the social sciences, particularly geography. Given the time lag before the new ideas were being expressed and debated, it is no surprise to find that, even before 'processual archaeology' had been given full consideration, new conceptual fashions were already at work (see Chapter 6). However, while only a handful of archaeologists with interests in the later medieval period undertook explicit applications of 'processual' thinking and even fewer published their research, it would be quite wrong to dismiss 'processual archaeology' as having a limited influence on thinking and practice. Medieval archaeology did not merely roll on heedlessly, even if some were uncertain as to the precise benefits of the new philosophy and others were entirely ignorant of its arguments and methods.

alarmed by some of the new techniques being developed by archaeologists. 'Sampling', he noted, 'horrifies truffle hunters . . . as medieval archaeologists in dinosaur-like mood confirm at annual meetings of the Society for Medieval Archaeology' (Hodges 1989).

Processual ideas were applied regularly to 'statements of policy' and research designs. Martin Carver argued against strategies for medieval urban excavation based wholly on historical preconceptions and in favour of new readings of archaeological deposits which made fuller use of sampling procedures (Carver 1981). Roger Leech advocated themes such as social organisation, subsistence and technology for the study of medieval towns in north-west England (Leech 1981). Statements of policy with regard to specific excavations were much rarer though, curiously, Wharram Percy was twice the target. In 1976 Martin Carver set out an elegant 'project management' chart which lightly employed the vocabulary of theory to suggest an orderly progress from trench to publication (Rahtz 1981b). Then, in 1980 and 1981 Philip Rahtz designed two editions of the *Wharram Percy Data Sheets* for the benefit of staff and students, as a basis for further research, to stimulate problem-orientation in excavation and data analysis, and to promote discussion. Like Leech's agenda for north-west towns, the Wharram sheets took their lead from work by the Wessex Archaeological Committee (WAC 1981) and were designed to be used 'as a preliminary base and archive from which to begin a structured systemic approach to Wharram' (Rahtz 1980: Figure 5.11). The reaction was predictably apathetic, even hostile.

What did Hodges, Rahtz and others see in processual archaeology? Above all it was the promise of a more objective, science-based discipline freed from narrative, textually-based, 'kings and queens' history (Austin 1985). Such a contribution would be distinctive and distance archaeology from history, where archaeologists had long been considered (or considered themselves) subservient. Rather than 'recognising [medieval archaeology's] essential interrelationship with history' as Platt (1978a: xv) had done in his highly regarded synthesis, theoretical converts saw no reason to fit archaeology to:

> very narrow and immeasurably partial view extrapolated from one type of artefact, the written sources. This is as ludicrous as attempting to relate the remainder of material remains to a framework of the past constructed on the basis of metal analyses.
>
> (Arnold 1986)

'New Archaeology' claimed to be able to trace the 'processes' which lay behind events and 'give history back to the people of the past' (Moreland 1991). Such a claim was empowering to a young discipline still fighting for an identity but it was not all new. The idea that medieval archaeology could provide independent evidence of how ordinary people lived had been suggested by Christopher Hawkes fifty years previously (Hawkes 1937) and Hurst and others had restated it and practised it in their work at Wharram Percy (Beresford and Hurst 1971: 78). What *was* novel was the outright rejection of the superiority of history, for 'processualists' only archaeology could provide the fuller, purer range of evidence needed to investigate the top *and* bottom of medieval society. A documentary record ciphered as élite, selective and subjective was thus pitched somewhat crudely against the 'objectivity' claimed for the archaeological record (Biddick 1993).

Few other archaeologists with an interest in the later medieval period showed much enthusiasm and those who did, like Philip Dixon, tended to be influenced by their research on earlier periods. Colin Platt's *Medieval England:*

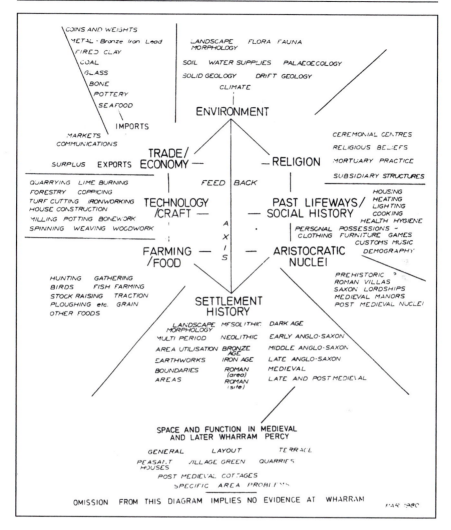

Figure 5.11 Wharram: data and interpretation. The Wharram Percy Data Sheets were compiled by Philip Rahtz in 1980 and 1981 and intended 'to stimulate problem-orientation in excavation and data analysis, and to promote discussion'. It was hoped that 'younger members of staff' might attempt 'a structured systemic approach to Wharram' but reaction was disappointing. (Rahtz 1980).

A Social History and Archaeology (1978a), the first synthesis of archaeology and history for the later medieval period, was unreferenced to theoretical developments elsewhere in archaeology. Throughout the 1970s and early 1980s not one article on new theory appeared in the pages of *Medieval Archaeology*. The reasons are not difficult to divine. Many practitioners of later medieval archaeology were practising historians, drawn from a firmly empirical tradition of scholarship whose reputation rested on a command of primary sources. Most archaeologists, educated in the culture history school, were simply not interested; 'doing' archaeology was more important than dwelling on its meaning in the abstract. *Medieval Archaeology* seemed to reflect this mood and tended to fill its pages with excavation reports which carried grant-aid. Review articles were offered all too rarely, in spite of some goading (Mytum 1986). A further source of rancour was the latest 'gimmicky' language of archaeologists, choked with quantification and statistical testing. Few had the mathematical background, or interest, to pursue the arguments of sampling strategies and locational models. To outsiders, the new brusque and confident tone was unfamiliar, inelegant, poorly expressed and exclusive.

For the conservative, 'a deliberate policy of demolishing disciplinary boundaries, bringing in by the cartload new 'models' and practical techniques developed in other disciplines' (Bintliff 1986b) was incautious, at worst a cynical attempt to posture in the latest conceptual fashion and tap into new sources of funding. 'The main weakness of . . . archaeologists, which it seems to me to limit their use for the historian', wrote Hobsbawn (1979), 'is, if you will excuse the word, a certain amount of "Status-seeking" by stressing the specific and scientific nature of the discipline'. In particular, historians were suspicious of over-grandiose statements, criticising 'the over-ambition and myopia of some of archaeology's leading spokesmen' and the lack of synthetic works (Lloyd 1986: 42). 'If this is the way forward in archaeological reporting', wrote Platt (1978b), 'it is clearly time for some of us to get off'.

Changes were evident in subtle ways. Some fields of research now became somewhat less fashionable, including art history/archaeology corpora of 'élite' sculpture, heraldry and grand buildings. In contrast, there was new scientific rigour in methodological exactness on site, in recording systems and sampling strategies. Medieval archaeology now drew regularly upon botanical, environmental, geographical and zoological studies. Mick Aston's *Interpreting the Landscape* (1985), for example, written as a general guide 'for those who want to know about the English landscape', contained various figures showing theoretical relationships between settlements, 'focal places' and land use. The deliberately 'neutral' lexicon reduced the distinction between the medieval and prehistoric periods, removing obfuscating historical jargon and expressing relationships graphically rather than in narrative form. Many similar examples could be cited, Chris Taylor's use of the term 'polyfocal settlement' among them (Taylor 1977; Figure 5.12).

Over and above changes in terminology, and what might be described broadly as a heightened awareness in human ecology and land use, there are three main areas in which 'processual archaeology' was influential in medieval studies. The first was to increase interest in how the archaeological record was created. While medievalists carried out few social studies of modern 'traditional' societies, they did draw upon ethnographical and archaeological

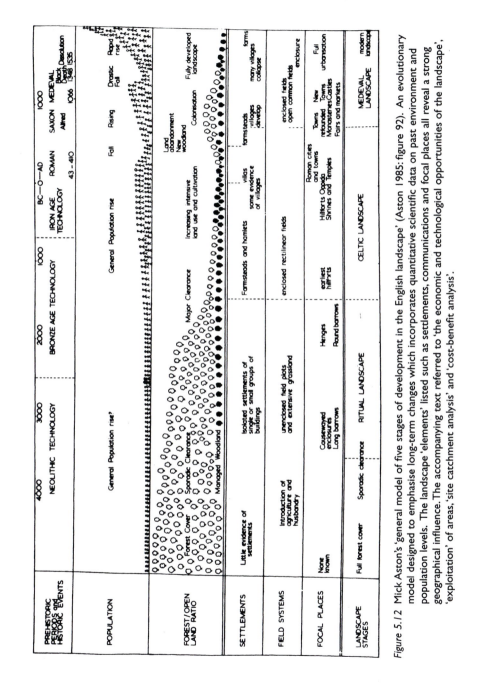

Figure 5.12 Mick Aston's 'general model of five stages of development in the English landscape' (Aston 1985: figure 92). An evolutionary model designed to emphasise long-term changes which incorporates quantitative scientific data on past environment and population levels. The landscape 'elements' listed such as settlements, communications and focal places all reveal a strong geographical influence. The accompanying text referred to 'the economic and technological opportunities of the landscape', 'exploitation' of areas, 'site catchment analysis' and 'cost-benefit analysis'.

evidence, for example in their attempts to make replica pots (MacDonald 1988). Experimental pottery kiln firings at Leeds and Barton-on-Humber examined alternative kiln superstructures (Bryant 1977) and tile kiln reconstructions and firings have a long history (Loyd Haberly 1937; Bradford and Dan 1975; Greene and Johnson 1978; Hudson 1989). Some experimental building was undertaken too, such as the peasant house at the Weald and Downland Museum (Sussex) but, on the whole, such ventures were expensive and reconstructions were confined to paper.

The second area in which processual archaeology was influential might be bracketed under the heading of spatial analysis. In a number of studies, beginning with Ellison and Harriss' (1972) discussion of settlement spacing and boundaries, attention was drawn to the size of medieval rural settlements, settlement density, hierarchies and spacing (e.g. Roberts 1977). Higher up the settlement hierarchy, larger market centres were also found to exhibit regularity in their spacing. The results were not exactly as locational models had predicted but sufficient to suggest a high degree of imposed planning and resource management (Austin 1986 for Durham; Gerrard 1987 for Somerset). Halsall (1989: 123–4) drew overlays of Theissen polygons to examine 'spheres of influence' of religious houses in north Yorkshire and then used the results to reflect upon late medieval land holding and lay charity (Figure 5.13). For the most part, straightforward extrapolations of geographical theory were not found to be overly useful but they did encourage careful scrutiny of spatial patterns and highlighted the importance of factors other than consumer behaviour as a determining factor in the spacing and ranking of sites (e.g. Fowler 1976; Wool 1982).

Spatial studies also considered the layout of monuments and settlements. Gilyard-Beer used 'planning analysis' in his investigation of De Ireby's Tower at Carlisle Castle (Cumb.), building upon the work of Faulkner in the 1950s (Hillier and Hanson 1984; see Chapter 6), while the topographical analysis of town property boundaries continued the earlier traditions of Conzen and others (Aston and Bond 1976; Slater 1987). The composition of settlement territories also came under scrutiny. O'Connor, reflecting on the sizable faunal collections at Lincoln and York, debated the huge economic impact of medieval cities upon their surrounding countryside (O'Connor 1982) and the historical geographer Brian Roberts drew up maps of schematic land use around medieval villages (Roberts 1977). More specific methods of territorial analysis such as 'site catchment analysis' found little favour, however. This technique assumed that each settlement subsisted within its own territory (Vita-Finzi and Higgs 1970), but even a cursory examination of the medieval evidence suggested that different areas would have specialised to some extent and exchanged their products through markets and fairs.

Finally, another new area of research combined methods of artefact analysis with geographical modelling and quantification techniques in the study of exchange systems. Alan Vince showed how distributional data could be com-

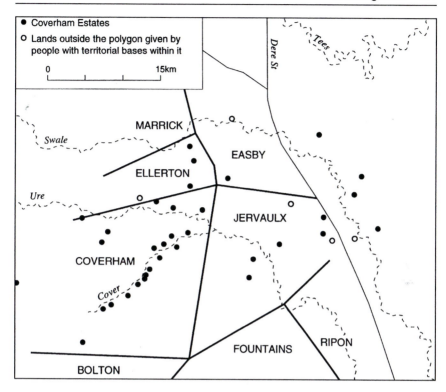

Figure 5.13 Spatial analysis and medieval archaeology. This figure shows the location of important religious houses in North Yorkshire overlain by a network of Theissen polygons. While no abbey exercised a monopoly over its theoretical territory, the bulk of the estates of the Premonstratensian abbey at Coverham were acquired within this limited 'sphere of influence'. (After Halsall 1989: figure 7).

pared for medieval ceramics and used to identify changing trading patterns (e.g. Vince 1977 for the Malvern region). In a number of sophisticated applications this author showed how quantities of a traded object could be plotted against distance from source and the resulting curve used to predict the mechanisms of distribution (Vince 1984). Such studies proved to be too easily influenced by bias in the initial collection of the archaeological information and the final interpretation assumed a great deal about the conduct of undifferentiated groups of 'consumers'. Studies of distribution patterns for other medieval products encountered similar problems of inadequate data sets and made simplistic assumptions about relationships between production, supply and consumption (e.g. for building stone, Gerrard 1985). In particular, the difficulties of understanding the highly complex commercial, tenurial and social networks behind medieval artefact distributions were exposed in a series of important articles by Stephen Moorhouse (1981; 1983a).

By the end of the 1980s medieval archaeologists were more numerous and numerate, more theoretically informed but rarely conceptually explicit, less hostile and more confident. Most continued to adopt a largely pragmatic approach to their data but seemed willing to view documents as 'but one source of evidence rather than the touchstone of confirmation for all the other lines of approach' (Bintliff 1986b). Historians too drew more routinely on archaeological data, particularly for urban life and living conditions (e.g. Reynolds 1977). Above all, three things had changed. First, largely thanks to the rescue excavations undertaken in the 1970s and 1980s there was now more data to work with and a greater variety of scientific techniques to offer new perspectives. At least basic levels of descriptive knowledge had been acquired for most monument classes, if not for all regions or periods (the what? questions). Second, medieval archaeology was by now firmly part of the wider archaeological scene; an equal partner technically, even if conceptually a weaker playmate. Some archaeologists had, for some time, been concerning themselves with the more intellectually demanding activity of picking out patterns of similarity and difference, spotting correlations between sites and identifying gaps in the data (the how? questions). Third, an even smaller band of archaeologists were now leaving descriptive levels of enquiry behind in favour of fuller engagement with theoretical issues with which they hoped to justify their purpose (the why? questions). Even as the 1980s drew to a close, the nature of these questions was already changing.

Part 3

Winds of change

Where nationally important archaeological remains, whether scheduled or not, and their settings, are affected by proposed development there should be a presumption in favour of their physical preservation.

(*Planning Policy Guidance Note 16*, Paragraph 8, 1990)

We all use theory, whether we like it or not . . .

(Johnson 1993: 7)

It is not a matter of the spade being mute, but rather that we seldom ask it the right questions, or understand its answers.

(Gilchrist 1994: 10)

An archaeological dig has started on the site of a controversial supermarket in Richmond in advance of the development work. The area is the site of an old friary church dating back to 1270, but no major discoveries are expected.

(*Darlington Northern Echo*, 8 August 1997)

In the late 1990's ceramic assemblages are usually too small to allow much more than the characterisation of a site and its deposits and sometimes even that is not attempted.

(Brown 1997: 95)

'Interesting nothing' at water meadow dig. Excavations in an historic water meadow in Bury St Edmunds have failed to provide evidence of the medieval town wall.

(*East Anglian Daily Times*, 8 April 1998)

Naked truth of Godiva's gold ring. A twelfth-century gold and amethyst ring has been found during excavations in Coventry, but archaeologists found no evidence to link the ring with Lady Godiva.

(*Birmingham Post*, 26 January 1999)

If archaeology were to visit the Well Discipline clinic the medics might be recommending a change of lifestyle.

(Richard Morris 1999, IFA AGM debate, *The Archaeologist* 34: 18)

Chapter 6

Retrospect and prospect

Medieval archaeology today
(1990 to the present)

The past decade has brought opportunity and concern in equal measure. New archaeology and planning policies have had a significant impact on the volume and nature of excavation undertaken in Britain and altered previously established patterns of funding and employment. On the one hand, there is now a higher level of public interest in archaeology, greater numbers of archaeologists at work and more resources to work with. Developers pay to record the archaeological deposits which might be damaged by their schemes and diminishing government funding has been channelled into other areas such as post-excavation costs. On the other hand, there is competition, uncertainty and little fieldwork is research-driven. Post-processual archaeologies have affected a growing proportion of writing and some field practice which, in turn, has been the subject of further technical innovation.

Excavation and fieldwork

Urban life

In the 1990s most medieval archaeology was urban and dictated in location and scale by the needs of development. A new emphasis on preservation *in situ* meant that many sites, which perhaps might have undergone major excavation ten or fifteen years previously, were left untouched by archaeologist and developer alike. Medieval features, such as pits or surfaces, were often recorded in evaluative trenches and watching briefs, but at such a small scale, little of significance could be learned. The value of this work lay in the careful accumulation of minor clues to the depth and extent of deposits rather than in the 'research' merit of any one individual exercise.

Bristol, Canterbury, Chester, Gloucester, Hereford, Oxford, Plymouth, Southampton and York all saw larger scale projects; a familiar list of historic towns prominent during the 'rescue' years. London remained the dominant centre for excavation and waterfront investigations, for instance at Fleet Valley, Bull Wharf, Vintners Place and 1 Poultry, continued to be rewarding. A typical specification combined detailed sample excavation with extensive watching briefs and, as before, pottery, leather, bone and wooden artefacts were all recovered in quantities together with the well-preserved timber revetments so important for dating and an understanding of medieval shipping

(Marsden 1996). Substantial new excavation was also undertaken away from the waterfront (e.g. at Cheapside; Nenk *et al.* 1992: 229).

The geographical range and variety of urban sites under excavation was extensive. Especially impressive was the increase in urban excavation in Wales. Investigations in Newport and at New Radnor (Powys) were promptly published to a high standard (Murphy 1994; Jones 1998) and a long-running series of excavations in Monmouth (Gwent) in advance of development revealed burgage plots, defensive features, metalworking sites and stone buildings (e.g. Nenk *et al.* 1991: 233). Smaller towns in England also saw higher levels of development-led archaeological work and are likely to see more in the future. At the riverside port of Bawtry (Yorks.), evaluation in October 1990 led on to a fifteen-week excavation which revealed tenement and building histories of the thirteenth century onwards (Dunkley and Cumberpatch 1996), while at Pershore and Evesham (Worcs.) major urban monuments, crafts and industries were examined (Dalwood 2000).

Opportunities were created by renewed financial support for post-excavation work. Among the major 'rescue' campaigns brought to publication were those at Chepstow (1973–4; Shoesmith 1991), Hull (1975–6; Evans 1993), Norwich (1985; Ayers 1994), Trowbridge (1977, 1986–8; Graham and Davies 1993) and Usk (1965–76; Courtney 1994). These results made possible two exceptional syntheses, one for towns generally (Schofield and Vince 1994) and another for medieval urban housing (Schofield 1994a).

Rural life

With the completion of the 41st and final season of excavations at Wharram Percy in 1990, the era of large-scale excavations at medieval village sites seemed to be drawing to a close. At Stratton (Beds.) over four hectares were mechanically stripped and selectively excavated in 1991 (Nenk *et al.* 1992: 193–4), but this was exceptional. Elsewhere, monuments were partially examined but few produced either lengthy or complete structural sequences and inevitably many issues were left unresolved on site in spite of the considerable ingenuity of archaeological contractors. Among a handful of more substantial projects was the excavation of a thirteenth- to fifteenth-century hamlet at Sourton Down (Devon; Nenk *et al.* 1992: 219–20) in advance of road construction, and the Wood Hall Moated Manor Project (Yorks.), funded by National Power, which took as its aim the near-complete excavation of a moated site within a wider landscape study. This research-led investigation promises to be a model of its kind and should act as a reminder that one intensive long-term project like Wood Hall can still undermine long-held perceptions (Metcalf 1997).

'Settlement' was a major theme of the Leeds International Medieval Congress in July 1998 which also marked the 50th anniversary of Maurice Beresford's first visit to Wharram Percy. The greatest advances in medieval settlement studies continued to come from detailed investigations of places and regions, making use of a variety of disciplines ranging from architectural history to environmental studies (Dyer 1992; 1997; Roberts 1993). The origin and development of nucleated villages remained a central issue (e.g. for the Shapwick Project in Somerset; Aston and Gerrard 1999; Figure 6.1), but a more inclusive agenda now embraced dispersed settlement, surviving villages and seasonal settlements (Fox 1996), such as sheepcotes (Dyer 1995) and coastal fishing hamlets (Gardiner 1996). The resurgence of interest in rural settlement studies in Scotland and Wales both at conferences and in publication was notable (e.g. Hingley 1993), as has been a trend towards the re-examination of published evidence (e.g. Gardiner 2000).

Studies at different scales sought to explain differences in settlement form, from a multi-county Leverhulme-funded project into the origins of the Midland Village (Lewis *et al.* 1997), to regional surveys such as the Compton Bassett Area Research Project (Reynolds 1994) and a number of valuable local case studies (e.g. Dyer 1990a). A new long-term study, the Whittlewood Project, began to examine the formation, function and contraction of settlements in parishes on the Northamptonshire and Buckinghamshire border (Dyer 1999a). As Jope recognised many years ago, the choice of a region as a unit of study

Figure 6.1 The Shapwick Project 1989–99. Excavations in 1996 on the emparked areas of the village to the south of Shapwick House. This trench was located with the benefit of geophysics plots, shovel-pit testing, map evidence and the results of a watching brief on a nearby pipeline. One of 42 excavations which form part of this wide-ranging landscape investigation. (Photo: Peter Jacobs).

bridges the gulf between isolated microstudies at the local level and national surveys which may gloss over conflicting trends. It also has the advantage of being small enough and well enough documented to be precise in both historical and geographical terms.

Good archaeology takes time to process and interpret. It is a curiosity of the discipline that, even while the results of major projects are still being processed and brought to publication, new projects get underway. There is a constant overlap between cycles of project design, execution and dissemination. Thus, while the South Manor at Wharram Percy was brought to successful publication (Stamper and Croft 2000) and other Wharram sites now near completion, they emerge into a far more diverse culture of developer-led and research-led projects to that in which they were conceived. On one hand the pace of the work at Wharram may now seem slow for a 6 per cent excavated sample of that settlement; on the other, the quality and clarity of academic reflection will be hard to match.

A fast growing literature on landscape archaeology continued to move the thrust of research away from excavation and the investigation of individual sites. Thematic Royal Commission inventories of a high standard continued to be issued, revealing just how incomplete our knowledge of medieval settlements other than deserted villages and moated sites could be (e.g. Everson *et al.* 1991; RCAHMS 1994). There was a continuing appetite too for the exploration of medieval landscapes, such as ancient woodlands (Day 1993), uplands (e.g. Fleming 1998) and reclaimed wetland (Eddison and Draper 1998; Rippon 1997a; 1997b; 1998). These studies integrated palaeo-environmental studies with excavation, map regression, documentary and place-name study in innovative ways, dovetailing research with conservation and management issues.

Developer-led fieldwork also produced evidence for new sites, mostly through fieldwalking programmes associated with landscaping for golf courses, forestry replantation (e.g. in south-east Suffolk; Nenk *et al.* 1992: 265), pipelines and bypasses. Linear developments often affected lynchets, wood banks and park pales (e.g. Nenk *et al.* 1992: 191) and, while seemingly of 'minor' interest, sometimes produced unexpected results. The survey and selective excavation of medieval post settings, woven fishtraps and fishbaskets in advance of the Second Severn River Crossing, for example, provided detailed evidence for estuarine fishing (Godbold and Turner 1994).

Churches and monasteries

Large numbers of small-scale investigations at church sites are recorded in the pages of *Medieval Archaeology*. The excavation and watching brief at St Mary's Church in Norton (Cleveland), for example, revealed wall foundations, mortar floors and intact medieval wall plaster (Nenk *et al.* 1992: 205).

These exercises were mostly related to drainage improvements or to liturgical rearrangements. Other work took place in advance of conservation measures, for example fabric recording was undertaken at Exeter Cathedral, Westminster Abbey and at many other sites (Nenk *et al.* 1992: 209; Tatton-Brown 1995; Cocke *et al.* 1996) and a programme of dendrochronological analysis on church timbers was funded by English Heritage. Only occasionally were large-scale investigations possible, as at Glasgow Cathedral when archaeological work in advance of the installation of heating ducts produced new evidence for burials and earlier structures on the site (Nenk *et al.* 1993: 305).

Future research directions have been explored in a recent edited volume (Blair and Pyrah 1996) and, while the excavation of parish churches continues to reveal sequences of building and burial, new options for research are now developing. These include the analysis of church settings (Morris 1989), regional differences between architectural styles (Brown *et al.* 1996; Rodwell 1996b), questions of medieval technology, the archaeology of ritual, burial, liturgy and the use of space (Morris 1996). Much of this work will not necessarily involve large-scale fieldwork except in cases where sites are threatened. The recent publication of Grimes' post-war excavations at St Bride's church (London; Milne 1997) is a reminder that bringing earlier excavations to publication must remain a priority.

Monastic sites continued to be affected by urban redevelopment, notably the sites of 'lesser' urban religious houses. A Dominican friary was excavated at Blackfriars in Gloucester (Nenk *et al.* 1992: 225–56) and Franciscan friaries have recently been examined at Greyfriars in Carmarthen (T. James 1997) and at the Central Library site in Lincoln, where a large portion of the southern range of the friary was uncovered (Nenk *et al.* 1995: 228–30). Excavations on Augustinian precincts ranged from those at Merton Priory (Surrey; Nenk *et al.* 1991: 155) where a medieval wharf and slipway were among the elements examined, to the friary in Hull where most of the ground plan was uncovered at the site of the Magistrates Court in one of the largest excavations ever undertaken in the city (Nenk *et al.* 1997: 271–3). Hospitals too have come under scrutiny, most notably at St Mary Spital in London where over 8,000 medieval burials were excavated, some in individual graves, others in mass burial pits, together with a charnel house, church and substantial quantities of medieval finds from pits (Thomas *et al.* 1997). Similarly, there was a happy coincidence of research and planning interests in Colchester (Essex) when the site of the demolished hospital of St Mary Magdalen was threatened by new housing (Olivier 1999: 105–6).

As previously, those rural monasteries affected by development were on the suburban fringe. Work of some scale was undertaken at the Cistercian abbeys at Hulton (Staffs.; Nenk *et al.* 1991: 185) and at Stratford Langthorne (Essex) which was affected by the Jubilee Line extension (Nenk *et al.* 1992: 231). The Bordesley Abbey Project continued, though the main thrust now shifted to post-excavation analysis and publication. An ongoing research programme on the Bordesley granges involving documentary and map-based assessment as well as earthwork survey will help to set the results within a regional context, and further underlines the tremendous value which can be gained from long-term programmes of archaeological research (Bordesley Abbey Project website).

Many monastic projects comprised either fabric analysis of buildings prior to their conversion (e.g. the gatehouses at Canonsleigh Abbey, Devon; Nenk *et al.* 1993: 251–53) or archaeological work in advance of improvements to presentation and visitor facilities, as at the Augustinian priory at Haverfordwest in Dyfed (Nenk *et al.* 1991: 230). Excavation connected with these improvement schemes, while not infrequent, tended to be modest in scale. The Templar and Hospitaller site at Cressing Temple (Essex), for example, saw some twenty-five separate fieldwork projects between 1987 and 1992. Of these only six were not subject to restrictions on the depth of excavation, thereby greatly limiting any interpretative potential (Robey 1993).

Work on monasteries over the past decade has therefore echoed the plight of other fields of medieval archaeology. Only occasionally have developer work or conservation projects led on to excavation on any scale, mostly where there has been some degree of State involvement. At Eynsham Abbey (Oxon.) the Oxford Archaeological Unit began a 3,000-metre-square rescue excavation in 1989 at the site of the Benedictine abbey when the existing cemeteries were to be extended. With the help of English Heritage funding, this work broadened out into a research project designed to improve the protection of the site as a whole. A complex of buildings was examined on the south side of the cloister and complementary survey work of the surviving earthworks was carried out by the Royal Commission (Keevil 1995). Similar rescue, research and management issues are behind the English Heritage project at another Benedictine house at Whitby (Yorks.; Nenk *et al.* 1995: 261) where earthwork and geophysical surveys preceded excavation. Similarly, Historic Scotland also sponsored large-scale investigation at the Cistercian abbey at Melrose (Borders; Nenk *et al.* 1997: 321–2).

Elsewhere, interest has largely been sustained through the publication of several important 'backlog' projects including the Benedictine nunnery and Dominican Friary at Chester (1964, 1974, 1976–81; Ward 1990), the Benedictine priory at Leominster (1979–80; Brown and Wilson 1994), St Bartholomew's Hospital in Bristol (1976–8; Price 1998), Thelsford Priory (1966–72; Gray 1993) and Lewes Priory (1969–82; Lyne 1997). New research has tended to be redirected into areas other than fieldwork, for example there have been several works of synthesis (e.g. Aston 1993; Coppack 1990; Greene 1992) and an inclination towards European perspectives (e.g. Bond 1993). One primary task has become the reconstruction of daily life, particularly the liturgical dimension. This has required a fuller integration of existing architectural and archaeological scholarship, as opposed to new data from excavation, and has been informed by new perspectives drawn from archaeological theory (e.g. Gilchrist 1992; 1994).

Castles

The closing of excavations at Hen Domen in 1992 (Nenk *et al.* 1993: 310–12) foreshadowed a rash of small-scale work at castle sites, though not all produced inconsequential results. Rescue excavations in Norwich on the fabric and structure of the castle bridge provided an excellent illustration of what could be achieved from a fleeting development opportunity and established the main phases of the bridge's evolution (Shelley 1996). Generally, however, those excavations with a stronger research bias which took place in Guildford (Nenk *et al.* 1992: 267), Stamford (Nenk *et al.* 1991: 185) and, most notably, at the Tower of London (Nenk *et al.* 1997: 264–8) only underlined the fact that castle excavation needed to be on a larger scale to produce results. This point was grasped particularly in Wales where castle excavations were a notable feature of the decade. At Dolforwyn (Powys; e.g. Nenk *et al.* 1992: 304–5) the twentieth and final season of excavation was completed in July 2000, and large scale excavations were also undertaken at Laugharne in Dyfed (Nenk *et al.* 1991: 231) as well as in Scotland, for example at Dunstaffnage (Strathclyde; Nenk *et al.* 1993: 305).

Renovation, emergency repairs and public display all justified additional recording. Numerous historic fabric surveys were undertaken, usually with stone-by-stone drawings based on a photogrammetric template, as at Wardour Castle (Wilts.; Reilly 1998; Figure 6.2). Surveys of Carlisle Castle (McCarthy 1990) and Norham Castle (Nhumbs.; Dixon and Marshall 1993) are two examples of this genre published to a high standard, recording areas of archaeological and architectural significance, illustrating major phases of construction and generating drawings which will inform all future conservation and research. As at Pevensey (Surrey; Nenk *et al.* 1995: 252–3), architectural recording was accompanied occasionally by excavation or combined with geophysics and topographical survey as at Aberedw (Powys; Nenk *et al* 1995: 289–90) and Wigmore Castle (Heref.; Olivier 1999: 41–4).

Castles were also the subject of several excellent synthetic volumes, characterised by a welcome tendency towards explanation rather than description (Higham and Barker 1992; Kenyon 1990; McNeill 1992, 1997). All these rightly stressed the major advances in knowledge since 1945 of earthwork castles and the importance of long-term personal and research commitments as at Hen Domen. Regional surveys also continued (e.g. for earthwork castles in Glamorgan; RCAHMW 1991) and significant efforts were made to bring earlier excavation campaigns to publication. Some achieved the transition from trowel to paper with admirable rapidity (e.g. Caergwrle Castle, Clwyd; Manley 1994) while others such as Caerlaverock (1955–66; Dumfries.; MacIvor and Gallagher 1999) took longer to germinate. The Ludgershall Castle report, in particular, is an advertisement for the way in which castle studies have developed. To an original text based largely on excavations between 1964 and 1972 were added new chapters designed to bring the

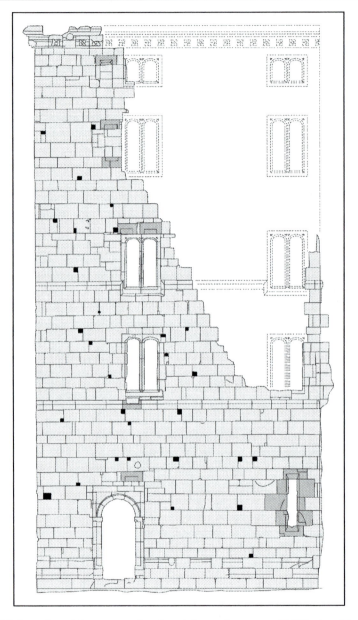

Figure 6.2 Recording of the western elevation of the north tower at Old Wardour Castle (Wilts.) by the Central Archaeology Service. A late fourteenth-century structure 'modernised' after 1570, substantially damaged during the Civil War and treated as a romantic ruin in eighteenth-century landscape design (Chapter 2). Building fabric recording like this is frequently carried out as a preliminary to programmes of conservation and repair but can also improve our interpretation of the monument in significant ways. (Reilly 1998) (English Heritage Copyright).

report into line with current directions of research. These examined the wider landscape and 'ornamental' setting of the castle as well as discussing the prehistoric and later post-medieval phases of occupation (Ellis 2000).

Ludgershall Castle is one of a remarkable series of earthworks surveys undertaken by the English Royal Commission which are beginning to open out the research agenda for castles from limited architectural and archaeological study to a detailed study of their surrounding landscape. At Bodiam Castle (Sussex) survey established the remains of gardens and water features which seemed designed to add a sense of theatre to the castle architecture (Taylor et al. 1990). This appreciation of the building in its wider setting underlined both the value of 'non-excavational' field survey as well as the contribution of new theoretical influences. It is perhaps here, in changing perceptions of castles and their cultural context, that future work will focus.

Buildings

The rate of work on standing buildings seems undiminished, contributions ranging from multiple tree-ring analyses of timbers to the wider implications for the medieval woodland economy (e.g. Rackham 1993) and the publication of valuable field guides (Alcock et al. 1996). The principles of structural analysis have been extended to medieval buildings of all kinds, including palaces (e.g. Turner 1997), bastles (Ryder 1992) and timber-framed buildings (e.g. Crook 1993). Much of this work will provide a basis for conservation decisions. Links between status, building form and dating have also been widely discussed and to particularly good effect in regional surveys such as that carried out in Kent by the Royal Commission (e.g. Barnwell and Adams 1994). In contrast, the main contribution of recent excavation to the study of buildings can confidently be expected to be for urban housing, largely as a consequence of backlog publications becoming available (e.g. Hannan 1998).

Thematic projects on particular building types have extended our knowledge of understudied monument classes such as palaces (Dunbar 1999), bishops' houses (Thompson 1998) and 'greater' medieval houses (e.g. Emery 1996). Some of this work led to striking reinterpretations, as has been the case with 'first-floor halls', now seen as surviving chamber-blocks once accompanied by free-standing open halls (Blair 1993). At the same time, a growing body of new work suggests how differences in the plans of houses might reflect social influences and steer practices in everyday life. Notions of privacy and segregation are seen as driving forces behind changes to internal arrangements (e.g. Alcock 1994). A comprehensive discussion of these new approaches (Grenville 1997) indicates their debt to recent developments in archaeological theory and several important case studies are now available including Matthew Johnson's study of traditional architecture in western Suffolk (1993).

Artefacts and industry

Over the past decade some understudied industries such as medieval salterns have received attention for the first time (McAvoy 1994). A handful of well-excavated sites such as the Bedern foundry in York (Richards 1993) and pottery workshops at Pound Lane in Canterbury (Cotter 1997) have also been brought to publication. Otherwise, distinctive trends in research are hard to identify except to say that this is one area of medieval archaeology where the overall sample of excavated sites remains small and a single excavation can still change long-held perceptions. Experimental work goes on (e.g. for floor-tile kilns; Kent and Dawson 1998) and historically-weighted studies continue to be produced for a variety of different building materials (Alexander 1995; Hare 1991; Stopford 1993) as well as for medieval industry generally (Blair and Ramsey 1991). A landscape approach has been brought to bear, one which considers the wider environment of production and consumption. Local programmes of field survey have played an important role here, the Dartmoor Tinworking Research Group (Nenk *et al.* 1991: 142; Passmore 1999) and the Medieval Potteries Survey around Hanley Castle (Nenk *et al.* 1993: 266), for example. Sometimes survey has led on to excavation, as for iron smelting sites in the Pennines (Nenk *et al.* 1996: 263–4). Foard (1991), for instance, has examined the medieval pottery industry of Rockingham Forest in Northamptonshire, noting relationships between pottery workshops and woodland resources.

One of the outstanding achievements of the decade in medieval archaeology has been the major finds reports published from earlier urban excavations. Drawings, descriptions and discussions of collections of over 6,000 non-ceramic artefacts from the Winchester excavations 1961–71 (Biddle 1990), finds from London (Egan and Pritchard 1991; Egan 1998; Figure 6.3), and from Norwich 1971–8 (Margeson 1993) are already standard reference works. More modest projects have also catalogued important groups of material, such as the collection of pilgrim badges from Salisbury (Spencer 1990) and there have been major thematic studies of understudied artefact types such as bone and antler (MacGregor *et al.* 1999) and decorative ironwork (Geddes 1999), as well as practical handbooks dedicated to improving best practice in recording (e.g. Stopford 1990 for floor tiles). The British Academy has also continued to support major reference works such as the cataloguing of coins and stained glass (e.g. Marks 1998).

Taken together, these publications help establish terminologies and explain how accessories were used. Crucially, because many of the finds are from stratified archaeological layers, they can be more closely dated than was previously the case and may be tied directly to their social context (e.g. Tyson 2000). Rather than reporting on exceptional objects or solely on aspects of dating or manufacture, a fuller picture of daily life can now be explored which seeks to place artefacts into a wider cultural context (e.g. Cherry 1992).

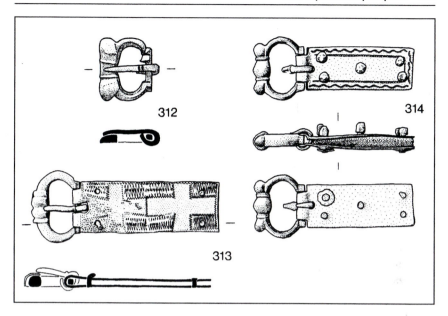

Figure 6.3 Ornate oval buckles with plates, late twelfth to late fourteenth-century, from a variety of sites in London including Billingsgate lorry park (1982–83), Seal House (1974) and Swan Lane (1981). Illustrated in the third volume on medieval finds from excavations in the City of London undertaken by the Department of Urban Archaeology, Museum of London. (Egan and Pritchard 1991: figure 46).

To facilitate this, finds are more often catalogued according to use and function rather than by material type, following the tradition of the 1940 London Museum Medieval catalogue (see Chapter 3).

The wide range of modern pottery studies being produced was well illustrated in John Hurst's second *Festschrift* volume (Gaimster and Redknap 1992). Another highlight was David Gaimster's substantial survey of German and related stonewares (1997a). All catalogues are a quarry for pottery specialists but this volume stands out for the breadth of its social and economic context, as well as its attention to technical and artistic developments. A number of other studies also began to incorporate innovative approaches. A series of articles by, among others, Duncan Brown (Brown *et al.* 1997) and Chris Cumberpatch (1997b) deliberately sought out new perspectives on the deployment of pots in the medieval household and on contemporary perceptions of colour and design.

Such bold initiatives were far from the whole story, however, as a review of medieval ceramic studies discovered (Mellor 1994). Severe limitations on specialist finds analysis and reporting are often imposed by developer-led archaeology (Blinkhorn and Cumberpatch 1998). Nor have all areas seen the benefits of publications of large backlog excavations or suites of dendrochronological dates, though more modest work has continued on regional chronologies and the identification of production sites. In Scotland, for example, only a handful of pottery workshops has been documented so far (Will 1997). The Medieval Pottery Research Group has been working with, among others, English Heritage, to try to remedy these lacunae. A new guide to medieval ceramic forms has been issued which aims to improve recognition skills and will help standardise nomenclature (MPRG 1998); a national bibliography for medieval pottery studies has been made available online; national and regional training days for medieval pottery have been instituted in order to spread best practice; a 'minimum standards' document for post-Roman ceramics encouraged further standardisation (Slowikowski *et al.* 2001); and a useful guide to scientific resources for ceramic study has been issued (Barclay 2001). Such a commitment to furthering understanding could usefully be extended to other artefact groups and demonstrates the impact that a special interest group can have on the direction of research when that commitment is backed with proper funding.

Techniques and scientific applications

According to one alternative chronology for the past, 'prehistory' can be defined as anything pre-1945 and the 'Middle Ages' placed between 1982 and 1992 (Rawlins 1997: 59). This was, of course, a history of the world based on information technology and most medieval archaeologists have been affected in some way over the past decade by digital advances in quantification, recording, archiving, publishing, education and communication. Useful tools include e-mail, Teaching and Learning Technology Programmes, virtual libraries, online journals, websites for national and local authorities (including county SMR records and museum collections in some cases) and archaeological discussion lists such as Britarch, where 1,440 members exchange news and views (source: Britarch December 2000). The latest information on several ongoing projects (e.g. Bordesley Abbey, the Shapwick Project) is available first online and excavations can be followed 'remotely'. Excavations and fieldwork at West Heslerton in north Yorkshire use 'clickable plans', section drawings, photographs and video-clips as well as digitally-archived information about contexts and phasing, artefacts and environmental details (Powlesland 1997).

Off site

Resistivity and magnetometry are now standard tools for subsurface detection (Gaffney *et al.* 1991) and the presentation of field data has become steadily more sophisticated with improved software and computer graphics. The power and portability of survey equipment has continued to develop and the speed of survey has quickened (David 1995). Recent work at Fountains Abbey illustrates the variety of purposes to which results can be put, both for management purposes and to further knowledge of below-ground archaeology (Coppack *et al.* 1992). Even previously disappointing targets such as rural medieval settlements (e.g. Aspinall *et al.* 1994) and iron-working sites (e.g. Vernon *et al.* 1998) have produced promising geophysics results (Figure 6.4).

Other forms of prospection are viewed with more ambivalence. Applications of new technology such as resistive tomography and ground probing radar to rural sites (Szymanski *et al.* 1992) and in urban areas (e.g. in Carlisle, Nenk *et al.* 1991: 138) have not been altogether convincing, but there is clearly some potential for identifying buried archaeology in otherwise unsympathetic terrains, as work near the Norman castle in Gloucester has demonstrated (Atkin and Milligan 1992). Possibilities are also offered by geochemistry; phosphate analysis still seems underused in later medieval archaeology (Crowther 1997) and the analysis of topsoil concentrations of elements such as lead and copper seems promising as a prospection tool for the future (Aston *et al.* 1998; Rippon 1998; Figure 6.5). Likewise, soil

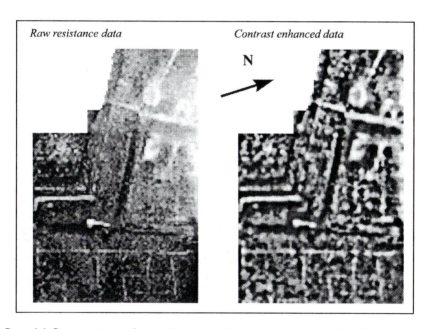

Figure 6.4 Greytone image of raw and contrast enhanced earth resistance data from the geophysical survey conducted by the Ancient Monuments Laboratory of English Heritage at Mohun Castle, South Perrot, Dorset, July 1997, in advance of the possible extension of the local churchyard. The rectilinear pattern of resistance within the moated area suggests wall footings, though there are no remains visible on the surface today. This is one of several geophysics plots available online from the English Heritage website. (Copyright: English Heritage).

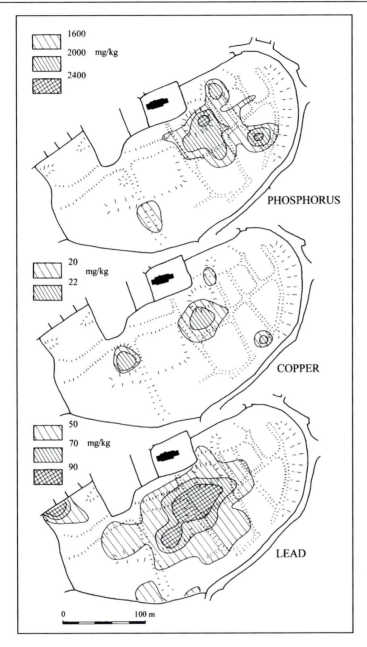

Figure 6.5 Soil chemistry survey undertaken by Andrew Jackson at Church Field, Puxton, for the North Somerset Levels Project. The three plots show marked concentrations to the south-east of the church, suggesting a focus for domestic occupation there. This interpretation is corroborated by spreads of tenth- to thirteenth-century pottery. (Rippon 1997c: figure 11).

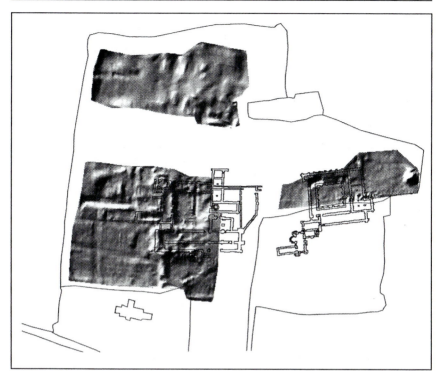

Figure 6.6 Combined GIS model and excavation plan of the nuns' cloister at Watton Priory in the Vale of York. (Copyright: Humber Wetlands Project, Univ. of Hull).

micromorphology (Foster and Smout 1994) and lipid biomarkers can provide detailed evidence of past land use, the latter being used recently to suggest manure composition and patterns of application in a case study from Orkney (Simpson *et al.* 1999).

The recording of earthworks has been speeded up and simplified by the introduction of Electronic Distance Measuring equipment ('EDMs' or 'total' stations) and Geographical Positioning Systems ('GPS'), particularly when large areas have to be surveyed, as in the case of deserted settlement earthworks. 'Hard' detail such as standing buildings is often mapped electronically to provide an accurate framework for survey, with 'soft' detail such as earthworks being added using plane tables or traditional tape-and-offset methods (Bowden 1999). Three-dimensional information can also generate Digital Terrain Models (DTMs) to supplement traditional illustration techniques. Several medieval sites have already been published which make use of this new technology, including studies of ridge and furrow (Fletcher and Spicer 1992) and a recent survey of the Gilbertine Priory of St Mary at Watton (Yorks.), a site originally excavated at the end of the nineteenth century by Hope (1900; Fenwick 2000; Figure 6.6).

Other important initiatives for medieval archaeology include the National Mapping Programme for England, which began in 1987 and will eventually provide aerial photographic coverage for the whole of England at 1:10,000 scale (Featherstone *et al.* 1999). Projects using complementary techniques are underway in Scotland and Wales and significant numbers of new sites and relict landscapes will be added to the national record as a result. The aerial photographic transcription of prehistoric, medieval and later remains on Bodmin Moor, for example, identified 37 deserted and shrunken medieval settlements, 62 herders' huts, 227 medieval field systems and a variety of ecclesiastical sites within 193 one-kilometre squares of moorland (Johnson and Rose 1994). But while there will always be a place for low level photography in archaeology, new techniques are also being developed as hardware and software costs fall (Bewley *et al.* 1999). Satellite imagery and multispectral data, for example, seem to offer complementary data and thermal detection methods have also produced results, even at unpromising locations (for example, Bosworth battlefield, Leics.; Donoghue 2001: 560).

High technology should be not necessarily be preferred over low technology. For their ten-year project at Roystone Grange (Derbys.), Richard Hodges' team examined local drystone walls, producing a typology for the prehistoric period onwards, and dug 'test-pits' at regular intervals to show the spread of finds across the landscape (Hodges 1991). No one survey can provide a 'blueprint' however, and suites of archaeological techniques cannot be universally applied. Fieldwalking is one cheap prospection tool which can be effective under the right circumstances and is now used on many 'landscape' projects. Surveys which once simply plotted densities of finds by field may now take account of frequencies of different wares, sherd size and abrasion, walker and environmental effects (Gerrard 1997), while the effect of ploughing on artefacts in the plough soil is now better understood (Boismier 1997; Schofield 1991). European and Mediterranean surveys remain an important source of inspiration (e.g. Astill and Davies 1997; Barker 1995).

Much of the challenge in interpreting field survey results lies in deconstructing and overlaying spatial patterns from different data sets. GIS (Geographic Information Systems) now hold huge potential for the presentation and interpretation of these types of results (Lock and Harris 1992) and have seen widespread adoption in UK archaeology. For example, the distribution of meadow and grassland can be examined in relation to settlement and field patterns when mapping historic landscape types (Olivier 1999: 8–12). At the site level, GPS has been used at Whitby Abbey to link local survey grids with the National Grid and so to Ordnance Survey digital data. Using GIS, stereoscopic aerial photographs of the headland and nearby coastline can all be overlain on the same mapped grids (Nenk *et al.* 1995: 261).

Advances in prospection methods and in the processing and interpretation of results are common to all periods of archaeology. Particular benefits have been brought to medieval archaeology by the development of digital mapping and plotting software, such as CAD systems, which are now used in most fabric surveys of historic buildings. The decreasing cost of three-dimensional graphics has also generated new interest in reconstruction modelling. The first fully animated tour of an archaeological model was for the Old Minster in Winchester, produced for the British Museum's 'Archaeology in Britain' exhibition in 1987. More recent projects undertaken at two Cistercian abbeys, Furness (Wood and Chapman 1992) and Kirkstall (Reilly 1992), show how visually sophisticated modelling has become, but photo-realistic visualisation can also have a serious research purpose, for example when investigating different lighting conditions within simulated medieval interiors (Brown *et al.* 1997).

On site

Archaeological fieldwork undertaken on a contractual basis now follows a staged path, beginning with a desk-based assessment of available sources and followed by field evaluation which combines invasive and non-invasive techniques, typically aerial photography, geophysics, fieldwalking, test pitting and machined trial trenches (Champion *et al.* 1995). Reports are mainly factual in content and can be used to support a planning application, a Scheduled Monument Consent or an Environmental statement (Darvill and Gerrard 1994: 157). Excavation normally only happens on a larger scale where remains cannot be preserved *in situ* and sometimes takes place even while construction progresses, as at the Central Library in Lincoln (Nenk *et al.* 1995: 228–30).

Most of the medieval archaeology reported over the past decade has been identified at the evaluation stage, much of it in narrow trial trenches or small test pits, and mostly with one aim in mind: to provide sufficient archaeological information to allow a well-reasoned and justifiable verdict to be reached on development proposals. Many such evaluations are substantial operations in their own right, involving kilometres of trenches, and they may make subtle use of suites of techniques. A recent investigation of a medieval fishery site involved intensive fieldwalking and metal detector survey on a 5 metres grid (Lucas 1998). Bulk samples for macro-botanical and micro-faunal remains were taken on a 10 metres grid. The excavated area was then machine-stripped in spits and dry sieved and a deep sondage excavated for environmental samples. Subsequent interpretation was based largely upon artefact distribution patterns. Elsewhere, phosphate analysis and soil micromorphology are just two of the techniques used to good effect to examine the detailed composition of medieval occupation debris (e.g. Crowther 1995; Milek 1997).

Appropriate methods for the study and recording of archaeology and architecture continue to be debated. Grenville (1997: 3–4) has documented the long debate over the advantages offered by differing archaeological and art/architectural history approaches to the recording of standing buildings.

Archaeology, represented by technical rigour, objectivity and pro-forma recording (Ferris 1989), has been pitched against the need for broader, more subjective consideration of cultural context and artistic merit (Fernie 1988). This tussle has rolled on for several years in articles, conferences, standards documents (RCHME 1996) and technical papers (e.g. Hurman and Steiner 1995) and was an early taste of concerns about the validity of archaeological recording methods which surfaced fully much later in the decade (e.g. Hodder 1999). There is now considerable doubt about the merit of 'value-free' observation espoused by positivists and this will doubtless lead to changes in the way excavations and buildings are recorded and interpreted in the future. Video, for example, has already been experimented with on medieval sites (Locock 1990).

Archaeological science

Despite the occasional use of archaeomagnetic dating and the promise of thermoluminescence, no single dating technique has had the same impact on later medieval archaeology as dendrochronology (Hillam 1998). Large regional samples of timbered buildings have been systematically analysed (e.g. in Kent; Pearson 1994) and the technique continues to have important implications for the dating of artefacts and sites. Dates obtained from timbers from the waterfronts at Bristol and Dublin (Nicholson and Hillam 1987), for example, led to the complete revision of previously accepted dates for Ham Green pottery. These Bristol wares had previously been dated 1240–1300 but the new dendrochronology dates pushed the start of production back to 1120 with significant implications for the dating of local sites and for trade with Ireland and Wales (Ponsford 1991).

During the 1990s the need to process bulk materials, like ceramics, quickly and accurately led to more widespread use of mineralogical analysis. At the same time, compositional analysis, such as NAA (neutron activation analysis) and the different methods of ICPS (inductively-coupled plasma spectrometry), became cheaper and were more commonly applied (Barclay 2001). Sustained programmes of scientific work on medieval artefacts, such as that by Mike Hughes at the British Museum on the major tin-glaze pottery industries in Europe (Hughes 1995), have been much rarer. Novel techniques of analysis also attracted attention, such as usage studies. For example, the first residue analyses on pots for which complete pottery profiles were available were undertaken on late Saxon/medieval pots. The identification of beeswax and animal fat among the contents showed promise for the study of medieval diet and confirmed that common vessel forms could have specific functions in the medieval household (Charters *et al.* 1995).

Animal bone specialists have continued to work on faunal assemblages recovered during the previous two decades. The major results were for towns such as medieval York (Rogers 1997; Bond and O'Connor 1999) and Lincoln

(Dobney *et al.* 1995). These dwelt on economic, industrial and social activities both within and outside the medieval town, adopting more sophisticated approaches to dating and chronology. The Lincoln report included sections on butchery, craft and industry, biometry and pathology of the wild and domestic species present. As further data accumulated so meaningful regional reviews of animal bone data became possible. In Oxford, for example, assemblages from urban areas (e.g. from Church Street; Hassall *et al.* 1984; 1989) were compared against local rural manors such as Middleton Stoney (Levitan 1983) and Faccombe Netherton (Sadler 1990) exposing economic difference and exploring urban-rural relationships (Wilson 1994).

Medieval data sets for faunal remains are woefully inadequate for some medieval monument classes. Monastic sites have produced little material (O'Connor 1993) and well-stratified material from rural sites is hard to come by. Ironically, while a great deal is understood about the medieval rural economy from historical documents, very little is known about the animals which made up the fabric of everyday country life and were not bought and sold. Future agendas must seek to correct these deficiencies (Bayley 1998). There is considerable potential in archaeologists and historians working together on their evidence (Albarella 1999) with a fuller understanding of social context (e.g. Gardiner 1997), but in the near future contributions will come from sites excavated in the 1980s rather than from more recent field-work (e.g. Albarella 1996 for West Cotton, Northants.; Albarella and Davies 1996 for Launceston Castle, Devon).

The publication of several large human bone assemblages is eagerly awaited, especially those for rural populations such as Wharram Percy churchyard where nearly 700 skeletons were recovered. Among the themes to be investigated here are demographic structures and burial practices but there is also considerable potential for comparison between the Wharram population and urban populations from York, especially for detecting variations in physique, demography and pathology (Mays 1997). Few regions can boast sufficient large-scale later medieval cemetery excavations to make regional comparison worthwhile (Daniell 1997: 143). There has also been a growing interest in forensic science, palaeopathology, diet and genetics. Exceptional in this respect was the excavation and prompt publication of a mass grave from the battle of Towton in 1461, where many individuals with horrific battle injuries seem to have died in a frenzy of hand-to-hand combat (Yorks.; Fiorato *et al.* 2000). The recovery of genetic DNA information from well-preserved thirteenth-century material from the medieval cemetery at Abingdon has longer term implications (Hagelberg *et al.* 1989). This technique will provide a significant new source of data for the study of past medieval populations as recent studies at Wharram Percy (Olivier 1999: 55) and Hulton Abbey have begun to demonstrate (Klemperer 1992).

Botanical studies can suggest living conditions, diet and resource exploit-ation and more rigorous specifications for methods of retrieval on excavations encourage excavators to explore these themes and to consult with specialists prior to undertaking their fieldwork. Some investigations do provide a broader landscape context but closely dated sequences of pollen remain a priority for most areas (e.g. Isle of May; Nenk *et al.* 1995: 273–4) and the systematic coring of medieval earthworks in order to evaluate their preservation potential seems a useful initiative (e.g. Fenwick 1997). Excavations of moated sites, such as Wood Hall (Yorks.) offer the best potential for reconstructing vegetational history, particularly where past agricultural practices are better documented (Finden-Browne 2000). Enough work has now been carried out to suggest that the survival of suitable medieval deposits is actually rather rare (Gearney *et al.* 1997), though one unexpectedly rich source of information about crops and weeds has come from the recent study of smoke-blackened thatch buried beneath later re-thatching on late medieval buildings (Letts 1999). Above all, perhaps because so many reports are produced on a site-by-site basis, this is one area of medieval archaeology which badly requires synthesis (and textbooks) so that strengths and weaknesses in the data can be acted upon. At present it would seem that we are not in a position to identify either regional or chronological variations.

Post-excavation and publication

How best to communicate its results is one dilemma which medieval archaeology shares with the discipline as a whole (e.g. Historic Scotland 1996; Olivier 1999: 74–5). Continuing worries about the format of publication were sparked off again by the price of the *Object and Economy in Medieval Winchester* in 1990. This volume retailed at £200 hardback, a price well beyond most potential purchasers, and the choice of a 1200-page, two-volume hardback format was questioned (Gaimster 1992). No solution seems ideal, given the wide range of expectations and uses for archaeological data and the rate at which technology is now moving. The London finds volumes (e.g. Egan and Pritchard 1991) suggested one alternative, by publishing related material from a wide range of sites in a single affordable softback volume, though this inevitably divorced finds from their archaeological context as well as different categories of finds from each other.

In the traditional field of academic book publication, useful series included 'The Archaeology of Medieval Britain' by the Leicester University Press series (e.g. Kenyon 1990) as well as an expanding Routledge archaeology output. Monograph series carrying medieval information were maintained by the Council for British Archaeology, the Society for Medieval Archaeology, Oxbow Books, British Archaeological Reports and by a number of units such as Wessex and York. Style has improved and better use is now made of colour (e.g. Ward 1990). Hybrid books serving both 'popular' and academic markets include those in the English Heritage and Historic Scotland/Batsford series, the new range of Oxbow and Tempus publications and some museum publications (e.g. Jennings 1992). Generally speaking, archaeology is well-placed to benefit from both electronic archiving and publication because it is a specialised, data-intensive discipline in which most data is already produced in machine-readable form (Rahtz *et al.* 1992). New initiatives include alternative publication media such as the CD-ROM (e.g. Calkins 1998 for medieval architecture) and the Internet. Some theses and project designs are already posted privately on websites and most medieval societies, units, local authorities and special interest groups maintain an Internet presence. It is still the case, however, that a great deal of the electronic data generated by archaeologists is unpublished and difficult to access, sometimes being stored in outmoded formats. Here, the role of the Archaeology Data Service (ADS) in collecting, archiving and encouraging the reuse of digital data is becoming an important one (Richards 1997) and the archives for several medieval projects can already be found at the ADS website.

Lack of publication is a cause for acute anxiety, especially since the initial cost of 'winning' the archaeological material through excavation when added to post-excavation processing had reached an average of £120,000 per cubic metre of finds by 1992 (Payne 1992)! Outstanding excavation projects of major importance such as Caldecote deserted medieval village, Glastonbury Abbey, Launceston Castle, South Witham preceptory, as well as components of the Wharram Percy and Winchester projects, have been forthcoming for many years and the extent to which this will diminish their final scholarly impact is uncertain. Today most writing-up of developer-led projects takes place on a project-by-project basis in order to comply with funding and planning requirements. The advent of standard word processing packages, desk-top publishing and laser printers allows archaeologists to produce inexpensive fieldwork reports in typescript form. Their extremely limited circulation is of some concern and the annual round-ups in *Medieval Archaeology*, CBA regional group annual listings and county annual reviews have become essential guides to recent work, complemented by the English Heritage and Bournemouth University initiative to collate the results of field evaluation work into an accessible annual database of archaeological investigations in England (e.g. Russell 2000). Summaries of work in Scotland have been published by the Council for Scottish Archaeology since 1955 and in Wales by CBA Group 2/Wales since 1961.

New threats, new funding

Cultural resource management

The advent of PPG 16 (Planning Policy Guidance Note 16: Archaeology and Planning) in November 1990 has been hailed as one of the most significant events in twentieth-century British archaeology. The high profile events in London and York which led up to the issue of new guidance have been well charted (e.g. G. J. Wainwright 1989; 2000) and, a decade later, the longer term effects are now being felt. To contrast with the situation in 1984 (Clarke 1984), in many respects archaeology is now in a much stronger position; as a conservation-led discipline the preservation of archaeological sites *in situ* is favoured over 'preservation by record' or excavation. This philosophy now permeates both Scottish and Welsh government advice and local and regional plans. At the same time, the volume of work, especially if quantified as a simple numerical count of 'interventions', has not diminished (Pagoda Projects 1992) and strategies for excavation are more fully considered and controlled. Field archaeologists can claim considerable creativity both in their use of different suites of evaluation methods and in seeking appropriate mitigation strategies. Meanwhile, the boost of funding from the private sector has released public money for other initiatives such as backlog publication.

Nonetheless, Clarke's fundamental criticism remains. Excavations are still undertaken in response to threatened redevelopment, so the excavation 'agenda' is still largely governed in volume by economic cycles affecting the construction industry and in location by the decisions of planners and developers (Biddle 1994). Some have argued that archaeology is impoverished as a result (Olivier 1996: 31–3), with technical description taking precedence over research goals leading to a conservative, anti-intellectual excavation culture (Chadwick 2000), one which is 'fundamentally uninterested in its basic purpose' (Baker 1999: 16). The preservation ideal espoused in PPG 16 seems a good idea, but nagging doubts remain about its impact on research and public support. If excavation is always to be small in scale, as much of it seems to have been over the past decade, then we might congratulate ourselves on the decrease in the rate of destruction but what will be the impact on research? The new trends are already with us. Among them a continuing surge of resource and management-related projects, an increasing weight placed on non-destructive survey, the re-visiting and quarrying of earlier archives (particularly those in electronic form), and a move towards those areas of archaeology which can (but ought not to) function independently of excavation data, such as historiography and theory.

PPG 16 was followed in 1994 by PPG 15 (Planning Policy Guidance Note 15: Planning and the Historic Environment) which has encouraged the recording of standing buildings prior to alteration and repair. As yet the two PPGs have not been enforced with equal vigour and the full impact of PPG 15 has yet to be felt. Nevertheless, one outcome has been a dramatic increase in the recording of buildings, often involving photogrammetry and dendrochronology. Among the other heritage matters which have or will have an impact on medieval archaeology are the adoption of the 1970 UNESCO Convention on trade in antiquities, the signing of the Valletta Convention, the compilation of non-statutory registers of monuments requiring special protection (e.g. battlefields, historic landscapes of Wales, parks and gardens), the 1996 Treasure Act and the subsequent Portable Antiquities Recording Scheme which provides for more comprehensive recording of metal detecting finds. All these will promote higher standards of archaeological conservation and recording.

Funding

PPG 16 enshrined fundamental changes in the way archaeology is funded. In England, while central government funding of archaeology had declined to £4.87 million in 1996–7, developers now carry the burden of cost for work related to construction projects, some £35 million in 1996–7 (Darvill and Fulton 1998). These resources are not, however, evenly spread. There is more development pressure and so more archaeological investigation in larger historic towns than there is in smaller towns or in rural areas. More archaeological work is undertaken in the south-east than it is in the north-east of England. These imbalances seem likely to continue into the foreseeable future.

The freeing up of public money administered through English Heritage has permitted a redirection of resources towards archaeological work required outside the planning process. This includes threats from natural agencies, such as the coastal erosion which revealed tile in the cliff face at Quarr Abbey (Isle of Wight) and led to the excavation of a fourteenth-century tile kiln (Nenk *et al.* 1995: 221–2), 'implications surveys' for the management and protection of landscapes and medieval monument types, such as the Buildings at Risk register launched in 1998, 'strategic projects' such as artefact reviews (e.g. Mellor 1994 for medieval ceramics), training initiatives, and the analysis and dissemination of pre-PPG 16 excavations. Though costly, this last initiative has been significant for medieval archaeology; £6.7m was spent on urban post-excavation programmes between 1992/3 and 1996/6 (English Heritage 1997: 79–82). The Greater London Publication Programme provides an excellent illustration of the way a huge volume of post-excavation and publication work can be structured and managed (Hinton and Thomas 1997).

Not all initiatives were either developer- or state-funded during the 1990s. The National Trust, for example, undertook excavation and recording when the Treasurer's House at Martock (Som.) was refurbished (Nenk *et al.* 1996: 278–9). Historic fabric surveys, usually a prelude to emergency repairs, were plentiful. Other sources of funding were provided by the Heritage Lottery, local authorities, national parks and millennium projects, including sponsorship of the second largest excavated area in Norwich (Bradley *et al.* 1999: 270). Many projects blended several sources of funding. Excavation at Guildford Castle, for example, was sponsored by Surrey County Council, Surrey Archaeological Society, the Society of Antiquaries and others (Nenk *et al.* 1992: 267). In the future the European Community is likely to be an important source of funds and the Raphael programme (budget £8.27 million for 1997) already encourages co-operation between several countries. Such programmes are likely to focus on widespread and visible monument classes, such as castles and monasteries, and will mainly address issues of public access to and awareness of cultural heritage. But, inevitably, they will also stimulate academic debate about common European phenomena during the later medieval period and, indeed, the extent to which Europe might be an appropriate unit for study (Austin 1990: 19–20).

Within higher education, the success rate of applications for funding for archaeology projects from the Arts and Humanities Research Board (AHRB) and its predecessors fell steadily. Among the medieval projects which met with favour were studies of the cemeteries of London's medieval religious houses, English place-names and the digitalisation of photographic archives of medieval stained glass. The Whittlewood Project on rural settlement is one of very few recent initiatives which involve new fieldwork. Overall, levels of practical involvement by universities in medieval archaeology seem to be dropping away due in part to the emphasis now being placed upon rapid cycles of publication and a rise in academic bureaucracy. Similar concerns were expressed for the funding of science-based archaeology after responsibility was transferred to the Natural Environment Research Council (NERC) in the mid-1990s (Jubb 2000).

There are no agreed national research agendas for archaeology. For the medieval period the statement of the period Society remains relevant (SMA 1987), but should now be read in conjunction with English Heritage's period-based objectives set out in *Exploring our Past* (1991a) together with an updated agenda (English Heritage 1997). Similar kinds of policy and achievement documents were issued in Scotland (e.g. Barclay 1997) and Wales (CADW 1994), but these are far from the only guidance available. A recent survey of research frameworks was able to gather some sixty-plus documents specific to the medieval period, more than for any other period (Olivier 1996). They range from local agendas (FWA 1993) to thematic ones (e.g. for rural settlement; MSRG 1996). That they should exist at all must reflect the vitality of the subject but their numbers might also suggest a marked anxiety within the profession about the direction of current research, or the lack of it, and an urgent wish for control. There are signs, however, of a shift away from this 'top down' approach. The regional assessments of archaeological resource currently underway are a promising opportunity for medieval archaeology (e.g. for eastern counties; Glazebrook 1997) and, if they are successful, should put in place a tiered structure of regional and national priorities which reflects better the plurality of the subject.

Threats and responses

The need to improve archaeological resource management in towns was first recognised in the 1960s and 1970s (Chapters 4 and 5) and has been given priority again in the 1990s. Historic Scotland have worked on a range of initiatives aimed at identifying excavation priorities, minimising the backlog of unpublished urban sites and, through the Scottish Burgh Survey, improving information available to planners and curators (Barclay 1997). Similarly, English Heritage commissioned three pilot projects on larger urban areas at Cirencester, Durham and York (Darvill and Gerrard 1994; Lowther *et al.* 1993; Ove Arup and Partners 1991) which set out some possible ways forward and coverage has now been extended to Bristol, Lincoln and a number of other historic towns. These 'intensive urban surveys' collated the results of archaeological work, engineering boreholes, documentary data, historic maps, much of it gathered over the past thirty years during rescue projects, into a consistent format. The debt owed to earlier work on urban archaeology by Biddle and Carver, amongst others, is obvious in the procedures and nomenclatures adopted. However, the results are not only of 'strategic' use when evaluating development proposals but also of considerable academic value (e.g. Stocker and Vince 1997 for Lincoln), particularly where no earlier surveys or Victoria County History coverage exist (e.g. Ches.; Olivier 1999: 17–19).

Smaller towns have been covered by 'extensive urban surveys' employing a slightly different range of techniques developed during pilot projects in Shropshire and in Hereford and Worcester (Dalwood 2000). The Central Marches Historic Towns Survey (1992–6) drew particularly upon plan-form analysis (see Chapter 5), pinpointing areas of archaeological sensitivity as a platform for planning decisions and conservation policies. The detailed analysis of a range of sources has completely revised our understanding of the archaeological potential of some towns, particularly those which suffered large-scale redevelopment in the 1960s and 1970s where the archaeological potential had previously been assumed to be low. As a result, the number of recommendations for archaeological investigations in smaller towns has risen, in one case doubling the recommendations for evaluations prior to the determination of planning applications and tripling recommendations for developer-funded watching briefs over a three-year period (Dalwood and Atkin 1998 for the County of Hereford and Worcester). Over time, and as similar urban surveys get underway elsewhere (e.g. Essex, Cheshire; Olivier 1999: 93–4), this upswing in archaeological work in smaller towns will have a considerable academic impact too.

Some 'resource' surveys targeted understudied parts of the landscape. One of these is the intertidal zone where a wealth of archaeology has been discovered along the foreshore of coastline estuaries, sometimes with notable medieval discoveries (e.g. the thirteenth-century Magor Pill boat from south Wales; Nayling 1996). Wetland projects have mostly had a prehistoric focus but the potential of the medieval landscape has not been excluded (e.g. Fenwick 2000 for the Hull valley). Field survey for the Fenland Project (1976–88) in eastern England covered a massive 420,000 hectares and was coupled with aerial photographic work and a wide-ranging environmental programme. The results were multiperiod but there was abundant evidence of medieval activity and four medieval sites were included in the excavation programme which followed (Hall and Coles 1994; Coles and Hall 1997). Medieval salterns, a 'fishing station', a port at Downham Hythe and two fishing platforms on Whittlesea Mere were evaluated in order to inform programmes for their future management (Lucas 1998).

Among the important publications which drew attention to under-protected aspects of the medieval resource was David Hall's work on the open field systems of Northamptonshire (1993), commissioned by the Monuments Protection Programme and now extended to the whole of the Midlands. By comparing aerial photographs taken in the late 1940s against the modern situation, this study calculated the very rapid rate of loss of ridge-and-furrow in a single county as a result of changes in agricultural practice. The report laid down criteria for the selection of areas of preservation, calling for new legislation as a matter of urgency and identifying those townships with the best survival for future management and preservation (Olivier 1999: 85–6). Most monument-based resource studies of this kind have academic as well as strategic implications. For example, the Nottinghamshire Village Earthwork Survey resulted in a more than 200 per cent increase in the numbers of known earthworks vulnerable to infill in villages and hamlets (Bishop and Challis 1999), while another MPP initiative is ensuring that regional diversity is reflected in the stock of medieval settlement sites recommended for protection (Stocker *et al.* 1993).

The Dyfed Archaeological Trust's Historic Settlement Project (1992–5) is one of a number of broad-based local resource assessments undertaken across Britain. These enhance existing records, identify sites at risk within a particular region and suggest fieldwork strategies (Kissock 1992). In Cornwall, for example, 'Rapid Identification Survey' comprised desk-based survey followed by a brief but intensive period of fieldwork in one selected area. This proved cost-effective in the identification of new sites such as shrunken and shifted medieval settlement (Nenk *et al.* 1995: 191–2). Work of a similar nature has been undertaken for designated landscapes such as Areas of Outstanding Natural Beauty (e.g. Ellis 1992), Environmentally Sensitive Areas (e.g. for Scotland, Hingley and Foster 1994; the Breckland Archaeological Survey, Nenk *et al.* 1997: 285–6), and areas included in Countryside Stewardship and the 'Survey Grants for Presentation' scheme run by English Heritage (e.g. Bradley and Gaimster 2000: 311; **Box 6.1**).

Evolving roles and new groups

Today there are more archaeologists than ever before. Numbers within the profession are growing and are expected to continue to do so. Adding together all the consultants, contractors, local government posts, universities and colleges, national heritage societies, museums and employees of archaeological societies, there were estimated to be 4,425 professional archaeologists in the UK in 1999. Most of these archaeologists, with the possible exception

Box 6.1 Auditing the resource

Today the national archaeological database recognises over 60,000 monuments of later medieval date (AD 1000–1540) in England alone, roughly 21 per cent of all the archaeological monuments known in the country. The highest densities occur in towns and cities, but there are rural 'hot-spots' in the north Pennines, the west Midlands and on Dartmoor, all areas where recent surveys have raised the numbers of sites recorded (Darvill and Fulton 1998). Initial research suggests some 6,500 excavations on later medieval sites (RCHME 1991), so perhaps around 8 per cent of known medieval monuments have been investigated in all. For moated sites, for example, 684 have been 'excavated' in some way, about 12 per cent of the total of 5,532 recorded sites (figures for 1996; Trow 1996: 93). 'Census' or 'audit' information of this kind helps to gauge where the archaeology is, what threats it might be prone to, and how much of it can be protected. Overall, well excavated and published sites are probably rather fewer than we lead ourselves to believe.

A complex hierarchy of legislation, guidance and designations identifies a handful of internationally recognised World Heritage Sites of later medieval date such as the Tower of London and Canterbury Cathedral. In 1995 about 3,500 later medieval monuments were 'scheduled' or protected under the terms of the Ancient Monuments and Archaeological Areas Act 1979 and so recognised to be of national archaeological importance. This is approximately 5 per cent of the total number of known later medieval monuments; only Bronze Age sites make up a higher proportion of scheduled sites. However, some monument types are better protected than others; 89 per cent of all Welsh castles are now scheduled (Avent 2000). In England, the Monuments Protection Programme has been reconsidering the list of scheduled sites to ensure a balance of protected monuments by type, period and region (Darvill et al. 1987).

Figure 6.7 Seventeenth-century and earlier manor house near Worth Maltravers in Dorset. Here being surveyed by one of the MARS field survey teams. (Darvill and Fulton 1998). (Photo: MARS Archive).

of some holders of university posts who might be specialists fixed in another field, regularly encounter medieval archaeology. However, a generous estimate of how many of these 4,425 individuals consult primary medieval data and read regularly on this topic might be between 300 and 500 individuals. If recent surveys are anything to go by they are more likely to be male, in their mid-thirties and poorly paid (Aitchison 1999).

With the integration of archaeology into the planning process the vast majority of all fieldwork done today is undertaken by commercial units. Archaeology has become more 'professional', with more structured approaches to project planning (English Heritage 1991b), employment and management (e.g. Cooper 1995), quality, regulation and standards and commercial practice (e.g. Darvill and Atkins 1991). Less positively, a great deal of excavation is routine and largely standardised (Faulkner 2000), contracts are often short, managers may go many months without a trowel in their hands and soon find that their contribution to the broader development of the discipline cannot easily be maintained. The absence of a research culture is keenly felt and must be reflected in the quality and range of work undertaken in the field.

Effectively, within the last twenty-five years the curatorial role undertaken by national statutory agencies such as English Heritage has been devolved down to local authority level. A pivotal role in the 'archaeological management cycle' is now played by archaeologists working in local authorities, who scrutinise planning applications, draw up specifications for projects and invigilate standards of fieldwork (ACAO 1993). Since they are at the forefront of archaeological investigation they will have an important role to play in the way research goals for medieval archaeology are reached in the future. In addition, the Sites and Monuments Records, besides providing information for planning purposes, have evolved into an essential research tool to complement the National Monuments Record (RCHME 1993). Some counties have made abbreviated versions of their records available on online.

All the national agencies have experienced significant change over the past decade. In the face of budgetary restrictions and changing patterns of funding brought about by PPG 16, money has been redirected towards what have been termed 'strategic' considerations and we have seen some of the impact of this realignment. At the same time, greater public accountability means that more information must be made widely available and all costs carefully justified. As one example of the former, the Royal Commission on Historical Monuments of Scotland placed their Sites and Monuments Record online in 1998, a free research tool which is now available the world over. As an example of the latter, in April 1999 the Royal Commission on Historical Monuments (England) was integrated with English Heritage (HBMCE), and, in the final few months of the twentieth century, English Heritage became the single lead body for the historic environment in England. This move is significant in making the curation of architecture and archaeology in England more coherent and it will inevitably place further emphasis on making the past accessible, on education and 'access', and providing information to the public. Academically, the benefits of this move remain to be assessed in the longer term.

The 36 staff in Departments of Archaeology in 1995 who identified themselves as having later medieval research interests (Heyworth 1995) had, by 2001, grown again to 45 with 11 professors among them (data compiled from higher education internet sites), a threefold increase since 1979. This is only a small percentage of the 371 archaeologists registered as research-active in the 1996 Research Assessment Exercise (Jubb 2000) but most institutions retain at least one member of staff in Archaeology covering the later medieval period with more significant groupings of scholars, sometimes in several different departments, to be found at the Universities of Birmingham, Bristol, Durham, Leicester and York. These universities, together with Cardiff and Glasgow, also offer related specialist MA courses in medieval archaeology but they are far from being the only higher education providers with strong medieval teaching (e.g. King Alfred's College, Winchester). A wider perspective on the teaching of medieval archaeology in higher education has been provided by the European Symposium of Teachers of Medieval Archaeology (ESTMA) which met at Budapest and Caen, following an inaugural meeting in Lund in 1990.

While academic presence is largely healthy, some topics receive only cursory attention. Vernacular architecture, for example, is barely touched upon by most universities while many seem disinclined to undertake fieldwork or post-excavation work. The cost of practical work, both in money and time, the difficulties of integrating excavation into a modular teaching programme, and the trend towards 'world' and therefore international archaeology all provide partial explanations. Long-term excavation and post-excavation projects do not chime well with the five-year cycle of the Research Assessment Exercise, through which academic 'productivity' is periodically 'measured'. That there were only two PhDs on aspects of medieval pottery underway in British universities in 2001 (Gutiérrez pers. comm.) graphically reflects the current separation of theory from practice and the feelings of fragmentation felt by many both inside and outside universities (Olivier 1996: 23–5). For a sub-discipline which is dependent for so much of its best research on the interplay of ideas *between* departments, some medieval archaeologists seem surprisingly isolated (Albarella 1999). Few have the courage to attempt broad synthesis, Hinton's well-balanced textbook being a rarity (1990).

It is one of the ironies of British field archaeology that, while the public may pay for developer-led archaeology through higher property prices and have so often taken an important role in projects in the past, they are now more excluded than they have ever been from participation in fieldwork. Not all fieldwork projects exclude the amateur workforce. Many have continued to build upon the traditions established by the Leicestershire Museums Service which particularly focused on recording medieval earthworks and landscapes (e.g. Hartley 1984). The Shapwick Project (Som.)

made 'community archaeology' the core of its approach (1989–9; Aston and Gerrard 1999) while work in Hanbury (Worcs.; Dyer 1991) drew on the enthusiasm of extra-mural classes to record earthworks, undertake field-walking and compile historical information. Some excavation projects have also encouraged local people to work alongside professionals, as at Wood Hall Moated Manor (Yorks.) and the Hyde Abbey Community Archaeology Project in Winchester. Generally though, public commitment is no longer so actively fostered through extra-mural teaching departments, many of which have been closed down or absorbed. Medieval archaeology has been fortunate to have had so many prominently placed extra-mural lecturers and course co-ordinators (e.g. Aston, Barker, Fowler, and Rowley) but award-bearing certificates, part-time and distance-learning courses have not attracted the same numbers.

Nevertheless, public interest in later medieval archaeology continues to manifest itself in many ways. Newspaper coverage in the *Independent*, *Guardian* and *Times* has been partly responsible for the upturn in public interest in archaeology in the past few years and the public appeal of the Middle Ages has never been confined to scholarly debate but has a long tradition in literature, television and cinema (**Box 6.2**). Mass popular culture is precisely many people's point of entry into the subject, however hard archaeologists may try to distance themselves from this side of their subject.

In 1998 three of the top ten tourist attractions in England were medieval monuments: the Tower of London (2,551,459 visitors), Canterbury Cathedral and Windsor Castle (English Tourism Council web site). Unregistered visits to parish churches must account for many more. Innovative new public attractions include the opening of the ARC (Archaeological Resource Centre) by the York Archaeological Trust in 1990 and Barley Hall in 1992. This late medieval building in the centre of York has been carefully returned to its appearance in *c.*1483 by removing all later features (Addyman 2000). While the public have been appreciative and much was learnt from the reconstruction exercise, the scheme was controversial, re-opening discussion about the principles of preservation established by SPAB in the late nineteenth century (Chapter 2). Elsewhere, medieval sites are used in a wide range of educational activities (e.g. Copeland 1990) where, generally speaking, rather less weight of interpretation is now placed upon the visitor. Kenilworth Castle (Warwicks.) houses an Education Centre which provides sheltered teaching spaces, audio-visual equipment and even replica costumes and models. Different activities explore standing structures, archaeological and documentary evidence and encourage children to exchange findings and make independent observations, all in a safe and spacious environment (Hancock 1991). The presentation of medieval monuments is now far removed from the approach adopted by Peers in the first half of the twentieth century, but because so many monuments were taken into guardianship during that period and 'cleared', medieval archaeology will always remain trapped in its

Box 6.2 A popular past?

The back catalogue of film with a medieval theme ranges widely from costume romance and epic drama to comedy, 'sword and sorcery sci-fi fantasy' and Disney (Harty 1999). Some characters and events, notably the private and political life of Henry VIII, Robin Hood and the discovery of the Americas, are revisited regularly, most successfully in *A Man for all Seasons* (1966). Fewer came lower budget than *The Black Knight* (1954), more epic than *El Cid* (1961), funnier than *Monty Python and the Holy Grail* (1975), more absurd than *Captain Kronos – Vampire Hunter* (1972) or more portentous than Ingmar Bergman's *The Seventh Seal* (1956). Credit for a more convincing representation of medieval life is due to *The Name of the Rose* (1986), a medieval whodunnit adapted from Umberto Eco's book (1984) of the same name which struck a chord in academic circles as well as being advertised on New York subway cars (Coletti 1988), and *Le Retour de Martin Guerre* (1982) which portrayed rural life in mid-sixteenth-century France. Genuine medieval monuments do occasionally figure, such as Wardour Castle (Wilts.) in *Robin Hood: Prince of Thieves* (1991), but medieval detail can rarely be relied upon. Unsurprisingly perhaps, medieval archaeologists are rarely seen themselves. Sean Connery's portrayal in *Indiana Jones and the Last Crusade* (1989) was a less honest portrayal of a normal working day than the 1987 screen version of J. L. Carr's novel *A Month in the Country*.

Time-travel seems to offer the best possibility of exploring the medieval world. An unpromising start was made by the time-travelling call-girls in Roger Corman's odyssey *The Undead* (1957), the set being an abandoned Los Angeles supermarket filled with fog and plastic shrubbery. Modest improvements were made for the time-travelling dwarfs in *Time Bandits* (1981), the time-travelling machos in *Highlander* (1986) and a time-travelling discount-store employee in *Army of Darkness* (1993) who finds himself stranded in the thirteenth century with only his car, his shotgun and a chainsaw. In *The Navigator: A Medieval Odyssey* (1988) a Cumbrian mining community attempt to evade the Black Death only to find they have travelled both forward in time and to the other side of the world to modern New Zealand. A parallel is drawn between the horrors of medieval plague and probable modern nuclear Armageddon. This kind of ploy, in which a medieval celluloid past is made relevant to a modern political and social situation, is a popular one. Best remembered are Olivier's patriotic call-to arms in *Fire over England* (1936) and *Henry V* (1944), or more recently *Braveheart* (1995). Joan of Arc has also personified French patriotism and resistance, against both foreign occupation (in Marco de Gastyne's 1916 version) and cultural takeover (in Luc Besson's 2000 version, *The Story of Joan of Arc*).

There are several widely-differing versions of the Middle Ages from which different groups take their past; the academic world represents only one small audience. Unlike language theorists like Umberto Eco (1986), medieval archaeologists have yet to address the issues raised by 'alternative writings' nor have they sought to consider the upswing in public interest in their period (Brown 1991; Cantor 1991: 37). In contrast to prehistory, the practice of medieval archaeology has attracted little attention and serious attempts to reconstruct a

Figure 6.8 The Grail legend and the Knights of the Round Table are popular subjects for cinematic make-over. They offer romance and the archaeology contributes the scenery (Scottish in this case) for the action. *Monty Python and the Holy Grail* (1975) blends a debunking of 'medievalism' in the movies with comment on scholarly narratives of the medieval past, not to mention some memorable comedy. (Photo: British Film Institute Stills, Posters and Designs).

medieval setting for social life are few and far between. There is no medieval Butzer. Instead, the medieval past is more often linked with the present in order to reflect upon modern practice; a use which should not surprise us given the frequency with which the Middle Ages have been revisited in the past for precisely that purpose.

Television is often a key source of information for the general public. History, we read, is the new 'gardening' for schedulers and both *Meet the Ancestors* and *Time Team* have regularly figured medieval subjects. The latter, first broadcast on Channel 4 in 1994, has had considerable impact on public understanding of aims and methods in archaeology and is watched regularly by 3.5 million viewers. By the end of 2001, eighty-one *Time Team* programmes had been made, of which twenty-seven had a later medieval theme. However 'vulgar' some archaeologists might find the commercial appeal of television, it has had the considerable virtue of making archaeology more accessible and less academically exclusive.

own conservation history even though modern approaches are less uniform. The recent conservation of Wigmore Castle (Heref.) reflects new philosophies of repair and display in which intervention has been minimised and the ruinous appeal of the site deliberately retained, for example (Coppack 1999).

The numbers of new groups starting up has slowed, though in 1990 two new Special Interest Groups were founded within the Institute of Field Archaeologists. The IFA Finds Group has considered guidelines and professional standards in finds work in the light of the rise of developer funding (Buteux 1990) while the Buildings Special Interest Group also encourages good practice (Wood 1994). Outside the IFA, many 'interested' members of the general public continue to be members of the period society or one of the many medieval special interest groups. These groups, through their committees, can have an important input into national and regional research agendas, just as the Medieval Settlement Research Group have advised English Heritage's Monuments Protection Programme on descriptions of medieval settlement. An over-arching role continues to be played by the Society for Medieval Archaeology. The conference in November 1996 at the British Museum, run jointly with the Society for Post-Medieval Archaeology was among the more influential of the decade, examining the sometimes over-rigid divisions between 'medieval' and 'modern' through wide-ranging discussions of daily life, artefacts, diet and housing (Gaimster and Stamper 1997). The Society also has a part to play in co-ordinating the Medieval Europe conference (first held in York in 1992 and in Bruges in 1997) and its members participated in the Ruralia conference (first held in Prague in 1995) which serves those with an interest in medieval rural settlement in Europe. International links continue to build with North American and Canadian organisations, notably the Medieval Institute at Kalamazoo and the Center for Medieval and Early Renaissance Studies at Binghamton.

National groups such as RESCUE and the CBA continue to play important roles, articulating between all of the groups mentioned above, between archaeologists of varying period interests and between archaeologists and the outside world. In 1996 the CBA established a single UK-wide Research and Conservation Committee to replace its specialist committees and continues its role as lobbyist, publisher, in education and in advancing best practice through its Practical Handbook series. Later medieval archaeology figures in every one of these important initiatives.

Challenging concepts and ideas

Even as some medieval archaeologists were toying with 'processual' approaches in the late 1970s and early 1980s, alternative philosophies were being applied elsewhere in the social sciences. Human geographers and historians attacked the massive scale of data-collection, the application of inappropriate and complex mathematical methods and called for greater behavioural emphasis and less consensual views of society (e.g. Herbert and Johnston 1978; Stone 1979). Some archaeologists followed suit, broadly mimicking the same criticisms and experimenting with a wide range of theoretical agendas, many of them derived from social and critical theory such as structuralism, feminism and gender studies, neo-Marxism and phenomenology (Johnson 1999). These widely differing approaches were grouped together by archaeologists under the label of 'post-processualist' or 'interpretative'.

The first inkling of this debate spilling over into medieval archaeology was a short paper by Steve Driscoll in the *Scottish Archaeological Review* (1984). This amounted to a critique of what was described as Rahtz's 'casual and misdirected' theoretical stance and his call for 'New Medieval Archaeology'. Driscoll's promotion of alternative structuralist readings of historical archaeology was novel. He specifically mentioned Henry Glassie's *Folkhousing in Middle Virginia* (1975) as a model and pointed out just how rarely medieval archaeology had been employed to 'illuminate ritual behaviour or medieval ideology'. In the very next paper in the same volume, Rahtz (1984) claimed that his only wish had been to 'set the ball rolling' and that it was his 'job to make provocative statements'. His tone seems to vary from wounded innocence to a more robust defence of his position based on huge experience, but the overall flavour was of 'open and friendly debate'.

In response to these conceptual rustlings, the great mass of medieval archaeologists remained theoretically inert. The 1986 Theoretical Archaeology Group (TAG) conference did include a session entitled 'This is Medieval Archaeology?' which resulted in a set of six papers, again published in the *Scottish Archaeological Review*, and provocatively introduced by Duncan Brown (1988). The papers were offered partly in the spirit of an exciting remedy to what were (once again) perceived as the safe but dull musings of some members of the Society for Medieval Archaeology. Similarly, in Rahtz's account of events at the 1986 World Archaeological Congress at Southampton he portrayed himself as being sidelined in 'descriptive and particularistic' medieval sessions while 'mind-boggling papers and discussions on subjects of real relevance to the study of the human past' took place elsewhere (Ucko 1987: 180–2). Medieval archaeology once again found itself cast in the role of stranger at the party and, predictably, frustration was vented in print. The most forceful statements were made in an introductory foreword to a volume in the *One World Archaeology* series (Ucko 1990) in which medieval archaeologists were accused of complacency and of peddling an 'historically dominated programme of research design':

> Without significant change in the nature and aims of medieval archaeological enquiry, it seems at least questionable whether it should really remain accepted within the mainstream of the archaeological discipline.
>
> (Ucko 1990: xii)

It was promised that contents of the volume which followed would cause 'shudders . . . through the breasts . . . of those who currently feel protected by . . . their attitudes to the all but sanctified pre-eminence of the written record' (Ucko 1990: xii). In response, some medieval archaeologists, mildly irritated at being accused of having their heads in the theoretical sand once again and not recognising this gloomy prognosis, politely ignored the taunts. No published response was made. Most others missed out on this offer of 'overdue emancipation' partly because of the high price of the volume in question and partly because of its place of publication. That quite another response might have been voiced had the foreword and the two papers which followed it appeared in *Medieval Archaeology* says much about the conservative choice of reading for most practitioners at the time. It also reflected a widely-held view that previous approaches were not wrong, merely different and, at worst, no longer fashionable.

Two substantial and theoretically explicit articles in the *From the Baltic to the Black Sea* edited volume (Austin and Alcock 1990) were among the first wave of articles in the late 1980s to promote post-processual ideas (Austin 1990; Austin and Thomas 1990). They remain key polemical texts but other explicit applications were also emerging at exactly the same time. Among these was Pam Graves' paper on the use of space in English parish churches (Graves 1989). Her text which, tellingly, was first presented as a paper at an inter-disciplinary conference on social space held in Denmark in 1987, acknow-ledged the advisory role of a prehistorian (John Barrett), as well as the writing of social theorists. In the same year the TAG conference in Newcastle held two sessions entitled 'The Social Archaeology of Houses' and 'Making Sense of Space' which proved to be the precursor to an influential set of edited papers (Samson 1990). The broad spectrum of influences at play is also apparent from two summaries, one by Harold Mytum (1989) on theoretical approaches to monastic archaeology, and the other by John Moreland (1991) on the wider possibilities of medieval archaeology. This last article set out very clearly the main criticisms of 'New Archaeology', its promotion of an objective past, objectively recorded, its lack of anthropological perspective and failure to recognise either the active role of individuals or material culture.

Broadly speaking, the new influences operating on writing in later medieval archaeology came from four directions. First, some read prehistoric texts and were persuaded by new currents in theoretical development which had already been alive in other parts of the discipline for some years (e.g. the writing of Barrett, Bradley, Shanks, Tilley, Thomas and others). This was as true for postgraduates as it was for their lecturers. Second, historical archae-ologists from the United States including Deetz, Glassie, Leone, and Yentsch were by now more widely read and their anthropological, ethnographical and sociological concerns have been increasingly reflected in the writing of British scholars (e.g. Johnson 1996: 14–17). Third, as we have seen, not all medieval archaeologists were atheoretical and a minority now began to read social theory for themselves and became conversant with key texts at first hand (e.g. Bourdieu 1977; Giddens 1984), quickly finding parallel debates underway in other countries, in Scandinavia for example (Andersson *et al.* 1997). Finally, as the rejection of positivism became more widespread, medieval archaeologists came into contact with historians, art historians, museums curators and other colleagues with related interests in multiple interpretations, gender issues, etc.

Post-processual influences and cognitive approaches have become steadily more powerful during the course of the decade. A list of positive initiatives might include a greater interest in disadvantaged and dominated groups, a fuller appreciation of the active role of material culture in moulding social relations, a greater emphasis on meaning and a growing awareness of the role of the medieval past in modern society (**Box 6.3**). But to be successful, theory cannot be a separate branch of medieval archaeology, as it seemed to be treated at the Medieval Europe conference in Bruges in 1997, for example. Impact is needed in mainstream journals and, significantly, in 1999 *Medieval Archaeology* carried five articles with strong theoretical underpinning, on buildings, castles, art history, ethnicity and another on conceptual terminology. Several of these papers had been presented in other arenas such as the Theoretical Archaeology Group and the Society for Medieval Archaeology conference in Glasgow in 1997. Each raised substantial issues and made use of different perspectives which can be best illustrated by examining a selection of common themes.

Identity and society

Neo-Marxist approaches place class struggle and strategies of power at the centre of theoretical explanation (Hodder 1986: 59–61), emphasising social inequality, ethnicity, domination, non-conformity and gender, while focusing upon 'disenfranchised' and 'liminal' groups as a counterweight to dominant medieval ideologies. These topics have had some airing in historical texts (e.g. Goodich 1998; Richards 1990), but have not so far been fully explored through archaeological evidence (e.g. Jones 1997). Nevertheless, an interest in the fuller diversity of late medieval life has been more fully reflected in new agendas for fieldwork of all kinds. Church archaeologists, for example, have recently invited more detailed consideration of religious practice 'on the margins', that is activity *outside* the major parish churches at chapels and cult centres such as holy wells (Rosser 1996). This tension between authority and dissent, between conformism and individualism, is one which might be illuminated through studies of medieval material culture. Such studies are likely to recognise 'agency' more fully and the ability of the individual to influence events, rather than generalising too broadly about social groups.

The archaeology of particular ethnic groups in later medieval England has also been the subject of a number of studies. The excavation of the Jewish

Box 6.3 Middle Ages, modern politics

Even in the recent past, later medieval archaeology has been at the mercy of contemporary politics. The timing of the raising of the Tudor warship the *Mary Rose* in 1982, for example, at a low point in the political fortunes of the Thatcher government during the Falklands War, did not go unnoticed (Wright 1985). Medieval heritage can still be a powerful symbol in nationalist narratives. In Scotland, the site of the battle of Bannockburn was the rallying point of the Scottish National Party from the 1950s until 1981, 'an icon of Scottish nationhood' which has since been adopted by more radical nationalists and militarist-religious groups (McCrone *et al.* 1995). The Stone of Destiny, a symbol of Caledonian nationhood removed from Scotland by the English King Edward I in 1296, was stolen from Westminster Abbey on Christmas morning 1950. Police roadblocks and border patrols failed to prevent it crossing back into Scotland and it was two weeks before the stone was located at Arbroath Abbey. As a sop to greater Scottish political autonomy the Stone was finally returned to Edinburgh Castle in 1996. Even local feelings can ride high, as Historic Scotland discovered when campaigns began to have the casket allegedly containing the heart of Robert the Bruce returned to Melrose Abbey after it was removed by archaeologists to Edinburgh. The casket was reburied at Melrose in June 1999.

A very different kind of debate was inspired by the fire in the Upper Ward of Windsor Castle in November 1992 which destroyed 9,000 square metres. The five-year restoration project was billed as the largest-ever at £37 million. The fire provided new opportunities for archaeological investigation and fabric survey (Brindle and Kerr 1997) but it also sparked rows about royal fire insurance and tax bills as well as provoking a crisis about the possible role of modern architecture in the reinstatement. In the event a (typically British?) compromise was reached when five of the nine principal rooms affected were reinstated as they had been before the fire and new designs were called for in the remaining areas.

cemetery at Jewbury on the north-east side of York (Lilley *et al.* 1994) not only revealed more about the topography of Jewish communities (Isserlin 1992) but also provoked discussion about the distinctiveness of burial practice and population characteristics. This raised questions about how ethnic identity might have been expressed or repressed and the extent to which such aspirations might be reflected in the archaeological record (Jones 1997). While Schofield (1992) has drawn attention to the distinctive stone housing in medieval jewries as an example of a statement of group membership by immigrant groups, other forms of material culture, such as pottery imports, do not seem to have been adopted as 'badges' of ethnic identity (Gutiérrez 2000: 188–94). The situation is a complex one, but it is already clear that the selection of material culture, whether house form or pottery, is not always used as an expression of difference.

The study of ethnicity has emerged as a feature of archaeology via feminist theory and women's studies. Until quite recently, most later medieval archaeologists ignored the issue in their writing of a 'gender-neutral past' (Gilchrist 1997), in spite of contributions in the related fields of social and feminist history (e.g. Hanawalt 1986). Nevertheless, a series of influential studies by Roberta Gilchrist on monasteries (e.g. 1988; 1994) has demonstrated the potential of available sources for the medieval period (Figure 6.9). She has argued for the influence of gender on the form and development of monastic buildings, as well as on their symbolic content and iconography. Aside from these exclusive 'gender domains', she has shown how gender, social status and age might impact more widely upon contemporary experience, for example in

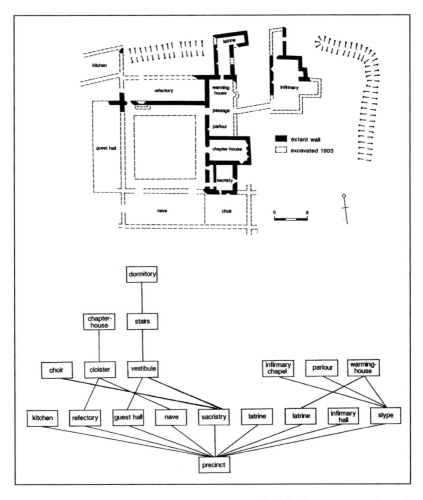

Figure 6.9 Formal spatial analysis of the nunnery at Burnham (Beds.). The rooms were located at four levels of access from the precinct, with the nuns' dormitory located in the deepest, most inaccessible space. (Gilchrist 1994: figure 68).

life in castles (Gilchrist 1999b: 109–45). This analysis, while it is grounded in a wide reading of archaeological and documentary evidence, demonstrates how far medieval archaeologists have crossed over in their reading into cognate areas such as history of art (e.g. Binski 1996), medicine (e.g. Rawcliffe 1995) and religious studies (e.g. Bynum 1987). Gender studies can no longer be equated with feminist critiques, nor do they necessarily seek to promote the role of women in the past, rather they are concerned with wider social definitions of gender which embrace both male and female roles.

This ambition to make the 'invisible' players visible again is one of the themes of post-processualist approaches (Scott 1997). However, it does not only embrace the significance of female agency, it might also include the very young, the infirm, and the old. Here debates in later medieval archaeology currently lag behind, though that is beginning to change (Scott 1999: 120–2). Large exhibitions of medieval and later toys were held in London in 1996 and in Stratford upon Avon in 1997 (Egan 1996, 1997) and placed childhood artefacts into a wider family and household context, for example. As medieval archaeologists come to realise how incomplete their scholarship has been and adopt new analytical categories for their work, more research on the fuller diversity of medieval life will surely follow.

Artefacts and meaning

The majority of analyses of medieval artefacts are concerned with questions of dating and provenance. Recent reactions against this restricted agenda show a shift towards behavioural modes of study which first developed in psychology and later found applications in human geography in the mid-1960s (Herbert and Johnston 1978: 16). The pedigree of these recent trends in later medieval archaeology is varied. A focus upon the individual, the subjective, and the 'lived worlds' of experience strongly echoes the interests of earlier historians, Eileen Power among them (Chapter 3), and would include, for example, John Keegan's moving and remarkable account of the battle of Agincourt (Keegan 1976: 79–116). At the same time, renewed interest in these themes has depended for its vitality less upon the direct influence of history or geography, but more upon broader discussions relevant to archaeology as a whole, often held at Theoretical Archaeology Group conferences (Cumberpatch and Blinkhorn 1997).

One aim of this approach has been to try to perceive objects as they might originally have been experienced and engaged with in the home. This 'phenomenological' perspective stresses the physical attributes of medieval artefacts and their environments; the colour, texture and decoration of glass, pottery, textiles, wood and so on (Cumberpatch 1997a). Inventories provide unrivalled detail for the use of historic artefacts in the domestic environment, though they are mostly sixteenth to eighteenth century in date (e.g. Shammas 1990; Weatherill 1996). The artefacts found on archaeological sites are thought of against this colourful backdrop of cloths, bedding and cushions and exactly how different artefacts might have looked under different lighting conditions can now be visualised more easily with the aid of three-dimensional modelling of medieval interiors (e.g. Brown *et al.* 1997). It is clear that lighting conditions, for example, might have affected the way in which medieval objects in the home were seen and designed. This is not an aspect of the medieval past which has hitherto been considered by archaeologists, though it is an approach familiar enough to art historians.

At the household level it must be admitted that our understanding of the ways in which artefacts were deployed remains crude. It is rare for an excavator to claim that a particular collection of historic artefacts was assembled in a certain suite of rooms, rarer still that household items are actually *in situ* (Beresford 1979; Margeson 1993). In some medieval buildings, activities would have taken place on the upper floors which are lost to the excavator. Many artefacts, particularly the more valuable or the most cared for, have been removed or recycled. Documents too have their idiosyncrasies, of course, some inventories mis-identify objects or judged them of too little value to be listed at all. Nevertheless, the broad current of these new studies must be welcome; to seek insight into social practice through the archaeological data rather than to focus exclusively on dating and typology.

Post-processual studies emphasise that material culture, usually artefacts or buildings, should be thought of as a 'text' which can be 'read' as a record of past social discourse. The role of signs and symbols is stressed as a means of conveying messages and meaning, so that material culture is seen as central to the playing out of social relationships. In medieval archaeology, the extent to which different colours and designs might have carried 'meaning' has been much debated over the past few years, particularly in the field of pottery studies (e.g. Gaimster and Nenk 1997: 175). These studies employ archaeological, historical and art historical sources to consider the symbolic role of ceramics in the home, 'the ideological matrix in which they performed' (Gaimster 1997b). One recent application has investigated the possible religious associations of the decorative colour schemes on medieval imports of decorated Mediterranean pottery (Gutiérrez 2000). The reinterpretation of Islamic objects found in the medieval church treasuries of the Christian west is a reminder that the symbolic meaning of an object can change according to the context in which it is found (Shalem 1996).

A related concept introduced recently to the study of medieval objects is *habitus* (Bourdieu 1977; 1990: 53). *Habitus* is concerned with the mental templates which structure the actions of everyday life and which are often unconscious, unregulated and the product of long custom. They may change from one generation to the next. One recent study has explored the concept of *habitus* in relation to medieval pottery from south Yorkshire (Dunkley and Cumberpatch 1996: 56–8) and suggested changing correlations between colour, texture, shape and use, particularly in the fifteenth and sixteenth centuries, at an important time of transition for both material culture and society. While the value of basic sorting and quantification is not denied, observations of this sort are widening the focus of pottery studies to look at broader patterning in the data. In time, this will have practical implications for the recording of pottery and affect the scale of research which, for these purposes, might be best set at the regional level rather than being undertaken on a site-by-site basis.

Patterns of consumption and socio-cultural behaviour are also of interest for the later medieval period, though far more work has been carried out for later periods, usually through the analysis of probate inventories and other historical documents which reflect ownership and spending (Glennie 1995). Concepts such as 'trickle-down' theory, which seeks to describe how different social groups emulate each other and how higher groups might respond by adopting new fashions, have not thus far been adopted with much enthusiasm (McCracken 1988). Again, a broad regional approach is required to detect such patterns, large artefact collections from a range of excavated monuments in rural and urban situations are needed to provide a statistically meaningful sample. This is only now becoming possible for some areas of medieval Britain, such as Southampton where sufficient data is now available for the social significance of imported medieval pottery to be considered (Brown 1997).

Architecture and use of space

The general move away from economic explanation towards social explanation is nowhere better seen than in studies of buildings and is by no means restricted to archaeologists (e.g. Pounds 1990) nor to the 1990s (e.g. Coulson 1979). A useful summary of the many applications of theory to the archaeological study of buildings is provided by Grenville (1997: 14–22). A long tradition of spatial and functional analysis of later medieval buildings has been based on the proposition that the use of space reflects the social organisation of the household (e.g. Faulkner 1958 for castle planning). This has been highlighted by schematic diagrams which display the arrangement of interconnected spaces. More recently, new methods of access and plan analysis have revived interest in these spatial techniques (Hillier and Hanson 1984) and a number of medieval buildings have been studied to good effect (e.g. Fairclough 1992; Schofield 1994b).

These dissections of buildings depend upon the kind of detailed picture of their architectural development perfected by the large numbers of historic fabric surveys produced over the past decade. That the recording and interpretation of buildings was the subject of a major session at the IFA annual conference in 1991, at which these new techniques of spatial analysis were fully aired, shows the extent to which theory, practice and funding have become more fully enmeshed, at least in some areas. Common systems of proportions in buildings and plans, for example, have long been noted (e.g. Fernie 1976), but their more systematic examination (e.g. Gallagher 1994) may be attributed in part to improved and increased recording as well as to a greater appetite for interpretation generally.

Spatial analysis proves to be a distinctive set of applications with a long pedigree in medieval archaeology. More recently, a series of influential case studies of different classes of medieval building have adopted structuralist principles. Here culture is perceived to be underlain by deeper codes and rules, and archaeologists seek to make these hidden mental structures explicit, often by looking for common patterns in several classes of evidence. Schofield (1992; 1994b), for example, discusses the use of social space in towns in terms of changing percentages of land use devoted to religious vs. secular use, public vs. private, and other binary oppositions. To do this he uses the evidence compiled from sets of early lease-plans dated to around 1600. Austin and Thomas (1990) also discuss 'conceptual structures' in terms of oppositions such as upper/lower, private/public and human/animal, this time using archaeological evidence for medieval longhouses on Dartmoor (Figure 6.10). These oppositions generate, in their own words, 'the rhythm of the house', suggesting what different spaces might have meant to the medieval occupants, how they might have been used and who by. People, actions and thoughts are the basis of their archaeological agenda.

Other influences on the study of standing buildings are derived from social theory, such as the concept of *habitus* mentioned above in which the relationship between space and ideology might be investigated (e.g. Graves 1989; Gilchrist 1994). Most applications of post-processual theory, however, combine several different theoretical strands and multiple sources of evidence, of which standing buildings might be just one. Gilchrist's analysis of the Military Orders, to take one example, made use of archaeology and architecture in a description of building and plan layouts but also included a discussion of iconography. Her aim was to draw attention to monastic plans which differ from the standard and to analyse the way in which identity (social, gender and religious) might be signalled through church dedications, church plans of unusual form, two-storey halls and churches, and preceptory layouts (Gilchrist 1992). These ideas were later expanded in a number of longer studies (Gilchrist 1994; 1995) which emphasise how far meaning and messages can be manipulated in architecture and material culture.

Likewise, two books by Matthew Johnson (1993; 1996) have been influential in demonstrating the value of applying explicit theory to the study of the medieval domestic environment and addressing more ambitious themes such as the transition from feudalism to capitalism. For example, *Housing Culture* (1993) is an exercise in contextual archaeology because, while its central theme may be traditional houses in western Suffolk between 1400 and 1700, it seeks to compare spatial changes observed there with other forms of archaeological and historical evidence. In doing so, Johnson identifies

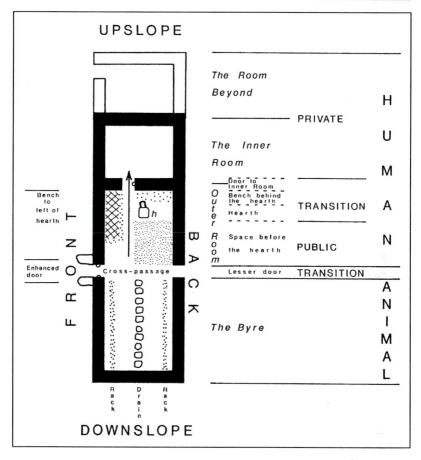

Figure 6.10 An analysis of spatial organisation in medieval domestic buildings on Dartmoor using archaeological data to suggest how space might have been conceptualised and ordered by its inhabitants. The rest of this case study, which was undertaken by a medieval archaeologist and a prehistorian working together, explores the wider physical context of farmyard and landscape. (Austin and Thomas 1990: figure 2.2).

common processes of segregation, drawing parallels between subdivisions in the use of space in houses and the enclosure of open fields. In contrast to much other work on vernacular architecture this book relates its findings to wider issues. As the title of the book suggests, it is the cultural dimension to housing which is emphasised as well as the 'mentality' of the occupants, as opposed to the practical and economic considerations which have dominated so many studies in the past (Dyer 1997). At the same time, these new approaches also have implications for field practice and Johnson's ideas have recently been applied to excavated structures (Dunkley and Cumberpatch

1996: 199–200). Even small-scale evaluation, in parish churches for example, can help to pinpoint spatial divisions within the chancel, the position of altars, the division between nave and chancel, seating arrangements and internal burials (Peters 1996).

Landscapes

Landscapes cannot be interpreted in economic terms alone and it is their social role which has been stressed recently, the place of human agency as against the influence of the physical environment (e.g. Feinman 1999). As an illustration, one recent study has examined the theological symbolism reflected in the location of later medieval and early post-medieval rabbit-warrens (Stocker and Stocker 1996). These earthworks have long been taken to be indicators of high status and their position within monastic precincts has been noted. Their important economic role is not contested but, given that rabbits were widely perceived as symbols of the salvation of man, it is argued persuasively that their siting may have an additional symbolic value, a sacred meaning echoed in medieval manuscripts and texts.

Most interest has been shown in how the medieval landscape might have dramatised expressions of power. A Marxist perspective on the manipulation of space in medieval villages, for example, interpreted regular plot sizes and the dominant location of the manor house as an expression of lordly control (e.g. Saunders 1990). A flurry of recent studies has also investigated later medieval 'designed' or 'created' landscapes, what have been termed 'stage sets for social theatre' (Locock 1994: 9). The analysis of earthworks has been of particular importance in recognising medieval gardens (Everson 1998) and in the reinterpretation of landscapes around major monuments, for example at Bodiam Castle (Sussex; Taylor *et al.* 1990), Ludgershall Castle (Wilts.; Everson *et al.* 2000), and Somersham Palace (Cambs.; Taylor 1989). These studies reveal fresh information about the use of space, the siting of well-known monuments and the manipulation of landscapes which are seen as being infused with meaning. Through a combination of phenomenology, spatial studies and social interpretation some unexpected insights are created into the presentation of medieval buildings which immerse the modern reader in the contemporary experience of viewing the site. There are important influences too from art history and history on the symbolic value of architecture (e.g. Binski 1986) and, indeed, specifically on Bodiam (e.g. Coulson 1991), so the choice of subject matter is not always novel (Stocker 1992).

The range of monuments treated in this way is expanding. One researcher is investigating how the inhabitants of medieval settlements might have expressed their attitudes towards and responded to the 'natural' landscapes of Dartmoor and Bodmin Moor (Altenberg 1999), another has extended the approach to consider the siting of medieval churches (Corcos 2001). Ultimately, there must be applications here for GIS and DTM modelling, which can convey a better impression of landscapes experienced on the ground than maps or air photographs (e.g. Llobera 1996), so here theory will continue to impact on the development of new techniques.

Time

Finally, it may seem self-evident that medieval archaeologists should think in terms of calendar dates as the hook on which to hang their observations, but dates are only one way of thinking about time and may not always be the most useful. The French historian Fernand Braudel suggested that time might be measured at three different scales (1972): the 'long-term' seen in environmental or landscape archaeology; 'social time', which measures the history of groups of people, perhaps every twenty-five years in the case of most medieval archaeology; and 'individual time', the history of events. A number of archaeologists feel that they are well placed to contribute at these different scales. 'Landscape' projects, for example, are well-suited to the discussion of long-term change (e.g. Barker 1995) whereas documents can provide high resolution dating for more rapid social changes in the later medieval period (e.g. Astill and Davies 1997) and, as we have seen in the last section of this book, post-processual archaeologies tend to emphasise 'individual time' (Austin and Thomas 1990: 51–53). Medieval archaeology can provide evidence of different processes operating at varying rates and, unlike the prehistorian who may be faced with significant problems of chronological resolution, the medievalist is more fortunate.

Conclusion

Though it has roots which stretch back to the Victorians and beyond, medieval archaeology is a relative newcomer as an academic discipline. For the most part, it is a conservative field of study. Resistance to change, it might be argued, is at least as strong, if not stronger, than forces for change. Excavations accumulate data, new information comes to light which adds to the detailed picture, chronologies are further refined, new sites located. These activities continue and might be broadly characterised as the presentation of empirical data. Processualism has also left a positive legacy, notably the stress placed on problem-orientated fieldwork and in the use of quantitative methods. 'Soft' processualism, too, in the form of hypothetical 'models' of landscape development remains useful, though as a general storyboard rather than as a predictive tool (e.g. Rippon 1999: fig. 4). Against this background, post-processual archaeologies have informed a wide variety of applications and interpretations of medieval archaeological data for more than a decade.

Medieval archaeology is pluralistic, diverse in its traditions but eclectic in its participation in theory. In so far as it is forging new ground, recent years have seen a revision of ideas rather than a revolution, to some extent revisiting much earlier themes (e.g. Bond 1914 on ecclesiastical symbolism; Power 1922 on gender). The number of medieval archaeologists demonstrating their conceptual allegiance is small, perhaps not as many as fifty, not enough to promote a significant sense of critical self-awareness. It can appear that some ideas have been abandoned before they have been fully explored. Nevertheless there is some evidence that medieval archaeologists *are* listening to what the material really has to say and then presenting it, as was urged a decade ago (Austin and Thomas 1990: 43). The absence of any consensus is a concern for those who perceive fragmentation in theory and practice and an ever increasing sub-division and specialisation encouraged by special interest groups. On the other hand, the contribution of post-processual archaeology is that it has linked medieval archaeology with debates in other parts of the discipline and in the social sciences generally. The time lag in the uptake of theoretical stances in the 1960s, 1970s and 1980s in different branches of archaeology is unlikely to be repeated in the future.

Links between history and archaeology are diverse. The tone of recent publications suggests that the relationship between medieval archaeology and history is less competitive, that the merits of fieldwork in medieval archaeology are long since proven, that what we share in common is more important than what divides us. The many advantages conferred by post-processual archaeology do not negate the relevance of recent developments in economic history which have much to offer the medieval archaeologist (Courtney 1997). Colin Platt's weaving of social history and archaeology remains relevant (Platt 1978a) while recent historical writing also considers themes such as identity, belief and symbolic order (Lineham 2001). There is no longer any novelty in proclaiming the advantages of multi-disciplinarity, though there is still uncertainty about how this can best be achieved (Coones 1985). Debates about archaeology as art or science seem less relevant with the introduction of post-processual ideas and the maturing of medieval archaeology. Some archaeologists and historians are united in their suspicion of positivism and fully content to recognise the contribution which can be made by the other discipline. Both *The Cambridge Urban History of Britain* (Palliser 2000) and the medieval volumes of *The Agrarian History of England and Wales* (Miller 1991; Thirsk 1988) demonstrate considerable collaboration between archaeologists and historians and, for some fields at least, archaeology has helped to shape the historians' agenda (Dyer 1990b).

There has been much to welcome in the past decade. With the advent of post-processual archaeology, medieval archaeologists have begun to stray with greater regularity beyond routine description. A common language of debate and discourse is being formed and used on a daily basis; there is no shortage of case studies, though these are widely spread. Much has been learnt from other disciplines and is now being applied to the large data-sets which have been accumulating for over forty years. Bruce-Mitford, Dunning,

Jope, Harden, Hoskins and Ward-Perkins would surely find much to please them, though there is still plenty to be done. It will take time to discover if a truly distinctive contribution to debates about social and economic issues is being made or whether sophistication of argument is being confused with real achievement.

Bibliography

Abbreviations

ACAO	Association of County Archaeological Officers
BAR	British Archaeological Reports (British Series unless otherwise stated)
CAS	Congress of Archaeological Societies
CBA	Council for British Archaeology
CUP	Cambridge University Press
DoE	Department of Environment
EUP	Edinburgh University Press.
HBMC	Historic Buildings and Monuments Commission
HMSO	Her Majesty's Stationery Office
IFA	Institute of Field Archaeologist
JBAA	Journal of the British Archaeological Association
LUP	Leicester University Press
MOLAS	Museum of London Archaeology Service
MPRG	Medieval Pottery Research Group
MSRG	Medieval Settlement Research Group
MVRG	Medieval Village Research Group
MUP	Manchester University Press.
OUP	Oxford University Press
PBA	Proceedings of the British Academy
PCAS	Proceedings of the Cambridge Antiquarian Society
PHFC	Proceedings of the Hampshire Field Club and Archaeological Society
PSANHS	Proceedings of the Somerset Archaeology and Natural History Society
PSAS	Proceedings of the Society of Antiquaries of Scotland
RCHME	Royal Commission on Historical Monuments (England)
RCAHMW	Royal Commission on Ancient and Historical Monuments (Wales)
RCAHMS	Royal Commission on Ancient and Historical Monuments (Scotland).
SMA	Society for Medieval Archaeology
TBGAS	Transactions of the Bristol and Gloucestershire Archaeological Society
UCL	University College London

Aberg, F. A. 1978. Introduction. In F. A. Aberg (ed.) *Medieval Moated Sites*, 1–4. CBA Research Report 17. London: CBA.

Aberg, F. A. and Brown, A. E. (eds.) 1981. *Medieval Moated Sites in North-West Europe*. BAR International Series 121. Oxford.

ACAO. 1993. *Model Briefs and Specifications for Archaeological Assessments and Field Evaluations*. Bedford: ACAO.

Addyman, P. V. 2000. Barley Hall. An experiment in archaeological interpretation. *Public Archaeology* 1 (1): 85–7.

Addyman, P. V. and Biddle, M. 1965. Medieval Cambridge: recent finds and excavations. *PCAS* 58: 74–137.

Addyman, P. V. and Priestley J. 1978. Baile Hill, York. In D. Parsons (ed.) *Five Castle Excavations. Reports on the Institute's Research Project into the Origins of the Castle in England*: 115–56. Leeds: Royal Archaeological Institute Monograph.

Aitchison, K. 1999. *Profiling the Profession. A Survey of Archaeological Jobs in the UK*. York: CBA, English Heritage and IFA.

Aitken, M. J. 1992. Introduction. In A. M. Pollard (ed.), New developments in archaeological science. A joint symposium of the Royal Society and the British Academy February 1991. *PBA* 77: 1–2. Oxford: OUP for British Academy.

Aitken, M. J. and Harold, M. R. 1959. Magnetic dating II. *Archaeometry* 2: 17–20.

Aitken, M. J. and Hawley, H. N. 1967. Archaeomagnetic measurements in Britain IV. *Archaeometry* 10: 129–35.

AJK. 1831. Notes on the excavations for the New London Bridge. *Gentleman's Magazine* 1831: 387–390.

Albarella, U. 1996. The animal economy of rural settlements: a zooarchaeological case study from Northamptonshire. *Medieval Settlement Research Group Annual Report* 9 (1994): 16–17.

—— 1999. 'The mystery of husbandry': medieval animals and the problem of integrating historical and archaeological evidence. *Antiquity* 73: 867–75.

Albarella, U. and Davies, S. 1996. Mammals and bird bones from Launceston Castle: decline in status and the rise of agriculture. *Circaea* 12 (1), 1996 for 1994: 1–156.

Alcock, N. W. 1994. Physical Space and Social Space: The interpretation of vernacular architecture. In M. Locock (ed.) *Meaningful Architecture: Social Interpretations of Buildings*. Worldwide Archaeology Series 9: 207–30. Aldershot: Ashgate Publishing.

Alcock, N. W., Barley, M. W., Dixon, P. W. and Meeson R. A. 1996. *Recording Timber Framed Buildings: An Illustrated Glossary*. London: CBA.

Alexander, J. 1995. Building stone from the East Midlands quarries: sources, transportation and usage. *Medieval Archaeology* 39: 107–35.

Alexander, M. J. and Roberts, B. K. 1978. The deserted village of Low Buston, Northumberland. A study in soil phosphate analysis. *Archaeologia Aeliana* series 5, VI: 107–16.

Allan, J. P. 1984. *Medieval and Post-Medieval Finds from Exeter, 1971–1980*. Exeter: Exeter City Council and the Univ. of Exeter.

Allcroft, A. H. 1908. *Earthwork of England: Prehistoric, Roman, Saxon, Danish, Norman, and Medieval*. London: Macmillan.

Allen, B. S. 1937. *Tides in English Taste (1619–1800), vol. 2*. Cambridge, Mass: Harvard Univ. Press.

Allen, R. 1999. The pageant of history: a re-interpretation of the 13th-century building at King John's House, Romsey, Hampshire. *Medieval Archaeology* 43: 74–14.

Allen, T. 1994. A medieval grange of Abingdon Abbey at Dean Court Farm, Cumnor, Oxon. *Oxoniensia* 59: 219–448.

Allibone, T E. (ed.) 1970. *The Impact of the Natural Sciences on Archaeology*. London: British Academy.

Allin, C. E. 1981. The leather. In J. E. Mellor and T. Pearce *The Austin Friars, Leicester*. Leicestershire Archaeological Field Unit Report. CBA Research Report 35: 145–65. London: CBA.

Allison, K. J., Beresford, M. W. and Hurst, J. G. 1965. *The Deserted Villages of Oxfordshire*. Leicester Univ.: Dept. of English Local History Occasional Papers, 1st series, 17.

Altenberg, K. 1999. Space and community on medieval Dartmoor and Bodmin Moor: interim report. *Medieval Settlement Research Group Annual Report* 14: 26–8.

Andersson, H., Carelli, P. and Ersgård, L. (eds) 1997. *Visions of the Past. Trends and Traditions in Swedish Medieval Archaeology*. Lund Univ.: Lund Studies in Medieval Archaeology 19.

Anon. 1744. A description of the church found lately under ground at Monkton Farley, in the county of Wilts. *Gentleman's Magazine* 14: 139–40.

Anon. 1796. Salisbury. *Gentleman's Magazine* 66: 185–6.

Anon. 1857. Annual reports and notes. *Archaeologia Aeliana*, new series 1, ii.

Anon. 1930. Bradenstoke Barn demolished. *Wiltshire Archaeological and Natural History Magazine* 45: 80–1.

Anon. 1953. *Penrhyn Castle, Bangor, Caernarvonshire*. London: Country Life Limited for The National Trust.

Anon. 1961. Editorial Notes. *Past and Present* 19: 1–6.

Archer-Thomson, J. 1987. Hedgerows. In L. Keen and A. Carreck (eds.) *Historic Landscape of Weld. The Weld Estate, Dorset*: 72–6. East Lulworth: Dorset County Council.

Armitage, E. 1912. *The Early Norman Castles of the British Isles*. London: John Murray.

Arnold, C. J. 1986. Archaeology and History: The shades of confrontation and cooperation. In J. L. Bintliff and C. F. Gaffney (eds.) *Archaeology at the Interface: Studies in Archaeology's Relationships with History, Geography, Biology and Physical Science*: 32–9. Oxford: BAR International Series 300.

Aslet, C. 1980. St Donat's Castle, South Glamorgan. The property of the United World College of the Atlantic. *Country Life* CLXVIII, 4335: 942–4.

Aspinall, A., Heron, C. and Pocock, J. A. 1994. Topographical and Geophysical Survey of a rural medieval complex. *Medieval Archaeology* 38: 177–82.

Astill, G. G. 1993. *A Medieval Industrial Complex and its Landscape: the Metalworking Watermills and Workshops of Bordesley Abbey*. CBA Research Report 92. London: CBA.

Astill, G. G. and Davies, W. 1997. *A Breton Landscape*. London: UCL Press.

Astill, G. G. and Grant A. (eds) 1988. *The Countryside of Medieval England*. Oxford: Blackwell.

Aston, M. 1973. English ruins and English history: the Dissolution and the sense of the past. *Journal of the Warburg and Courtauld Institutes* 36: 231–55.

Aston, M. A. 1983a. The making of the English landscape: the next 25 years. *The Local Historian* 15: 323–32.

—— 1983b. Deserted farmsteads on Exmoor and the Lay Subsidy of 1327 in West Somerset. *PSANHS* 127: 71–104.

—— 1985. *Interpreting the Landscape: Landscape Archaeology in Local Studies*. London: Batsford.

—— (ed.). 1988 *Medieval Fish, Fisheries and Fishponds in England*. Oxford; BAR 182.

—— 1989. A regional study of deserted settlements in the west of England. In M. Aston, D. A. Austin and C. Dyer (eds) *The Rural Settlements of Medieval England*: 105–28. Oxford: Blackwell.

—— 1993. *Monasteries*. London: Batsford.

Aston, M. A., Austin, D. A. and Dyer, C. (eds.) 1989. *The Rural Settlements of Medieval England*. Oxford: Blackwell.

Aston, M. A. and Bond, C. J. 1973. Sketch planning: an introduction. *CBA Group 9 Newsletter* 3: 8–12.

—— 1976. *The Landscape of Towns*. London: Dent.

Aston, M. A. and Gerrard, C. 1999. 'Unique, traditional and charming'. The Shapwick Project, Somerset. *Antiquaries Journal* 79: 1–58

Aston, M. A. and Rowley, T. 1974. *Landscape Archaeology: An Introduction to Fieldwork Techniques on Post-Roman Landscapes*. Newton Abbot: David and Charles.

Aston, M. A., Martin, M. H. and Jackson, A. W. 1998. The potential for heavy metal soil analysis on low status archaeological sites at Shapwick, Somerset. *Antiquity* 72: 838–46.

Atkin, M. and Evans, D. H. 1984. Population, profit and plague: the archaeological interpretation of buildings and land use in Norwich. *Scottish Archaeological Review* 3 (2): 92–8.

Atkin, M., Carter, A. and Evans, D. H. 1985. *Excavations in Norwich 1971–78, Part II*. East Anglian Archaeology Report No. 26. Norwich: Centre for East Anglian Studies.

Atkin, M. and Milligan, R. 1992. Ground-probing radar in archaeology: practicalities and problems. *The Field Archaeologist* 16: 288–91.

Atkinson, C. 1946. *Field Archaeology*. London: Methuen and Co.

Aubrey, J. 1847. *Natural History of Wiltshire (written between 1656 and 1691)*. London: printed by J. B. Nichols and Son.

Austin, D. A. 1980. Barnard Castle, Co. Durham. Second interim report: Excavation in the Inner Ward 1976–8: the later medieval period. *JBAA* 133: 74–96.

—— 1985. Medieval Archaeology and the landscape. *Landscape History* 7: 53–6.

—— 1986. Central Place Theory and the Middle Ages. In E. Grant (ed.) *Central Places, Archaeology and History*: 95–104. Sheffield: Dept. of Archaeology and Prehistory, Univ. of Sheffield.

—— 1987. The future of archaeology in British Universities. *Antiquity* 61: 227–38.

—— 1988. Excavations and survey at Bryn Cysegrfan, Llanfair Clydogan, Dyfed, 1979. *Medieval Archaeology* 32: 130–65.

—— 1989. *The Deserted Medieval Village of Thrislington, County Durham, Excavations 1973–74*. Lincoln: SMA Monograph Series 12.

—— 1990. The 'proper study' of medieval archaeology. In D. A. Austin and L. Alcock (eds.) *From the Baltic to the Black Sea. Studies in Medieval Archaeology*: 9–42. London: Unwin Hyman.

Austin, D. A. and Alcock, L. (eds.) 1990. *From the Baltic to the Black Sea. Studies in Medieval Archaeology*. London: Unwin Hyman.

Austin, D. A., Daggatt, R. H. and Walker, M. J. C. 1980. Farms and fields in Okehampton Park, Devon: the problems of studying medieval landscape. *Landscape History* 2: 39–57.

Austin, D. A., Gerrard, G. A. M. and Greeves, T. A. P. 1989. Tin and agriculture in the Middle Ages and beyond: landscape archaeology in St Neots Parish, Cornwall. *Cornish Archaeology* 28: 5–251.

Austin, D. A. and Thomas J. 1990. The 'proper study' of medieval archaeology: a case study. In D. A. Austin and L. Alcock (eds) *From the Baltic to the Black Sea: Studies in Medieval Archaeology*: 43–78. London: Unwin Hyman.

Austin, D. A. and Walker, M. J. C. 1985. A new landscape context for Houndtor, Devon. *Medieval Archaeology* 29: 147–52.

Avent, R. 2000. CADW and castle conservation. *Castle Studies Group Newsletter* 1999–2000.

Ayers, B. S. 1987. Excavations at St Martin-at-Palace Plain, Norwich, 1981. *East Anglian Archaeology*, Report No. 37. Gressenhall: Norfolk Arch. Unit.

—— 1994. *Excavations at Fishergate, Norwich, 1985*. East Anglian Archaeology Report No. 68. Dereham: Field Archaeology Division, Norfolk Museums Service.

Ayloffe, J. 1786. An Account of the Body of King Edward the First, as it appeared on opening his Tomb in the Year 1774. *Archaeologia* 3: 76–431.

Baggs, A. P. 1994. Architectural guides and inventories. In C. R. J. Currie and C. P. Lewis (eds) *A Guide to English County Histories*: 26–31. Sutton: Stroud.

Baker, A. R. H. and Butlin, R. A. 1973. *Studies of Field Systems in the British Isles*. London: CUP.

Baker, D. 1970. Excavations in Bedford 1967. *Bedfordshire Archaeological Journal* 5: 67–100.

—— 1971. Excavations at Elstow Abbey, 1968–70: third interim report. *Bedfordshire Archaeological Journal* 3: 22–30.

—— 1999. Contexts for collaboration and conflict. In G. Chitty and D. Baker (eds) *Managing Sites and Buildings. Reconciling Presentation and Preservation*: 1–21. London: Routledge.

Baker, D. and Baker, E. 1989. Research designs: timber phases and outbuildings with special reference to Elstow Abbey and Grove Priory, Bedfordshire, with a note about availability of information. In R. Gilchrist and H. Mytum (eds) *The Archaeology of Rural Monasteries*. Oxford: BAR 203: 261–276.

Baker, D., Baker E., Hassall, J, and Simco, A. 1979. *Excavations in Bedford 1967–1977*. Bedfordshire Archaeological Journal 13.

Baker, J. N. L. 1952. The development of historical geography in Britain during the last hundred years. *Advancement of Science* 8: 406–12.

Bale, J. 1557–59. *Scriptorum illustrium maioris Brytannie . . . Catalogus*. Basle.

Banham, J. 1984. 'Past and present': images of the Middle Ages in the early nineteenth century. In J. Banham and J. Harris (eds.) *William Morris and the Middle Ages*: 17–31. Manchester: MUP.

Banham, J. and Harris, J. (eds) 1984. *William Morris and the Middle Ages*. Manchester: MUP.

Barclay, G. J. 1997. *State-Funded 'Rescue' Archaeology in Scotland*. Historic Scotland Ancient Monuments Division Occasional Paper 2. Edinburgh: Historic Scotland.

Barclay, K. 2001. *Scientific Analysis of Archaeological Ceramics. A Handbook of Resources*. Oxford: Oxbow Books for English Heritage.

Baring-Gould, S. 1892–3. An ancient settlement on Trewortha Marsh. *Journal of the Royal Inst. Corn.* 11: 57–70.

Barker, G. (ed.) 1995. *A Mediterranean Valley. Landscape Archaeology and Annales History in the Biferno Valley*. London: LUP.

Barker, K. and Darvill, T. C. 1997. *Making English Landscapes, Changing Perspectives: Papers Presented to Christopher Taylor at a Symposium Held at Bournemouth University on 25 March 1995*. Oxford: Oxbow Books.

Barker, P. A. 1964. Pontesbury Castle mound; emergency excavations 1961 and 1964. *Transactions of the Shropshire Archaeological Society* 57: 206–30.

—— 1968–9. The origins of Worcester. *Transactions of the Worcester Archaeological Society* 3, ser. 2.

—— 1969a. The deserted medieval hamlet of Braggington. *Transactions of the Shropshire Archaeological Society* 58: 122–39.

—— 1969b. Some aspects of the excavation of timber buildings. *World Archaeology* 1: 220–35.

—— 1977. *Techniques of Archaeological Excavation*. London: Batsford.

—— P. A. 1987. Rescue: antenatal, birth and early years. In H. Mytum and K. Waugh (eds) *Rescue Archaeology. What's Next?* Univ. of York Monograph 6: 7–10. York: Dept. of Archaeology, Univ. of York Monograph and Rescue, The British Archaeological Trust.

Barker, P. A. and Barton, K. J. 1978. Excavations at Hastings Castle, 1968. In D. Parsons (ed.) *Five Castle Excavations. Reports on the Institute's Research Project into the Origins of the Castle in England*: 80–100. Leeds: Royal Archaeological Institute Monograph.

Barham, R. H. 1837–43. *The Ingoldsby Legends or Mirth and Marvels*. London: Macmillan and Co.

Barley, M. W. 1961. *The English Farmhouse and Cottage*. London: Routledge.

—— (ed.) 1975. *The Plans and Topography of Medieval Towns in England and Wales*. CBA Research Report 14. London: CBA.

—— (ed.) 1977. *European Towns: Their Archaeology and Early History*. London: Academic Press for the CBA.

Barley, M. W., Rogers, A. and Strange, P. 1969. The medieval parsonage house, Coninsby, Lincolnshire. *Antiquaries Journal* 49: 346–66.

Barnwell, P. S. and Adams, A. T. 1994. *The House Within. Interpreting Medieval Houses in Kent*. London: RCHME.

Baron, J. 1883. On a hoard of gold nobles found at Bremeridge Farm, Westbury, Wilts. *Archaeologia* 47: 137–56.

Barraclough, G. 1979. *Main Trends in History*. New York: Holmes and Meier.

Barton, K. J. 1969. Pickwick Farm, Dundry, Somerset. *Proceedings of the Univ. of Bristol Spelaeological Society* 12: 99–112.

—— 1979. *Medieval Sussex Pottery*. London: Phillimore.

Barton, K. J. and Holden, E. W. 1978. Excavations at Bramber Castle, Sussex, 1966–67. In D. Parsons (ed.) *Five Castle Excavations. Reports on the Institute's Research Project into the Origins of the Castle in England*: 11–79. Leeds: Royal Archaeological Institute Monograph.

Bayley, J. (ed.) 1998. *Science in Archaeology: an Agenda for the Future*. London: English Heritage.

Bell, R. D. and Beresford, M. W. 1987. *Wharram Percy: The Church of St Martin*. London: SMA Monograph 11.

Bennett, P. 1988. Archaeology and the Channel Tunnel. *Archaeologia Cantiana* 106: 1–24.

Bennett, P., Frere, S. S. and Stow, S. 1982. *Excavations at Canterbury Castle*. The Archaeology of Canterbury 1, Maidstone.

Bennett, R. and Elton, J. 1898–1904. *History of Corn Milling*, 4 vols. London: Simpkin, Marshall and Co. Ltd.

Benson, D. 1972. A museum: Oxfordshire. In E. Fowler (ed.) *Field Survey in British Archaeology*: 16–21. London: CBA.

Benson, D. and Cook, J. 1966. *City of Oxford Redevelopment: Archaeological Implications*. Oxford: Oxford City and County Museum.

Beresford, G. 1975. *The Medieval Clay-Land Village: Excavations at Goltho and Barton Blount*. Society for Medieval Archaeology Monograph 6. London: SMA.

—— 1979. Three deserted medieval settlements on Dartmoor, a report on the late E. Marie Mintner's excavations. *Medieval Archaeology* 23: 98–158.

—— 1987. *Goltho: The Development of an Early Medieval Manor, c.850–1150*. London: HBMCE.

Beresford, M. W. 1954. *The Lost Villages of England*. London: Lutterworth Press.

—— 1957. *History on the Ground*. London: Lutterworth Press.

—— 1966. Fallowfield, Northumberland: an early cartographic representation of a deserted medieval village. *Medieval Archaeology* 10: 164–7.

—— 1967a. East Layton, Co. Durham in 1608. Another early cartographic representation of a deserted medieval village site. *Medieval Archaeology* 11: 257–66.

—— 1967b. *New Towns of the Middle Ages, Town Plantation in England, Wales and Gascony*. London: Lutterworth Press.

—— 1970. Herbert Finberg: an appreciation. In J. Thirsk (ed.) *Land, Church and People. Essays Presented to Professor H. P. R. Finberg*, vii-xii. Reading: British Agricultural History Society.

—— 1981. Obituary: Sir Michael Postan. *Medieval Village Research Group* 29: 4.

—— 1985. Mapping the medieval landscape: forty years in the field. In S. R. J. Woodell (ed.) *The English Landscape. Past, Present and Future*: 106–28. Oxford: OUP.

—— 1986-7. Forty Years in the Field: An Exaugural Lecture. *The Univ. of Leeds Review* 29: 27–46.

—— 1989. A review of historical research (to 1968). In M. W. Beresford and J. G. Hurst (eds). *Deserted Medieval Villages*: 3–75. Gloucester: Alan Sutton.

—— 1994. Obituary: Professor J. K. S. St. Joseph. *Medieval Settlement Research Group. Annual Report* 9: 53.

Beresford, M. W. and Hurst, J. G. 1971. *Deserted Medieval Villages*. Woking: Lutterworth Press.

—— 1990. *Wharram Percy Deserted Medieval Village*. London: Batsford.

Beresford, M. W., Hurst, J. G. and Sheail, J. 1980. MVRG: The first thirty years. *Medieval Village Research Group Annual Report* 28: 36–39.

Beresford, M. W. and St Joseph, J. K. 1958. *Medieval England: An Aerial Survey*. Cambridge: CUP.

Bewley, R. H., Donoghue, D. N. M., Gaffney, V. and Van Leusen, M. and Wise, A. 1999. *Archiving Aerial Photography and Remote Sensing Data: a Guide to Good Practice*. Archaeological Data Service. Oxford: Oxbow Books.

Biddick, K. 1993. Decolonizing the English past: readings in medieval archaeology and history. *Journal of British Studies* 32: 1–23.

Biddle, M. 1961-2. The deserted medieval village of Seacourt, Berkshire. *Oxoniensia* 26/27: 70–201.

—— 1964. The excavation of a motte and bailey castle at Therfield, Hertfordshire. *J. Brit. Archaeol. Ass.* 27: 53–91.

—— 1968. Archaeology and the history of British towns. *Antiquity* 42: 109–16.

—— 1970. Excavations at Winchester, 1969. Eighth interim report. *Antiquaries Journal* 50: 277–326.

—— 1972. Excavations at Winchester 1970. *Antiquaries Journal* 52: 93–131.

—— 1974. The future of the urban past. In P. A. Rahtz (ed.) *Rescue Archaeology*: 95–112. Harmondsworth: Penguin Books.

—— 1983. The study of Winchester: archaeology and history in a British town, 1961–1983. *PBA* 59: 93–135.

—— 1989. The Rose reviewed: a comedy (?) of errors. *Antiquity* 63: 753–60.

—— (ed.) 1990. *Object and Economy in Medieval Winchester. Artefacts from Medieval Winchester, Part II*. Winchester Studies 7.ii. Oxford: OUP.

—— 1994. *What Future for British Archaeology?* Oxbow Lecture 1. Oxford: Oxbow Books.

—— 1997. Obituary: Rupert Bruce Mitford, 1914–1994. *Medieval Ceramics* 21: 119–22.

Biddle, M. and Hudson, D. 1973. *The Future of London's Past*. Worcester: Rescue Publications.

Biddle, M. and Kjølbye-Biddle, B. 1969. Metres, areas and robbing. *World Archaeology* 1: 208–19.

Biek, L. 1963. *Archaeology and the Microscope*. London: Lutterworth Press.

Binford, S. R. and Binford, L. R. (eds) 1968. *New Perspectives in Archaeology*. Chicago: Aldine Pub. Co.

Binski, P. 1986. *The Painted Chamber at Westminster*. London: Society of Antiquaries of London.

—— 1996. *Medieval Death: Ritual and Representation*. London: British Museum Press.

Bintliff, J. 1986a. Introduction. In J. Bintliff (ed.) *European Social Evolution. Archaeological Perspectives*: 13–39. Bradford: Univ. of Bradford.

—— 1986b. Archaeology at the interface: an historical perspective. In J. L. Bintliff and C. F. Gaffney (eds) *Archaeology at the Interface: Studies in Archaeology's Relationships with History, Geography, Biology and Physical Science*: 4–31. Oxford: BAR International Series 300.

Bishop, M. and Challis, K. 1999. Village earthwork survey in Nottinghamshire. *Medieval Settlement Research Group. Annual Report* 13: 26–32.

Blair, J. 1993. Hall and chamber: English domestic planning 1000–1250. In G. Meirion-Jones and M. Jones (eds) *Manorial Domestic Buildings in England and Northern France*: 1–21. London: Society of Antiquaries of London.

Blair, J. and Pyrah, C. (eds) 1996. *Research Designs for Church Archaeology*. CBA Research Reports 104. York: CBA.

Blair, J. and Ramsay, N. (eds) 1991. *English Medieval Industries*. London: Hambledon Press.

Blake, H. and Davey, P. 1983. *Guidelines for the Processing and Publication of Medieval Pottery from Excavations*. Directorate of Ancient Monuments and Historic Buildings Occasional Paper 5. London.

Blinkhorn, P. W., and Cumberpatch, C. G. 1998. The interpretation of artefacts and the tyranny of the field archaeologist. *Assemblage* 4 (online journal: assemblage@sheffield.ac.uk).

Bliss, P. (ed.) 1869. *The Remains of Thomas Hearne . . .*, II. London.

Boddington, A. 1985. Idle thoughts of a post-excavator. *The Field Archaeologist* 4: 49–50.

—— 1996. *Raunds Furnell. The Anglo-Saxon Church and Churchyard*. London: English Heritage.

Bogdan, N. Q. and Wordsworth, J. W. 1978. *The Medieval Excavations at the High Street, Perth, 1975–76: An Interim Report*. Perth: Perth High Street Archaeological Excavation Committee.

Boismier, W. A. 1997. *Modelling the Effects of Tillage Processes on Artefact Distribution in the Ploughzone: A Simulation Study of Tillage-Induced Pattern Formation*. Oxford: BAR 259.

Bond, C. J. 1979. The estates of Abingdon Abbey. *Landscape History* 1: 59–75.

—— 1989a. Water management in the rural monastery. In R. Gilchrist and H. Mytum (eds) *The Archaeology of Rural Monasteries*. Oxford: BAR 203: 83–112.

—— 1989b. Grassy Hummocks and stone foundations: fieldwork and deserted medieval settlements in South-West Midlands, 1945–1985. In M. Aston, D. A. Austin, C. Dyer (eds) *The Rural Settlements of Medieval England*: 129–48. Oxford: Blackwell.

—— 1993. The Premonstratensian order: a preliminary survey of its growth and distribution in medieval Europe. In M. Carver (ed.) *In Search of Cult. Archaeological investigations in Honour of Philip Rahtz*: 153–85. Woodbridge: Boydell Press.

—— 1995. *Medieval Windmills in South-Western England*. The Wind and Watermill Section of the Society for the Protection of Ancient Buildings (SPAB). Occasional Publication 3. Needham Market: SPAB.

Bond, C. J. and Tiller, K. 1987. *Blenheim. Landscape for a Palace*. Stroud: Alan Sutton.

Bond, F. 1905. *Gothic Architecture in England*. London: Batsford.

—— 1908. *Fonts and Font Covers*. London: Henry Frowde.

—— 1910. *Wood Carvings in English Churches*. London: Henry Frowde.

—— 1914. *Dedications and Patron Saints of English Churches: Ecclesiastical Symbolism: Saints and their Emblems*. London: OUP.

—— 1916. *The Chancel of English Churches*. London: Humphrey Milford.

Bond, J. M. and O'Connor, T. P. 1999. *Bones from Medieval Deposits at 16–22 Coppergate and Other Sites in York*. The Archaeology of York, 15/5. York: York Archaeological Trust and CBA.

Bordesley Abbey website: www.rdg.ac.uk/archaeology/Research/bordesley

Borenius, T. 1932. *St Thomas Becket in Art*. London: Methuen.

Borenius, T. and Tristram, E. W. 1927. *English Medieval Painting*. Paris: Pegasus Press.

Bourdieu, P. 1977. *Outline of a Theory of Practice*. Cambridge: CUP.

—— 1990. *The Logic of Practice*. Oxford: Polity Press.

Bowden, M. 1991. *Pitt Rivers. The Life and Archaeological Work of Lieutenant-General Augustus Henry Lane Fox Pitt Rivers, DCL, FRS, FSA*. Cambridge: CUP.

—— (ed.) 1999. *Unravelling the Landscape. An Inquisitive Approach to Archaeology*. Stroud: Tempus.

Bradford, G. and Dan, J. 1975. The experimental production of tiles. In P. J. Drury and G. D. Pratt, A late thirteenth and early fourteenth-century tile factory at Danbury, Essex. *Medieval Archaeology* 19: 148–9 (92–164).

Bradley, J. and Gaimster, M. 2000. Medieval Britain and Ireland in 1999. *Medieval Archaeology* 44: 235–354.

Bradley, J., Gaimster, M. and Haith, C. 1999. Medieval Britain and Ireland in 1998. *Medieval Archaeology* 43: 226–302.

Bradley, J. L. 1986. Introduction. In J. L. Bradley (ed.) *John Ruskin. The Critical Heritage*: 1–29. London: Routledge and Kegan Paul.

Brakspear, H. 1907. Stanley Abbey, Wiltshire. *Archaeologia* 60 (2): 493–515.

Braudel, F. 1972. *The Mediterranean and the Mediterranean World in the Age of Philip II*. London: Collins.

Brentnall, H. C. 1935–7. Marlborough Castle. *Wiltshire Archaeological Magazine* 47: 543.

Brewster, T. C. M. 1969. Tote Copse Castle, Aldinbourne, Sussex. *Sussex Archaeological Collections* 107: 141–91.

Bridge, M. C. 1988. The dendro dating of buildings in southern England. *Medieval Archaeology* 32: 166–74.

Brindle, S. and Kerr, B. 1997. *Windsor Revealed: New Light on the History of the Castle*. London: English Heritage.

Brinklow, D. A. and Warren, S. E. 1975. Analyses of some medieval and later copper alloys from recent excavations in York. In *Symposium on Archaeometry and Geophysical Prospection* (Oxford 1975). Oxford: The Laboratory.

British Museum, Working Party of the, 1982. *Selection and Retention of Environmental and Artefactual Material from Excavations*. Circulated copy of the 'Longworth Report'.

Britton, J. 1807–26. *Architectural Antiquities of Great Britain*. London: Longman, Hurst, Rees and Orme.

Britton, J. 1814–35. *Cathedral Antiquities*. London: Longman, Hurst, Rees and Orme.

Broadway, J. 1999. *William Dugdale and the Significance of County History in Early Stuart England*. Dugdale Society Occasional Papers 39. Stratford-upon-Avon: Dugdale Society in association with the Shakespeare Birthplace Trust.

Brooke, C. J. 1989. Ground-based Remote Sensing. *Institute of Field Archaeologists Technical Paper No. 7*. London: IFA.

Brooke, C. N. L. 1975. David Knowles 1896–1974. *PBA* 61: 439–77.

Brooks, C. 1998. Introduction: historicism and the nineteenth century. In V. Brand (ed.) *The Study of the Past in the Victorian Age*: 1–19. Oxbow Monograph 73. Oxford: Oxbow Books.

Brooks, F. W. 1939. A medieval brick-yard at Hull. *JBAA*, series 3 (4): 151–74.

Brothwell, D. R. 1972. *Digging up Bones: the Excavation, Treatment and Study of Human Skeletal Remains*. London: British Museum.

Brown, A., Peters, C., and Rosser, G. 1996. The late medieval English church: parish devotion in buildings and the landscape. In J. Blair and C. Pyrah (eds) *Church Archaeology. Research Directions for the Future*. CBA Research Report 104: 63–84. York: CBA.

Brown, C. 1991. Today's Middle Ages: a child's perspective. *Scottish Archaeological Review* 8: 149–53.

Brown, D. H. 1988. Some medieval archaeology. *Scottish Archaeological Review* 5: 95–7.

—— 1997. The social significance of imported medieval pottery. In C. G. Cumberpatch and P. W. Blinkhorn (eds) *Not so Much a Pot, More a Way of Life*. Oxbow Monograph 83: 95–112. Oxford: Oxbow Books.

Brown, D. H., Chalmers, A. and MacNamara, A. 1997. Light and the culture of colour in medieval pottery. In G. De Boe and F. Verhaege (eds) *Method and Theory in Historical Archaeology*. Pre-printed papers of the Medieval Europe Brugge 1997 Conference, vol. 10: 145–47. Zellik: Medieval Europe Brugge.

Brown, D. H. and Wilson, D. 1994. Leominster Old Priory: Recording of standing buildings and excavations 1979–80. *Archaeological Journal* 151: 307–68.

Brown, M. R. and Harris, E. C. 1993. Interfaces in archaeological stratigraphy. In E. C. Harris, M. R. Brown and G. J. Brown (eds) *Practices of Archaeological Stratigraphy*: 7–20. London: Academic Press.

Brown, R. 1841. *Domestic Architecture: Containing a History of the Science, and the Principles of Designing Public Edifices . . . Also . . . Laying Out and Ornamenting Grounds*. London: G. Virtue.

Brown, R. A. 1970. An historian's approach to the origins of the castle in England. *Archaeological Journal* 126: 131–48.

Brownsword, R. and Pitt, E. E. H. 1984. X-Ray Fluorescence analysis of English 13th-16th century pewter flatware. *Archaeomtery* 26 (2): 237–44.

Bruce-Mitford, R. L. S. 1939. The archaeology of the site of the Bodleian Extension in Broad Street, Oxford. *Oxoniensia* IV: 89–146.

—— 1940a. Excavations at Seacourt. *Oxoniensia* V: 31–40.

—— 1940b. Medieval tripod pitchers. *Antiquaries Journal* 20: 103–12.

—— 1948. Medieval archaeology. *The Archaeological News Letter* 6: 1–4.

—— 1964. A National Reference Collection of medieval pottery. *Medieval Archaeology* 8: 229–30.

Brunskill, R. W. 1971. *Illustrated Handbook of Vernacular Architecture*. London: Faber and Faber.

Bryant, G. F. 1977. Experimental kiln firings at Barton-on-Humber, England, 1968–1975. *Medieval Archaeology* 21: 106–23.

Buckland, P. C. 1974. Archaeology and environment in York. *Journal of Archaeological Science* 1: 303–16.

Buckland, P. C., Dolby, M. J., Hayfield, C. and Magilton, J. R., 1979. *The Medieval Pottery Industry at Hallgate, Doncaster*. The Archaeology of Doncaster 2.1, Doncaster.

Burton, J. 1758. *Monasticon Eboracense and the Ecclesiastical History of Yorkshire*. York: printed for the author by N. Nickson.

Burton, J. 1979. *Yorkshire Nunneries in the Twelfth and Thirteenth Centuries*. Borthwick Papers 45. York: Borthwick Institute of Historical Research.

Burton, W. 1622. *The Description of Leicester Shire, Containing Matters of Antiquitye, Historye, Armorye and Genealogy*. London.

Buteux, V. 1990. *Finds Research and the Institute of Field Archaeologists Finds Special Interest Group*. Finds Research Group 700–1700, Datasheet 13.

Butler, L. A. S. 1960. Excavations at Black Friars, Hereford, 1958. *Trans Woolhope Natur Fld Club* 36, 334–70.

—— 1983. Church archaeology and the work of the Council for British Archaeology's Churches Committee. In D. A. Hinton (ed.) *Twenty Five Years of Medieval Archaeology*, 117–26. Sheffield: Dept. of Archaeology and Prehistory, Univ. of Sheffield and SMA.

—— 1987. Medieval urban religious houses. In J. R. Schofield and R. Leech (eds) *Urban Archaeology in Britain*. CBA Research Report 61, 167–76. London: CBA.

—— 1989a. Dolforwyn Castle, Montgomery, Powys. First report: the excavations 1981–1986. *Archaeol Cambrensis* 138: 78–98.

—— 1989b. The archaeology of rural monasteries in England and Wales. In R. Gilchrist and H. Mytum (eds) *The Archaeology of Rural Monasteries*. Oxford: BAR 203, 1–28.

—— 1993. The archaeology of urban monasteries in Britain. In R. Gilchrist and H. Mytum (eds) *Advances in Monastic Archaeology*. Oxford: BAR 227, 79–86.

Bynum, C. W. 1987. *Holy Feast and Holy Fast: the Religious Significance of Food to Medieval Women*. Berkeley CA: Univ. of California Press.

Cadman, G. 1983. Raunds 1977–1983: An excavation summary. *Medieval Archaeology* 27: 107–122.

Cadman, G. and Foard, G. 1984. Raunds, manorial and village origins. In M. Faull (ed.) *Studies in Late Anglo-Saxon Settlement*, 81–100. Oxford: Oxford Univ. Dept. for External Studies.

CADW 1994. *Strategic Framework for Funding Archaeological Work in Wales*. Cardiff: CADW.

Calkins, R. G. 1998. *Medieval Architecture in Western Europe: From AD 300 to 1500*. New York: OUP.

Camden, W. 1607. *Remaines Concerning Brittaine*. London: printed by G. E. for Simon Waterson.

Cameron, K. 1961. *English Place-Names*. London: Batsford.

Cantor, L. (ed.) 1982. *The English Medieval Landscape*. Philadelphia: Univ. of Pennsylvania Press.

—— 1983. *The Medieval Parks of England: A Gazetteer*. Loughborough: Loughborough Univ. of Technology.

Cantor, N. F. 1991. *Inventing the Middle Ages: the Lives, Works and Ideas of the Great Medievalists of the 20th Century*. New York: W. Morrow.

Caple, C. 1990. The castle and lifestyle of a 13th century independent Welsh lord; excavations at Dryslwyn Castle 1980–1988. *Château Gaillard* 14: 47–59.

Carley, J. P. 1985. John Leland at Somerset Libraries. *PSANHS* 129: 141–54.

Carlyle, T. 1843. *Past and Present*. London: Dent.

Carter, A. 1978. Sampling in a medieval town: the study of Norwich. In J. F. Cherry, C. Gamble and S. Shennan (eds) *Sampling in Contemporary British Archaeology*: 263–78. Oxford: BAR 50.

Carter, J. 1795–1814. *The Ancient Architecture of England. Part I. Orders of Architecture during the British, Roman, Saxon and Norman Aeras*. London.

Carus-Wilson, E. M. 1957. The significance of the secular sculptures in the Lane Chapel, Cullompton, Devon. *Medieval Archaeology* 1: 104–17.

Carver, M. O. H. 1978. Early Shrewsbury: an archaeological definition in 1975. *Transactions of the Shropshire Archaeological Society* 59: 225–63.

—— (ed.) 1980. *Medieval Worcester, an Archaeological Framework*. Transactions of the Worcestershire Archaeological Society, 3rd Series, 7. Worcester: Worcestershire Archaeological Society.

—— 1981. Sampling towns: an optimistic strategy. In P. Clack and S. Haselgrove (eds) *Approaches to the Urban Past*. Dept. of Archaeology, Durham Univ. Occasional Paper No. 2: 65–92. Durham: Durham Univ.

—— 1983. Forty French Towns: an essay on archaeological site evaluation and historical aims. *Oxford Journal of Archaeology* 2: 339–78.

—— 1993. *Arguments in Stone. Archaeological Research and the European Town in the First Millennium*. Oxbow Monograph 29. Oxford: Oxbow Books.

—— (ed.) 1995. *Excavations at York Minster I*. London: CBA

Casey, D. A. 1931. Lydney castle, Gloucestershire. *Antiquaries Journal* 11: 240–61.

Caygill, M. 1997. Franks and the British Museum: the Cuckoo in the Nest. In M Caygill and J. Cherry (eds) *A. W. Franks. Nineteenth-century Collecting and the British Museum*: 51–114. London: British Museum Press.

CBA Publications Committee. 1976. *Signposts for Archaeological Publication: a Guide to Good Practice in the Presentation and Printing of Archaeological Periodicals and Monographs*. London: CBA.

Celoria, F. and Spencer, B. W. 1966–70. Eighteenth century fieldwork in London and Middlesex. *Transactions of the London and Middlesex Archaeological Society* 22: 22–31.

Chadwick, A. 2000. Taking English archaeology into the next millennium: a personal review of the state of the art. *Assemblage* 5 (online journal: assemblage@sheffield.ac.uk).

Chaffers, W. 1850. On medieval earthenware vessels. *JBAA* 5: 23–39.

Champion, S. 1973. *Andover. The Archaeological Implications of Development*. Andover and District Excavation Committee.

Champion, T. C. 1996. Protecting the monuments: archaeological legislation from the 1882 Act to PPG 16. In M. Hunter (ed.) *Preserving the Past. The Rise of Heritage in Modern Britain*: 38–56. Stroud: Sutton.

Champion, T. C., Shennan, S. and Cuming, P. 1995. *Planning for the Past, volume 3*. London: Univ. of Southampton and English Heritage.

Chandler, A. 1971. *A Dream of Order. The Medieval Ideal in Nineteenth-century English Literature*. London: Routledge and Kegan Paul.

Chandler, J. (ed.) 1993. *John Leland's Itinerary: Travels in Tudor England*. Stroud: Sutton.

Chapelot, J. and Fossier, R. 1980. *The Village and House in the Middle Ages*. London: Batsford.

Chaplin, R. E. 1971. *The Study of Animal Bones from Archaeological Sites*. London and New York: Seminar Press.

Charles, F. W. B. 1967. *Medieval Cruck-building and its Derivatives*. SMA Monograph 2. London: SMA.

Charleston, R. J. 1975. The glass. In C. Platt and R. Coleman-Smith (eds) *Excavations in Medieval Southampton, 1953–1969*, vol 1: 204–26. Leicester: LUP.

Charlton, J. 1936. Excavations at Dunstanburgh Castle. *Archaeologia Aeliana* 25: 181–96.

Charters, S., Evershed, R. P., Blinkhorn, P. W. and Denham, V. 1995. Evidence for mixing of fats and waxes in archaeological ceramics. *Archaeometry* 37 (1): 113–27.

Chater, A. G. and Major, A. F. 1909. Excavations at Downend. *PSANHS* 4: 162–73.

Cherry, J. 1986. Technology, towns, castles and churches AD 1100–1600. In I. Longworth and J. Cherry (eds) *Archaeology in Britain Since 1945*: 161–96. London: British Museum Press.

—— 1992. The breaking of seals. *Medieval Europe 1992, Art and Symbolism, pre-printed papers, vol. 7*: 23–27. York: Medieval Europe.

—— 1997. Franks and the medieval collections. In M. Caygill and J. Cherry (eds) *A. W. Franks. Nineteenth-century Collecting and the British Museum*: 184–200. London: British Museum Press.

Chorley, R. J. and Haggett, P. (eds) 1967. *Models in Geography*. London: Methuen.

Christie, P. M. and Coad, J. G. 1980. Excavations at Denny Abbey. *Archaeological Journal* 137: 138–279.

Church, A. H. 1884. *English Earthenware: a Handbook to the Wares Made in England During the Seventeenth and Eighteenth Centuries as Illustrated by Specimens in the National Collections*. London: Chapman and Hall Ltd.

City of Bristol Museum and Art Gallery. 1979. *Rescue Archaeology in the Bristol Area: 1*. Monograph No. 2. Bristol: City of Bristol Museum and Art Gallery.

Clapham, A. W. 1922. Haverfordwest Priory. Report on the excavations of June 1922. *Archaeologia Cambrensis* 77: 327–34.

—— 1934. *English Romanesque Architecture after the Conquest*. Oxford: OUP.

Clark, A. 1891–1900. *The Life and Times of Anthony Wood*. Oxford: Clarendon Press.

—— 1987. *Scientific Dating Techniques*. IFA Technical Paper No. 5. London: IFA.

—— 1990. *Seeing Beneath the Soil*. London: Routledge.

Clark, G. T. 1850. Castell Coch, Glamorgan. *Archaeologia Cambrensis*, new series, 1: 241–250.

—— 1884. *Mediaeval Military Architecture in England*. London: Wyman and Sons.

Clark, J. (ed.) 1995. *The Medieval Horse and Its Equipment, c.1150–c.1450*. London; HMSO.

Clark, K. 1950 (revised and enlarged edn). *The Gothic Revival: an Essay in the History of Taste*. London: Constable. (1st edn 1928).

Clarke, D. L. 1968. *Analytical Archaeology*. London: Methuen

—— 1977. Spatial information in archaeology. In D. L. Clarke (ed.) *Spatial Archaeology*: 1–32. London: Academic Press.

Clarke, H. 1981. The medieval waterfront at King's Lynn. In G. Milne and B. Hobley (eds) *Waterfront Archaeology in Britain and Northern Europe* 132–35. CBA Research Report 41. London: CBA.

—— 1984. *The Archaeology of Medieval England*. London: British Museum Press.

Clarke, H. and Carter A. 1977. *Excavations in Kings Lynn 1963–1971*. SMA Monograph 7. London.

Cleere, H. 1971. Iron-making materials. In J. H. Money, Medieval iron-workings in Minepit Wood, Rotherfield, Sussex. *Medieval Archaeology* 15: 103–07 (86–111).

Cobbett, W. 1824–6. *History of the Protestant Reformation*. London: Charles Clement.

Cocke, T. 1973. Pre-19th century attitudes in England to Romanesque Architecture. *JBAA* 36: 72–97.

—— 1987. The wheel of fortune: the appreciation of Gothic since the Middle Ages. In J. Alexander and P. Binski (eds) *Age of Chivalry. Art in Plantagenet England 1200–1400*, 183–91. London: Royal Academy of Arts.

—— 1998. Robert Willis: the religious revival and its impact on architecture. In V. Brand (ed.) *The Study of the Past in the Victorian Age*: 93–102. Oxbow Monograph 73. Oxford: Oxbow Books.

Cocke, T., Findlay, D., Halsey, R. and Williamson, E. 1996. *Recording a Church: an Illustrated Glossary*. Practical Handbooks in Archaeology No. 7. London: CBA.

Coldstream N. and Draper, P. 1980. *Medieval Art and Architecture at Durham Cathedral*. British Archaeological Association Conference Transactions 3. London: British Archaeological Association.

Coleman, D. C. 1987. *History and the Economic Past. An account of the Rise and Decline of Economic History in Britain*. Oxford: Clarendon Press.

Coleman-Smith, R. J. and Pearson T. 1988. *Excavations in the Donyatt Potteries*. Chichester: Phillimore.

Coles, J. and Hall, D. 1997. The Fenland Project: from survey to management and beyond. *Antiquity* 71: 831–44.

Coles, R. 1935. The past history of the forest of Essex. *Essex Naturalist* 24: 115–33.

Coletti, T. 1988. *Naming the Rose. Eco, Medieval Signs, and Modern Theory*. Ithaca and London: Cornell Univ. Press.

Colleton Rennie, C. G. 1876. Account of excavations at Basing House. *Proceedings of the Society of Antiquaries* 6: 461–65.

Collinson, J. 1791. *The History and Antiquities of the County of Somerset*. Bath: printed by R. Cruttwell and sold by C. Dilly.

Collis, J. 1979. Foreword. In M. Maltby *Faunal Studies on Urban Sites. The Animal Bones from Exeter 1971–1975*. Exeter Archaeological Reports 2: ix-x. Sheffield: Dept. of Prehistory and Archaeology, Univ. of Sheffield.

Colvin, H. M. (ed.) 1963. *The History of the King's Works: Volumes 1–2. The Middle Ages*. London: HMSO.

—— (ed.) 1971. *Building Accounts of King Henry III*. Oxford: Clarendon Press.

—— (gen. ed.) 1975. *The History of the King's Works: Volume III, 1485–1660 (Part I)*. London: HMSO.

—— (gen. ed.) 1982. *The History of the King's Works: Volume IV, 1485–1660 (Part II)*. London: HMSO.

CAS 1910. *Report of the Committee on Ancient Earthworks and Fortified Enclosures, July 6th 1910*. CAS in union with the Society of Antiquaries of London. London: Congress of Archaeological Sciences.

—— 1926. *Report of the 34th Congress and of the Earthworks and Research Committees*. London: Congress of Archaeological Societies.

—— 1930. First Report of the Research Committee. In *Report of the 38th Congress and of the Earthworks and Research Committees*: 29–36. London: Congress of Archaeological Societies.

Conzen, M. R. G. 1960. *Alnwick, Northumberland. A Study in Town-Plan Analysis*. London: The Institute of British Geographers Publications 27.

—— 1968. The use of town plans in the study of urban history. In H. J. Dyos (ed.) *The Study of Urban History*: 113–30. London: Edward Arnold.

Cook, R. M. and Belshé, J. C. 1958. Archaeomagnetism: a preliminary report on Britain. *Antiquity* 32: 167–178.

Coones, P. 1985. One landscape or many? A geographical perspective. *Landscape History* 7: 5–12.

Cooper, M. A. (ed.) 1995. *Managing Archaeology*. Stroud: Alan Sutton.

Cooper, N. 1988. The recording of threatened buildings: an aspect of the work of the Royal Commission on the Historical Monuments of England. *Transactions of the Ancient Monuments Society*, 32: 28–45.

Copeland, T. 1990. *Kenilworth Castle. A Handbook for Teachers*. Colchester: English Heritage.

Coppack, G. 1989. Thornholme Priory: the development of a monastic outer court. In R. Gilchrist and H. Mytum (eds) *The Archaeology of Rural Monasteries*. Oxford: BAR 203: 185–222.

—— 1990. *Abbeys and Priories*. London: Batsford and English Heritage.

—— 1991. *Mount Grace Priory*. London: English Heritage.

—— 1999. Setting and structure. The conservation of Wigmore Castle. In G. Chitty and D. Baker (eds) *Managing Historic Sites and Buildings. Reconciling Presentation and Preservation*: 61–70. London: Routledge.

Coppack, G., Emerick, K., Wilson, K., Dittmar, J. K., Szymanski, J. E, Tsourlos, P. and Giannopoulos, A. 1992. Recent archaeological discoveries at the medieval site of Fountains Abbey. *Medieval Europe 1992. Religion and Belief, Pre-Printed Papers* vol. 6: 47–54.

Corcos, N. 2001. Churches as pre-historic ritual monuments: a review and phenomenological perspective from Somerset. *Assemblage* 6 (online journal: assemblage @sheffield.ac.uk).

Cotter, J. 1997. *A Twelfth-Century Pottery Kiln at Pound Lane, Canterbury*. Canterbury Archaeological Trust Occasional Paper no. 1. Canterbury: Canterbury Archaeological Trust.

—— 2000. *Post-Roman Pottery from Excavations in Colchester, 1971–85*. Colchester: Colchester Archaeological Trust.

Cotton, M. A. 1962. The Norman bank of Colchester Castle. *Antiquaries Journal* 42: 57–61.

Coulson, C. 1979. Structural symbolism in medieval castle architecture. *JBAA* 132: 73–90.

——— 1991. Bodiam Castle: truth and tradition. *Fortress* 10: 3–15.

Courtney, P. 1994. *Medieval and Later Usk. Report on the Excavations at Usk 1965–76*. Cardiff: Univ. of Wales Press.

——— 1997. After Postan: English medieval archaeology and the growth of commerce before the Black Death. In D. De Boe and F. Verhaeghe (eds) *Method and Theory in Historical Archaeology*. Pre-printed papers of the Medieval Europe Brugge 1997 Conference, vol. 10: 175–180. Zellik: Medieval Europe Brugge.

Cowgill, J., De Neergard, M. and Griffiths, N. 1987. *Medieval Finds from Excavations in London: 1. Knives and Scabbards*. London: HMSO.

Cox, C. J. 1916 *Bench Ends in English Churches*. London: OUP.

Cox, J. C. 1905. *The Royal Forests of England*. London: Methuen.

Cram, R. A. 1906. *The Ruined Abbeys of Great Britain*. London: Gay and Bird.

Crawford, O. G. S. 1921. *Man and his Past*. London: OUP.

——— 1925. Air photograph of Gainstrop, Lincs. *Antiquaries Journal* 5: 432–434.

——— 1928. *Air Survey and Archaeology*. Ordnance Survey Professional Papers New Series No. 7. Southampton: HMSO.

——— 1942. Buildings and monuments of historical and architectural value. In S. D. Ashead and H. T. Cook *The Replanning of Southampton*. Southampton: County Borough Council.

——— 1953. *Archaeology in the Field*. London: Phoenix House.

——— 1960. *Archaeology in the Field*. London: Phoenix House.

Crawford, O. G. S. and Keiller, A. 1928. *Wessex from the Air*. Oxford: OUP.

Crittall, E. 1975. *A History of Wiltshire*. Victoria History of the Counties of England, vol. X. Oxford: OUP.

Croad, S. 1989. Architectural Records in the Archive of the Royal Comission on the Historical Monuments of England. *Transactions of the Ancient Monuments Society* 33: 23–44.

Croft, R. A. and Mynard, D. C. 1993. *The Changing Landscape of Milton Keynes*. Buckinghamshire Archaeological Society Monograph 5. Aylesbury: Buckinghamshire Archaeological Society.

Crook, J. 1993. The medieval roof of Marwell Hall, Hampshire. *Antiquaries Journal* 73: 69–75.

Crook, J. M. 1970. Introduction. In C. Eastlake *A History of the Gothic Revival*: 13–60. New York: LUP.

——— 1987. *The Dilemma of Style: Architectural Ideas from the Picturesque to the Post-Modern*. London: Murray

Crossley, D. W. 1975. *The Bewl Valley Ironworks, Kent, c.1300–1730*. London: Royal Archaeological Institute Monograph.

——— (ed.) 1981. *Medieval Industry*. CBA Research Report 40. London: CBA.

Crowfoot, E., Pritchard, F. and Staniland, K. 1992. *Medieval Finds from Excavations in London:* vol. 4. *Textiles and Clothing*. London: HMSO.

Crowther, J. 1995. Soils and ditch sediments from excavations at Westbury. In R. Ivens, P. Busby, and N. Shepherd *Tattenhoe and Westbury. Two Deserted Medieval Settlements in Milton Keynes*. Buckinghamshire Archaeology Society Monograph Series 8: 454–61. Aylesbury: Buckinghamshire Archaeology Society.

——— 1997. Soil phosphate surveys: critical approaches to sampling, analysis and interpretation. *Archaeological Prospection* 4: 93–102.

Cruden, S. 1951–2. Scottish medieval pottery: the Bothwell Castle Collection. *PSAS* 86: 140–170.

—— 1952–3. Scottish medieval pottery: the Melrose Abbey Collection. *PSAS* 87: 161–75.

Crummy, P. 1987. Presenting the results: the popular publication. In H. Mytum and K. Waugh (eds) *Rescue Archaeology. What's Next?* Univ. of York Monograph 6: 59–71. York: Dept. of Archaeology, Univ. of York Monograph and Rescue, The British Archaeological Trust.

—— 1988. *Reducing Publication Costs.* IFA Archaeologist Technical Paper No.6. Stockbridge: IFA.

Crummy, N., Crummy, P. and Crossan, C. 1993. *Excavations of Roman and Later Cemeteries, Churches amd Monastic Sites in Colchester, 1971–88.* Colchester Archaeological Reports 9. Colchester: Colchester Archaeological Trust.

Cumberpatch, C. G. 1997a. Towards a phenomenological approach to the study of medieval pottery. In C. G. Cumberpatch and P. W. Blinkhorn (eds) *Not so Much a Pot, More a Way of Life.* Oxbow Monograph 83: 125–52. Oxford: Oxbow Books.

—— 1997b. Concepts of economy and 'habitus' in the study of later medieval ceramic assemblages. *Archaeological Review from Cambridge,* vol. 14.2: 9–22.

Cumberpatch, C. G. and Blinkhorn, P. W. 1997. Introduction. In C. G. Cumberpatch and P. W. Blinkhorn (eds) *Not so Much a Pot, More a Way of Life.* Oxbow Monograph 83: v–vi. Oxford: Oxbow Books.

Cunliffe, B. W. 1982. *The Report of a Joint Working Party of the Council for British Archaeology and the Department of the Environment.* London: DoE.

—— 1985. *Heywood Sumner's Wessex.* Wimborne: Roy Gasson Associates.

Currie, C. R. J. and Lewis C. P. (eds) 1997. *A Guide to English County Histories.* Stroud: Sutton.

Dalwood, H. 2000. The archaeology of small towns in Worcestershire. *Transactions of the Worcestershire Archaeological Society* 17: 215–21.

Dalwood, H. and Atkin, M. 1998. *The Impact of Extensive Urban Survey in Hereford and Worcester.* Unpublished typescript report, Hereford and Worcester County Archaeological Service.

Damon, P. E., Donahue, D. J., Gore, B. H., Hatheway, A. L., Jull, A. J. T., Linick, T. W., Sercel, P. J., Toolin, L. J., Bronk, C. R., Hall, E. T., Hedges, R. E. M., Housley, R., Law, I. A., Perry, C., Bonani, G., Trumbore, S., Woelfli, W., Ambers, J. C., Bowman, S. G. E., Leese, M. N. and Tite, M. S. 1989. Radiocarbon dating of the Shroud of Turin. *Nature* 337: 611–15.

Daniel, G. 1981. *A Short History of Archaeology.* London: Thames and Hudson.

Daniell, C. 1997. *Death and Burial in Medieval England 1066–1550.* London: Routledge.

Darby, H. C. 1932. Human geography of the Fenland before the drainage. *Geographical Journal* 80: 400–35.

—— 1934. Domesday woodland in East Anglia. *Antiquity* 8: 185–99.

—— 1940. *The Draining of the Fens.* Cambridge: CUP.

—— 1951. Changing English Landscape. *Geographical Journal* 117: 377–94.

—— 1952. *The Domesday Geography of Eastern England.* Cambridge: CUP.

—— 1953. On the relations of geography and history. *Transactions and Papers of the Institute of British Geographers* 19: 1–11.

Dark, K. 1995. *Theoretical Archaeology.* London: Duckworth.

Darvill, T. C. 1993. Working practices. In J. Hunter and I. Ralston (eds) *Archaeological Resource Management in the UK. An Introduction*: 169–83. Stroud: Sutton.

Darvill, T. C. and Atkins, M. 1991. *Regulating Archaeological Work by Contract.* IFA Technical paper 8. Birmingham: IFA.

Darvill, T. C., Burrow, S. and Wildgust, D. A. 1995. *Planning for the Past vol. 2. An Assessment of Archaeological Assessments, 1982–91.* London: English and Heritage and Bournemouth Univ.

Darvill, T. C. and Fulton, A. 1998. *MARS: The Monuments at Risk Survey of England. Main Report.* Bournemouth and London: Bournemouth Univ. and English Heritage.

Darvill, T. C. and Gerrard, C. M. 1994. *Cirencester: Town and Landscape.* Cirencester: Cotswold Archaeological Trust.

Darvill, T., Gerrard, C. M. and Startin, B. 1993. Identifying and protecting historic landscapes. *Antiquity* 67: 563–74.

Darvill, T. C., Saunders, A. and Startin, B. 1987. A question of national importance: approaches to the evaluation of ancient monuments for the Monuments Protection Programme in England. *Antiquity* 61: 393–408.

Davey, P. and Hodges, R. 1983. *Ceramics and Trade. The Production and Distribution of Later Medieval Pottery in North-West Europe.* Sheffield: Dept. of Prehistory and Archaeology, Univ. of Sheffield.

David, A. 1995. *Geophysical Survey in Archaeological Field Evaluation.* English Heritage Research and Professional Services Guideline 1. London: English Heritage.

Davison, B. K. 1969. Normandy field survey, 1969. *Archaeologial Journal* 126: 179–80.

—— 1972. Castle Neroche: an abandoned Norman fortress in south Somerset. *PSANHS* 116: 116–58.

—— 1978. Excavations at Sulgrave, Northamptonshire, 1969–76: an interim report. In D. Parsons (ed.) *Five Castle Excavations. Reports on the Institute's Research Project into the Origins of the Castle in England*: 105–14. Leeds: Royal Archaeological Institute Monograph.

Dawes, J. D. and Magilton, J. R. 1980. *The Cemetery of St Helen-on-the-Walls, Aldwark. The Archaeology of York: The Medieval Cemeteries 12/1.* York: CBA.

Day, S. P. 1993. Origins of medieval woodland. In P. Beswick and I. D. Rotherham (eds) *Ancient Woodlands, Their Archaeology and Ecology, a Coincidence of Interest.* Sheffield: Landscape Conservation Forum.

Defoe, D. 1742 (3rd edn). *A Tour thro' the Whole Island of Great Britain.* London: printed for J. Osborn.

Delaney, T. G. 1977. The archaeology of the Irish town. In M. W. Barley (ed.) *European Towns and Their Archaeology and Early History*: 47–64. London: Academic Press for CBA.

Dellheim, C. 1982. *The Face of the Past. The Preservation of the Medieval Inheritance in Victorian England.* Cambridge: CUP.

Démians d'Archimbaud, G. 1975. Monnaies, céramiques et chronologie: essai d'analyse des fouilles de Rougiers (Var). *Provence Historique* 25, fascicule 100: 227–41.

Dickins, B. 1961. The progress of English place-name studies since 1901. *Antiquity* 25: 281–85.

Dickinson, F. H. (ed.) 1889. *Kirby's Quest for Somerset, etc.* Somerset Record Society 3. London: Harrison and Sons.

Dickinson, R. E. 1949. Rural settlements in the German lands. *Annals of the Association of American Geographers* 39: 239–63.

Dimbleby, G. 1967. *Plants and Archaeology.* London: John Baker.

Dixon, P. and Marshall, P. 1993. The Great Tower in the twelfth century: the case of Norham Castle. *Archaeological Journal* 150: 410–32.

Dobney, K. M. Jaques, S. D. and Irving, B. G. 1995. *Of Butchers and Breeds: Report on Vertebrate Remains from Various Sites in the City of Lincoln*. Lincoln Archaeological Studies 5. Lincoln: Lincoln Archaeology Unit.

DoE 1975. *Principles of Publication in Rescue Archaeology*. Report by a Working Party of the Ancient Monuments Board for England, Committee for Rescue Archaeology. London: DoE.

—— 1990. *Planning Policy Guidance 16: Archaeology and Planning*. London: DoE and HMSO.

Donoghue, D. N. M. 2001. Remote sensing. In D. R. Brothwell and A. M. Pollard (eds) *Handbook of Archaeological Science*: 555–63. Chichester: John Wiley and Sons.

Donaldson, A. 1979. Plant life and plant use. In M. O. H. Carver, Three Saxo-Norman tenements in Durham City, 55–60. *Medieval Archaeology* 23: 55–60 (1–80).

Donaldson, A. M., Jones, A. K. G. and Rackham, D. J. 1980. Barnard Castle, Co. Durham. A dinner in the Great Hall: Report on the contents of a fifteenth-century drain. *JBAA* 133: 86–96.

Donkin, R. A. 1963. The Cistercian order in medieval England: some conclusions. *Transactions and Papers of the Institute of British Geographers* 33: 181–98.

Down, A. 1974. *Chichester Excavations 2*. Chichester. Phillimore for Chichester Civic Society Excavations Committee.

Down, A. and Rule, M. 1971. *Chichester Excavations 1*. Chichester: Chichester Civic Society.

Drewett, P. L. 1976. *An Extensive View of Plough Damage to Known Archaeological Sites in West and East Sussex*. London: Institute of Archaeology.

Driscoll, S. T. 1984. The New Medieval Archaeology: Theory vs. History. *Scottish Archaeological Review* 1984: 104–8.

Driver, J C., Rady, J. and Sparks, M. 1990. *Excavations in the Cathedral Precincts, 2 Linacre Garden, 'Meister Omers' and St Gabriel's Chapel*. The Archaeology of Canterbury, vol. IV. Gloucester: Canterbury Archaeological Trust.

Duby, G. 1974. *Early Growth of the European Economy*. London: Weidenfeld and Nicholson.

Duffy, E. 1992. *The Stripping of the Altars*. New Haven and London: Yale Univ. Press.

Dugdale, W. 1656. *The Antiquities of Warwickshire*. London: printed by Thomas Warren.

Duignan, W. H. 1902. *Notes on Staffordshire Place-Names*. London: OUP.

Dunbar, J. G. 1999. *Scottish Royal Palaces: The Architecture of the Royal Residences during the Late Medieval and Early Renaissance Periods*. East Linton: Tuckwell Press, Historic Scotland.

Dunkley, J. A. and Cumberpatch, C. G. 1996. *Excavations at 16–20 Church Street, Bawtry, South Yorkshire*. Oxford: BAR 248.

Dunning, G. C. 1936. Alstoe Mount, Burley, Rutland. *Archaeological Journal* 26: 396–411.

—— 1942. A medieval jug and its contents. *The Lancet* 11 July: 56.

—— 1961. A group of English and imported medieval pottery from Lesnes Abbey, Kent and the trade in early Hispano-Moresque to England. *Antiquaries Journal* 41: 1–12.

Dyer, C. C. 1986. English peasant buildings in the later Middle Ages. *Medieval Archaeology* 30: 19–45.

—— 1989. *Standards of Living in the Later Middle Ages. Social Change in England c.1200–1520.* Cambridge: CUP.

—— 1990a. Dispersed settlements in medieval England. A case study of Pendock, Worcestershire. *Medieval Archaeology* 34: 97–121.

—— 1990b.The past, the present and the future in medieval rural history. *Rural History* 1 (1): 36–49.

—— 1991. *Hanbury: Settlement and Society in a Woodland Landscape.* Leicester: Univ. of Leicester, Dept. of English Local History Occasional Papers, 4th series, 4.

—— 1992. Current study of medieval rural settlements in England. In Medieval Europe 1992. *Rural Settlement,* pre-printed papers vol. 8: 227–31. York: Medieval Europe 1992.

—— 1995. Sheepcotes: evidence for medieval sheepfarming. *Medieval Archaeology* 39: 136–64.

—— 1997. Recent developments and future prospects in research into English medieval rural settlements. In G. De Boe and F. Verhaege (eds) *Rural Settlements in Medieval Europe,* Pre-printed papers of the Medieval Europe Brugge 1997 Conference, vol. 6: 55–61. Zellick: Medieval Europe Brugge.

—— 1999a. The Medieval Settlement Research Group Whittlewood Project. *Medieval Settlement Research Group Annual Report* 14: 16–17.

—— 1999b. The lost villages of England, 1954–1998. In M. Beresford *The Lost Villages of England,* repr.: xii–xxviii. Trowbridge: Sutton.

Eames, E. 1980. *Medieval Leadglazed Earthenware Floor Tiles in the Department of Medieval and Later Antiquities.* London: British Museum Catalogue, 2 vols.

Earl, J. 1996. London government: a record of custodianship. In M. Hunter (ed.) *Preserving the Past. The Rise of Heritage in Modern Britain*: 57–76. Stroud: Sutton.

Earle, J. 1633. *Microcosmographie.* London: Methuen and Co.

Eastlake, C. L. 1872. *A History of the Gothic Revival.* London: Longmans, Green and Co.

Eco, U. 1984. *The Name of the Rose.* London: Picador.

—— 1986. Dreaming of the Middle Ages. In U. Eco (ed.) *Travels in Hyper Reality,* trans. William Weaver. San Diego: Harcourt Brace Jovanovich.

Eddison, J. and Draper, G. 1998. A landscape of medieval reclamation: Walland Marsh, Kent. *Landscape History* 19: 75–88.

Egan, G. 1996. *Playthings from the Past.* London: Jonathan Horne (exhibition catalogue).

—— 1997. Children's pastimes in past time: medieval toys found in the British Isles. In G. De Boe and F. Verhaeghe (eds) *Material Culture in Medieval Europe, Papers of the Medieval Europe Brugge 1997 Conference,* Pre-printed papers of the Medieval Europe Brugge 1997 Conference, vol. 7: 413–21. Zellik: Medieval Europe Brugge.

—— 1998. *Medieval Finds from Excavations in London 6. The Medieval Household: Daily Living c.1150–c.1450.* London: HMSO and Museum of London.

Egan, G. and Pritchard, F. 1991. *Medieval Finds from Excavations in London 3. Dress Accessories.* London: HMSO.

Ekwall, E. 1922. *The Place-Names of Lancashire.* Manchester: MUP.

—— 1951. *Concise Oxford Dictionary of English Place-Names.* Oxford: OUP.

Ellis, P. 1992. *Mendip Hills. An Archaeological Survey of an AONB.* Taunton and London: Somerset County Council and English Heritage.

—— (ed.) 1993. *Beeston Castle, Cheshire, a Report on the Excavations 1968–85 by Lawrence Keen and Peter Hough.* HBMC Archaeological Report 23. London: English Heritage.

—— (ed.) 2000. *Ludgershall Castle, Wiltshire. A Report on the Excavations by Peter Addyman, 1964–1972*. Wiltshire Archaeological and Natural History Society Monograph 2. Devizes: Wiltshire Archaeological and Natural History Society.

Ellison, A. and Harriss, J. 1972. Settlement and land use in the prehistory and early history of southern Britain: a study based on locational models. In D. Clarke (ed.) *Models in Archaeology*: 911–62. London: Methuen.

Emery, A. 1970. *Dartington Hall*. Oxford: OUP.

—— 1996. *Greater Medieval Houses of England and Wales 1300–1500. Vol. 1: Northern England*. Cambridge: CUP.

Emery, F. V. 1962. Moated settlements in England. *Geography* 47: 378–88.

English Heritage 1991a. *Exploring Our Past: Strategies for the Archaeology of England*. London: English Heritage.

—— 1991b. *Management of Archaeological Projects 2*. London: RCHME.

—— 1997. *English Heritage Archaeology Division Research Agenda (Draft)*. London: English Heritage.

Evans, D. H. (ed.) 1993. *Excavations in Hull 1975–6*. East Riding Archaeologist 4, Hull Old Town Reports Series 2. Hull: East Riding Archaeological Society and the Archaeological Unit, Humberside County Council.

Evans, D. H. and Jarrett, M. G. 1987 The deserted village of West Whelpington, Northumberland: third report, part one. *Archaeologia Aeliana*, 5th series, 15: 199–308.

Evans, D. H., Jarrett, M. G. and Wrathmell, S. 1988. The deserted village of West Whelpington, Northumberland: third report, part two. *Archaeologia Aeliana*, 5th ser, 16: 139–92.

Evans, J. 1949. The Royal Archaeological Institute: a retrospect. *Archaeological Journal* 106: 1–11.

—— 1956. *A History of the Society of Antiquaries*. Oxford: OUP.

—— 1961. Anniversary Address. *Antiquaries Journal* 41: 149–53.

Evelyn, J. 1706. *An Account of Architects and Architecture*. London.

Everson, P. 1989. Rural monasteries within the secular landscape. In R. Gilchrist and H. Mytum (eds) *The Archaeology of Rural Monasteries*: 141–6. Oxford: BAR 203.

—— 1998. 'Delightfully surrounded with woods and ponds': Field evidence for medieval gardens in England'. In P. Pattison (ed.) *There by Design. Field Archaeology in Parks and Gardens*: 32–7. Oxford: BAR 267.

Everson, P., Brown, G. and Stocker, D. 2000. The Castle earthworks and landscape context. In P. Ellis (ed.) *Ludgershall Castle. A Report on the Excavations by Peter Addyman*: 95–117. Wiltshire Archaeological Society Monograph 2. Devizes: Wiltshire Archaeological and Natural History Society.

Everson, P., Taylor, C. C. and Dunn, C. J. 1991. *Change and Continuity: Rural Settlements in North-West Lincolnshire*. London: HMSO.

Evison, V. I., Hodges, H. and Hurst, J. G. 1974. A Bibliography of the works of G. C. Dunning. In Evison, V. I., Hodges, H. and Hurst, J. G. (eds) *Medieval Pottery from Excavations. Studies Presented to Gerald Clough Dunning with a Bibliography of his Works*: 17–32. London: John Baker.

Eyre, S. R. 1955. The curving plough strip. *Ag. Hist. Rev.* 3: 80–94.

Fairbrother, J. M. 1990. *Faccombe, Netherton: Excavations of a Saxon and Medieval Complex*. Occasional Paper of the British Museum 74. London: British Museum.

Fairclough, G. 1992. Meaningful constructions: spatial and functional analysis of medieval buildings. *Antiquity* 66: 348–66.

Fairholt, F. W. 1846. *Costume in England: A History from the Earliest Period till the Close of the Eighteenth Century.* London: Chapman and Hall.

Fasham, P. J. 1984. *Groundwater Pumping Techniques for Excavation,* Institute of Field Archaeologists Technical Paper No. 1. London: IFA.

Fasham, P. J., Schadla-Hall, R. T., Shennan, S. J., and Bates, P. J. 1980. *Fieldwalking for Archaeologists.* Winchester: PHFC.

Faulkner, N. 2000. Archaeology from below. *Public Archaeology* 1 (1): 21–33.

Faulkner, P. 1980. *Against the Age. An introduction to William Morris.* London: George Allen and Unwin.

Faulkner, P. A. 1958. Domestic planning from the twelfth to the fourteenth centuries. *Archaeological Journal* 115: 150–83.

—— 1963. Castle planning in the fourteenth century. *Archaeological Journal* 120: 215–35.

Faull, M. and Moorhouse, S. A. (eds) 1981. *West Yorkshire: an Archaeological Survey to AD 1500,* 4 vols. Wakefield: West Yorkshire Metropolitan County Council.

Featherstone, R., Horne, P., Macleod, D. and Bewley, R. 1999. Aerial reconnaissance over England in summer 1996. *Archaeological Prospection* 6: 47–62.

Fehring, G. P. 1991. *The Archaeology of Medieval Germany: An Introduction.* London: Routledge.

Feinman, G. M. 1999. Defining a contemporary landscape approach: concluding thoughts. *Antiquity* 73: 684–85.

Fenwick, H. 2000. Medieval sites in the Hull Valley: distribution and modelling. In R. Van de Noort and S. Ellis (eds) *Wetland Heritage of the Hull Valley*: 183–92. Hull: Univ. of Hull.

—— 1997. The wetland potential of medieval moated sites in the Humberhead Levels. In R. Van de Noort and S. Ellis (eds) *Wetland Heritage of the Humberhead Levels*: 429–38. Hull: Univ. of Hull.

Ferguson, S. 1849. Unsigned review in the Dublin University Magazine July 1849, 34: 1–14. In J. L. Bradley (ed.) *Ruskin. The Critical Heritage*: 99–110. London: Routledge and Kegan Paul.

Fergusson, P. 1984. *Architecture of Solitude: Cistercian Abbeys in Twelfth-Century England.* Princeton: Princeton Univ. Press.

Fergusson, P. and Harrison, S. 1999. *Rievaulx Abbey. Community, Architecture and Memory.* New Haven and London: Yale Univ. Press.

Fernie, E. C. 1976. The ground plan of Norwich Cathedral and the square root of two. *JBAA* 129: 77–86.

—— 1988. Contrasts in methodology and interpretation of medieval ecclesiastical architecture. *Archaeological Journal* 145: 344–64.

Ferrers, Earl. 1987. Chairman's Foreword. RCHME *Churches of South-East England.* London: HMSO.

Ferris, I. M. 1989. The archaeological investigation of standing buildings. *Vernacular Architecture* 20: 12–17.

Field, J. 1989. *English Field Names: A Dictionary.* Stroud: Sutton.

Fieldhouse, R. 1996a. University adult education. In R. Fieldhouse (ed.) *A History of Modern British Adult Education*: 199–223. Leicester: National Institute of Adult Continuing Education (England and Wales).

—— 1996b. An overview of British adult education in the twentieth century. In R. Fieldhouse (ed.) *A History of Modern British Adult Education*: 46–76. Leicester: National Institute of Adult Continuing Education (England and Wales).

Finberg, H. P. R. 1957. *Roman and Saxon Withington: A Study in Continuity*. Leicester: Dept. of English Local History, Leicester Univ., Occasional Papers, first series, no. 8.

Finberg, H. P. R. and Skipp, V. H. T. 1967. *Local History. Objective and Pursuit*. Newton Abbot: David and Charles.

Finden-Browne, H. 2000. The vegetational history of Oldhall Copse, Old Woking. *Surrey Archaeological Collections* 87: 157–68.

Finds Research Group. 1999. *Datasheets 1–24. A Consolidated Reprint of Datasheets Issued by the Finds Research Group between 1985 and 1988*. Oxford: Finds Research Group 700–1700.

Fiorato, V., Boylston, A. and Knusel, C. (eds) 2000. *Blood Red Roses: The Archaeology of a Mass Grave from the Battle of Towton AD 1461*. Oxford: Oxbow Books.

Fleming, A. 1998. *Swaledale: The Valley of the Wild River*. Edinburgh: EUP.

Fleming, A. and Ralph, N. 1982. Medieval settlement and land use on Holne Moor, Dartmoor: the landscape evidence. *Medieval Archaeology* 26: 101–37.

Fletcher, M. and Spicer, D. 1992. The display and analysis of ridge-and-furrow from topographically surveyed data. In P. Reilly and S. Rahtz (eds) *Archaeology and The Information Age. A Global Perspective*: 97–122. London and New York: Routledge.

Flower, R. 1935. Lawrence Nowell and the discovery of England in Tudor times. *PBA* 21: 47–73.

Foard, G. 1991. The medieval pottery industry of Rockingham Forest, Northamptonshire. *Medieval Ceramics* 15: 13–20.

Fojut, N. 1987. A different approach: the situation in Scotland. In H. Mytum and K. Waugh (eds) *Rescue Archaeology. What's Next?* Univ. of York Monograph 6: 105–110. York: Univ. of York Monograph and Rescue, The British Archaeological Trust.

Ford, S. 1987. *East Berkshire Archaeological Survey*. Berkshire: Dept. of Highways and Planning, Berkshire County Council Occasional Paper 1.

Foreman, M. 1996. *Further Excavations at the Dominican Priory, Beverley 1986–89*, Sheffield Excavation Reports 4. Sheffield: Sheffield Academic Press.

Foster, S. and Smout, C. (eds) 1994. *The History of Soils and Field Systems*. Aberdeen: Aberdeen Scottish Cultural Press.

Fowler, G. 1934. Extinct waterways of the Fenlands. *Geographical Journal* 83: 30–36.

Fowler, P. J. (ed.) 1970. *Archaeology and the Landscape*. London: John Baker.

—— 1972a. Field archaeology in the future. In P. J. Fowler (ed.) *Archaeology and Landscape: Essays for L. V. Grinsell*: 96–126. London: John Baker.

—— 1972b. Field archaeology on the M5 motorway 1969–71. Some provisional results, analyses and implications. In E. Fowler (ed.) *Field Survey in British Archaeology*: 28–37. London: CBA.

—— 1976. Rural settlement and agriculture. In D. Wilson (ed.) *The Archaeology of Anglo-Saxon England*: 23–48. London: Methuen.

—— 1980. Tradition and objectives in British field archaeology. *Archaeological Journal* 137: 1–21.

Fowler, P. J. and Blackwell, I. 1998. *The Land of Lettice Sweetapple*. Stroud: Tempus.

Fox, A. 1937. Dinas Noddfa, Gellygaer Common, Glamorgan: Excavations in 1936. *Archaeologia Cambrensis* 93: 247–68.

—— 1939. Early Welsh homesteads on Gellygaer Common, Glamorgan: excavations in 1938. *Archaeologia Cambrensis* 94: 163–99.

—— 2000. *Aileen: A Pioneering Archaeologist*. Leominster: Gracewing.

Fox, C. 1923. *The Archaeology of the Cambridge Region*. Cambridge: CUP.

—— 1932. *The Personality of Britain. Its Influence on Inhabitant and Invader in Prehistoric and Early Historic Times*. Cardiff: National Museum of Wales.

Fox, C. and Fox, A. 1934. Forts and farms on Margam Mountain, Glamorgan. *Antiquity* 8: 395–413.

Fox, C. and Lord Raglan. 1951–4. *Monmouthshire Houses*. Cardiff: National Museum of Wales.

Fox, C. and Radford, C. A. R. with Dunning, G. C. 1933. Kidwelly Castle, Carmarthenshire; including a survey of the polychrome pottery found there and elsewhere in Britain. *Archaeologia* 83: 93–138.

Fox, H. S. A. (ed.) 1996. *Seasonal Settlement*. Leicester: Univ. of Leicester, Dept. of Adult Education.

Fox, L. 1997. *The Shakespeare Birthplace Trust. A Personal Memoir*. Norwich: Shakespeare Birthplace Trust.

Francis, E. B. 1913. Rayleigh Castle: new facts in its history and recent explorations on its site. *Transactions of the Essex Archaeological Society* 12: 147–86.

Frankl, P. 1960. *The Gothic. Literary Sources and Interpretations Through 8 Centuries*. Princeton Univ. Press. Offprint from The Art Bulletin 45.

Freeman, E. A. 1871. *Historical Essays* vol. IV. London: Macmillan.

Freestone, I. C. 1991. Extending ceramic petrology. In A. Middleton and I. Freestone (eds) *Recent Developments in Ceramic Petrology*. British Museum Occasional Paper 81: 399–410. London: British Museum.

Frere, S. 1988. Roman Britain since Haverfield and Richmond. A lecture delivered in All Souls College on 23 October 1987. *History and Archaeology Review* 3: 31–6.

Frew, J. 1980. An aspect of the early Gothic revival: the transformation of medievalist research, 1770–1800. *Journal of the Warburg and Courtauld Institutes* 43: 174–85.

FWA 1993: Forum for Wessex Archaeology. 1993. *Wessex and Archaeology: Opportunities, Priorities and Management in the 1990s and the New Millennium*. Salisbury: Forum for Wessex Archaeology.

Gaffney, C. and Gater, J. with Ovenden, S. 1991. *The Use of Geophysical Techniques in Archaeological Evaluations*. Institute of Field Archaeologists Technical Paper 9. London: IFA.

Gaimster, D. 1992. The publication of finds from medieval towns: Winchester Reviewed. *Medieval Archaeology* 36: 309–14.

—— 1997a. *German Stoneware 1200–1900. Archaeology and Cultural History*. London: British Museum Press.

—— 1997b. 'Distant voices, still-lifes'. Late medieval religious panel painting as a context for archaeological ceramics. In G. De Boe and F. Verhaeghe (eds) *Method and Theory in Historical Archaeology*. Pre-printed papers of the Medieval Europe Brugge 1997 Conference, vol. 10, 37–46. Zellik: Medieval Europe Brugge.

Gaimster, D., Margeson, S. and Barry, T. 1989. Medieval Britain and Ireland in 1988. *Medieval Archaeology* 33: 161–241.

Gaimster, D. and Nenk, B. 1997. English households in transition *c*.1450–1550: the ceramic evidence. In D. Gaimster and P. Stamper (eds) *The Age of Transition. The Archaeology of English Culture 1400–1600*. SMA Monograph 15. Oxford: SMA.

Gaimster, D. and Redknap, M. (eds) 1992. *Everyday and Exotic Pottery from Europe c.650–1900: Studies in Honour of John G. Hurst*. Oxford: Oxbow Books.

Gaimster, D. and Stamper, P. (eds) 1997. *The Age of Transition: The Archaeology of English Culture 1400–1600*. SMA Monograph 15. Oxford: Oxbow Books.

Gallagher, D. B. 1994. The planning of Augustinian monasteries in Scotland. In M. Locock (ed.) *Meaningful Architecture: Social Interpretations of Buildings*. Worldwide Archaeology Series 9: 167–87. Aldershot: Ashgate Publishing.

Gardiner, M. 1996. A seasonal fisherman's settlement at Dungeness, Kent. *Medieval Settlement Research Group. Annual Report 11*: 18–20.

—— 1997. The exploitation of sea-mammals in medieval England: bones and their social context. *Archaeological Journal* 154: 173–95.

—— 2000. Vernacular buildings and the development of the later medieval domestic plan in England. *Medieval Archaeology* 44: 159–80.

Garner, T. and Stratton, A. 1929 (2nd edn). *Domestic Architecture of England during the Tudor Period*. London: Batsford.

Gaskell Brown, C. (ed.) 1986. *Plymouth Excavations: the Medieval Waterfront: Woolster Street, Castle Street. The Finds*. Plymouth Museum Archaeological Series 3. Plymouth: Plymouth City Museum.

Gathercole, P. W. 1958. Excavations at Oakham Castle. *Transactions of the Leicestershire Archaeological and Historical Society* 34: 17–38.

Gearney, B. R., West, S. and Charman, J. 1997. The landscape context of medieval settlement on the south-western moors of England. Recent palaeoenvironmental evidence from Bodmin Moor and Dartmoor. *Medieval Archaeology* 41: 195–210.

Geary, P. J. 1978. *Furta Sacra. Thefts of Relics in the Central Middle Ages*. Princeton, New Jersey: Princeton Univ. Press.

Geddes, J. 1999. *Medieval Decorative Ironwork in England*. London: Society of Antiquaries of London.

Gelling, M. 1978. *Signposts to the Past: Place-Names and the History of England*. London: Dent.

Gelling, P. S. 1962–3. Medieval shielings in the Isle of Man. *Medieval Archaeology* 6/7: 156–72.

Gent, T. 1730. *Ancient and Modern History of the Famous City of York, and in a Particular Manner of its Magnificent Cathedral*. London.

—— 1733. *The Ancient and Modern History of the Loyal Town of Ripon*. York: T. Hammond.

Gerrard, C. M. 1985. Ham Hill stone: a medieval distribution pattern from Somerset. *Oxford Journal of Archaeology* 4: 105–15.

—— 1987. *Trade and Settlement in Medieval Somerset. An Application of Some Geographical and Economic Models to Historical Data*. Unpublished PhD thesis, Univ. of Bristol.

—— 1997. Misplaced faith? Medieval pottery and fieldwalking. *Medieval Ceramics* 21: 61–72.

Gerrard, G. A. M. 1988. Phosphate analysis of Buildings 1–4. In D. A. Austin, Excavations and survey at Bryn Cysegrfan, Llanfair Clydogan, Dyfed, 1979. *Medieval Archaeology* 32: 130–65.

Giddens, A. 1984. *The Constitution of Society*. Cambridge: Polity Press.

Gilchrist, R. 1988. The spatial archaeology of gender domains: a case study of medieval English nunneries. *Archaeological Review from Cambridge* 7: 21–8.

—— 1992. Knight Clubs: an archaeology of the Military Orders. *Medieval Europe 1992, Religion and Belief*, pre-printed papers, vol. 6: 65–70. York: Medieval Europe 1992.

—— 1994. *Gender and Material Culture: the Archaeology of Religious Women*. London: Routledge.

—— 1995. *Contemplation and Action. The Other Monasticism*. London: LUP.

—— 1997. Ambivalent bodies: gender and medieval archaeology. In J. Moore and E. Scott (eds). *Invisible People and Processes. Writing Gender and Childhood into European Archaeology*: 42–58. London: LUP.

—— 1999a. Churches, castles and monasteries. In J. Hunter and I. Ralston (eds) *The Archaeology of Britain*: 228–46. London: Routledge.

—— 1999b. *Gender and Archaeology. Contesting the Past*. London: Routledge.

Gilchrist, R. and Mytum, H. (eds) 1989. *The Archaeology of Rural Monasteries*. Oxford: BAR 203.

Gilchrist, R. and Mytum, H. (eds) 1993. *Advances in Monastic Archaeology*. Oxford: BAR 227.

Gillies, K. J. S. and Cox, G A. 1983. Medieval window glass: its composition and decay. In A. Aspinall and S. E. Warren (eds) *Proceedings of the 22nd Symposium on Archaeometry*: 181–83.

Gilmour, B. J. J. and Stocker, D. A. 1986. *St Mark's Church and Cemetery*. The Archaeology of Lincoln XIII–1. Lincoln.

Gilpin, W. 1782. *Observations on the River Wye, etc., relative chiefly to Picturesque Beauty, made in the Summer of 1770*, London: printed for R. Blamire.

Gingell, C. 1976. *Archaeology in the Wiltshire Countryside: a Report Prepared for the Wiltshire Archaeological and Natural History Society*. Devizes: Devizes Museum.

Girling, M. 1981. The environmental evidence. In J. E. Mellor and T. Pearce *The Austin Friars, Leicester*. Leicestershire Archaeological Field Unit Report. CBA Research Report 35: 169–72. Leicester: Leicestershire County Council.

Glassie, J. 1975. *Folk Housing in Middle Virginia*. Knoxville: Tenessee Press.

Glazebrook, J. (ed.) 1997. *Research and Archaeology: a Framework for the Eastern Counties. 1. Resource and Assessment*, East Anglian Archaeology, Occasional Paper 3. Norwich: Scole Archaeological Committee.

Glenn, T. A. 1915. Prehistoric and historic remains at Dyserth Castle. *Archaeologia Cambrensis*, 6 ser., 15: 47–86.

Glennie, P. 1995. Consumption within historical studies. In D. Miller (ed.) *Acknowledging Consumption. A Review of New Studies*: 164–203. London and New York: Routledge.

Godbold, S. and Turner, R. C. 1994. Medieval fishtraps in the Severn Estuary. *Medieval Archaeology* 38: 19–54.

Godfrey, W. H. 1928. *The Story of Architecture in England, I*. London: Batsford.

—— 1953. Sir Alfred Clapham, 1883–1950. *PBA* 39: 351–54.

Gomme, G. L. (ed.) 1890. *Sacred and Medieval Architecture. A Classified Collection of the Chief Contents of 'The Gentleman's Magazine' from 1731–1868. Volume I*. London: Elliot Stock.

Good, G. L. and Tabraham, C. J. 1981. Excavations at Threave Castle, Galloway, 1974–78. *Medieval Archaeology* 25: 90–140.

Goodburn, D. 1992. Woods and woodland: carpenters and carpentry. In G. Milne (ed.) Timber Building Techniques in London c.900–1400. *London and Middlesex Archaeological Society Special Papers* 15: 106–30.

Goodich, M. 1998. *Other Middle Ages: Witnesses at the Margins of Society*. Pennsylvania: Pennsylvania Univ. Press.

Gough, R. 1768. *Anecdotes of British Topography, or, An Historical Account of What Has*

Been Done for Illustrating the Topographical Antiquities of Great Britain and Ireland. London: printed by W. Richardson and S. Clark.

—— 1786–96. *Sepulchral Monuments in Great Britain, Applied to Illustrate the History of Families, Manners, Habits and Arts, at Different Periods from the Norman Conquest to the Seventeenth Century* 2 vols. London: printed by J. Nichols for the author.

Gover, J. E. B., Mawer, A. and Stenton, F. M. 1931–2. *The Place-Names of Devon.* English Place-Name Society VIII–IX. Cambridge: CUP.

Graham, A. H. and Davies, S. 1993. *Excavations in Trowbridge, Wiltshire, 1977, and 1986–88.* Salisbury: Wessex Archaeology.

Gransden, A. 1994. The alleged incorruption of the body of St Edmund, King and Martyr. *Antiquaries Journal* 74: 169–210.

Grant, A. 1985. The large mammals. In B. W. Cunliffe and J. Munby, *Excavations at Portchester Castle. Volume IV: Medieval, the Inner Bailey*: 244–56. London: Society of Antiquaries of London.

Grant, R. 1991. *The Royal Forests of England.* Stroud: Sutton.

Graves, P. 1989. Social space in the English parish church. *Economy and Society* 18 (3): 297–322.

Gray, H. St G. 1903. Excavations at Castle Neroche, Somerset. *PSANHS* 49 (2): 23–53.

Gray, M. 1993. *The Trinitarian Order in England. Excavations at Thelsford Priory.* Oxford: BAR 226.

Green, F. J. 1983. The Palaeobotanical Evidence. In K. S. Jarvis, *Excavations in Christchurch 1969–1980*: 98. Dorset Natural History and Archaeological Society Monograph 5. Dorchester.

—— 1992. The Palaeobotanical Evidence. In I. Horsey, *Excavations in Poole 1973–1983*: 182–86. Dorchester: Dorset Natural History and Archaeological Society Monograph 11.

Greene, J. P. 1989. *Norton Priory: the Archaeology of a Medieval Religious House.* Cambridge: CUP.

—— 1992. *Medieval Monasteries.* London: LUP.

Greene, J. P. and Johnson, B. 1978. An experimental tile kiln at Norton Priory, Cheshire. *Medieval Ceramics* 2: 31–42.

Greenfield, B. W. 1892. Encaustic tiles of the Middle Ages, especially those found in the South of Hampshire. *PHFC* II: 141–66.

Greenslade, M. W. 1997. Introduction: County History. In C. R. J. Currie and C. P. Lewis (eds) *A Guide to English County Histories*: 9–25. Stroud: Sutton.

Grenville, J. 1997. *Medieval Housing.* London: LUP.

Grew, F. and de Neergaard, M. 1988. *Shoes and Pattens.* Medieval Finds from Excavations in London 2. London: HMSO.

Greig, J. 1981. The investigation of a medieval barrel-latrine from Worcester. *Journal of Archaeological Science* 8: 265–82.

—— 1986. The archaeobotany of the Cowick medieval moat and some thoughts on moat studies. *Circaea* 4: 43–50.

Greig, J. and Osborne, P. J. 1984. Plant and insect remains at Taunton Priory. In P. Leach (ed.) *The Archaeology of Taunton.* Western Archaeological Trust Excavation Monograph 8: 160–67. Gloucester: Western Archaeological Trust.

Grimes, W. F. 1956. *Excavations in the City of London.* In R. L. S. Bruce-Mitford (ed.) *Recent Archaeological Excavations in Britain*: 111–44. London: Routledge and Kegan Paul.

—— 1968. *The Excavation of Roman and Medieval London*. London: Routledge.

Grose, F. 1773–87. *Antiquities of England and Wales*. 6 vols.

Gunton, S. 1686. *A History of the Church of Peterborough*. Peterborough: printed by J. Jacob.

Gutiérrez, A. 2000. *Mediterranean Pottery in Wessex Households (12th–17thC)*. Oxford: BAR 306.

Haberly, L. 1937. *Medieval English Paving Tiles*. London.

Hagelberg E., Hedges, R. and Sykes, B. 1989. Ancient bone DNA amplified. *Nature* (30 November) 342: 485.

Hall, D. 1993. *The Open Fields of Northamptonshire: The Case for the Preservation of Ridge and Furrow*. Northampton: Northampton Heritage.

Hall, D. and Coles, J. 1994. *Fenland Survey. An Essay in Landscape and Persistence*, English Heritage Archaeological Report 1. London: English Heritage.

Hall, R., McGregor, H. and Stockwell, M. 1988. *Medieval Tenements in Aldwark, and Other Sites*, Archaeology in York 10/2. London: CBA.

Halsall, G. 1989. Coverham Abbey: its context in the landscape of late medieval north Yorkshire. In R. Gilchrist and H. Mytum (eds) *The Archaeology of Rural Monasteries*: 113–39. Oxford: BAR 203: 113–139.

Hamilton Thompson, A. 1912. *Military Architecture in England during the Middle Ages*. London: Henry Frowde.

Hanawalt, B. 1986. *The Ties That Bound: Peasant Families in Medieval England*. Oxford: OUP.

Hancock, A. 1991. *Goodrich Castle. A Handbook for Teachers*. Colchester: English Heritage.

Hannan, A. P. 1977. Northamptonshire: a policy for Archaeology. In R. T. Rowley and M. Breakell (eds) *Planning and the Historic Environment II*: 120–130. Oxford: Oxford Univ. Dept. of External Studies.

—— 1998. Tewkesbury and the Earls of Gloucester: excavations at Holm Hill, 1974–5. *TBGAS* 15: 79–231.

Harden, D. B. 1957. The Society for Medieval Archaeology. *Medieval Archaeology* 1: 1–3.

Hare, J. N. 1986. *Battle Abbey. The Eastern Range and the Excavations of 1978–80*. HBMC Archaeological Report no. 2. London: HBMC.

—— 1991. The growth of the roof-tile industry in later medieval Wessex. *Medieval Archaeology* 35: 86–103.

Harris, E. C. 1975. The stratigraphic sequence: a question of time. *World Archaeology* 7: 109–21.

Harris, J. 1984a. William Morris and the Middle Ages. In J. Banham and J. Harris (eds) *William Morris and the Middle Ages*: 1–16. Manchester: MUP.

—— 1984b. Medieval dress in pre-Raphaelite painting. In J. Banham and J. Harris (eds) *William Morris and the Middle Ages*: 46–58. Manchester: MUP.

Harrison, J. F. C. 1961. *Learning and Living, 1790–1960*. London: Routledge.

Harte, N. B. 1971. The making of economic history. In N. B. Harte (ed.) *The Study of Economic History. Collected Inaugural Lectures 1893–1970*: xi–xxxix. London: Frank Cass.

Hartley, R. F. 1984. *The Medieval Earthworks of North West Leicestershire. A Survey*. Archaeological Report No. 9. Leicester: Leicester Museums, Art Galleries and Records Service.

Hartshorne, R. 1939. *The Nature of Geography*. Lancaster, PA: Association of American Geographers.

Harty, K. J. 1999. *The Reel Middle Ages*. London: McFarland and Company.

Harvey, D. 1969. *Explanation in Geography*. London: Edward Arnold.

Harvey, J. 1954. *English Medieval Architects*. London: Batsford.

—— 1981. *Medieval Gardens*. London: Batsford.

Harvey, J. H. 1969. *William Worcestre: Itineraries [of]*. Oxford: Clarendon Press.

Haskell, F. 1993. *History and its Images. Art and the Interpretation of the Past*. New Haven and London: Yale Univ. Press.

Hassall, J. 1979. *17–19 St Mary's Street (BSM72 38)*. In D. Baker, E. Baker, J. Hassall and A. Simco, Excavations in Bedford 1967–1977. *Bedfordshire Archaeological Journal* 13: 137–43.

Hassall, T. G. 1977. The Battle of Wallingford Castle 1971–1977. In R. T. Rowley and M. Breakell (eds) *Planning and the Historic Environment II*: 156–68. Oxford: Oxford Univ. Dept. of External Studies.

—— 1978. Current approaches to the historic environment. In T. C. Darvill, M. Parker Pearson, R. W. Smith and R. M. Thomas. *New Approaches to Our Past. An Archaeological Forum*: 127–38. Southampton: Dept. of Archaeology, Univ. of Southampton.

Hassall, T. G., Halpin, C. E. and Mellor, M. 1984. Excavations in St Ebbe's, Oxford, 1967–1976: Part II. *Oxoniensia* 49: 153–275.

—— 1989. Excavations in St Ebbe's, Oxford, 1967–1976: Part I. *Oxoniensia* 54: 71–278.

Hawkes, C. F. C. 1937. Lecture on October 29, 1937. *First Annual Report of the Institute of Archaeology* 47–69.

Hawkes, C. F. C., Myres, J. N. L. and Stevens, C. G. 1930. *Saint Catharine's Hill, Winchester*. PHFC 11.

Hayfield, C. 1987. *An Archaeological Survey of the Parish of Wharram Percy, East Yorkshire 1. The Evolution of the Roman Landscape*. Oxford: BAR 172.

—— 1990. *Wharram Remembered. A Social View of 40 Years of Excavations at Wharram Percy, East Riding of Yorkshire*. Birmingham: Kingate Press.

HBMC. 1989. *English Heritage Report and Accounts 1988–1989*. London: HBMC.

Headley, G. and Meulenkamp, W. 1986. *Follies. A Guide to Rogue Architecture in England, Scotland and Wales*. London: Jonathan Cape.

Heath, C. 1793. *Historical and Descriptive Accounts of Tintern Abbey, Monmouthshire*. Monmouth: printed by the author.

Hebditch, M. 1968. Excavations on the medieval defences, Portwall Lane, Bristol, 1965. *TBGAS* 87: 131–43.

Hedges, J. 1977. Development control and Archaeology. In R. T. Rowley and M. Breakell (eds) *Planning and the Historic Environment II*: 32–51. Oxford: Oxford Univ. Dept. of External Studies.

Heighway, C. 1972 *The Erosion of History*. London: CBA.

Hennicker, J. M, 1796. *Two Letters on the Origin of Norman Tiles*. London: John Bell.

Henson, D. 2000. Archaeology in Higher Education. *The Archaeologist*, Spring 2000, No. 37: 19–20.

Henstock, A. 1997. Nottinghamshire. In C. R. J. Currie and C. P. Lewis (eds) *A Guide to English County Histories*: 312–22. Stroud: Sutton.

Herbert, D. T. and Johnston, R. J. 1978. Geography and the urban environment. In D. T. Herbert and R. J. Johnston (eds) *Geography and the Urban Environment. Progress in Research and Applications. Vol. 1*: 1–34. Chichester: John Wiley and Sons.

Herteig, A. E. 1981. The medieval harbour of Bergen. In G. Milne and B. Hobley (eds) *Waterfront Archaeology in Britain and Northern Europe*. CBA Research Report 41: 80–7. London: CBA.

Hewett, C. A. 1962–3. Structural carpentry in medieval Essex. *Medieval Archaeology* 6–7: 240–71.

—— 1980. *English Historic Carpentry*. Chichester: Phillimore.

Heyworth, M. 1995. *British Archaeological Yearbook 1995–6*. York: CBA.

Higham, R. A. 1977. Excavations at Okehampton Castle, Devon. Part I: the motte and bailey. *Proceedings of the Devon Archaeological Society* 35: 3–42.

—— 1982. Dating in medieval archaeology: problems and possibilities. In B. Orme (ed.) *Problems and Case Studies in Archaeological Dating*. Exeter Studies in History No. 4, Exeter Studies In Archaeology No. 1: 83–107. Exeter: Univ. of Exeter.

Higham, R. A. and Allan, J. P. 1980. Excavations at Okehampton Castle, Devon. Part II: the bailey. A preliminary report. *Proceedings of the Devon Archaeological Society* 38: 49–51

Higham, R. A. and Barker, P. 1992. *Timber Castles*. London: Batsford.

—— 2000. *Hen Domen, Montgomery: a Timber Castle on the English-Welsh Border*. Exeter: Univ. of Exeter Press.

Hillam, J. 1981. An English tree-ring chronology AD 404–1216. *Medieval Archaeology* 25: 31–44.

—— 1987. Dendrochronology: 20 years on. *Current Archaeology* 107: 358–63.

—— 1998. *Dendrochronology: Guidelines on Producing and Interpreting Dendrochronological Data*. London: English Heritage.

Hillam, J. and Morgan, R. A. 1981. 'What value is dendrochronology to waterfront archaeology? In G. Milne and B. Hobley (eds) *Waterfront Archaeology in Britain and northern Europe*. CBA Research Report 41: 39–46. London: CBA.

Hillier, B. and Hanson, J. 1984. *The Social Logic of Space*. Cambridge: CUP.

Hills, C. 1987. Archaeology and the Media. In H. Mytum and K. Waugh (eds) *Rescue Archaeology. What's Next?* Univ. of York Monograph 6: 73–7. York: Univ. of York Monograph and Rescue, The British Archaeological Trust.

Hingley, R. (ed.) 1993. *Medieval and Later Rural Settlement in Scotland. Management and Preservation*. Historic Scotland Occasional Publication No. 1. Edinburgh: Historic Scotland.

—— 2000. *Roman Officers and English Gentlemen. The Imperial Origins of Roman Archaeology*. London and New York: Routledge.

Hingley, R. and Foster, S. 1994. Medieval or later rural settlement in Scotland. Defining, understanding and conserving an archaeological resource. *Medieval Settlement Research Group. Annual Report 9*: 7–11.

Hinton, D. A. 1969. Excavation at Bicester Priory, 1969. *Oxoniensia* 34: 21–8.

—— 1977. Rudely made earthen vessels. In D. P. S. Peacock (ed.) *Pottery and Early Commerce*: 221–36. London: Academic Press.

—— (ed.) 1983. *Twenty Five Years of Medieval Archaeology*. Sheffield: Dept. of Archaeology and Prehistory, Univ. of Sheffield and SMA.

—— 1990. *Archaeology, Economy and Society: England from the Fifth to the Fifteenth Century*. London: Seaby.

Hinton, P. and Thomas, R. 1997. The Greater London Publication Programme. *Archaeological Journal* 154: 196–213.

Hirst, S. M. 1976. *Recording on Excavations. I. The Written Record*. Hertford: RESCUE.

Hirst, S. M., Walsh, D. A. and Wright, S. M. 1983. *Bordesley Abbey II*. Oxford: BAR 111.

Historic Scotland. 1996. *Publication and Archiving of Archaeological Projects*. Edinburgh: Historic Scotland.

Hoare, R. C. 1810–21. *History of Ancient Wiltshire*. London: published by W. Miller, printed by W. Bulmer and Co.

—— 1837. *History of Modern Wiltshire, v, part i*. London.

Hobsbawn, E. 1979. An historian's comments. In B. C. Burnham and J. Kingsbury (eds) *Space, Hierarchy and Society*: 247–52. Oxford: BAR International Series 59.

Hobson, R. L. 1902. Medieval pottery found in England. *Archaeological Journal* 54: 1–16.

—— 1903. *Catalogue of the Collection of English Pottery in the Department of British and Medieval Antiquities . . . of the British Museum*. London: British Museum Press.

Hodder, I. 1986. *Reading the Past. Current Approaches to Interpretation in Archaeology*. Cambridge: CUP.

—— 1999. *The Archaeological Process*. Oxford: Blackwell.

Hodder, M. A. 1991. *Excavations at Sandwell Priory and Hall 1982–88*. South Staffordshire Archaeological and Historical Society 31.

Hodgen, M. 1939. Domesday watermills. *Antiquity* 13: 261–79.

Hodges, R. 1982a. Method and theory in medieval archaeology. *Archeologia Medievale* 8: 7–37.

—— 1982b. *Dark Age Economics: the Origins of Towns and Trade, AD 600–1000*. London: Duckworth.

—— 1989. Parachutists and truffle-hunters: At the frontiers of Archaeology and History. In M. Aston, D. A. Austin and C. Dyer (eds) *Rural Settlements of Medieval England: Studies dedicated to Maurice Beresford and John Hurst*: 287–306. Oxford: Basil Blackwell.

—— 1990. Rewriting the rural history of early medieval Italy: twenty-five years of medieval archaeology reviewed. *Rural History*, 1 (1): 17–36.

—— 1991. *Wall-to-Wall History. The Story of Roystone Grange*. London: Duckworth.

Holden, E. W, 1963. Excavations at the deserted medieval village of Hangleton, part 1. *Sussex Archaeological Collections* 101: 54–181.

Holdsworth, J. 1978. *Selected Pottery Groups AD 650–1780*. The Archaeology of York. The Pottery 16/1. London: York Archaeological Trust.

Holton-Krayenbuhl, A. 1997. The infirmary complex at Ely. *Archaeological Journal* 154: 118–172.

Hope, W. H. St J. 1900. Watton Priory, Yorkshire. *Transactions of the East Riding Antiquarian Society* 8: 70–07.

Hope, W. H. St J. and Brakspear, H. 1906. The Cistercian Abbey of Beaulieu in the County of Southampton. *Archaeological Journal* 63: 129–86.

Hope-Taylor, B. 1956. The excavation of a motte at Abinger in Surrey. *Archaeological Journal* 107: 15–43.

Hooper, M. D. 1970. Hedges and history. *New Scientist* 48: 598–600.

Horn, P. 1970. The potential and limitations of radiocarbon dating in the Middle Ages: the art historian's view. In R. Berger (ed.) *Scientific Methods in Medieval Archaeology*. UCLA Center for Medieval and Renaissance Studies Contributions IV: 23–88. Los Angeles, London: Univ. of California Press.

Horsman, V. and Davison, B. 1989. The New Palace Yard and its Fountains: Excavations in the Palace of Westminster 1972–4. *Antiquaries Journal* 69: 279–97.

Hoskins, W. G. 1937. The fields of Wigston Magna. *Transactions of the Leicester Archaeological Society* 19: 163–69.

—— 1944–45. The deserted villages of Leicestershire. *Transactions of the Leicester Archaeological Society* 22: 241–65.

—— 1954. *Devon*. London: Collins.

—— 1955. *The Making of the English Landscape*. London: Hodder and Stoughton.

—— 1959. *Local History in England*. London: Longmans.

—— 1962. Foreword. In J. West, *Village Records*, vii–viii. London: Macmillan and Co. Ltd.

—— 1967. *Fieldwork in Local History*. London: Faber and Faber.

Howarth, D. 1997. *Images of Rule. Art and Politics in the English Renaissance, 1485–1649*. London: Macmillan.

Hudson, J. 1989. The York Medieval Tile-making Project. A Potter's Tale. *Medieval Ceramics* 13: 43–52.

Hudson, K. 1981. *A Social History of Archaeology. The British Experience*. London: Macmillan.

Huggins, P. J. 1970. Excavation of a medieval bridge at Waltham Abbey, Essex, in 1968. *Medieval Archaeology* 14: 126–47.

—— The excavation of an 11th-century Viking hall and 14th-century rooms at Waltham Abbey, Essex, 1969–71. *Medieval Archaeology* 20: 75–133.

Hughes, M. 1989. Hampshire castles and the landscape: 1066–1216. *Landscape History* 11: 27–60.

Hughes, M. J. 1995. Application of scientific analytical methods to Spanish medieval ceramics. In C. M. Gerrard, A. Gutiérrez and A. G. Vince (eds) *Spanish Medieval Ceramics in Spain and the British Isles*: 359–66. Oxford: BAR International Series 610.

Hume, Revd A. 1863. *Ancient Meols: Antiquities from the Sea Coast of Cheshire*. London: J. R. Smith.

Hunter, M. 1971. The Royal Society and the Origins of British Archaeology I. *Antiquity* 65: 113–21.

Hurman, B. and Steiner, M. (eds) 1995. *The Survey and Recording of Historic Buildings*. Exeter: Association of Archaeological Illustrators and Surveyors Technical Paper 12.

Hurst, J. G. 1955. Saxo-Norman pottery in East Anglia, part 1, general discussion and St Neots ware. *PCAS* 49: 49.

—— 1961. The kitchen area of Northolt Manor, Middlesex. *Medieval Archaeology* 5: 211–99.

—— 1962–3. White Castle and the dating of medieval pottery. *Medieval Archaeology* 6–7: 135–55.

—— 1963. Post-Roman archaeological dating and its correlation with archaeological results. *Archaeometry* 6: 81–2.

—— 1965. The medieval peasant house. In A. Small (ed.) *The Fourth Viking Congress, 1961*: 190–6. Aberdeen: Aberdeen Univ. Studies 149.

—— 1966. Post-Roman archaeological dating and its correlation with archaeological results. *Archaeometry* 9: 198–99.

—— 1971. A review of archaeological research (to 1968). In M. W. Beresford and J. G. Hurst *Deserted Medieval Villages*: 76–144. Woking: Lutterworth Press.

—— 1974. Sixteenth- and seventeenth-century imported pottery from the Saintonge. In V. I. Evison, H. Hodges and J. G. Hurst (eds) *Medieval Pottery from Excavations*.

Studies Presented to Gerald Clough Dunning, with a Bibliography of his Works: 221–55. New York: St Martin's Press.

—— 1977. Spanish pottery imported into medieval Britain. *Medieval Archaeology* 21: 68–105.

—— 1980. Research priorities in medieval villages. *Medieval Village Research Group Twenty-Eighth Annual Report*: 42.

—— 1982. Gerald Dunning and his contribution to Medieval Archaeology. *Medieval Ceramics* 6: 3–20.

—— 1983. Medieval archaeology twenty-five years on: summing up. In D. A. Hinton (ed.) *25 Years of Medieval Archaeology*: 132–5. Sheffield: Univ. of Sheffield.

—— 1986. The medieval countryside. In I. Longworth and J. Cherry (eds.) *Archaeology in Britain since 1945*: 197–236. London: British Museum.

—— 1989. A Review of Archaeological Research (to 1968). In M. W. Beresford and J. G. Hurst (eds) *Deserted Medieval Villages*: 76–144. Stroud: Alan Sutton.

—— 1991. Antiquarian finds of medieval and later pottery. In E. Lewis (ed.) *Custom and Ceramics: Essays Presented to Kenneth Barton*: 7–21. Wickham: APE.

—— 1994. Obituary: Donald Harden 1901–1994. *Medieval Archaeology* 38: 182–3.

—— 1999. Axel Steensberg 1 June 1906–3 March 1999. *Medieval Settlement Research Group Annual Report* 14: 13–15.

Hurst, J. G. and Golson, J. 1955. Excavation of St Benedict's Gates, Norwich 1951 and 1953. *Oxoniensia* 4: 89–146.

Hurst, J. G. and Hurst D. G. 1967. Excavation of two moated sites: Milton, Hampshire and Ashwell, Hertfordshire. *JBAA*, 3rd series, 30: 48–86.

Hurst, J. G., Neal, D. S. and Van Beuningen, H. J. E. 1986. *Pottery Produced and Traded in North-West Europe, 1350–1650*. Rotterdam Papers 6. Rotterdam: Museum Boijmans Van Beuningen

Hutchinson, G. 1994. *Medieval Ships and Shipping*. London: LUP.

IFA 1993a *Draft Standards and Guidance for Archaeological Desk-Based Studies*. Birmingham: IFA.

—— 1993b *Draft Standards and Guidance for Archaeological Field Evaluations*. Birmingham: IFA.

Ingrams, J. 1846. Medieval pottery. *Archaeological Journal* 3: 62–4.

Innocent, C. F. 1916. *The Development of English Building Construction*. Cambridge: CUP.

Isherwood, J. 2000. The Society for the Protection of Ancient Buildings campaign to save Holy Trinity Church, Penton Mewsey. *PHFC* 55: 79–88.

Isserlin, R. M. J. 1992. Aspects of English and Continental Jewries. *Medieval Europe 1992, Religion and Belief*, pre-printed papers, vol. 6: 37–42. York: Medieval Europe 1992.

Ivens, R., Busby, P. and Shepherd, N. 1995. *Tattenhoe and Westbury. Two Deserted Medieval Settlements in Milton Keynes*. Buckinghamshire Archaeology Society Monograph Series 8. Aylesbury: Buckinghamshire Archaeology Society.

Jacques, D. 1983. *Georgian Gardens: The Reign of Nature*. London: Batsford.

James, T. 1997. Excavations at Carmarthen Greyfriars, 1983–1990. *Medieval Archaeology* 41: 100–94.

James, T. B. 1989. Visitors to Coombe Bissett and Clarendon Palace 1930–39. *Hatcher Review* 28: 407–15.

—— 1990. *The Palaces of Medieval England c.1050–1500*. London: Seaby.

—— 1997. *Book of Winchester*. London: Batsford.

James, T. B. and Robinson, A. M. 1988. *Clarendon Palace*. London: Society of Antiquaries.

Jarrett, M. G. and Evans, D. H. 1987. The deserted village of West Whelpington, Northumberland. Third report, part 1. *Archaeologia Aeliana* 5th series 15: 199–308.

Jefferies, J. S. 1977. *Excavation Records. Techniques in use by the Central Excavation Unit.* Directorate of Ancient Monuments and Historic Buildings Occasional Paper No. 1. London: DoE.

Jenkinson, H. 1938. A new great seal of Henry V. *Antiquaries Journal* 18: 382–90.

Jennings, S. 1981. *Eighteen Centuries of Pottery from Norwich*. East Anglian Archaeology Report 13. Norwich: Centre of East Anglian Studies.

—— 1992. *Medieval Pottery in the Yorkshire Museum*. York: Yorkshire Museum.

Johnson, C. J. 1980. The statistical limitations of hedge dating. *Local Historian* 14: 28–33.

Johnson, M. 1993. *Housing Culture. Traditional Architecture in an English Landscape.* Washington DC: Smithsonian Institution Press.

—— 1996. *An Archaeology of Capitalism*. Oxford: Blackwell.

—— 1999. *Archaeological Theory*. Oxford: Blackwell.

Johnson, N. and Rose, P. 1994. *Bodmin Moor: An Archaeological Survey. Volume 1: The Human Landscape to c.1800.* London: English Heritage, RCHME and Cornwall Archaeological Unit.

Jones, B. 1984. *Past Imperfect. The Story of Rescue Archaeology*. London: Heinemann.

Jones, G. R. J. 1961. Early territorial organisation in England and Wales. *Geografiska Annaler* 43: 174–81.

Jones, N. W. 1998. Excavations within the medieval town at New Radnor, Powys, 1991–92. *Archaeological Journal* 155: 134–206.

Jones, R. H. 1980. *Medieval Houses at Flaxengate, Lincoln*. The Archaeology of Lincoln, 11/1. London: CBA.

Jones, R. and Ruben, I. 1987. Animal bones, with some notes on the effects of differential sampling. In G. Beresford, *Goltho: The Development of an Early Medieval Manor, c.850–1150*: 197–206. London: HBMC.

Jones, S. 1997. *The Archaeology of Ethnicity. Constructing Identities in the Past and Present.* London: Routledge.

Jope, E. M. 1947. Medieval pottery in Berkshire. *Berkshire Archaeological Journal* 50: 49–76.

—— 1948. Note on Oxford City. *Oxoniensia* 13: 171.

—— 1952a. 'Medieval pottery' and 'Regional character in west country pottery'. In H. E. O'Neil, Whittington Court Villa, Whittington, Gloucestershire. *TBGAS* 71: 61–97.

—— 1952b. Excavations in the City of Norwich, 1948. *Norfolk Archaeology* 30: 287–322.

—— 1953–4. Medieval pottery kilns at Brill, Bucks. *Records of Buckinghamshire* 16: 39–42.

—— 1963. The regional cultures of medieval Britain. In I. L. Foster and L. Alcock (eds) *Culture and Environment. Essays in Honour of Sir Cyril Fox*: 327–50. London: Routledge and Kegan Paul.

—— 1972. Models in medieval studies. In D L Clarke (ed.) *Models in Archaeology*: 963–90.

Jope, E. M. and Dunning, G. C. 1954. The use of blue slate for roofing in medieval England. *Antiquaries Journal* 34: 209–17.

Jope, E. M. and Hodges, H. W. M. 1956. The technique of pottery-making, as seen on Carlisle pottery. *Transactions of the Cumberland and Westmorland Antiquarian and Archaeological Society* 55: 102–7.

Jope, E. M. and Pantin, W. A. 1958. The Clarendon Hotel. *Oxoniensia* 23: 1–129.

Jope, E. M. and Threlfall, R. I. 1958. Excavation of a medieval settlement at Beere, North Tawton, Devon. *Medieval Archaeology* 2: 112–40.

Jope, E. M. and Threlfall, R. I. 1959. The 12th century castle at Ascot D'Oilly, Oxfordshire: its history and excavation. *Antiquaries Journal* 39: 219–74.

Jubb, M. 2000. The AHRB and the funding of archaeology. *Antiquity* 74: 343–48.

Kames, Lord. 1762. *Elements of Criticism*. Edinburgh: printed for A. Miller, London.

Keegan, J. 1976. *The Face of Battle*. London: Jonathan Cape.

Keeley, H. C. M. 1987. *Environmental Archaeology: A Regional Review*. London: HBMC Occasional Paper No. 1.

Keene, D. 1985. *Survey of Medieval Winchester*. Winchester Studies, vol. 2. Oxford: OUP.

Keevil, G. D. 1995. *In Harvey's House and in God's House: Excavations at Eynsham Abbey 1991–3*. Thames Valley Landscapes Monograph 6. Oxford: Oxford Archaeological Unit.

Kenawell, W. W. 1965. *The Quest at Glastonbury. A Biographical Study of Frederick Bligh Bond*. New York: Helix Press.

Kendrick, T. D. 1950. *British Antiquity*. London: Methuen and Co.

Kendrick, T. D. and Hawkes, C. F. C. 1932. *Archaeology in England and Wales 1914–1939*. London: Methuen and Co.

Kent, J. P. C. 1968. Excavations at the motte and bailey castle of South Mimms, Herts. 1960–1967. *Barnet District Local History Society Bulletin* 15, whole issue.

Kent, O. and Dawson, D. 1998. The packing of medieval floor-tile kilns. *Medieval Archaeology* 42: 45–53.

Kenyon, J. R. 1988. *Raglan Castle*. Cardiff: CADW.

—— 1990. *Medieval Fortifications*. London: LUP.

Ker, N. R. 1955. Sir John Prise. *The Library*, 5th series, 10: 1–24.

Kerridge, E. 1951. Ridge and furrow and agrarian history. *Economic History Review* 4 (n.s.): 14–36.

—— 1955. A reconsideration of former husbandry practices. *Agricultural History Review* 3: 26–40.

King, D. J. C. 1983. *Castellarium Anglicanum: An Index and Bibliography of the Castles in England, Wales and the Islands* (2 vols). New York: Kraus International.

—— 1988. *The Castle in England and Wales. An Interpretative History*. London: Routledge.

King, D. J. C. and Alcock, L. 1969. Ringworks of England and Wales. *Château Gaillard* 3: 90–127.

Kissock, J. 1992. Recent research into the medieval landscape of south west Wales: the Dyfed Archaeological Trust's Historic Settlement Project. *Medieval Settlement Research Group Annual Report* 7: 10–12.

Klemperer, W. D. 1992. The study of burials at Hulton Abbey. In *Medieval Europe 1992, Death and Burial*. Pre-printed papers, vol. 4: 85–92.

Klindt-Jensen, O. 1975. *A History of Scandinavian Archaeology*. London: Thames and Hudson.

Klingelhofer, E. C. 1974. *The Deserted Medieval Village of Broadfield, Hertfordshire.* Oxford: BAR 2.

Knight, J. K. 1977. *Tintern and the Romantic Movement.* London: DoE.

Knoop, G. and Jones, G. P. 1933. *The Medieval Mason.* Manchester: MUP.

Knowles, M. D. 1940. *The Monastic Order in England.* Cambridge: CUP.

—— 1948–59. *The Religious Orders in England.* Volumes 1–3. Cambridge: CUP.

—— 1974. William Abel Pantin, 1902–1973. *PBA* 60: 447–58.

Knowles, M. D. and Hadcock, R. N. 1953. *Medieval Religious Houses. England and Wales.* London: Longmans, Green and Co.

—— 1971 (2nd ed.). *Medieval Religious Houses. England and Wales.* London: Longmans, Green and Co.

Knowles, M. D. and St Joseph, J. K. 1952. *Monastic Sites from the Air.* Cambridge: CUP.

Kristiansen, M. S. and Mahler, D. L. D. 1998. Some perspectives in Danish Medieval Archaeology. *Medieval Settlement Research Group. Annual Report* 12: 21–26.

Kuhn, T. 1962. *The Structure of Scientific Revolutions.* Chicago: Univ. of Chicago Press.

Lacey, R. and Danziger, D. 1999. *The Year 1000.* London: Little, Brown and Company.

Lada-Grodzicka, C. n.d. *A Lecture on the Life and Work of Professor Tancred Borenius* (unpublished manuscript).

Ladurie, E. L. R. 1975. *Montaillou.* Paris: Editions Gallimard.

Laking, G. F. 1920–2. *A Record of European Armour and Arms through Seven Centuries*, 5 vols. London: G. Bell and Sons.

Lambarde, W. 1576. *Perambulation of Kent.* London.

Lambrick, G. and Mellor, M. 1980. The medieval and later pottery. In G. Lambrick, Excavations in Park Street, Towcester. *Northamptonshire Archaeology* 15: 98–102.

Lambrick, G. and Woods, H. 1976. Excavations on the second site of the Dominican Priory, Oxford. *Oxoniensia* 41: 168–231.

Lane, L. 1966. A plan for a new metropolitan city. Humber. Counter-magnet to London and showcase for Britain. *Architects Journal* 19: 168–216.

Langley, B. 1728 *New Principles of Gardening* (unspec. publ.).

Le Patourel, H. E. J. 1968. Documentary evidence and the medieval pottery industry. *Medieval Archaeology* 12: 101–26.

—— 1972. Medieval Moated Sites Research Group. *Local Historian* 11: 89–93.

—— 1973. The moated site at East Haddlesey, West Riding. In H. E. J. Le Patourel (ed.) *The Moated Sites of Yorkshire.* SMA Monograph 5: 23–36. London: SMA.

—— 1983 Documentary evidence for the pottery trade in north-west Europe. In P. Davey and R. Hodges (eds) *Ceramics and Trade. The Production and Distribution of Later Medieval Pottery in North-West Europe*: 27–35. Sheffield: Univ. of Sheffield.

—— 1992. John G. Hurst: a potted bibliography. In D. Gaimster and M. Redknap (eds) *Everyday and Exotic Pottery from Europe. Studies in Honour of John G. Hurst*: 1–6. Oxford: Oxbow Books.

Leach, P. 1984. *The Archaeology of Taunton. Excavations and Fieldwork to 1980.* Western Archaeological Trust Excavation Monograph 8. Bristol: Western Archaeological Trust.

Lee, F. and Magilton, J. 1989. The cemetery of the hospital of St James and St Mary Magdalene, Chichester: a case study. *World Archaeology* 21 (2): 273–82.

Leech, R. H. 1975. *Small Towns in Avon: Archaeology and Planning.* Bristol: Committee for Rescue Archaeology in Avon, Gloucestershire and Somerset. Survey 1.

—— 1981. Medieval urban archaeology in the northwest: problems and response. In P.

Clack and S. Haselgrove (eds) *Approaches to the Urban Past*. Dept. of Archaeology, Univ. of Durham Occasional Paper No. 2: 55–64. Durham: Durham Univ.

Leeds, E. T. 1936. An adulterine castle on Faringdon clump, Berkshire. *Antiquaries Journal* 16 (2): 165–78.

—— 1947. A Saxon village at Sutton Courtenay, Berkshire. Third report. *Archaeologia* 92: 79–93.

Leigh, D. 1982. The selection, conservation and storage of archaeological finds. *Museums Journal* 5 (2): 115–16.

Leighton, W. 1933. The Black Friars, Now Quaker's Friars, Bristol. *TBGAS* 55: 151–90.

Leland, J. 1546. *The Laboryouse Journey and Serche of Johan Leylande for Englandes Antiquitees*. London: printed by J. Bale.

Letts, J. B. 1999. *Smoke-Blackened Thatch: a Unique Source of Late Medieval Plant Remains from Southern England*. London: English Heritage.

Leveson Gower, G. W. G. 1891. Report of a paper read to the Society on 12th February 1891. *Proceedings of the Society of Antiquaries of London*, 2 series, 13: 247–51.

Levine, P. 1986. *The Amateur and the Professional. Antiquarians, Historians and Archaeologists in Victorian England, 1838–1886*. Cambridge: CUP.

Levitan, B. 1983. The vertebrate remains. In S. P. Q. Rahtz and T. Rowley, *Middleton Stoney: Excavation and Survey in a North Oxfordshire Parish 1970–1982*: 108–72. Oxford: Oxford Univ. Dept. for External Studies.

Levy, F. J. 1967. *Tudor Historical Thought*. San Marino, CA: Huntington Library.

Lewis, C. 1989. *Particular Places. An Introduction to English Local History*. London: British Library.

Lewis, C., Mitchell-Fox, P. and Dyer, C. 1997. *Village, Hamlet and Field. Changing Medieval Settlements in Central England*. Manchester: MUP.

Lewis, J. M. 1978. *Medieval Pottery and Metalware in Wales*. National Museum of Wales guidebook.

Lewis, W. S. (ed.) 1955. *The Correspondence of Horace Walpole*, volume xxix. London: OUP.

Lilley, J. M, Stroud, G., Brothwell, D. R., and Williamson, M. H. 1994. *The Jewish Burial Ground at Jewbury. The Medieval Cemeteries*. The Archaeology of York 12/3. York: CBA.

Lineham, P. (ed.) 2001. *The Medieval World*. London: Routledge.

Lingard, J. 1819. *History of the Middle Ages*. London: J. Mawman.

Llobera, M. 1996. Exploring the topography of mind: GIS, social space and archaeology. *Antiquity* 70: 612–22.

Lloyd, J. A. 1986. Why should historians take archaeology seriously? In J. L. Bintliff and C. F. Gaffney (eds) *Archaeology at the Interface: Studies in Archaeology's Relationships with History, Geography, Biology and Physical Science*: 40–51. Oxford: BAR International Series 300.

Lock, G. and Harris, T. 1992. Visualizing spatial data: the importance of Geographic Information Systems. In P. Reilly and S. Rahtz (eds) *Archaeology and the Information Age. A Global Perspective*: 81–96. London and New York: Routledge.

Locock, M. 1990. The use of the video camera for archaeological recording a practical evaluation at Dudley Castle, West Midlands. *Scottish Archaeological Review* 7: 146–49.

—— 1994. *Meaningful Architecture: Social Interpretations of Buildings*. Aldershot: Avebury.

Long, W. H. (ed.) 1888. *The Oglander Memoirs*. London: Reeves and Turner.

Lowther, P., Ebbartson, L., Ellison, M. and Millett, M. 1993. The city of Durham: an archaeological survey. *Durham Archaeological Jurnal* 9: 27–119.

Lucas, G. 1998. A medieval fishery on Whittlesea Mere, Cambridgeshire. *Medieval Archaeology* 42: 19–44.

Lucy, S. J. 1998. *The Early Anglo-Saxon Cemeteries of East Yorkshire. An analysis and reinterpretation*. Oxford: BAR 272.

—— 2000. *The Anglo-Saxon Way of Death*. Stroud: Sutton.

Lugar, R. 1805. *Architectural Sketches*. London.

Lunde, O. 1985. Archaeology and the medieval towns of Norway. *Medieval Archaeology* 29: 120–135.

Lyne, M. 1997. *Lewes Priory. Excavations by Richard Lewis 1969–82*. Lewes: Lewes Priory Trust.

Lysons, S. 1804. *Collection of Gloucestershire Antiquities*. London: printed for T. Cadell and W. Davies.

Macaulay, J. 1975. *The Gothic Revival 1795–1845*. Glasgow and London: Blackie.

Macaulay, R. 1953. *Pleasure of Ruins*. London: Thames and Hudson.

Macaulay, T. 1849. *History of England* 4 vols. London: Longmans, Brown, Green, Longmas and Roberts.

MacDonald, A. 1988. An attempt to make a replica 14th century Lincoln ware jug. *Medieval Ceramics* 12: 23–31.

MacGregor, A. 1985. The cabinet of curiosities in seventeenth-century Britain. In O. Impey and A. MacGregor (eds) *The Origins of Museums. The Cabinet of Curiosities in Sixteenth- and Seventeenth-century Europe*: 147–58. Oxford: Clarendon Press.

—— 1998. Antiquity Inventoried: Museums and National Antiquities in the Mid-Nineteenth Century. In V. Brand (ed.) *The Study of the Past in the Victorian Age*. Oxbow Monograph 73: 125–37. Oxford: Oxbow Books.

MacGregor, A., Mainman, A. J. and Rogers, N. S. H. 1999. *Craft, Industry and Everyday Life. Bone, Antler, Ivory and Horn from Medieval York*. York: York Archaeological Trust and CBA.

MacIvor, I. and Gallagher, D. 1999. Excavations at Caerlaverock Castle, 1955–66. *Archaeological Journal* 156: 143–245.

Mackintosh, 1830–1831. *History of England*. London.

Mahany, C. 1982. *Excavations in Stamford, Lincolnshire, 1963–1969*. SMA Monograph 9. London: SMA.

Maitland, F. W. 1897. *Domesday Book and Beyond*. Cambridge: CUP.

Maltby, M. 1979. *Faunal Studies on Urban Sites. The Animal Bones from Exeter 1971–1975*. Sheffield: Dept. of Prehistory and Archaeology.

Mandler, P. 1997. *The Fall and Rise of the Stately Home*. New Haven and London: Yale Univ. Press.

Manley, J. 1994. Excavations at Caergwrle Castle, Clwyd, North Wales: 1988–1990. *Medieval Archaeology* 38: 83–133.

Mann, J. G. 1932. Instances of Antiquarian Feeling in Medieval and Renaissance Art. *Archaeological Journal* 89: 254–74.

Margeson, S. 1993. *Norwich Households: The Medieval and Post-medieval Finds from Norwich Survey Excavations 1971–1978*, East Anglian Archaeology Report 58. Norwich: Norwich Survey.

Marks, R. 1998. *The Medieval Stained Glass of Northamptonshire*. Corpus Vitrearum Medii Aevi, summary catalogue 4. Oxford: OUP.

Marsden, P. 1996. *Ships of the Port of London, Twelfth to Seventeenth Centuries AD*. London: English Heritage.

Marshall, J. D. 1997. *The Tyranny of the Discrete. A Discussion of the Problems of Local History in England*. Aldershot: Scolar Press.

Marshall, K. 1951. Excavations in the City of Bristol 1948–51. *TBGAS* 70: 5–50.

Mawer, A. 1929. *Problems of Place-Name Study*. Cambridge: CUP.

Mawer, A. and Stenton, F. M. 1925. *The Place-Names of Buckinghamshire*. Cambridge: CUP.

Mawer, A. and Stenton, F. M. 1933. *Introduction to the Survey of English Place-Names*. Cambridge: CUP.

Mayes, P. 1965. A medieval tile kiln at Boston, Lincolnshire. *JBAA* 28: 86–106.

Mayes, P. and Butler, L. A. S. 1983. *Sandal Castle Excavations 1964–1973: a Detailed Archaeological Report*. Wakefield: West Yorkshire Archaeology.

Mayes, P. and Scott, K. 1984. *Pottery Kilns at Chilvers Coton, Nuneaton*. SMA Monograph 10. London: SMA.

Mays, S. 1997. Life and death in a medieval village. In G. De Boe and F. Verhaeghe (eds) *Death and Burial in Medieval Europe*. Pre-printed papers of the Medieval Europe Brugge 1997 Conference, vol. 2: 121–25. Zellik: Medieval Europe Brugge.

—— 1998. *The Archaeology of Human Bones*. London: Routledge.

Mays, S., Lees, B. and Stevenson, J. C. 1998. Age-dependent bone loss in the femur in a medieval population. *International Journal of Osteoarchaeology* 8 (2): 97–106.

McAvoy, F. 1994. Marine salt extraction: the excavation of salterns at Wainfleet St Mary, Lincolnshire. *Medieval Archaeology* 38: 134–63.

McCarthy, M. R. 1979. The pottery. In J. H. Williams, *St Peter's Street, Northampton: Excavations 1973–6*: 151–229. Northampton: Northampton Development Corporation Archaeological Monograph 2.

—— 1990. *Carlisle Castle. A Survey and Documentary History*. Historic Buildings and Monuments Commission Archaeological Report 18. London: English Heritage.

McCarthy, M. R. and Brooks, C. M. 1988. *Medieval Pottery in Britain AD 900–1600*. Leicester: LUP.

McCracken, G. 1988. *Culture and Consumption. New Approaches to the Symbolic Character of Consumer Goods and Activities*. Bloomington: Indiana Univ. Press.

McCrone, D., Morris, A. and Kiely, R. 1995. *Scotland: the Brand. The Making of Scottish Heritage*. Edinburgh: EUP.

McGarvie, M. 1983. John Strachey, F.R.S. and the Antiquities of Wessex in 1730. *Transactions of the Ancient Monuments Society* 27: 77–104.

McKisack, M. 1971. *Medieval History in the Tudor Age*. Oxford: Clarendon Press.

McLees, D. 1998. *Castell Coch*. Cardiff: CADW.

McNeil, R. 1983. Two 12th-century Wich Houses in Nantwich, Cheshire. *Medieval Archaeology* 27: 40–88.

McNeill, T. 1992. *Book of Castles*. London: Batsford and English Heritage.

—— 1997. *Castles in Ireland: Feudal Power in a Gaelic World*. London: Routledge.

Mead, W. R. 1954. Ridge and furrow in Bucks. *Geographical Journal* 120: 34–42.

Mellor, A. S. 1940–2. Record of a buried cruciform structure at Mount's Patch, Bromham, Wilts. *Wiltshire Archaeological Magazine* 49: 383–85.

Mellor, J. E. 1988. MSC – What next? The adult training initiative and the role of archaeological bodies. *Rescue News* 45: 3.

Mellor, J. E. and Pearce, T. 1981. *The Austin Friars, Leicester*. Leicestershire Archaeological Field Unit Report. CBA Research Report 35.

Mellor, M. 1994. *Medieval Ceramic Studies in England. A Review for English Heritage*. London: English Heritage.

Mercer, E. 1975. *English Vernacular Houses: A Study of Traditional Farmhouses and Cottages*. London: HMSO.

Mecuri, P. 1860–1. *Costume historique des XIIe, XIIIe, XIVe et XVe siècles: tirés des monuments les plus authentiques de peinture et de sculpture*. Paris: Lévy.

Metcalf, D. M. and Schweizer, F. 1971. The metal contents of the silver pennies of William II and Henry I (1087–1135). *Archaeometry* 13: 177–90.

Metcalf, V. M. 1997. Wood Hall Moated Manor Project. In G. De Boe and F. Verhaege (eds) *Environment and Subsistence in Medieval Europe*. Pre-printed papers vol. 9: 195–201. Zellik: Medieval Europe Brugge 1997.

Meyrick, S. R. M. 1824. *A Critical Inquiry into Ancient Armour, as it existed in Europe, but particularly in England, from the Norman Conquest to the Reign of Charles II*. London: Jennings.

Miele, C. 1996. The first conservation militants: William Morris and the Society for the Protection of Ancient Buildings. In M. Hunter (ed.) *Preserving the Past. The Rise of Heritage in Modern Britain*: 17–37. Stroud: Sutton.

—— 1998. Real antiquity and the ancient object: the science of gothic architecture and the restoration of medieval buildings. In V. Brand (ed.) *The Study of the Past in the Victorian Age*. Oxbow Monograph 73: 103–24. Oxford: Oxbow Books.

Milek, K. B. 1997. Micromorphology and the medieval urban environment: examples from Ely and Peterborough, Cambridgeshire, England. In G. De Boe and F. Verhaege (eds) *Environment and Subsistence in Medieval Europe*. Pre-printed papers vol. 9: 155–68. Zellik: Medieval Europe Brugge.

Millard, L. 1971. The Blackfriars, Canterbury. *Archaeologia Cantiana* 86: 215–19.

Miller, E. 1991. *The Agrarian History of England and Wales*. Cambridge: CUP.

Millett, M. 1987. Universities and the future of achaeology in Britain. In H. Mytum and K. Waugh (eds) *Rescue Archaeology. What's Next?* Univ. of York Monograph 6: 29–33. York: Univ. of York Monograph and Rescue, The British Archaeological Trust.

Milne, G. 1992a. Medieval riverfront reclamation in London. In G. Milne, From Beach market to Hanseatic kontore: a study of the London waterfront. In *Medieval Europe 1992, Maritime Studies, Ports and Ships*, pre-printed papers vol. 2: 145–6. York: Medieval Europe 1992.

—— 1992b. *Timber Building Techniques in London c.900–c.1400*. London and Middlesex Archaeological Society Special Paper 15.

—— 1997. *St Bride's Church, London. Archaeological Research 1952–60 and 1992–5*. English Heritage Archaeological Report 11. London: English Heritage.

Milne, G. and Hobley, B. (eds) 1981. *Waterfront Archaeology in Britain and Northern Europe*. CBA Research Report 41. London: CBA.

Milne, G. and Milne, C. 1978. Excavations on the Thames waterfront at Trig Lane, London 1974–6. *Medieval Archaeology* 22: 84–104.

Milne, G. and Milne, C. 1982. *Medieval Waterfront Development at Trig Lane, London*. London and Middlesex Society Special Paper 5. London.

Milner, J. 1797. Discovery at Winchester. *Gentleman's Magazine* 67: 397.

—— 1800. The means necessary for further illustrating the ecclesiastical architecture of the Middle Ages. In J. Tayloe (ed.) *Essays on Gothic Architecture by the Revd T. Warton, Revd J. Bentham, Captain Grose and the Revd J. Milner*. London: printed by S. Gosnell for J. Taylor.

Mitchell, J. B. 1954. *Historical Geography*. London: English Universities Press.

Moffat, B. 1986. The environment of Battle Abbey estates (East Sussex) in medieval times: a re-evaluation using analysis of pollen and sediments. *Landscape History* 8: 77–83.

Moir, E. 1964. *The Discovery of Britain: The English Tourist 1540–1840*. London: Routledge and Kegan Paul.

Money, J. H. 1971. Medieval iron-workings in Minepit Wood, Rotherfield, Sussex. *Medieval Archaeology* 15: 86–111.

Moorhouse, S. 1981. The medieval pottery industry and its markets. In D. Crossley (ed.) *Medieval Industry*: 96–125. CBA Research Report 40. London: CBA.

—— 1983a. Documentary evidence and its potential for understanding the inland movement of medieval pottery. *Medieval Ceramics* 7: 45–87.

—— 1983b. The medieval pottery. In P. Mayes and L. A. S. Butler (eds) *Sandal Castle Excavations 1964–73: A Detailed Archaeological Report*: 83–212. Wakefield: West Yorkshire Archaeology.

—— 1986. Non-dating uses of medieval pottery. *Medieval Ceramics* 10: 85–123.

—— 1989. Monastic estates: their composition and development. In R. Gilchrist and H. Mytum (eds) *The Archaeology of Rural Monasteries*: 29–82. Oxford: BAR 203.

Moorhouse, S. and Slowikowski, A. M. 1987. The pottery. In S. Moorhouse and S. Wrathmell, *Kirkstall Abbey, volume 1. The 1950–64 Excavations: A Re-Assessment*: 59–116. Wakefield: West Yorks Archaeological Service.

Moreland, J. 1991. Method and theory in medieval archaeology in the 1990s. *Archaelogia Medievale* 18: 7–42.

Morley, B. and Gurney, D. 1997. *Castle Rising Castle, Norfolk*. East Anglian Archaeology Report 81. Gressenhall: Field Archaeology Divison, Norfolk Museums Service.

Morris, E. 1980. Medieval and post-medieval pottery in Worcester: a type series. In M. O. H. Carver (ed.) *Medieval Worcester, an Archaeological Framework*. Transactions of the Worcestershire Archaeological Society, series 3 (7): 221–54.

Morris, R. 1977. Redundant churches and the historic environment. In R. T. Rowley and M. Breakell (eds) *Planning and the Historic Environment II*: 94–119. Oxford: Oxford Univ. Dept. for External Studies.

—— 1989. *Churches in the Landscape*. London: Dent.

—— 1996. Introduction. In J. Blair and C. Pyrah (eds) *Church Archaeology. Research Directions for the Future*. CBA Research Report 104: xv–xvi. York: CBA.

Morris, W. 1966. *The Collected Works of William Morris XXIII*. New York: Russell.

MPRG 1998. *A Guide to the Classification of Medieval Ceramic Forms*. MPRG Occasional Paper 1. Over Wallop: MPRG.

MSRG 1988. *Statement of Excavation Policy*. MSRG.

—— 1996. *Medieval Rural Settlements. A Policy on their Research, Survey, Conservation and Excavation*. MSRG.

Munby, J. and Renn, D. 1985. Description of the castle buildings. In B. W. Cunliffe and J. Munby (eds) *Excavations at Portchester Castle: 4 Medieval: the Inner Bailey*: 72–119. London: Society of Antiquaries of London.

Murphy, K. 1994. Excavations in three burgage plots in the medieval town of Newport, Dyfed, 1991. *Medieval Archaeology* 38: 55–82.

Murray, D. 1858. *A Handbook for Travellers in Kent and Sussex*. London: J. Murray.

Murray, P. 1984. Nikolaus Bernhard Leon Pevsner, 1902–1983. *Proceedings of the British Academy* 70: 501–14.

Murray-Threipland, L. 1946–8. Medieval farmstead in Bredon Hill. *TBGAS* 67: 415–18.

Museum of London. 1980. *Site Manual. Part 1: The Written Record*. London: Museum of London.

Musson, C. 1987. The Organisation of Regional and Rescue Archaeology in Wales. In H. Mytum and K. Waugh (eds) *Rescue Archaeology. What's Next?* Univ. of York Monograph 6: 99–104. York: Univ. of York Monograph and Rescue, The British Archaeological Trust.

Musty, J. W. G. 1966. *The Medieval Pottery Industry in Great Britain*. MA Thesis, Univ. of Bristol.

—— 1974. Medieval pottery kilns. In V. I. Evison, H. Hodges and J. G. Hurst (eds) *Medieval Pottery from Excavations*: 41–65. London: J. Baker.

Musty, J. W. G. and Algar, D. 1986. Excavations at the deserted medieval village of Gomeldon, near Salisbury. *Wiltshire Archaeological and Natural History Magazine* 80: 127–69.

Musty, J. W. G., Algar, D. and Ewence, P. 1969. The medieval pottery kilns at Laverstock, near Salisbury, Wiltshire. *Archaeologia* 102: 83–50.

Musty, J. W. G. and Rahtz, P. A. 1964. The Suburbs of Old Sarum. *Wiltshire Archaeological and Natural History Magazine* 59: 130–54.

Musty, J. W. G. and Thomas, L. C. 1962. The spectrographic examination of English and continental medieval glazed pottery. *Archaeometry* 5: 38–51.

Müller, U. 1996. *Holzfunde aus Freiburg und Konstanz*. Stuttgart: Kommissionsverlag K. Theiss.

MVRG 1983. *Preservation and Excavation of Moated Sites*. MVRG.

—— 1984a. *The Excavation of Medieval Settlement Sites*. MVRG.

—— 1984b. *The Preservation of Deserted Medieval Village Sites*. MVRG.

Mynard, D. C. 1971. Rescue excavations at the deserted medieval village of Stantonbury, Bucks. *Rec Buckinghamshire* 19: 17–41.

—— 1994. *Excavations on Medieval and Later Sites in Milton Keynes, 1972–1980*. The Buckinghamshire Archaeological Society Monograph Series 6. Aylesbury: Buckinghamshire Archaeological Society.

Mynard, D. C. and Zeepvat, R. J. 1991. *Excavations at Great Linford*. Aylesbury: Buckinghamshire Archaeological Society.

Myres, J. N. L. 1935. The medieval pottery at Bodiam Castle. *Sussex Archaeological Collections* 76: 223–30.

Mytum, H. 1986. Review of 'Ranking, Resource and Exchange: aspects of the archaeology of early European Society'. *Medieval Archaeology* 30: 219–20.

—— 1989. Functionalist and non-functionalist approaches in monastic archaeology. In R. Gilchrist and H. Mytum (eds) *The Archaeology of Rural Monasteries*: 339–61. Oxford: BAR 203.

Nayling, N. 1996. The Magor Pill Boat. *Current Archaeology* 149: 180–3.

Neale, J. M. 1843. *A Few Words to the Parish Clerks and Sextons of Country Parishes*. Cambridge: Stevenson.

Nenk, B. S., Margeson, S. and Hurley, M. 1991. Medieval Britain and Ireland in 1990. *Medieval Archaeology* 35: 126–238.

—— 1992. Medieval Britain and Ireland in 1991. *Medieval Archaeology* 36: 184–308.

—— 1993. Medieval Britain and Ireland in 1992. *Medieval Archaeology* 37: 240–313.

—— 1994. Medieval Britain and Ireland in 1993. *Medieval Archaeology* 38: 184–293.

—— 1995. Medieval Britain and Ireland in 1994. *Medieval Archaeology* 39: 180–293.

—— 1996. Medieval Britain and Ireland in 1994. *Medieval Archaeology* 40: 234–317.

Nenk, B. S., Haith, C. and Bradley, J. 1997. Medieval Britain and Ireland in 1996. *Medieval Archaeology* 41: 241–328.

Newton, R. G. 1971. The enigma of the layered crusts on some weathered glasses, a chronological account of the investigations. *Archaeometry* 13 (1): 1–9.

Nichols, J. G. 1845. *Examples of Decorative Tiles, Sometimes Termed Encaustic*. London: printed by J. B. Nichols and Son.

Nicholson, R. and Hillam, J. 1987. Tree-ring analysis of medieval oak timbers from Dundas Wharf, Redcliff Street, Bristol. *TBGAS* 105: 133–45.

Noddle, B. A. 1975. The animal bones. In C. Platt and R. Coleman-Smith (eds) *Excavations in Medieval Southampton, 1953–1969*, vol 1: 332–9. Leicester: LUP.

—— 1977. Mammal bone. In H. Clarke and A. Carter, *Excavations in King's Lynn 1963–1970*: 378–99. SMA Monograph Series 7. London: SMA.

—— 1985. The animal bones. In R. Shoesmith (ed.) *Hereford City Excavations Volume 3. The Finds*. CBA Research Report 56: 84–94. London: CBA.

Norden, J. 1728. *Speculi Britanniae Pars: a Topographical and Historical Description of Cornwall*. London.

O'Connor, T. P. 1982. *Animal Bones from Flaxengate, Lincoln, 870–1500. The Archaeology of Lincoln*, vol. XVIII–1. London: CBA.

—— 1993. Bone assemblages from monastic sites: many questions but few data. In R. Gilchrist and H. Mytum (eds) *Advances in Monastic Archaeology*: 107–12. Oxford: BAR 227.

Oldridge, D. 1998. *Religion and Society in Early Stuart England*. Aldershot: Ashgate.

Oliver, G. 1846. *Monasticon Dioecesis Exoniensis*. London: Longman, Brown, Greer and Longmans.

Olivier, A. 1996. *Frameworks for our Past. A Review of Research Frameworks, Strategies and Perceptions*. London: English Heritage.

—— 1999. *Archaeology Review 1997–98*. London: English Heritage.

O'Neil, B. H. St J. 1935a. Finds from Coity, Ogmore, Grosmont and White castles. *Antiquaries Journal* 15: 320–35.

—— 1935b. Pottery from Beaumaris Castle. *Archaeologia Cambrensis* 90: 141–3.

—— 1946a. The Congress of Archaeological Societies. *Antiquaries Journal* 26: 61–6.

—— 1946b. The castles of Wales. In V. E. Nash-Williams (ed.) *A Hundred Years of Welsh Archaeology*. Cambrian Archaeological Association, Centenary Volume 1846–1946: 129–40. Gloucester: Cambrian Archaeological Association.

—— 1948. War and Archaeology in Britain. *Antiquaries Journal* 28: 20–44.

Ordnance Survey. 1936. *Field Archaeology. Some Notes for Beginners Issued by the Ordnance Survey*. Ordnance Survey Professional Papers, new series No. 13. London: HMSO.

Ormsby Gore, W. G. 1936. Address on the work of HM Office of Works. In Congress of Archaeological Societies in union with the Society of Antiquaries of London. *Report of the 43rd Congress and of the Research Committee for the year 1935*: 7–12. London: Congress of Archaeological Sciences.

Orton, C. R. 1978. *Pottery Archive: Users' Handbook*. Dept. of Urban Archaeology Publications 1. London: Museum of London.

—— 1982. Computer simulation experiments to assess the performance of measures of quantities of pottery. *World Archaeology* 14 (1): 1–20.

—— 2000. *Sampling in Archaeology*. Cambridge Manuals in Archaeology. Cambridge: CUP.

Orton, C. R., Tyers, P. and Vince, A. 1993. *Pottery in Archaeology*. Cambridge Manual in Archaeology. Cambridge: CUP.

Orwin, C. S. and Orwin C. S. 1938. *The Open Fields*. Oxford: Clarendon Press.

Oswald, A. 1962–3. Excavation of a thirteenth-century wooden building at Weolley castle, Birmingham, 1960–1961. An interim report. *Medieval Archaeology* 6/7: 109–34.

Ove Arup and Partners. 1991. *York Development and Archaeology Study*. York: York City Council and English Heritage.

Oxley, J. 1986. *Excavations at Southampton Castle*. Southampton Archaeology Monographs 3. Southampton: Southampton City Museums.

Pagoda Projects. 1992. *An Evaluation of the Impact of PPG 16 on Archaeology and Planning*. London: report commissioned by English Heritage.

Paley, F. A. 1845. *A Manual of Gothic Mouldings*. London: Van Voorst.

Palliser, D. M. 2000 *The Cambridge Urban History of Britain*. Vol. 2: 1540–1840. Cambridge: CUP.

Pantin, W. A. 1962–3. Medieval English town-house plans. *Medieval Archaeology* 6/7: 202–39.

Parker, H. 1965. A medieval wharf in Thoresby College courtyard, King's Lynn. *Medieval Archaeology* 15: 73–85.

Parker, J. H. 1836. *Glossary of Gothic Architecture*. London.

—— 1871. On the English origins of Gothic Architecture. *Archaeologia* 43: 73–96.

Parsons, D. (ed.) 1978. *Five Castle Excavations. Reports on the Institute's Research Project into the Origins of the Castle in England*. Leeds: Royal Archaeological Institute Monograph.

—— 1994. The Church and its architecture before and after the Reformation. In B. Vyner (ed.) *Building on the Past. Papers Celebrating 150 Years of the Royal Archaeological Institute*: 264–82. London: Royal Archaeological Institute.

Passmore, A. 1999. Boveycombehedd, Chagford, Devon: an archaeological investigation of a diachronic landscape. *Rep. Trans. Devon. Ass. Advmt. Sci.* 131: 49–70.

Payne, S. 1992. To keep or to throw? The costs of long term storage of bulk finds. *Museum Archaeologists News* 16: 2–4.

Peacock, D. P. S. 1977. Ceramics in Roman and medieval archaeology. In D. P. S. Peacock (ed.) *Pottery in Early Comerce*: 21–34. London: Academic Press.

—— 1979. Petrography of fabrics A-H. In P. A. Rahtz, *The Saxon and Medieval Palaces at Cheddar. Excavations 1960–62*: 310–14. Oxford: BAR 65.

Pearce, J. E. and Vince, A. G. 1988. *A Dated Type-Series of London Medieval Pottery. Part 4: Surrey Whitewares*. London: London and Middlesex Archaeology Society.

Pearce, J. E., Vince, A. G. and Jenner, M. A. 1985. Medieval pottery. London-type ware. *London and Middlesex Archaeological Society* Special Paper No. 6.

Pearson, S. 1994. *The Medieval Houses of Kent*. London: RCHME.

Peers, C. A. 1929. A research policy for fieldwork. *Antiquaries Journal* 9: 349–53.

Petch, D. F. 1968. Earthmoving machines and their employment on archaeological excavations. *Journal of the Chester Archaeological Society* 55: 15–28.

Peters, C. 1996. Interior and furnishings. In J. Blair and C. Pyrah (eds) *Church Archaeology. Research Directions for the Future*: 68–75. York: CBA.

Pettigrew, T. J. 1851. On the study of archaeology, and the objects of the British Archaeological Association. *JBAA* 6: 163–77.

Pevsner, N. 1985a. *The Buildings of England. Wiltshire*. Harmondsworth: Penguin.

—— 1985b. *South and West Somerset*. London: Penguin.

Phillips, C. W. 1980. *Archaeology in the Ordnance Survey 1791–1965*. London: CBA.

—— 1987. *My Life in Archaeology*. Gloucester: Sutton.

Philp, B. 1968. *Excavations at Faversham 1965*. Kent Archaeological Research Groups Council Report 1: 1–61. Bromley: Kent Archaeological Research Groups' Council.

Phythian-Adams, C. 1992. Hoskin's England: a local historian of genius and the realisation of his theme. *Local Historian* 22 (4): 170–83.

—— 1997. Leicestershire and Rutland. In C. R. J. Currie and C. P. Lewis (eds) *A Guide to English County Histories*: 228–45. Stroud: Sutton.

Piggott, S. 1976. *Ruins in a Landscape. Essays in Antiquarianism*. Edinburgh: EUP.

Pike, A. W. and Biddle M. 1966. Parasite eggs in medieval Winchester. *Antiquity* 40: 293–6.

Pitt Rivers, A. H. L. F. 1883. Excavations at Caesar's Camp near Folkstone, conducted in June and July, 1878. *Archaeologia* 47 (II): 429–65.

—— 1884. Address to the Antiquarian Section at the Annual Meeting of the Archaeological Institute, held at Lewes. *Archaeological Journal* 41: 58–78.

—— 1890. *King John's House, Tollard Royal, Wilts*. Privately printed.

—— 1898. *Excavations in Cranborne Chase*. Privately printed.

Planché, J. R. 1834. *History of British Costume*. London: C. Knight.

Platt, C. 1969. *The Monastic Grange in Medieval England: A Reassessment*. New York: Fordham Univ. Press.

—— 1978a. *Medieval England: A Social History and Archaeology from the Conquest to 1600*. London: Routledge and Kegan Paul.

—— 1978b. Review of 'Excavations in King's Lynn 1963–1970' by Helen Clarke and Alan Carter. *Medieval Archaeology* 22: 201–303.

—— 1982. *The Castle in Medieval England and Wales*. London: Secker and Warburg.

Platt, C. and Coleman-Smith, R. (eds) 1975. *Excavations in Medieval Southampton. 1953–1969*, 2 vols. Leicester: LUP.

Plot, R. 1686. *The Natural History of Staffordshire*. Oxford.

Pollack, D. 1985. The Lunan Valley Project: medieval rural settlement in Angus. *Proceedings of the Society of Antiquaries of Scotland* 115: 357–99.

Ponsford, M. W. 1972. *Bristol Castle: A Short Summary of the Recent Excavations*. Bristol: Bristol City Museum.

—— 1991. Dendrochronological dates from Dundas Wharf, Bristol and the dating of Ham Green and other medieval pottery. In E. Lewis (eds) *Custom and Ceramics. Essays Presented to Kenneth Barton*: 81–103. Wickham: APE.

Posnansky, M. 1956. The Lamport post-mill. *Journal of the Northamptonshire Natural History Field Club* 33: 66–79.

Potter, G. 1992. The medieval bridge and waterfront, Kingston-upon-Thames, England. *Medieval Europe 1992. Technology and Innovation*. Pre-printed papers, vol. 3: 1–8. York: Medieval Europe.

Poulton, R. 1988. *Archaeological Investigations on the Site of Chertsey Abbey*. Surrey Archaeological Society Research Volume 11. Guildford: Surrey Archaeological Society.

Poulton, R. and Woods, H. 1984. *Excavations on the Site of the Dominican Friary at Guildford in 1974 and 1978*. Research Volume of the Surrey Archaeological Society No. 9. Guildford: Surrey Archaeological Society.

Pounds, N. J. G. 1990. *The Medieval Castle in England and Wales. A Social and Political History*. Cambridge: CUP.

Powell, A. 1963. *John Aubrey and his Friends*. London: Heinemann.

Power, E. 1922. *Medieval English Nunneries c.1275–1535*. Cambridge: CUP.

—— 1926. *Medieval People*. London: Methuen.

—— 1955. *The Wool Trade in English Medieval History*. London: OUP.

—— 1971. On medieval history as a social study. In N. B. Harte (ed.) *The Study of Economic History. Collected Inaugural Lectures 1893–1970*: 109–26. London: Frank Cass.

Powlesland, D. 1997. Publishing in the round: a role for CD-ROM in the publication of archaeological field-work results. *Antiquity* 71: 1062–66.

Price, R. 1998. *St Bartholomew's Hospital, Bristol: The Excavation of a Medieval Hospital 1976–8*. CBA Research Report 110. York: CBA.

Pryor, F. 1974. *Earthmoving on Open Archaeological Sites*. Nene Valley Archaeological Handbook 1. Peterborough: Nene Valley Research Committee.

Pugh, R. B. and Saunders, A. D. 1968. *Old Wardour Castle, Wiltshire*. London: HMSO.

Pugin, A. W. 1836. *Contrasts, Or a Parallel Between the Noble Edifices of the Middle Ages and the Corresponding Buildings of the Present Day, Showing the Present Decay of Taste*. London: published by the author.

Quiney, A. 1994. Medieval and post-medieval vernacular architecture. In B. Vyner (ed.) *Building on the Past. Papers celebrating 150 years of the Royal Archaeological Institute*: 228–43. London: Royal Archaeological Institute.

Rackham, B. 1948. *Medieval English Pottery*. London: Faber and Faber.

Rackham, B. and Read, H. 1924. *English Pottery: its Development from Early Times to the End of the Eighteenth Century*. London: Ernest Benn.

Rackham, O. 1975. *Hayley Wood: its History and Ecology*. Cambridge: Cambs. and Isle of Ely Naturalists' Trust.

—— 1976. *Trees and Woodland in the British Landscape*. London: Dent.

—— 1978. Archaeology and land-use history. In D. Corke (ed.) Epping Forest: the Natural Aspect? *Essex Naturalist NS* 2: 16–75.

—— 1980. *Ancient Woodland: its History, Vegetation and Uses in England*. London: Edward Arnold.

—— 1989. *The Last Forest: the Story of Hatfield Forest*. London: Dent.

—— 1993. Woodland management and timber economy as evidenced by the buildings at Cressing Temple. In D. D. Andrews (ed.) *Cressing Temple. A Templar and Hospitaller Manor in Essex*: 85–92. Chelmsford: Essex County Council.

Rackham, O., Blair, W. J. and Munby, J. T. 1978. The thirteenth-century roofs and floor of the Blackfriars Priory at Gloucester. *Medieval Archaeology* 22: 105–22.

Radford, C. A. R. 1953. Sir Charles Reed Peers, 1868–1952. *PBA* 39: 363–8.

Rahtz, P. A. 1959. Holworth, Medieval Village Excavation, 1958. *Proceedings of the Dorset Natural History and Archaeological Society* 81: 127–47.

—— 1969. Upton, Gloucestershire, 1964–1968. *TBGAS* 88: 74–126.

—— 1974. Rescue Digging Past and Present. In P. A. Rahtz (ed.) *Rescue Archaeology*: 53–72. Harmondsworth: Penguin Books.

—— 1979. *The Saxon and Medieval Palaces at Cheddar. Excavations 1960–62*. Oxford: BAR 65.

—— 1980. *Wharram Percy Data Sheet*. Medieval Villages Research Group. Privately circulated: Dept. of Archaeology, Univ. of York.

—— 1981a. *The New Medieval Archaeology*. Inaugural lecture: Univ. of York.

—— 1981b. *Wharram Percy Data Sheet*. Medieval Village Research Group. Privately circulated: Dept. of Archaeology, Univ. of York.

—— 1983. New approaches to medieval archaeology, part 1. In D. Hinton (ed.) *Twenty Five Years of Medieval Archaeology*: 12–23. Sheffield: Dept. of Archaeology and Prehistory.

—— 1984. The Nuer Medieval Archaeology. Comment on Theory vs. History. *Scottish Archaeological Review* 1984: 109–12.

—— 1985. *Invitation to Archaeology*. Oxford: Basil Blackwell.

—— 1993. *Glastonbury*. London: English Heritage and Batsford.

—— 2001. *Living Archaeology*. Stroud: Tempus.

Rahtz, P. A. and Colvin, H. 1960. King John's Palace, Clipstone, Notts. *Transactions of the Thoroton Society of Nottinghamshire* 64: 21–43.

Rahtz, P. A. and Greenfield, E. 1977. *Excavations at Chew Valley Lake, Somerset*. London: HMSO.

Rahtz, P. A. and Hirst, S. 1976. *Bordesley Abbey, Redditch, Hereford-Worcestershire*. Oxford: BAR 23.

Rahtz, P. A. and Rahtz, M. H. 1958. T40: Barrow and Windmill at Butcombe, North Somerset. *Proceedings of the Univ. of Bristol Speleological Society* 8: 89–96.

Rahtz, P. A. and Watts, L. 1984. Upton: deserted medieval village, Blockley, Gloucestershire 1973. *TBGAS* 102: 141–54.

—— 1997. *St Mary's Church, Deerhurst, Gloucestershire*. London: Society of Antiquaries Research Report.

Rahtz, S., Hall, W. and Allen, T. 1992. The development of dynamic archaeological publications. In P. Reilly and S. Rahtz (eds) *Archaeology and the Information Age. A Global Perspective*: 360–83. London and New York: Routledge.

Ramm, H. G., McDowall, R. W. and Mercer, E. 1970. *Shielings and Bastles*. London: HMSO.

Randall, H. J. 1934. *History in the Open Air*. London: G. Allen and Unwin.

Randsborg, K. 1980. *The Viking Age In Denmark: the Formation of a State*. New York: St Martin's Press.

Rawcliffe, C. 1995. *Medicine and Society in Later Medieval England*. Stroud: Sutton.

Rawlins, G. J. E. 1997. *Slaves of the Machine*. Cambridge MA: MIT Press.

RCAHMS 1994. *South-East Perth. An Archaeological Landscape*. London: HMSO.

RCAHMW 1991. *The Early Castles, from the Norman Conquest to 1217*, An Inventory of the Ancient Monuments in Glamorgan, vol. III, Part 1a. London: HMSO.

RCHME 1910. *An Inventory of Historic Monuments in the County of Hertfordshire*. London: HMSO.

—— 1912. *An Inventory of Historic Monuments in the County of Buckinghamshire. Vol. 1 South*. London: HMSO.

—— 1913. *An Inventory of Historic Monuments in the County of Buckinghamshire. Vol. II North*. London: HMSO.

—— 1916. *An Inventory of Historic Monuments in the County of Essex. Vol. 1 North-West*. London: HMSO.

—— 1960. *A Matter of Time: An Archaeological Survey of the River Gravels of England*. London: HMSO.

—— 1968. *An Inventory of Historic Monuments in the County of Cambridgeshire. Vol. 1 West*. London: HMSO.

—— 1969. *Peterborough New Town. A Survey of the Antiquities in the Areas of Development*. London: HMSO.

—— 1975. *An Inventory of Historic Monuments in the County of Dorset. Vol. V East.* London: HMSO.

—— 1977. *An Inventory of Historical Monuments in the Town of Stamford.* London: HMSO.

—— 1980. *Ancient and Historical Monuments in the City of Salisbury: Vol. 1.* London: HMSO.

—— 1981. *An Inventory of the Historical Monuments in the City of York. Vol. 5. The Central Area.* London: HMSO.

—— 1987. *Churches of South-East Wiltshire.* London: HMSO.

—— 1991. Excavations and Medieval England: The Excavation Index. *Medieval Archaeology* 35: 123–5.

—— 1993. *Recording England's Past.* London: RCHME.

—— 1996. *Recording Historic Buildings: A Descriptive Specification.* London: RCHME.

—— 1999. *Annual Report 1998/9. A History and Final Report.* Swindon: RCHME.

Redknap, M. 1988. The National Reference Collection for Medieval and Later Pottery for Wales. *Medieval and Later Pottery in Wales* 10: 33–9.

Redknap, M. and Dean, M. 1989. Underwater archaeology in Britain. *The Field Archaeologist* 10: 157–62.

Reilly, P. 1992. Three-dimensional modelling and primary archaeological data. In P. Reilly and S. Rahtz (eds) *Archaeology and the Information Age. A Global Perspective*: 147–76. London and New York: Routledge.

Reilly, S. 1998. Old Wardour Castle, Wilts. *Central Archaeological Service News* 9: 2–3.

Renn, D. F. 1968. *Norman Castles in Britain.* London: Baker.

Reynolds, A. 1994. The Compton Bassett Area Research Project: first interim report. *Institute of Archaeology Bulletin* 31: 169–98.

Reynolds, S. 1977. *An Introduction to the History of English Medieval Towns.* Oxford: Clarendon Press.

Rhodes, M. 1979. Methods of cataloging pottery in inner London: an historical outline. *Medieval Ceramics* 3: 81–108.

Richards, J. 1990. *Sex, Dissidence and Damnation. Minority Groups in the Middle Ages.* London: Routledge.

Richards, J. D. 1997. Preservation and re-use of digital data: the role of the Archaeology Data Servive. *Antiquity* 71: 1057–9.

—— 1993. *The Bedern Foundry.* The Archaeology of York 10/3. York: CBA.

Richardson, K. M. 1959. Excavations in Hungate, York. *Archaeological Journal* 116: 51–114.

Rickman, T. 1817. *An Attempt to Discriminate the Styles of Architecture in England from the Conquest to the Reformation.* London: Longman, Hurst, Rees, Orme and Brown.

Riden, P. 1983. *Local History. A Handbook for Beginners.* London: Batsford.

Rigold, S. 1956. *Nunney Castle, Somerset.* London: HMSO.

—— 1966. Some major Kentish timber barns. *Archaeologia Cantiana* 81: 1–3.

Rippon, S. (ed.) 1997a. *The Severn Estuary. Landscape Evolution and Wetland reclamation.* London: LUP.

—— 1997b. Wetland reclamation on the Gwent levels. In N. Edwards (ed.) *Landscape and Settlement in Medieval Wales.* Oxbow Monograph 81. Oxford: Oxbow Books.

—— 1997c. Roman and medieval settlement on the North Somerset Levels: the second season of survey and excavation at Banwell and Puxton, 1997. In S. Rippon (ed.) *The Severn Estuary. Landscape Evolution and Wetland reclamation*: 41–54. London: LUP.

—— 1998. Puxton (North Somerset) and early medieval 'infield' enclosures. *Medieval Settlement Research Group. Annual Report 12*: 17–20.

—— 1999. Landscapes in context: the exploitation and management of coastal resources in southern and eastern Britain during the 1st millennium AD. In C. Fabech and J. Ringtved (eds) *Settlement and Landscape*. Proceedings of a conference in Århus, Denmark, May 4–7 1998: 225–36. Denmark: Jutland Archaeological Society.

Roberts, B. K. 1965. Moated sites in Midland England. *Transactions and Proceedings of the Birmingham Archaeological Society* 80: 26–37.

—— 1977. *Rural Settlement in Britain*. Folkestone: Dawson.

—— 1987. *The Making of the English Village*. Harlow: Longman.

—— 1993. Some relict landscapes in Westmorland: a reconsideration. *Archaeological Journal* 150: 433–55.

Robey, T. 1993. The archaeology of Cressing Temple. In D. D. Andrews (ed.) *Cressing Temple. A Templar and Hospitaller Manor in Essex*: 37–50. Chelmsford: Essex County Council.

Robins, G. 1842. *A Catalogue of the Classic Contents of Strawberry Hill collected by Horace Walpole*. London: George Robins Auctioneers.

Robinson, D. M. 1980. *The Geography of Augustinian Settlement*, 2 vols. Oxford: BAR 80.

—— 1986. *Tintern Abbey*. Cardiff: CADW.

Robinson, P. F. 1827. *Designs for Ornamental Villas*. London: printed for J. Carpenter and Son.

—— 1830. *Village Architecture*. London: printed for J. Carpenter and Son.

Rodwell, W. J. 1976. The archaeological investigation of Hadstock Church, Essex: an Interim Report. *Antiquaries Journal* 56: 55–71.

—— 1984. Churches in the landscape: aspects of topography and planning. In M. L. Faull (ed.) *Studies in Late Anglo-Saxon Settlement*: 1–23. Oxford: Oxford Univ. Dept. for External Studies.

—— 1987. Rescue and research in churches and cathedrals. In H. Mytum and K. Waugh (eds.) *Rescue Archaeology. What's Next?* Univ. of York Monograph 6: 93–8. York: Univ. of York Monograph and Rescue, The British Archaeological Trust.

—— 1989. *Church Archaeology*. London: English Heritage and Batsford.

—— 1996a. Above and below ground: archaeology at Wells Cathedral. In T. Tatton-Brown and J. Munby (eds) *The Archaeology of Cathedrals*: 115–33. Oxford Univ. Committee for Archaeology Monograph No. 42. Oxford.

—— 1996b. Church archaeology in retrospect and prospect. In J. Blair and C. Pyrah (eds) *Church Archaeology. Research Directions for the Future*: 197–202. York: CBA.

Rodwell, W. J. and Rodwell, K. A. 1982. St Peter's Church, Barton-upon-Humber: Excavation and Structural Study, 1978–81. *Antiquaries Journal* 62: 283–315.

Rodwell, W. J. and Rodwell, K. A. 1985. *Rivenhall: Investigations of a Villa, Church and Village, 1960–77. Vol 1*. CBA Research Report 55. London: CBA.

Rogers, P. W. 1997. *Textile Production at 16–22 Coppergate, York*. Archaeology of York 17/11. York: CBA.

Rosser, G. 1996. Religious practice on the margins. In J. Blair and C. Pyrah (eds) *Church Archaeology. Research Directions for the Future*: 75–84. York: CBA.

Rowley, T. 1981. *The Origins of Open-Field Agriculture*. London: Croom Helm.

Rudder, S. 1779. *A New History of Gloucestershire*. Cirencester: printed by the author.

Ruding, R. 1817. *Annals of the Coinage of Britain and its Dependencies*. London: printed by Nichols, Son and Bentley.

Ruskin, J. 1849. *The Seven Lamps of Architecture*. London.

—— 1851–3. *The Stones of Venice*. London: Smith, Elder and Co.

Russell, B. E. (ed.) 2000. *Gazetteer of Archaeological Investigations in England 1998*. York: English Heritage and Bournemouth Univ.

Ryder, M. L. 1961. The livestock remains from four medieval sites in Yorkshire. *Agricultural History Review* 9: 105–10.

—— 1969. Remains of fishes and other aquatic animals. In D. Brothwell and E. Higgs (eds) *Science in Archaeology. A Survey of Progress and Research*: 376–94. London: Thames and Hudson.

Ryder, P. F. 1992. Bastles and bastle-like buildings in Allendale, Northumberland. *Archaeological Journal* 149: 351–79.

Sadler, P. 1990. Osteological remains. In J. M. Fairbrother, *Faccombe Netherton: Excavations of a Saxon and Medieval Complex*. Occasional Paper of the British Museum 74: 462–99. London: British Museum Press.

Salter, H. E. 1934. *Map of Medieval Oxford*. London: OUP.

Salzman, L. F. 1913. *English Industries of the Middle Ages*. London: Constable.

—— 1952. *Building in England down to 1540*. Oxford: OUP.

Sambrook, A. J. 1980. Netley and Romanticism. In A. H. Thompson, *Netley Abbey*. London: HMSO.

Samson, R. (ed.) 1990. *The Social Archaeology of Houses*. Edinburgh: EUP.

Samuel, R. 1984. Forum. *History Today*, May 1984: 6–9.

Sauer, C. O. 1941. Foreword to historical geography. *Annals of the Association of American Geographers* 31: 1–24.

Saunders, A. D. 1978. Introduction. In D. Parsons (ed.) *Five Castle Excavations. Reports on the Institute's Research Project into the Origins of the Castle in England*: 1–10. Leeds: Royal Archaeological Institute Monograph.

—— 1980. Lydford Castle, Devon. *Medieval Archaeology* 24: 123–87.

—— 1983. A century of Ancient Monuments Legislation 1882–1982. *Antiquaries Journal* 63: 11–33.

Saunders, P. and Saunders, E. (eds) 1991. *Salisbury Museum Medieval Catalogue. Part 1*. Salisbury: Salisbury and South Wiltshire Museum.

Saunders, T. 1990. The feudal construction of space: power and domination in the nucleated village. In R. Samson (ed.) *The Social Archaeology of Houses*: 181–96. Edinburgh: EUP.

Schiffer, M. B. 1987. *Formation Processes of the Archaeological Record*. Albuquerque: Univ. of Utah Press.

Schofield, J. A. 1983. The Council for British Archaeology's Urban Research Committee, 1970–81. In D. A. Hinton (ed.) *Twenty-five Years of Medieval Archaeology*: 83–9. Sheffield: Dept. of Archaeology, Univ. of Sheffield and the SMA.

—— (ed.) 1987. *The London Surveys of Ralph Treswell*. London Topographical Society 135. London.

—— (ed.) 1991. *Interpreting Artefact Scatters: Contributions to Ploughzone Archaeology*. Oxbow Monographs 4. Oxford: Oxbow Books.

—— 1992. The social perceptions of space. *The Field Archaeologist* 16: 299–301.

—— 1994a. *Medieval London Houses*. New Haven and London: Yale Univ. Press.

—— 1994b. Social perceptions of space in medieval and Tudor London houses. In M. Locock (ed.) *Meaningful Architecture: Social Interpretations of Buildings*. Worldwide Archaeology Series 9: 188–206. Aldershot: Ashgate Publishing.

—— 1999. Towns 1050–1500. In Hunter, J. and Ralston, I. (eds) *The Archaeology of Britain*: 210–27. London: Routledge.

Schofield, J. A., Palliser, D. and Harding, C. (eds) 1981. *Recent Archaeological Research in English Towns*. London: CBA.

Schofield, J. A. and Vince, A. 1994. *Medieval Towns*. London: LUP.

Scollar, I., Tabbagh, A., Hesses, A. and Herzog, I. 1990. *Archaeological Prospecting and Remote Sensing (Topics in Remote Sensing 2)*. Cambridge: CUP.

Scott, E. 1997. Introduction: On the incompleteness of archaeological narratives. In J. Moore and E. Scott (eds) *Invisible People and Processes. Writing Gender and Childhood into European Archaeology*: 1–12. London: LUP.

—— 1999. *The Archaeology of Infancy and Infant Death*. Oxford: BAR International Series 819.

Scott, I. R. 1996. *Romsey Abbey. Report on the Excavations 1973–1991*. Stroud: Hampshire Field Club and Test Valley Archaeological Trust.

Scott, W. 1810. *The Lady of the Lake*. Edinburgh: printed for J. Ballantyne and Co.

—— 1819. *Ivanhoe*. Edinburgh: printed for A. Constable and Co.

—— 1820. *The Monastery*. Edinburgh: Longman, Hurst, Rees, Orme and Brown.

Seebohm, F. 1883. *The English Village Community*. London: Longman.

Selkirk, A. 1975. Wharram Percy. *Current Archaeology* 49: 39–49.

Shackley, M. 1981. *Environmental Archaeology*. London: George Allen and Unwin.

Shalem, A. 1996. *Islam Christianized: Islamic Portable Objects in the Medieval Church Treasuries of the Latin West*. Frankfurt: Peter Lang.

Shammas, C. 1990. *The Pre-industrial Consumer in England and America*. Oxford: Clarendon Press.

Sharpe, E. 1848. *Architectural Parallels*. London: J. Van Voorst.

Shaw, H. 1836. *Specimens of Ancient Furniture Drawn from Existing Authorities*. London: W. Pickering.

—— 1843. *Dresses and Decorations of the Middle Ages*. London: W. Pickering.

Shelley, A. 1996. Norwich Castle Bridge. *Medieval Archaeology* 40: 217–26.

Shennan, S. 1985. *Experiments in the Collection and Analysis of Archaeological Survey Data: The East Hampshire Survey*. Sheffield: Univ. of Sheffield.

Shepard, A. O. 1956. *Ceramics for the Archaeologist*. Washington: Carnegie Institute of Washington.

Sheppard, F. H. W. (ed.) 1960. *Parish of Hackney (pt 1): Brooke House*. Survey of London vol. XXVII. London: Athlone Press.

Sherburn, G. 1956. *The Correspondence of Alexander Pope*. Oxford: Clarendon Press.

Shoesmith, R. 1985. *Hereford City Excavations 3: The Finds*. CBA Research Report 56. London: CBA.

Shoesmith, R. 1991. *Excavations at Chepstow 1973–1974*. Cambrian Archaeological Monographs 4. Bangor: Cambrian Archaeological Association.

Simpson, I. A., Dockrill, S. J., Bull, I. D. and Evershed, R. P. 1999. Lipid biomarkers of manuring practice in relict anthropogenic soils. *The Holocene* 9: 223–9.

Skeat, W. W. 1901. *Place Names of Cambridgeshire*. Cambridge: printed for the Cambridge Antiquarian Society.

—— 1913. *The Place-Names of Suffolk*. Cambridge: printed for the Cambridge Antiquarian Society.

Slade, C. F. 1973. Excavations at Reading Abbey 1964–67. *Berkshire Archaeological Journal* 66: 29–70.

Slater, T. R. 1987. Ideal and reality in English episcopal medieval town planning. *Transactions of the Institute of British Geographers* 12: 191–203.

Slowikowski, A., Nenk, B. and Pearce, J. 2001. *Minimum Standards for the Processing, Recording, Analysis and Publication of Post-Roman Ceramics*. MPRG Occasional Paper No. 2. Leigh-on-Sea: MPRG.

Smith, J. T. 1963. The long-house in Monmouthshire. In I. L. Foster and L. Alcock (eds) *Culture and Environment. Essays in Honour of Sir Cyril Fox*: 389–414. London: Routledge and Kegan Paul.

—— 1965. Timber-framed building in England: its development and regional differences. *Archaeological Journal* 122: 133–58.

Smith, L. 1985. *Investigating Old Buildings*. London: Batsford.

Smith, M. 1999. Abbey's Road. In *SF Weekly*. December 1999–January 2000.

SMA: Society for Medieval Archaeology. 1987. Archaeology and the Middle Ages. *Medieval Archaeology* 31: 1–12.

Soden, I. 1992. The Carthusians of Coventry, in Medieval Europe 1992. *Religion and Belief*. Pre-printed papers vol. 6: 77–82. York: Medieval Europe.

Southey, R. 1829. *Sir Thomas More; Or Colloquies on the Progress and Prospects of Society*. London: J. Murray.

Spearman, R. M. 1984. Scottish Urban Archaeology. Where do we go from here? *Scottish Archaeological Review* 3 (2): 99–103.

Speed, J. 1611. *History of Great Britaine*. Taunton: South West Regional Planning Conference.

Spence, C. 1993. Recording the archaeology of London: the development and implementation of the DUA recording system. In E. C. Harris, M. R. Brown and G. J. Brown (eds) *Practices of Archaeological Stratigraphy*: 23–46. London: Academic Press.

Spencer, B. 1990. *Salisbury Museum Medieval Catalogue Part 2: Pilgrim Souvenirs and Secular Badges*. Salisbury: Salisbury and South Wiltshire Museum.

Spillett, P. J., Stebbing, W. P. D. and Dunning, G. C. 1943. A pottery kiln site at Tyler Hill, near Canterbury. *Archaeologia Cantiana* 55: 57–64.

Stafford Borough Council. nd. *Stafford Castle. A Brief History*. Walsall: Stafford Borough Council.

Stamper, P. 1980. Barton Blount: climatic change or economic change: an addendum. *Report MSRG* 7: 43–6.

—— 1988. Woods and parks. In G. Astill and A. Grant (eds) *The Countryside of Medieval England*: 128–47. Oxford: Blackwell.

—— 1999. Rural settlement and manors. In J. Hunter and I. Ralston (eds) *The Archaeology of Britain*: 247–63. London: Routledge.

Stamper, P. A. and Croft, R. A. 2000. *The South Manor Area. Wharram, A study of Settlement on the Yorkshire Wolds VIII*. Univ. of York Archaeological Publications 10. Exeter: Univ. of York.

Steane, J. M. 1984. *The Archaeology of Medieval England and Wales*. London: Croom Helm.

Steane, J. M. and Bryant, G. F. 1975. Excavations at the deserted medieval settlement at Lyveden. *Journal of the Northants. Museum and Art Gallery* 12: 2–160.

Steedman, K., Dyson, T and Schofield, J. 1992. Aspects of Anglo-Norman London, III; Billingsgate and the bridgehead to 1200. London and Middlesex Archaeological Society Special Paper 14.

Steensberg, A. 1982. The development of open area excavation and its introduction into medieval archaeology: an historical survey. *Medieval Village Research Group Annual Report* 30: 27–30.

Stocker, D. 1992. The Shadow of the General's Armchair. *Archaeological Journal* 149: 415–20.

Stocker, D., Roberts, B. and Wrathmell, S. 1993. Medieval Rural Settlements in the Monuments Protection Programme: A Progress Report. *Medieval Settlement Research Group Annual Report* 8: 15.

Stocker, D. and Stocker, M. 1996. Sacred profanity: the theology of rabbit breeding and the symbolic landscape of the warren. *World Archaeology* 28(2): 265–72.

Stocker, D. and Vince, A. G. 1997. The early Norman castle at Lincoln and a re-evaluation of the original west tower of Lincoln Cathedral. *Medieval Archaeology* 41: 223–33.

Stoddart, D. R. 1986. *On Geography and its History*. Oxford: Blackwell.

Stone, J. F. S. and Charlton, J. 1935. Trial excavations in the east suburb of Old Sarum. *Antiquaries Journal* 15: 174–92.

Stone, L. 1979. The Revival of Narrative: Reflections on a New Old History. *Past and Present* 85: 3–24.

Stone, P. 1895–7. Recent discoveries in the Keep of Carisbrooke Castle. *Proceedings of the Society of Antiquaries* 16: 409–11.

—— 1912. Down pits in the Isle of Wight. *Proceedings of the Society of Antiquaries* 24: 67–78.

Stones, J. A. (ed.) 1989. *Three Scottish Carmelite Friaries: Excavations at Aberdeen, Linlithgow and Perth 1980–86*. Society of Antiquaries of Scotland Monograph 6. Edinburgh.

Stothard, C. A. 1817. *The Monumental Effigies of Great Britain*. London: printed by J. M'Creery for the author.

Stopford, J. 1990. *Recording Medieval Floor Tiles*. CBA Practical Handbook 10. London: CBA.

—— 1993. Modes of production among medieval tilers. *Medieval Archaeology* 37: 93–108.

Stopford, J. Hughes, M. J. and Leese, M. N. 1991. A scientific study of medieval tiles from Bordesley Abbey, near Redditch (Hereford and Worcester). *Oxford Journal of Archaeology* 10 (3): 349–60.

Straker, E. 1931. *Wealden Iron*. Newton Abbott: David and Charles.

Streeten, A. D. F. 1980a. Potters, kilns and markets in medieval Sussex; a preliminary study. In D. J. Freke (ed.) *The Archaeology of Sussex*. Sussex Archaeological Collections 118: 105–18.

—— 1980b. Potters, kilns and markets in medieval Kent: a preliminary study. In P. Leach (ed.) *Archaeology in Kent to AD 1500*. CBA 48: 87–95. London: CBA.

Stroud, G. and Kemp, R. L. 1993. *Cemeteries of the Church and Priory of St Andrew, Fishergate*. The Archaeology of York. The Medieval Cemeteries 12. York: CBA.

Strutt, J. 1796–9. *A Complete View of the Dress and Habits of the People of England: From the Establishment of the Saxons in Britain to the Present Time*. London: J. Nichols.

Stukeley, W. 1724. *Itinerarium Curiosum Centuria*, I. London: printed for the author.

—— 1770. Account of Lesnes Abbey. *Archaeologia* 1: 44–8.

—— 1882–7. The family memoirs of the Rev. William Stukeley, M.D. and the antiquarian and other correspondence of William Stukeley, Roger and Samuel Gale, etc. In *Publications of the Surtees Society*, 1882–87, III: 70.

Sumner, H. 1917. *The Ancient Earthworks of the New Forest*. London: Chiswick Press.

Sutherland, D. S. and Parsons, D. 1984. The petrological contribution to the survey of All Saints Church, Brixworth, Northamptonshire: An Interim Account. *JBAA* 137: 45–64.

Szymanski, J. E., Campbell, T., Dittmer, J. K., Giannopoulos, A., Tsourlos, P., Coppack, G., Emerick, K. and Wilson, K. 1992. Non-destructive Site Diagnosis at Medieval sites in the UK. *Medieval Europe 1992, Religion and Belief*. Pre-printed papers vol. 6: 201–6. York: Medieval Europe.

Tanner, T. 1722. *Notitia Monastica*. London.

Tatton-Brown, T. 1974. Excavations at the Custom House site, City of London, 1973. *Transactions of the London Middlesex Archaeological Society* 25: 117–219.

—— 1995. Westminster Abbey: archaeological recording at the West End of the Church. *Antiquaries Journal* 75: 171–88.

Tawney, R. H. 1912. *The Agrarian Problem in the Sixteenth Century*. London: Harper and Row.

Taylor, A. J. 1946. The greater monastic houses. In V. E. Nash-Williams (ed.) *A Hundred Years of Welsh Archaeology*. Cambrian Archaeological Association, Centenary Volume 1846–1946. Gloucester: Cambrian Archaeological Association: 140–7.

—— 1986. *Conwy Castle*. Cardiff: CADW.

Taylor, C. C. 1967. Whiteparish, a study of the development of a forest edge parish. *Wiltshire Archaeological and Natural History Magazine* 62: 79–102.

—— 1970. *The Making of the English Landscape: Dorset*. London: Hodder and Stoughton.

—— 1974a. *Fieldwork in Medieval Archaeology*. London: Batsford.

—— 1974b. Total archaeology or studies in the history of the landscape. In A. Rogers and T. Rowley (eds) *Landscapes and Documents*: 15–26. London: Bedford Square Press.

—— 1977. Polyfocal settlement and the English Village. *Medieval Archaeology* 21: 189–93.

—— 1981. The role of fieldwork in medieval settlement studies. *Medieval Village Research Group Annual Report* 29: 29–31.

—— 1983. Towards total archaeology? Aerial photography in Northamptonshire. In G. S. Maxwell (eds) *The Impact of Aerial Reconnaisaance on Archaeology*. CBA Research Report 49: 54–8. London: CBA.

—— 1987. Field Survey: Where did we go wrong? In H. Mytum and K. Waugh (eds) *Rescue Archaeology. What's Next?* Univ. of York Monograph 6: 23–7. York: Univ. of York Monograph and Rescue, The British Archaeological Trust.

—— 1989. Somersham Palace, Cambridgeshire: a medieval landscape for pleasure? In M. Bowden, D. Mackay, C. C. Taylor, P. Everson and W. R. Wilson-North, Bodiam Castle, Sussex. *Medieval Archaeology* 33: 112–33.

Taylor, C. C., Everson, P. and Wilson-North, R. 1990. Bodiam Castle, Sussex. *Medieval Archaeology* 34: 155–6.

Taylor, E. L. 1955. Parasitic helminths in medieval remains. *Vet. Rec.* 67 (12): 216.

Taylor, H. M. 1972. Structural criticism: a plea for more systematic study of Anglo-Saxon buildings. *Anglo-Saxon England* 1: 259–72.

Taylor, H. M. and Taylor, J. 1965. *Anglo-Saxon Architecture I-III*. Cambridge: CUP.

Thirsk, J. 1988 *Agrarian History of England and Wales*. Cambridge: Cambridge University Press.

Thomas, C., Sloane, B. and Phillpotts, C. 1997. *Excavations at the Priory and Hospital of St Mary Spital, London*. MOLAS Monograph 1. London.

Thomas, K. 1971. *Religion and the Decline of Magic*. London: Weidenfield and Nicolson.

Thomas, N. 1979. *Rescue Archaeology in the Bristol Area: 1*. Bristol: City of Bristol Museum and Art Gallery.

Thomas, R. 1993. English Heritage funding policies and their impact on research strategy. In J. Hunter and I. Ralston (ed.) *Archaeological Resource Management in the UK. An Introduction*: 136–48. Stroud: Sutton and IFA.

Thompson, F. H. 1962. Excavations at the Cistercian abbey of Vale Royal, Cheshire. *Antiquaries Journal* 42: 183–207.

Thompson, M. W. 1956. Excavation of a medieval moat at Moat Hill, Anlaby, near Hull. *Yorkshire Archaeological Journal* 39: 67–85.

—— 1967. *Novgorod the Great: Excavations at the Medieval City*. London: Evelyn, Adams and Mackay.

—— 1981. *Ruins. Their Preservation and Display*. London: British Museum Publications.

—— 1983. *The Journeys of Sir Richard Colt Hoare through Wales and England 1793–1810*. Gloucester: Sutton.

—— 1987. *The Decline of the Castle*. Cambridge: CUP.

—— 1996. Robert Willis and the Study of Medieval Architecture. In T. Tatton-Brown and J. Munby (eds) *The Archaeology of Cathedrals*. Oxford: Oxford Univ. Committee for Archaeology Monograph No. 42: 154–64.

—— 1957. Excavation of the fortified medieval hall of Hutton Colswain at Huttons Ambo, near Malton, Yorkshire. *Archaeological Journal* 114: 69–91.

—— 1977. *Kenilworth Castle, Warwickshire*. London: English Heritage.

—— 1998. *Medieval Bishops' Houses in England and Wales*. Aldershot: Ashgate.

Thoroton, R. 1677. *The Antiquities of Nottinghamshire*. London: printed by Robert White.

Thorpe, H. 1975. Air, ground, document. In Wilson, D. R. (ed.) *Aerial Reconnaissance for Archaeology*. London: CBA Research Report 12: 141–53.

Thorpe, W. A. 1935. *English Glass*. London: Black.

—— 1949 (2nd edn enlarged). *English Glass*. London: Black.

Tiller, K. 1992. *English Local History*. Stroud: Sutton.

Timms, S. 1985. The lessons of Barnstaple. *The Field Archaeologist* 4: 43–4.

Tingle, M. 1991. *The Vale of the White Horse Survey. The Study of a Changing Landscape in the Clay Lowlands of Southern England from Prehistory to the Present*. Oxford: BAR 218.

Tout, T. F. 1913–14. The present state of medieval studies in Great Britain. *PBA* (1913–14): 151–66.

Trevor-Roper, H. R. 1969. *The Romantic Movement and the Study of History*. The John Coffin Memorial Lecture. London: Athlone Press.

Trigger, B. G. 1989. *History of Archaeological Thought*. Cambridge: CUP.

Trow, S. 1996. Developing frameworks: archaeological research strategies for the next millennium. In D. A. Hinton and M. Hughes (eds) *Archaeology in Hampshire: A Framework for the Future*: 90–6. Salisbury: Hampshire County Council.

Turner, G. J. (ed.) 1901. *Select Pleas of the Forest*. Seldon Society 13. London: B. Quaritch.

Turner, R. C. 1997. The medieval palaces of the bishops of St Davids, Wales. In G. de Boe and F. Verhaege (eds) *Military Studies in Medieval Europe*. Pre-printed papers volume 11: 217–25. Zellik: Medieval Europe Brugge.

Turner, S. 1815–23. *History of England*. London: Longman, Hurst, Rees, Orme and Brown.

Turner, T. H. and Parker, J. H, 1851–9. *Some Account of the Domestic Architecture in England, vols. I–III*. Oxford: J. H. Parker.

Tylecote, R. F. 1959. An early medieval iron-smelting site in Weardale. *Journal of the Iron and Steel Institute* 192: 26–34.

Tyson, R. 2000. *Medieval Glass Vessels Found in England c.AD 1200–1500*. CBA Research Reports 121. York: CBA.

Ucko, P. 1987. *Academic Freedom and Apartheid. The Story of the World Archaeological Congress*. London: Duckworth.

—— 1990. Foreword. In D. A. Austin and L. Alcock (eds) *From the Baltic to the Black Sea. Studies in Medieval Archaeology*: ix–xii. London: Unwin Hyman.

van Bueningen, H. J. E. and Koldeweij, A. M. 1993. *Heilig en Profaan: 1000 laatmiddeleeuwse insignes uit de collectie H. J. E. van Beuningen*. Rotterdam Papers 8 (for pewter badges).

van de Put, A. 1904. *Hispano-Moresque Ware of the XV century*. London: Art Worker's Quarterly.

VCH. 1948. *Cambridgeshire II*. Oxford: OUP.

Vernon, R. W., McDonnell, G. and Schmidt, A. 1998. The geophysical evaluation of an iron-working complex: Rievaulx and environs, North Yorkshire. *Archaeological Prospection* 5: 181–201.

Vince, A. G. 1977. The medieval and post-medieval ceramic industry of the Malvern region: the study of a ware and its distribution. In D. P. S. Peacock (ed.) *Pottery and Early Commerce*: 257–305. London: Academic Press.

—— 1981a. The medieval pottery industry in southern England 10th to 13th centuries. In H. H. Howard and E. C. Morris (eds) *Production and Distribution: a Ceramic Viewpoint*: 309–21. Oxford: BAR 120.

—— 1981b. The use of petrology in the study of medieval ceramics: case studies from southern England. *Medieval Ceramics* 8: 31–45.

—— 1984. *The Medieval Ceramic Industries of the Severn Valley*. Unpublished PhD thesis, Univ. of Southampton.

—— 1985a. Pt 2: the ceramic finds. In R. Shoesmith, *Hereford City Excavations: the Finds*. CBA Research Report 56: 34–82.

—— 1985b. The Saxon and medieval pottery of London: a review. *Medieval Archaeology* 29: 25–93.

Vinogradoff, P. 1892 *Villainage in England. Essays in English Medieval History*. Oxford: Clarendon Press.

Viollet-le-Duc, E. 1854–68. *Dictionnaire raisonné de l'architecture française du XI au XVI siècle*. Paris.

Vita-Finzi, C. and Higgs, E. S. 1970. Prehistoric economy in the Mt. Carmel area of Palestine: site catchment analysis. *Proceedings of the Prehistoric Society* 36: 1–37.

Wade-Martins, P. 1980. *Village Sites in Launditch Hundred*. East Anglian Archaeology 10. Gressenhall: Norfolk Archaeological Unit.

Wainwright, G. J. 1978. Theory and Practice in Field Archaeology. In T. C. Darvill, M. Parker Pearson, R. W. Smith and R. M. Thomas (eds) *New Approaches to Our Past*.

An Archaeological Forum: 11–28. Southampton: Dept. of Archaeology, Univ. of Southampton.

—— 1989. Saving the Rose. *Antiquity* 63: 430–5.

—— 2000. Time please. *Antiquity* 74: 909–43.

Wall, J. C. 1908. *Ancient Earthworks*. London: Talbot.

Walpole, H. 1764. *The Castle of Otranto*. London: printed for W. Bathoe and Thomas Lowndes.

Ward, S. 1990. *Excavations at Chester. The Lesser Medieval Religious Houses: Sites Investigated 1964–1983*. Grosvenor Museum Archaeological Excavation and Survey Reports No. 6. Chester: Chester City Council.

Ward Perkins, J. B. 1937. English medieval embossed tiles. *Archaeological Journal* 94: 128–41.

—— (ed.) 1940. *London Museum Medieval Catalogue 1940*. London: Museum of London.

Warhurst, M. 1999. Norton Priory. A resource for the community. In G. Chitty and D. Baker (eds) *Managing Historic Sites and Buildings. Reconciling Presentation and Preservation*: 71–83. London: Routledge.

Watkins, D. J. 1994. *The Foundry: Excavations on Poole Waterfront 1986–87*. Dorset Natural History and Archaeological Society Monograph Series 14. Dorchester: Dorset Natural History and Archaeology Society.

Watkins, J. G. 1987. The pottery. In P. Armstrong and B. S. Ayers, *Excavations in High Street and Blackfriarsgate, Hull*. East Riding Archaeology 8: 53–183.

Watts, L. 1974. *Rescue Archaeology in the West Midlands. Past, Present and Future*. Birmingham: West Midlands Rescue Archaeology Committee.

Watts, L. and Rahtz, P. A. 1985. *Mary-le-Port, Bristol. Excavations 1962–3*. Bristol: City of Bristol Museum.

Weatherall, D. M. 1994. The British Archaeological Association: Its Foundation and Split. In B. Byner (ed.) *Building on the Past: Celebrating Years of the Royal Archaeological Institute*. London: Royal Archaeological Institute.

—— 1998. The Growth of Archaeological Societies. In V. Brand, *The Study of the Past in the Victorian Age*. Oxbow Monograph 73: 21–34. Oxford: Oxbow Books.

Weatherill, L. 1996. *Consumer Behaviour and Material Culture in Britain, 1660–1760*. London: Routledge.

Webster, G. 1963. *Practical Archaeology*. London: Black.

Weever, J. 1631. *Ancient Funerall Monuments within the united Monarchie of Great Britaine, Ireland, and the Ilands adiacent, with the dissolved Monasteries therin contained; their Founders, and what eminent Persons have beene in the same interred*. London.

Wells, C. 1982. The human bones: summary. In J. P. Roberts with M. Atkin (eds) *St Benedict's Church (Site 157N): Excavations in Norwich 1971–1978 Part 1*. East Anglian Archaeology Report 15: 25–7. Norwich: Centre for East Anglian Studies.

Wenham, L P., Hall, R. A., Briden, C. M. and Stocker, D. A. 1987. *St Mary Bishophill Junior and St Mary Castlegate*. The Archaeology of York. Anglo-Scandinavian York 8/2, York: CBA for the York Archaeological Trust.

WAC 1981: Wessex Archaeological Committee. 1981. *Towards a Policy for Archaeological Investigation in Wessex: 1980–1985*. Wessex: Wessex Archaeological Committee.

West, S. E. 1970. Brome; the excavation of a moated site, 1967. *JBAA* 33: 89–121.

Wheeler, R. E. M. 1940. Prefatory Note. In J. B. Ward Perkins, *London Museum Medieval Catalogue 1940*. London: Lancaster House.

—— 1954. *Archaeology from the Earth*. London: Clarendon Press.

Whellan, T. 1859. *History of York and the North Riding of Yorkshire*. Beverley.

White, G. M. 1935. Stonewall Farm, Bosham. *Sussex Archaeological Collections* 76: 193–200.

White, L. S. and Gardner, G. A. 1950. *Government Offices, Whitehall Gardens. The Special Problem of the Re-Siting of an Historic Building*. London: The Institution of Civil Engineering Paper No. 5765.

White, W. J. 1988. *Skeletal Remains from the Cemetery of St Nicholas Shambles, City of London*. London: London and Middlesex Archaeological Society.

Will, R. 1997. Cooking pots and the origins of the Scottish medieval pottery industry re-visited. In G. De Boe and F. Verhaege (eds) *Material Culture in Medieval Europe*: 323–32. Zellik: Medieval Europe Brugge.

Williams, A. 1946. A homestead moat at Nuthampstead, Hertfordshire. *Antiquaries Journal* 26: 138–44.

Williams, J. H. 1976. Excavations at Gravel Walk, Canterbury 1967. *Archaeologia Cantiana* 91: 119–43.

Williams, M. 1970. *The Draining of the Somerset Levels*. Cambridge: CUP.

Williams, S. 1889. *The Cistercian Abbey of Strata Florida: its History, and an Account of the Recent Excavations Made on this Site*. London: Whiting and Co.

—— 1892. The Cistercian Abbey of Strata Marcella. *Archaeologia Cambrensis*, 5th series, 9: 1–17.

—— 1894–5. The Cistercian abbey of Cwmhir, Rednorshire. *Transactions of the Society of Cymmrodorion* 1894–95: 61–98.

—— 1897. Excavations at Talley Abbey. *Archaeologia Cambrensis* 52: 229–47.

Williams-Freeman, J. P. 1915. *An Introduction to Field Archaeology as Illustrated by Hampshire*. London: Macmillan.

Willis, R. 1972–3. *Architectural History of Some English Cathedrals*, 2 vols. Newport Pagnell: Paul P. B. Minet.

Wilson, B. 1994. Mortality patterns, animal husbandry and marketing in an around medieval and post-medieval Oxford. In A. R. Hall and H. K. Kenward (eds) *Urban-Rural Connexions: Perspectives from Environmental Archaeology*. Symposia of the Association for Environmental Archaeology No. 12: 103–16. Oxford: Oxbow Books.

Wilson, J. 1846. Antiquities found at Woodperry, Oxfordshire *Archaeological Journal* 3: 116–28.

Wilson, T. 1995. Spanish pottery in the British Museum. In C. M. Gerrard, A. Gutiérrez and A. G. Vince (eds) *Spanish Medieval Ceramics in Spain and the British Isles*: 339–51. Oxford: BAR International Series 610.

Winbolt, S. E. 1933. *Wealden Glass*. Cambridge: Hove.

Wood, J. 1984. *Kempston*. Bedfordshire Parish Surveys 2. Bedford: Bedfordshire County Council.

Wood, J. 1992. Furness Abbey. An integrated and multi-discipinary approach to the survey, recording, analysis and interpretation of a monastic building. *Medieval Europe 1992, Religion and Belief*. Pre-printed papers, vol. 6: 163–70. York: Medieval Europe 1992.

—— (ed.) 1994. *Buildings Archaeology: Applications in Practice*. Oxbow Monograph 43. Oxford: Oxbow Books.

Wood, J. and Chapman, G. 1992. Three-dimensional computer visualization of historic buildings, with particular reference to reconstruction modelling. In P. Reilly and S. Rahtz (eds) *Archaeology and the Information Age. A Global Perspective*: 123–46. London and New York: Routledge.

Wood, M. E. 1965. *The English Medieval House*. London: Dent.

Woods, H. 1982. Excavations at Eltham Palace, 1975–9. *Transactions of the London and Middlesex Society* 33: 215–65.

Woodward, S. 1836. An account of some discoveries made in excavating the foundations of Wymondham Abbey, with a plan and description of the religious establishment. *Archaeologia* 26: 287–99.

Wool, S. 1982. *Fundus and Manerium: A Study of Continuity and Survival in Gloucestershire from Roman to Medieval Times*. Unpublished PhD thesis, Univ. of Bristol.

Wrathmell, S. 1989. *Wharram: A Study of Settlement on the Yorkshire Wolds, vol. 6: Domestic Settlement 2: Medieval Peasant Farmsteads*. York Univ. Archaeological Publications 8. York: Univ. of York.

Wright, P. 1985. *On Living in an Old Country: The National Past in Contemporary Britain*. London: Verso.

Young, C. R. 1979. *The Royal Forests of Medieval England*. Leicester: LUP.

Zeepvat, B. 1994. Not with a ten-foot barge pole . . . *The Field Archaeologist* 20: 403–5.

Index

Note: page numbers in *italics* denote illustrations or text in boxes